**DO NOT REMOVE
CARDS FROM POCKET**

The Stephen King Story

If you have an imagination, let it run free.
But if you have no imagination,
stop right here.
This book is not for you.

—Chris Chesley and Steve King, 1963

in *People, Places, and Things*

The
Stephen King
Story

George Beahm

Illustrated by Kenny Ray Linkous

Andrews and McMeel
A Universal Press Syndicate Company
Kansas City

Book design by Edward King.

Library of Congress Cataloging-in-Publication Data

Beahm, George W.
    The Stephen King story / George Beahm ; illustrated by Kenny Ray
Linkous.
      p.   cm.
    Includes bibliographical references and index.
    ISBN 0-8362-7989-1 : $16.95
    1. King, Stephen, 1947–   . 2. Novelists, American—20th century—
Biography. 3. Horror tales, American—History and criticism.
I. Title
PS3561.I483Z56   1991
813'.54–dc20   91–32063
[B]   CIP

This one is for

Michael R. Collings
Stephen J. Spignesi
Carroll F. Terrell

a drawing of the three
who know the territories well

**In the country of the story
the writer is king.**

Shirley Jackson,
"Notes for a Young Writer"

Contents

Introduction

The Persistence of Darkness— Shadows Behind the Life Behind the Story

by Michael R. Collings

Plot Summary

A handful of people have gathered in a building in the center of a small town. Inside, they have found safety . . . or at least the illusion of safety. Outside, there are only darkness, and fear, and death. Daylight is dying. With the night will come the monster. The people huddle close for warmth, for comfort. They know that by the time the sun dawns again, some, or most—or all—of them may be dead.

A plot outline for a Stephen King novel? A synopsis of "The Mist" perhaps? That would be a good guess. It seems logical. To a degree even possible. But "The Mist" was not the story I had in mind when I wrote that summary of a tale written down a bit before Stephen King assumed the mantle—willingly or not—of King of Terror. No, the story I remembered is older by more than a thousand years.

It is *Beowulf,* the oldest and greatest of the surviving Germanic epics, and the story of a small group of people confronted by horror and terror beyond their imaginings. The building is the golden meadhall, Heorot. The cluster of people is the warriors of the Germanic king Hrothgar. And the monster is Grendel. The monster has visited the great meadhall before, at night, and each time has left a trail of blood and death.

But it is intriguing and instructive to see how closely the two stories represent departures from a similar point. Both focus on a small group of people, a nexus of a culture that defines both the individual and the society. Both groups are isolated by physical darkness and by internal darkness. They are forced to come together for communal strength and protection—but their gathering does not work. In spite of everything, they must confront the darkness and their fear and the specter of death.

There are differences, of course. In *Beowulf* we quickly discover that the poet has discovered a hero, a single warrior with courage and power enough to combat the monster. The monster has devoured thirty of King

1

Hrothgar's retainers; the hero Beowulf, symmetrically enough, is endowed with the strength of thirty men. In the fury of single battle with Grendel, he rips the monster's arm from its body and nails the bloody trophy on the wall over the entry to Heorot.

In "The Mist" events do not proceed quite as smoothly. There is no hero. In a technologically oriented world such as ours, individual heroism is generally not encouraged; nor does King insult his reader's intelligence by importing one—not even from the distant, almost mythic shores of Geatland (Sweden). There are individual battles fought against the monsters that inhabit the mist, to be sure, but in King's vision there can be no simple ending. His characters are stripped of everything until all that remains is the courage of a few to face the darkness directly and to attempt to discover the extent of the mist . . . and the monsters.

And then the next wave of monsters strikes, in *Beowulf* as well in "The Mist." Even Beowulf, the impervious hero, ultimately suffers defeat in battle with the Firedrake. All that he has accomplished—the deaths of Grendel and Grendel's dam, the consolidation of his kingdom, his fifty years of faultless rule—all is called into doubt as his body burns and the forces of darkness gather once again. In "The Mist" the time frame has been condensed from fifty years to hours and days, but the effect is the same. Humanity may raise buildings, and construct moral and civil codes, and create a veneer of civility, but in the face of the darkness, most of that counts for little. The implications of both stories are consistent with a pervasive theme in Western literature, captured by the *Beowulf* poet and Stephen King: "Here there be tygers," here in the darkness of the human soul, and here in the darkness of the worlds we imagine.

Let's try another one.

Plot Summary

A frightened man confronts a midnight apparition, a specter that by all logic cannot exist, but does. He speaks to it, he conjures it to speak to him, and it reveals tales of darkness and fear and death. It grants him visions of murder, blood, revenge, and—again—death.

Does this describe *The Dark Half*? Or a segment of *IT*? Perhaps. Certainly the synopsis could apply equally to either of King's novels. But again, neither of those was the story I had in mind. Instead, I was thinking of *Hamlet*. There, three times in the course of what is almost universally hailed as the greatest tragedy in English literature (some would broaden that to include Western literature), we find . . . a ghost. A specter. A haunted shade whispering of murders past and murders to come.

From all accounts, the audiences of Shakespeare's day loved the play. They flocked to the Globe Theater to watch it, standing for the full four hours of its performance (unlike modern ones, those audiences were not subjected to editors and rewriters who knew more about dramaturgy than the Bard himself). They might have stood in the rain to see it. They might have paid the equivalent of a week's wages for the privilege.

Why? Did they come to watch a performance of the greatest play by the greatest English playwright?

Hardly.

F. E. Halliday begins his *Shakespeare and His Critics* by noting that at the time of Shakespeare's death, there were no popular newspapers to herald the tragic tidings from shore to shore; and even if there had been, "it is more than probable that the death in the provinces of a retired actor and writer of plays which could scarcely be considered as serious literature would have passed unnoticed."

No, the Elizabethan playgoers went to see a *drama,* and not coincidentally to see blood, and fear, and death . . . and a ghost. Samuel Johnson, writing over a century after Shakespeare's death about another of Shakespeare's theatrical successes, *Titus Andronicus,* urged that the play not be considered part of the master's canon: "The barbarity of the spectacles, and the general massacre, which are here exhibited, can scarcely be conceived tolerable to any audience; yet we are told by [Ben] Jonson, that they were not only borne, but praised. That Shakespeare wrote any part . . . I see no reason for believing." In spite of now being frequently excoriated as among Shakespeare's worst plays, *Titus Andronicus* was unusually and undeniably popular in its time. G. B. Harrison notes in his edition of the plays that it remained in the stage repertory for two full decades after it first appeared. Based on tales preserved for over a thousand years in classical myth and specifically in Seneca's Latin revenge tragedies (one of the popular genres of the Elizabethan period), the story was sensational and horrific even for the Elizabethans, full of graphic representations of blood and death. Many of the more objectionable episodes were eliminated in variants written by Shakespeare's contemporaries, but, again in Professor Harrison's words, "Shakespeare spared his audience nothing."

Mainstream critics today agree that the play fails miserably. Harrison writes:

Few critics can seriously defend *Titus Andronicus,* but its failure is not solely due to a revolting and fantastic story. Modern playgoers may regard rape, mutilation, and severed heads and hands as unsuitable for stage presentation; yet there are scenes quite as painful in plays which are among the very greatest—the blinding of Gloucester in *Lear* for instance or the conclusion of Sophocles' *Oedipus the King;* these are horrible but still justifiable in their contexts. The horrors in *Titus Andronicus* are too much; if ever presented on a modern stage they would move the audience not to shudders but to guffaws. Moreover, if a dramatist chooses to bring a drama of passion and revenge to a climax of horror when a parent unknowingly eats the flesh of his child, the episode should at least be adequately prepared and set off.

Shakespeare's audience—not being "modern playgoers" and lacking the foreknowledge that they were in the presence of a work by one of the premier dramatists of Westure culture—found nothing absurd in the presentation of horrors that included, among other bloody episodes, the on-stage removal of Titus Andronicus' hand, after which the character puns on multiple meanings of "giving one's hand" as a symbol of loyalty. One of my undergraduate Shakespeare professors, in fact, lectured at length on that scene, noting that the actor portraying Titus Andronicus would often wear a bladder of pig's blood beneath his arm and, at the climactic moment, spray blood onto the footlings surrounding the stage.

Whether by dramatizing ghostly visitations that lead to revenge and bloody death, or more directly by the on-stage removal of body parts, Shakespeare shows himself not unacquainted with the age-old techniques of fear, terror, and horror—including what King has described in his own works as the "gross-out."

This is not to argue simplistically that Stephen King is a twentieth-century Shakespeare (although a strong case for a similar contention has been made by Professor Carroll Terrell in his recent *Stephen King: Man and Artist*). It is to suggest, instead, that Shakespeare—and the *Beowulf* poet, for that matter—was an early Stephen King: that is, they were writers who knew the pulse of their audiences, who gave them what they wanted to see, and did so through stories so strong and compelling that they survive to this day.

And there is another similarity between King and these two eminent predecessors.

We know little about the private lives of either Shakespeare or the *Beowulf* poet. For the former, there are birth and death dates, some references, the names of his children . . . and the intriguing bit about the second-best bed. But about Shakespeare's day-to-day activities, about his home life, even about his personal, religious, or political affiliations, the records remain largely silent. It is perhaps a measure of the critics' need for biographical insights that many of them feel driven to read the sonnets, for example, as revealing—alone of Shakespeare's works—his private, emotional biography. In those poems, it is asserted, and unlike in the plays, the poet "wears his heart on his sleeve."

About the *Beowulf* poet, we know even less for certain. The transcriber of the poem was Christian. He was aware of the conflicting values of the old world views and the new, of Germanic paganism—with its elevation of loyalty and courage and warfare—and of Christianity. But other than that, we know little.

Paradoxically (since we are a nation of celebrity hunters, and he is very much in the public eye), although admittedly to a lesser extent, the case is similar with Stephen King. King is (and deserves to be) a private man. He rarely allows prolonged glimpses behind the public, media-oriented facade of "Stephen King, the Titan of Terror." When he appears in public, it is as if he has donned a persona, the mask of King the phenomenon, King the showman, King the literary equivalent of a "Big Mac and fries." Of the King behind the hype, we see little.

In some senses, of course, that is as it should be. We have his books, after all—and according to at least some critics, they should suffice. As *Different Seasons* warns its readers, "It is the tale, not he who tells it."

But with King, there is often a strong sense that his own history has entered those books, often transformed and transmuted in an alchemical process by which life becomes art. Biographical backgrounds to "The Body," or "Gramma," or "The Woman in the Room," or *IT,* for example, are important not because they intrude into King's personal life, but because that private life has been carried over into the fiction. Knowing that King saw a dead body as a child, knowing that he was present when his grandmother died, knowing that he struggled with the barren and painful fact of his mother's death by cancer, knowing that he was large and awkward and shy as a child—knowing these things can intensify the experience of reading his fiction.

It might seem pretentious, overweening, or at least premature to construct a meticulous, detailed, scholarly, definitive biography of a man who, at just over forty years of age, could be considered as midway in his career. And it is dangerous (albeit challenging and exhilarating) to promulgate critical dogma about living authors—they have a tendency to write subsequent works that prove the critics wrong. Certainly, it is safer and easier to write about people who are safely dead. Even so, the outlines of King's life *are* relevant to his fictions. His frequent dislocations as a child, the overt structure of his family life, his high school and college concerns all lend depth to his writings.

This is the level of biographical engagement that George Beahm has chosen in this approach to King. He does not treat King as a cultural icon, nor does he attempt to reconstruct a tabloid version of the secret sex life of "bestsellasaurus rex." Beahm focuses on those points where King's life history illuminates his fiction. He places King's writing into historical, social, and cultural contexts, indicating what else was happening in the world at the time King was writing certain novels and stories. He uses biography to suggest King's handling of themes and images and motifs.

The result is a new perspective, a distinct way of looking, not at King as person, but at the artifacts King has created. Beahm's title, *The Stephen King Story*, is, I think, purposely and fruitfully ambiguous. The book is, on the surface, the story of Stephen King, focusing on his life as an index to his fictions. But in a deeper sense, it is primarily the story of Stephen King's stories and King's sense of the importance of Story.

In "Fantasy and the Believing Reader," Orson Scott Card refers to critical studies as one individual's story about the fictions a particular writer has created. That "critickal" story may illuminate the fictions or it may obscure them; it may open them wider, or close them down and lock them away from change. It may suggest that its vision is definitive and exclusive, or it may remain open-ended, intending to ask more questions than it answers. But Card reminds us that any critical approach embodies only *one* of the many stories that may be told about the fictions. As long as readers (and critics) remember that single fact, the act of criticism remains fruitful.

Stephen King has told many stories. Like Story on its best, most functional levels, his stories are capable of changing their readers. What follows is one story about those stories, taking as its point of departure that, while the tale may be most important, rather than the teller, knowing something about the teller often strengthens, deepens, and illuminates the tale.

Thousand Oaks, California
March 1991

Preface

Bestsellasaurus Rex

I think that maybe the one value literary critics have is that they can chart a career after it's gone past a certain point. I don't think that I have reached that point—you can't chart a career for someone who has only been publishing for five years. But, ten years from now or fifteen years from now down the road, somebody can look at the books and say, "Well, he started out doing this and he developed into this."
— Stephen King, in 19, 1978

In many ways, his is the American dream come true.

To fellow Mainers, he's the local boy who made good, the one who put Maine—specifically, Bangor—on the literary map.

To his die-hard fans, he's a literary fix who always delivers.

To his publishers, he's the brand-name author who delivers on the promise of earning out his monstrous advances.

To the booksellers—from the small independents to the big chain stores—he's Mr. Productivity, averaging two bestselling books every year.

To critics—fan, academic, literary, and popular—he's the subject of endless discussion, as each new story is dissected for its themes, subtexts, and relative merits and demerits.

To the moguls in Hollywood, he's a luminary whose stories are easy to visualize but difficult to produce.

To the media, he's everything from the King of Horror, the Master of the Macabre, the Ghostmaster General, the "spooksman" (as *Famous Monsters of Filmland* publisher Forrest J. Ackerman might say) for the horror genre.

To *Time* magazine, he's the "master of pop dread," the "indisputable King of horror, a demon fabulist who raises gooseflesh for fun and profit. . . . [H]e seems to be the country's best-known writer."

To fellow writers of the *fantastique,* he's the writer who made horror respectable, a result comparable to the salutary effect of Robert A. Heinlein in science fiction, who popularized and elevated the genre.

To writers with less talent, he's what they want to be—but can't.

To readers worldwide, he holds the skeleton key to the dark half of our personalities: glimpses into nightmarish worlds through which we willingly walk, with King as the guide.

To his family and close friends, he's Steve King, who in public assumes the *Stephen King!* persona.

To the American public at large, he's a household name.

To himself, he's a "Bestsellasaurus Rex," a "middle-aged white rapper," a writer who doubts he'll ever "be taken seriously."

He is a one-man entertainment industry whose compulsion to write stories—a "marketable obsession," as he puts it—has become an international addiction.

He is "America's Horror Writer Laureate," according to the president of the American Bookseller's Association.

As the eighties drew to a close, it seemed that, more than anyone else's, King's fiction captured the texture of our times. A sharp contrast to the work of fellow babyboomers Steven Spielberg and George Lucas, who drew from the American myth pool to dream up stories that celebrated fantasy, heroic archetypes, and bittersweet adolescence, King's work reflected the decade's dark half, its nightmares: fear, not fun.

It was a decade symbolized by an aging actor (Ronald Reagan), a boy-toy turned ballsy entrepreneur (Madonna), and the self-appointed masters of the universe (Donald Trump and the wizards of Wall Street)—a decade whose fears became the realities of 1991: economic nightmares, social unrest, a domestic policy in chaos, and the specter of war that became a reality, with the U.S. and its coalition forces soundly defeating Iraq's Saddam Hussein in the Persian Gulf.

No wonder King's fears, expressed through his fiction, strike responsive chords in readers worldwide: his collective work is a metaphor for our troubled times.

Looking back at the decade, we note that of its twenty-five bestselling novels, seven were written by King. With twenty-eight books (and the inevitable TV and film adaptations) and dozens of short pieces of fiction and nonfiction to his credit, King, at age forty-three, is at the putative midpoint in his career. "America's literary boogeyman," as he perceives himself, is *too* well known. As he told *Entertainment Weekly*:

> All I can say is that I feel a bit overexposed. It's sort of like the character in that movie *The Seven Year Itch*—you know, Marilyn Monroe when the wind blows up her dress on the subway grating—and you look around and realize everybody is looking at you, and there's a lot to look at.

Despite the critics who can't agree on the merits (or demerits) of his work, King appears not to have let the money, the fame, or the adulation affect the primacy and privacy of doing what he does best—telling stories. As King wryly observed: "Nothing really changes. I'll still be told by my wife, 'Steve, we need a loaf of bread,' and so I'll go out shopping. And if I forget, and come back instead with an idea that I tell her will make us $2 million, she'll still say, 'Steve, I'm delighted, but we still need a loaf of bread.' "

As King explained in an introductory note to his most recent collection, *Four Past Midnight,* the more things change, the more they essentially remain the same. For King, money has never been the end; for him, it's the means by which he has bought time to be able to write.

On August 23, 1990, on the ABC television news program "Prime Time Live," cohost Diane Sawyer prefaced "King Fear," a personality profile on Stephen King, by acknowledging him as the "high priest of horror" with 140 million copies of his books in print worldwide. Sawyer went on to report that, according to *Forbes* magazine, King's net worth was $50 million, with an additional $30 million for a recent four-book deal.

In the profile, King patiently answered the stock questions with stock answers, conditioned responses to questions he's heard countless times.

In King's case, interviewers seldom ask the right questions, the revealing ones that shed new light. More typically, an interviewer starts out with what King calls "The Question," a tipoff that the interview will be just another personality profile. "Where do you get your ideas, Mr. King?"

In a fine, mad moment, I envision King turning on the interviewer and asking, "Where do you get your *questions?*"

Not surprisingly, those in the mainstream media who have interviewed King know little about him as a writer, or the traditions he works in, and even less about his work. Predictably, this was the case with this major profile.

Most disappointing. Depressing, even.

"Prime Time Live," ostensibly a news program with in-depth, hard-hitting investigative reportage, didn't give us what it promised: a fresh look at a genuine phenomenon.

Precisely for this reason—the growing mountain of material that focuses on King as a celebrity—I saw a need for a look at King and his work in a biographical framework, one that would attempt to bring together the wealth of information about him and his work in a chronological narrative.

Though there have been more books *about* him than *by* him, King has not had any comprehensive examinations of his life and work—the two are inseparable—since 1986, when Douglas E. Winter revised and updated his seminal study *Stephen King: The Art of Darkness,* which its author describes as "a critical appreciation . . . an intermingling of biography, literary analysis, and unabashed enthusiasm. . . ."

You should not read about King without reading Winter's book first, especially its second chapter, "Notes Toward a Biography: Living with the Boogeyman," a title that suggests a formal literary biography to follow, presumably with King's consent and full cooperation—a benefit Winter enjoyed when writing *The Art of Darkness.*

Neil Barron, editor of *Horror Literature,* observed that despite the number of books about King, a biography had yet to be written. Winter, I believe, will not only write that book, but do a thorough job. I look forward to reading his version of Stephen King's story.

In the interim, however, I felt now was the time to put King's work in context with his life, showing the relationship between the two. This book, then, is a literary profile: impressionistic sketches, not a mural.

At the midpoint in his career, King is in the comfortable (and enviable) position of being able to write whatever he wishes without the pressures of financial need. Despite the growing volume of letters from his fans urging him to write more of the same—like Beatle fans waiting for a reunion concert that can never be—King apparently trusts and listens only to that inner voice within him, the one that has compelled him to write since he was a teenager: "I feel a certain pressure about my writing, and I have an idea of who reads my books; I am concerned with my readership. But it's kind of a combination love letter/poison-pen relationship, a sweet-and-sour thing. I feel I ought to write something because people want to read something. But I think, 'Don't give them what they want—give them what you want.' "

Is it, as King himself asserts, the tale and not he who tells it? In part, yes; but you cannot divorce the man from his work, his values, his beliefs, and his environment—they are inseparable.

In truth, it's the tale *and* he who tells it—the subject of this book, where in the country of this story the writer is King.

GEORGE BEAHM

Williamsburg, Virginia
New Year's Day, 1991

Foreword

The Gambler

by Christopher Chesley

At the time of the telegram that changed his life forever, Stephen King was living in a double-wide on a side road the lonely highway rose to meet at the top of a long tall hill. I was living there too, taking a room and supper with the family, and hitching to and from the University of Maine campus.

On that spring day when I got back from school, Tabby ran out the front door and met me in the driveway. She handed me the telegram which said Doubleday bought *Carrie*. Happiness welled up in her. It would not let her stand still. It shone in her face, even making the tears in her eyes gleam.

A few days later Steve picked me up on my way home. Since our routines weren't the same, that didn't happen often. But sometimes while hitching, I'd see him coming, rolling on in his dark, sinister old Buick. His custom was to draw down on me, take aim using the high point of the hood, and plow into the shoulder right at me, raising the dust as he stopped right by my knee; or I'd walk into the road, daring this black prince of the white line not to slow down. It was a reminder of the old days back in Durham, when dodging cars was a sport. I got into the car and saw he'd bought himself a carton of cigarettes, a sign of new luxury. There were narrow times in the past when he'd had to roll his own.

We got home and sat down at the living room table with the carton. He broke the seal on a pack and offered me a cigarette. While he sat there feeling flush with the other packs half out of the carton and fanned around, we looked at the contract for *Carrie* Doubleday sent him. He stroked the neck of his beer and grinned like a pimp as I kept poking my finger at one pretty clause after another: percentage for foreign sales, percentage for film deal, percentage for T-shirts.

Stephen King sat and grinned like a man capable of high and fancy rolling.

He has always loved the chance and the bet, the room upstairs where the men go to separate winners from the losers. When he was a boy, he and the neighbor kids used the upper floor of the shed on the back side of his

11

house as a game room. Somebody had found some numbers that had come off an apartment door, and they nailed them up and called their place the "249 Club." There they'd all penny-ante the hot summer afternoons away, looking at high cards through blue-stained, smoky air, losers throwing smoldering butts at the winners, who raked in the change with their fingers.

Steve brought this hyperbolic sense of risk, a theatrical feel for high stakes, into his writing. He loved working at the typewriter spontaneously, and on his good days, more and more frequent as time passed, when what came out of his head would settle perfectly and almost simultaneously on the page, when the sound his typewriter made was more hum than stac-cato, his prose had not only a wonderful writerly assuredness but—more than that—an uncanny kind of allurement, as if reading it was to be drawn by some attractive luckiness imprinted on each word.

So maybe that day when we sat together looking over his contract for *Carrie* was the big payoff for the ultimate bet he'd made. At some time, years before, he had decided to chance himself, all his talent, all the writing skill he'd mastered, against the odds.

He always honored the bet, and, in a strange way, the house now and then offered a little respect. More than once during the hard times before the sale of *Carrie,* a check for a story he had sold to a magazine came in the mail, money at just the right desperate time, enough to cover some bills and stave off the wolf a little longer.

I remember looking up from the contract and watching him finish his beer. He started talking about the second draft of *Second Coming.* Soon he got up and went to work on it, down the hall in the little room with space enough only for him, his typewriter, the loud furnace, and the louder radio. The kids came in while he banged the keys. They rummaged and scrabbled, winding themselves around his legs.

As it got dark, in the kitchen Tabby sang along with Steve's radio.

I remember the carton of cigarettes still gracing the living room table, the packs fanned out, gleaming luxuriously under the ceiling light.

And now I know that Stephen King's ultimate bet did not end then. After all, a bet like that turns out to be its own payoff.

Pownal, Maine
March 1991

1

The Early Years

It was the end of the nightmare and the beginning of the American dream. World War II had ended and, like millions of other servicemen, Donald Edwin King—a master mariner in the Merchant Marine—headed home.

King returned to Croton-on-Hudson, New York, to be with his wife, Nellie Ruth Pillsbury King, whom he married six years ago when he was twenty-five, she twenty-six. On September 14, 1945, they adopted at birth David Victor King. Two years later, in Scarborough, Maine, Donald E. King—now a captain in the Merchant Marine—and Nellie King had their second son: Stephen Edwin King, born in Portland, Maine, on September 21, 1947, at the Maine General Hospital.

Like his older brother, Stephen was a war baby, one of the millions of babyboomers. A demographic anomaly, his generation would find its collective identity in popular culture: popular films, pop music, and television.

A child of the fifties, King grew up in the shadow of the atomic bomb—the technological wonder that ended the war would also throw its long shadow across the next four decades. Looking back at that time, King wrote in *Danse Macabre:* "We were fertile ground for the seeds of terror, we war babies; we had been raised in a strange circus atmosphere of paranoia, patriotism, and national hubris."

When Stephen King was two years old, his father, as the story goes, went out to get a pack of cigarettes and never returned. In *Danse Macabre* King recounted what happened afterward:

> After my father took off, my mother landed on her feet, scrambling. My brother and I didn't see a great deal of her over the next nine years. She worked at a succession of low-paying jobs: presser in a laundry, doughnut-maker on the night shift at a bakery, store clerk, housekeeper. She was a talented pianist and a woman with a great and sometimes eccentric sense of humor, and somehow she kept things together, as women before her have done and as other women are doing even now as we speak.

For Ruth King, books were her escape from the drudgeries of the workaday world. As Stephen recalled:

> I can remember one night coming in after she'd been to one of these little bookshops where you go and they had the recycled paper-backs—this was back in the early fifties, and she had a pile of her favorites, which were Agatha Christies and Erle Stanley Gardners piled up, which she had gotten for a nickel apiece—the covers were torn off—and they were stacked up by our TV, which at that time was a table model Motorola that weighed 5,000 pounds, black-and-white, that had a picture seven inches wide. And I said, "What have you got there?" And I still remember what she said: "I've got a pile of cheap, sweet vacations." And she was a lady who worked hard—she worked forty-four, fifty hours a week—and she read those Agatha Christies and Erle Stanley Gardners. She knew what she was going to get from me on her birthday and Mother's Day and everything else; it was always a Perry Mason or something like that.

For the next few years, the King family—Nellie, David, and Stephen—moved across the country, looking for a place to call home. David King, in an interview in *The Shape Under the Sheet,* remembered those transitory days when they stayed with relatives in Durham, Maine; Malden, Massachusetts; Chicago; West De Pere, Wisconsin; and Fort Wayne. Although they stayed with relatives on their father's side of the family, more often they lived with their mother's kin.

When Stephen King was six years old, he and his family moved to Stratford, Connecticut. Here they lived for four years, and here a young and impressionable Stephen King got his first exposure to horror.

As King recounted the story in *Danse Macabre,* he asked permission from his mother to hear the radio adaptation of Ray Bradbury's story "Mars Is Heaven!" His mother denied him permission, but he listened anyway. That night he slept "in the doorway, where the real and rational light of the bathroom bulb could shine on my face."

Years later King would observe: "This memory is interesting because it is *not* a memory of literature—one thing the memory says is that I did not come face to face with fantasy by way of print . . . it was rather a technological medium. . . ."

That early exposure to storytelling—oral, not written—made an indelible impression on the writer-to-be. What King discovered would become a fictional trademark in his storytelling techniques: tell the story in visual terms so it can be vividly imagined in the mind's eye.

Stephen King's earliest memory of exposure to the written tradition of storytelling was that of his mother reading to him and his brother. She read them "Classics Illustrated" comics—adaptations of classical works of literature—and children's classics like *Treasure Island*. But even then, at age seven, King preferred the darker fare. *The Strange Case of Dr. Jekyll and Mr. Hyde,* Robert Louis Stevenson's horrific tale, was an early favorite. As King recollected:

> She had a thin book from the library—obviously a grown-up book. You always knew the difference, because they were dull on the out-side, but sometimes interesting on the inside. I said, "What's that one about?" And she said, "Oh, you wouldn't like this one. This one's a really scary one. It's about a man who changes into someone else. It's called *Dr. Jekyll and Mr. Hyde."* And I said, "Read it to me." And she protested, but never very hard, because she loved that stuff; she absolutely adored it. If there was anything she loved better than that, it was passing the scare on to somebody else.
>
> That was a happy summer for me. We sat out on the porch at night, and she said she would smoke her Kool cigarettes to keep the bugs away, although I noticed she did quite a bit of inhaling, and she read me *Dr. Jekyll and Mr. Hyde.* I lived and died with that story, with Mr. Utterson and with poor Dr. Jekyll, and particularly with Dr. Jekyll's other side, which was every vestige of pretense of civilization thrown away. I can remember lying in bed, wakeful after that night's reading was done, and what I usually thought of was how Mr. Hyde walked over the little girl, back and forth, breaking her bones; and it was such a terrible image and I thought, *I have to do that; but I have to do that worse,* because it was the only way to get back to normal again.

On his own, King read Dr. Seuss, whose "grim situation comedy" *The 500 Hats of Bartholomew Cubbins* made a powerful impact on him: the idea that "sudden weirdness can happen to the most ordinary people, and for no reason at all." It was an idea that, years later, would become the cornerstone of virtually all of his major fiction.

King was also seven when first exposed to horror movies. Though accounts vary as to where he saw it—on television, or at a drive-in theater in the company of his mother and her date—King viewed *The Creature from the Black Lagoon,* a 1954 black-and-white movie that, as Leonard Wolf wrote in *Horror,* "is a darling of horror film aficionados."

Years later, King would observe: "I still see things cinematically. I write down everything I see. It seems like a movie to me, and I write that way."

According to Douglas E. Winter, in *The Art of Darkness,* King began his first fictional efforts at about this time, including his first horror story, which was imitative of the horror movies of the fifties: a dinosaur terrorizes a town, but a scientist saves the day. Because dinosaurs are allergic to leather, theorizes the scientist, we'll assault it with leather artifacts and it'll go away.

Though clearly derivative, the story foreshadowed many key elements of King's fiction to come—his storytelling stripped to its basic components: something happens for which there is no apparent explanation (a dinosaur suddenly appears); an off-the-wall solution is found through scientists, the high priests of technology (they come up with a scientific theory); and although the theory has no basis in fact (the dinosaur's allergy to leather), it works.

Three years later, on October 4, 1957, a ten-year-old King—raised in the euphoria of a postwar booming American economy—realized his age of innocence had come to an end. The Russians had launched *Sputnik I,* a twenty-two-inch, 184-pound satellite that ushered in the space race—a rude awakening for Americans who assumed that space, the final frontier, would be explored by them first; the Russians would have to settle for sloppy seconds.

Interestingly, King's recollections of this formative event conflict: In one account, in a college newspaper column, he wrote that he was "waiting in the barber shop to get a haircut when that happened. I thought it had to be a joke. . . . Americans were always first—we had been with the telephone, the electric light, the airplane—surely the Russians, who played dirty, could not have beaten us into space! It was degrading, it was frightening . . . well, it was downright embarrassing."

But in *Danse Macabre* King tells a far more dramatic version. He is at a Saturday matinee, watching *Earth vs. the Flying Saucers.* The house lights are brought up and the manager comes on stage to make an announcement: "I want to tell you that the Russians have put a space satellite into orbit around the earth. They call it . . . *Spootnik.*"

No matter which version is true, it was a pivotal moment in his life, as he wrote in *Danse Macabre:* "I am certainly not trying to tell you that the Russians traumatized me into an interest in horror fiction, but am simply pointing out that instant when I began to sense a useful connection between the world of fantasy and that of what *My Weekly Reader* used to call Current Events."

It was, for King and millions of other babyboomers, the end of innocence.

A year later, in 1958, when Stephen was eleven, the King family moved to Durham, Maine, where Ruth King would find herself not only raising her two sons on her own but also caring for her parents, Guy Pillsbury and Nellie Fogg Pillsbury, both in their eighties, both with failing health.

Durham Days

In the late fifties Durham was, as King's childhood friend Christopher Chesley recalled, "a working-class town—in a sense, a hard-luck town. Right around here was farming, but the majority of towners went out-of-town to Lewiston, Auburn, or Brunswick."

With a population then of under a thousand—a figure that hasn't changed much over the years—rural Durham has always been a place where you make your own fun.

The King family settled down in what was known locally as Methodist Corners, so named because of the proximity of the West Durham Methodist Church to a local crossroad. The modest two-story house Ruth King occupied with her family was the place where Stephen King's worldview was shaped, a view sharply circumscribed by the local geography.

Standing on the front porch of the King home, looking across the road that formed a right angle, you could look across a windswept field to see a brick house a quarter mile down the road, the home of King's aunt and uncle, Ethelyn Pillsbury Flaws and Oren Flaws. To the left, within an eighth mile, was Alex and Joyce Hall's home, whose three sons—Brian and twins Dean and Dana—were childhood friends of Stephen King. Between the Hall home and the King home were the one-room schoolhouse where King attended grammar school (fifth and sixth grades) and the West Durham Methodist Church, which according to a plaque outside the building is "the Second Oldest Methodist Church in Continuous Use in New England." (Today the church building is no longer used, but then it was a focal point for community activities for the children, including Stephen and David King, who attended Bible classes and church services on a regular basis; with other children, under the supervision of lay minister Charles Huff, they went on picnics to nearby Bradbury Mountain.)

By all accounts, the Kings lived a lower-middle-class life, not unlike that of other families in the area. Behind the house was the outhouse. "We didn't have desserts when I grew up," Stephen King recalled. "The house was always rented. Our outhouse was painted blue and that's where we contemplated the sins of life. Our well was always going dry and I remember lugging water from a far spring."

David King remembered that his mother "was taking care of her parents with support from her sisters, and sometimes, even when we were in Durham, she was getting Aid to Dependent Children."

Ruth King was largely on her own; likewise her sons were largely on their own. Stephen and David King were latchkey kids. Stephen King recalled: "My mother . . . worked at the bakery from eleven to seven, making the goods. So, she was home days. My brother David would tell me to be quiet; ma was trying to sleep. When I was a little older she worked in a laundry. In summer for the most part we were left to our own devices."

The next year, when Stephen King was twelve, he met Christopher Chesley, who lived a half mile down the street from the King residence. In Chesley, King would find a kindred spirit: another writer in the making.

Chesley, whose parents had transferred him from a one-room schoolhouse on the other end of town to the one-room schoolhouse near the King residence, remembered his first encounter with the twelve-year-old Stephen King. "He looked like a kid with those old-fashioned, black-rimmed glasses. His hair was kind of messy and he was kind of slow. He was chunky, but not fat."

Brian Hall echoed Chesley's comments. "Steve was a big, klutzy kid. . . . Uncoordinated. Walking down the road you knew he was going to fall down or walk into a sign, reading his book." David King's recollections, though, paint the most vivid picture: "He looked like Vern [Tessio] in the film *Stand by Me*."

At twelve, large for his age—six feet, two inches—Stephen King stood out physically, sometimes with comical results. Brian Hall told interviewer Jeff Pert that when he and King went to the Ritz theater in nearby Lewiston, the woman in the ticket booth took one look at a king-sized King and decided he couldn't get in for the reduced admission because he obviously was over-age. Frustrated, King—according to Hall—began showing up with a copy of his birth certificate in hand.

An early and lasting influence, the Saturday matinees at the Ritz opened up a new world for the young and impressionable writer looking to find his fictional voice. According to Chesley, King's admittedly cinematic style of writing can be attributed to the hours spent in the darkened Ritz theater where, larger than life, black-and-white movies unreeled. Chesley observed, "King, in effect, learned *how* to write from what he saw on the screen at the Ritz—the place where parents sent their kids on Saturday."

The movies, in fact, provided early inspiration for King's first attempts at writing. After seeing the 1961 American International film *The*

Pit and the Pendulum—directed by Roger Corman, king of the B-movies— King self-published his own version on his brother's mimeograph machine, one of several self-published works. Chesley recalled, "This was *not* a takeoff on the story. King had seen the film and in effect novelized that movie. We ran off copies and sold them in school for a dime or a quarter, but the teachers made us stop doing that."

Flushed with early success and encouragement—a literary license to steal, so to speak—Stephen King continued his early writing efforts. In another story, King playfully wove fact and fiction, using the real names of fellow students in a fictional hostage situation. "It was all of twenty pages," recalled Chesley, "and it was a story where he used real kids who had taken over the grammar school. Of course, the people that were in the story read the story; because of things like that, King was lionized. He could take real people and set them into this setting where we were heroes. In this story, we died fighting the National Guard. The kids he liked best 'died' last; so naturally, we were all wondering when we were going to 'die.' "

Though King was in a physical sense an outsider—a large and ungainly child—it didn't really matter to him. As he would tell interviewer Charles Platt years later, "I could write, and that was the way I defined myself, even as a kid."

More than King's way of self-identification, writing would be his ticket to ride. King's powers of perception heightened by an extraordinary imagination would eventually be King's one-way ticket out of the confines of rural Maine forever. As King later observed, "I grew up in a real rural environment, and I've been writing about it ever since. It was a quiet childhood and a lot of it went on inside. And when I started writing stories, I wanted to write about being a private eye in the big city or being a space jockey in the asteroid belt—anything to get away from Durham, Maine, where I grew up."

Ironically, it was his father, Donald E. King, who opened the way. In *Danse Macabre* King recounts the specific day—the turning point—when he first met the masters of horror. It was "a cold day in 1959 or 1960, the attic over my aunt and uncle's garage was the place where that interior dowsing rod suddenly turned over, where the compass needle swung emphatically toward some mental true north. That was the day I happened to come on a box of my father's books."

In what King termed the "family museum," the attic over the garage, King became reacquainted with his long-lost father, the father he knew principally through what his mother had told him, the father who was a rambling man, a merchant mariner who later traveled the Midwest to sell Electroluxes door to door—"the only man on the sales force who regularly demonstrated vacuum cleaners to pretty young widows at two o'clock in the morning," said King. The son described his father as being of "average height, handsome in a 1940s sort of way, a bit podgy, bespectacled." An aspiring writer who lacked persistence, Donald King submitted fiction to the men's magazines of his day but, even though he had received encouragement, never broke through. As his son later observed, "None of the stories sold and none survives."

In that box of books, including several Avon paperbacks, King discovered H. P. Lovecraft for the first time; that Lovecraft collection left an indelible mark on a young, impressionable King. Lovecraft "struck . . . with the most force, and I still think, for all his shortcomings, he is the best writer of horror fiction that America has yet produced." Later, King would write in *Danse Macabre:* "When Lovecraft wrote 'The Rats in the Walls' and 'Pickman's Model,' he wasn't simply kidding around or trying to pick up a few extra bucks; he meant it, and it was his seriousness as much as anything else which that interior dowsing rod responded to, I think."

Lovecraft—a lantern-jawed, dour-faced outsider in his own time—took his weird fiction seriously indeed, even outlining the æsthetics of horror in a long essay, *Supernatural Horror in Literature,* the first full-length study of its kind.

In some ways, Lovecraft was the Stephen King of his generation. The native New Englander, from Providence, Rhode Island, was an outsider in his own time. A voluminous reader, devouring print at an early age, Lovecraft self-published his early work and later explored the New England milieu through fictional constructs like Innsmouth and Arkham, Massachusetts. Exploring horror through myth—within the framework of the Cthulhu Mythos, a race of cosmic entities whose existence dwarfed man's insignificant place in the universe—Lovecraft found horror fiction the ideal vehicle for his groundbreaking work, which laid a foundation for the postwar *Weird Tales* writers like Fritz Leiber, the early Ray Bradbury, the early Robert Bloch, Charles Beaumont, Jack Finney, and Richard Matheson, all of whom were instrumental in bringing horror to everyday America, and all of whom influenced King.

Chris Chesley credited Lovecraft for showing King a new approach to fiction:

What Steve learned from Lovecraft was the possibility of taking the New England atmosphere and using that as a springboard. Lovecraft showed him a milieu that was definitely New England horror. *Dracula* could be moved to Durham, basically. He didn't keep on reading Lovecraft, but in terms of his development, he took that European kind of horror and set it on this continent.

King had been bitten by the horror bug, and bitten hard, especially when he discovered that he wasn't alone in his fascination for weird fiction. In an introduction to *Mr. Monster's Movie Gold*—a look at horror films by Forrest J. Ackerman—King wrote, "As a kid growing up in rural Maine, my interest in horror and the fantastic wasn't looked upon with any approval whatsoever—there went young Steve King, his nose either in a lurid issue of *Tales from the Vault* or an even more lurid paperback of some sort or other—I had gone from Robert Bloch to Frank Belknap Long and from Long to the rest of the so-called Lovecraft Circle. I was, as far as most of my elders were concerned, eating tomatoes . . . poison fruit."

Chesley, who recalled King's sense of isolation at that time, explained:

> Everybody thought—considering how much he read and how much he wrote—that he spent way too much time in his room, too much time in his imagination, and it was thought to be unhealthy and abnormal behavior.
>
> I think he felt that and was sensitive to it. It was very difficult for him to be who he was and be accepted for it. In that respect, I think Steve felt more alone; he felt a sense of isolation.
>
> Given who he was, though, the isolation was necessary to make him what he became.

When King first came across Ackerman's *Famous Monsters of Filmland,* he was pleasantly surprised to discover that all over the country there were kids just like him—mostly babyboomers—who shared his affinity with popular culture. The adults could call it junk, but Ackerman knew better. Ackerman, wrote King, "stood up for a generation of kids who understood that if it was junk, it was *magic* junk. He has always seen the fiction of the fantastic—the stories and the cinema—as a gateway to wonder. His love of the genre is a child's wonder, untouched by the sophistication which eventually corrupts. But this childish love which has been coupled with the enthusiasm of a man who had found the thing which God made him to do and is doing it with a unique style and an energy which never seems to flag."

For King, Durham was the place where it all began. Through the lens of his imagination, King saw a Durham that nobody else could see.

Pounding out stories on a manual typewriter in his cramped bedroom which he shared with his brother, Stephen King escaped from the ordinary world by transmuting it into an extraordinary world of fiction. As Chesley wrote, "The country dirt roads, the stands of pine trees, the hayfields run to seed, the antique-copper Maine sun, all of it common, and real enough; yet within King's room, as if an actual atmosphere, as if breathed out on the air directly from the imagination of the kid who owned the typewriter, extraordinary things were vivid and real enough—more real, for an afternoon, than all the prosaic territory outside."

To make the unreal real and the unbelievable believable —that, according to Chesley, is King's unique gift, which has been instrumental to his success:

> When I went to Stephen King's house to write stories with him, there was the sense that these things weren't just stories; when you walked inside the walls of his house, there was a sense of palpability, almost as if the characters in the stories had real weight.
>
> Imagination didn't make it real just for him—it made it real for *me.* To go inside his house was like being pulled into a different world unlike old, unimaginative Durham with its cowsheds. And that's what drew me to go see him. He had that ability. If you went inside those walls and you were at all susceptible, you would be drawn into that.
>
> And when you read stories with him, or read his writing, or participated and wrote stories with him, the stories took on weight.
>
> It was a world unto itself, and I was privileged to enter it. Even as a kid, as a teenager, King had the power to do that. It was an amazing thing.

That is the essence of storytelling: if the writer has done his job, the reader will slip effortlessly from the real world into the autohypnotic world of fiction; the transition is so smooth, the reader will never notice.

Years later, when delivering a public speech to a group in Truth or Consequences, New Mexico, King explained the magic behind the fictional transition:

> The reason I write this stuff is a sense of wonder, a sense that there could be something more, or there's a way to establish the world and the natural laws that govern the world.
>
> I call it the Narnia feeling.
>
> To me, the finest explication of that is a novel by C. S. Lewis, *The Lion, the Witch, and the Wardrobe,* which begins with kids playing hide-and-seek in a big old British house.

Lucy goes into a wardrobe (British-ese for closet) and she's stumbling back through these hanging garments, coats, and stoles. Suddenly, it's cold underneath her feet, and when she looks down, it's not dark there anymore—it's light. And when she reaches down, instead of boards, there's this cold stuff that she holds up and pushes against her face.

And it's snow.

For me, that's it. That's when everything trips over and I'm gone, and you say, "I fell through the world. I'm out of this crap. I'm somewhere else." For me, that's really a nice thing, like "Toto, I don't think we're in Kansas anymore." That's a wonderful moment and you say, "Thank God you're not, Dorothy, because it's a lot more fun over here. You'll meet people you've *never* met over there."

In January 1959 David King began publishing an informal community newspaper, *Dave's Rag*. The first issue had a minuscule print run of two copies, since each copy had to be typed individually. As David King said, "Until I get a mimeograph machine things are going to be rather rushed."

An admittedly modest effort—David King, after all, was only thirteen, and Stephen only eleven—*Dave's Rag* eventually garnered twenty paid subscriptions, once the young publisher acquired a mimeograph machine.

Mimeography is a printing process that is virtually extinct today: one types on a wax stencil, and the stencil is then placed on a rotating drum filled with ink; as the drum rotates and the ink forces its way through the stencil, sheets of paper are fed through the machine, which prints the finished copies.

Though mimeography is capable of producing beautiful work—multi-colored inks can be used and photographs and artwork can be electronically imaged on special stencils that can be pasted into the mimeograph stencil—*Dave's Rag* was more primitive: letter-size sheets printed in black ink only, with cartoons drawn directly on the stencil. A home-grown effort, *Dave's Rag* showcased Stephen King's first journalistic efforts. The one surviving copy from those days is dated "Summer 1959." In that issue David King appeared on the masthead as editor-in-chief and illustrator. Donald P. Flaws, a cousin, was its sports editor. Stephen King was a reporter, writing (in this issue, at least) about television:

Well, the fall T.V. season is in full swing, and it has the newest and best shows since the beginning of T.V. There's T.V. for every fan. Like adventure or espionage? Try the "Trouble Shooters" or "Five

Fingers." Westerns your preference? How about "The Deputy" or
"Man from Blackhawk." Westerns are the most numerous this sea-
son. Science fiction? Try "Man into Space" or "Twilight Zone."
Roughly *20* new fall shows. Happy Viewing. Steve King.

Jam-packed with news about summer vacation in West Durham,
classified ads, jokes, letters, sports news, and general news, *Dave's Rag* cost
a nickel a copy (without postage), or $1 for a long-term subscription.

In the classifieds, there were ads for photographic services (David
King offered "Pictures expertly taken of any subject, in color or black-
and-white. Professional looking prints or enlargements given at lowest
prices") and for local produce (The Hall's roadside stand featured pumpkins for a quarter, Indian corn for a dime, and "the FINEST squash,
potatoes, and pumpkins . . .").

Of special interest in the classifieds: an ad for a self-published book by
a local writer. "New book by STEVE KING! Thirty-One of the Classics!
Read KIDNAPPED, TOM SAWYER, and many others! If you order in
three weeks, only thirty cents."

It was not the first such fictional offering from a fledgling writer, for in
an earlier issue, in the classifieds, King offered for sale a book that from its
description sounded very similar to Edgar Rice Burroughs's novel *The
Land That Time Forgot*:

> WATCH FOR THE NEW KING STORY!!!! "Land of 1,000,000
> Years Ago." Exciting story of 21 people prisoners on an island that
> should have been extinct 1,000,000 years ago. Order through this
> newspaper.

In 1962 King began submitting fiction to professional markets, bang-
ing out short stories on his manual typewriter that were submitted to the
science-fiction magazines. Even then, though, the tales were essentially
horror, as King explained in *Dream Makers: Volume II* to interviewer Charles
Platt:

> I started to submit stuff when I was about twelve, to magazines like
> *Fantastic* or *Fantasy and Science Fiction*. These stories had the trappings of
> science fiction, they were set in outer space, but they were really horror
> stories. One of the few good ones was about an asteroid miner who
> discovered a pink cube, and all this stuff started to come out of the cube
> and drive him back further and further into his little space hut, breach-
> ing the airlocks one after the other. And the thing got him in the end.

Considered escapist fiction, the pulps, as they were derisively called, were
printed on cheap pulp paper. Often the stories were seldom better than the

paper they were printed on. (Respectable fiction was published in magazines with glossy paper stock, the "slicks.")

The stories went out—and came right back. David King, in *The Shape Under the Sheet,* told Stephen Spignesi that his brother was "constantly at the typewriter" and for his efforts "got lots of rejection slips. If I remember correctly, there was a nail pounded in the wall up in the bedroom, and he'd spear all the rejection slips on it." Chesley echoed his comments: "In an odd way, they were trophies. They depressed him, but he knew that he was paying his dues."

King, even at the beginning of his career, realized that what separated the amateur writer from the professional was the quantity and quality of the writing itself. As King observed later, "I think that writers are made, not born or created out of dreams or childhood trauma—that becoming a writer . . . is a direct result of conscious will. Of course there has to be some talent involved, but talent is a dreadfully cheap commodity, cheaper than table salt. What separates the talented individual from the successful one is a lot of hard work and study; a constant process of honing."

Early on King recognized that there was no substitute for the time spent at the typewriter. Years later Chesley reflected on the importance of King's self-imposed isolation necessary for any writing career:

> Stephen King is aware of what he needs to preserve himself—the time and space and distance that allow him to write. That's pretty much what he is, and that's pretty much the way it always was.
>
> He was certainly not a recluse. He had friends like the rest of us, but when he was done, he would always return to the typewriter.
> Watching him at his writing, you knew that's where he belonged.

Through King's imagination, Durham became a microcosm of the universe, where his "lens of imagination" focused on the people and their ways that, years later, would be fictionalized as Castle Rock, Maine, which King would put on the literary map.

King's assimilation of Durham, filtered through his overactive imagination, transformed its commonplace surroundings into the stuff of fiction.

Behind the King home was a shed where Stephen and David King and their friends would meet to "play cards, read magazines, things like that," as Chesley remembered. Called the "249 Club"—the numbers had fallen off an apartment building and were mounted on their shed—it foreshadowed King's fictional 249 Club in New York, a brownstone where members of an exclusive club meet to tell tales.

Near the Chesley home is the Harmony Grove Cemetery where, as Chesley recalled, he and King "went . . . under the light of the late, sinking summer moon" and "ran among the old markers . . . . Death's plain calling cards." Years later, in 'Salem's Lot, the cemetery would reappear as the fictionalized Harmony Hill cemetery.

Down the road from Chesley's home is Runaround Pond, where he, King, and a mutual friend saw a dead body pulled from the lake, a victim of a boating accident. Years later the lake and the body would be transmuted into "The Body," subsequently made into the movie Stand by Me.

Down the road from the King house is an old barn that used to be a house, where Chesley and King shot a home movie, after haunting the local theater:

> We got hold of a movie camera. We weren't seriously trying to make a movie; we were trying to figure out how you designed a shot to make it scary. We were trying to figure out how you got the person up and down the stairs, how you got the shadows.
>
> This house was the kind of place that had bad vibes. You didn't want to spend the night there. I don't think we ever got enough nerve to do that. It had enough feeling of previous occupancy so that you didn't want to hang around too long. It had the staircase that Steve mentions in 'Salem's Lot where Hubie Marsten hung himself.

Down the road from what Chesley believes to be the inspiration for the Marsten house is the Shiloh Temple, an odd multistoried building capped with what appears to be a rotunda, topped by a gold-colored crown. When the sun sets and its rays glint off the crown, its shadow is thrown down the long, straight road that leads up to it. At the base of the road is a cemetery, flanked by dark woods.

Years later Shiloh Temple would reappear in "The Body."

King, who had grown up in Durham, discovered that, in turn, Durham had grown on him. King came to know its distinctive small-town feel, its way of life that passed virtually unnoticed by outsiders and, often, the townfolk. In "It Grows on You," King wrote: "Outsiders think they are the same, these small towns—that they don't change. It's a kind of death the outsiders believe in, although they will call it 'tradition' simply because it sounds more polite. It's those inside the town who know the difference—they know it but they don't see it."

King saw it and it became the rock-bed of realism for his fiction, part of his Maine milieu. In King's mind, Castle Rock, Maine, *was* real because, in a real sense, he had grow up there for most of his young life. It was a motherlode of memories that, years later, would emerge full force in his fiction: "I was twelve going on thirteen when I first saw a dead human being. It happened in 1960, a long time ago . . . although sometimes it doesn't seem that long to me," King wrote in "The Body," set in Castle Rock, Maine, near "the surrounding towns of Motton and Durham and Pownal."

In spring 1962 King graduated from grammar school at the top of his class—one of only three graduates.

High School Daze

In the fall of 1962 Stephen King began his high school career at Lisbon High School in nearby Lisbon Falls, approximately six miles northeast of Durham. (David King attended Brunswick High, southeast of Durham.)

In an interview with Brian Hall, who attended high school with King, Jeff Pert wrote that "Durham couldn't afford a school bus for only a few kids, so they hired Mike's Taxi of Lisbon. Mike had an old limousine, and he'd haul the handful of Durham kids to school in that. Hall says one of the regular riders was one of two girls on whom King based the protagonist of *Carrie*. When the limo arrived, there was a rush to get the best seat. You didn't want to ride all the way to Lisbon with Carrie on your lap."

Chris Chesley, who attended a nearby prep school, recalled that he "saw Steve periodically on the weekends, but he never talked very much about his high school years. It was understood that we got together to talk about movies, TV, and books."

In many ways, King's high school career was rather ordinary. Academically, he was an above-average student; though he remembered getting "C's and D's in chemistry and physics," he did sufficiently well in other classes to make the honor roll twice, in his freshman and sophomore years.

A large teenager, King played left tackle on the football team; however, he probably had greater interest in the rock and roll band, in which he played the rhythm guitar. (A yearbook photo shows King in tuxedo at his high school prom, presumably with his girlfriend. Bearing a strong resemblance to Buddy Holly, King is playing the guitar and singing into the freestanding microphone in front of him.)

If anything drew attention to King in high school it was his writing talent—a two-edged sword, as he found out. Years later, in "Everything You Need to Know About Writing Successfully—In Ten Minutes," King recounted his misadventures as a satirist who self-published the *Village Vomit,* a parody of the school newspaper. As a staffer on the regular school's newspaper, King was the ideal writer to lampoon it. Every year but his first, he was on the staff of his high school newspaper; and in his third year, he was its editor.

As King explained, the *Village Vomit* poked fun at his teachers—even mentioning names, with a kind of innocent cruelty unique to children. His self-published effort drew immediate, unwanted attention—and the distinct possibility of a three-day suspension. King, though, lucked out. Rather than suspend him, the administration decided to channel his creative writing efforts into a more productive publication—a local newspaper, the *Lisbon Enterprise,* for which he covered high school sports for a half-cent per word.

John Gould, its editor, was the one "who taught me everything I know about writing in ten minutes," wrote King. Gould, as it turned out, was the first person to show King that excellence in writing meant rewriting.

During those four years King soaked up raw material for his work to come. King saw high school in its true light: a rigid caste system in which everyone knew his place. Years later King remarked:

> I would observe what happened to people who were totally left out
> and picked on constantly. One morning, you'd come in and there
> would be "Sally Delavera sucks" written across her locker . . . this
> constant barrage until finally the kid would drop out of school . . .
> because they just couldn't take it anymore. High school is the last
> chance, the last place where you're really allowed to use that totally
> naked, violent approach to people that you don't like.

During his high school years King made a distinction between works of literature like *Hamlet* and *Moby Dick* that teachers assigned him to read ("Gotta Read"), and the works of popular literature he read on his own volition ("Wanna Read").

Chesley recalled that King particularly enjoyed Ed McBain (who taught King "some of the stylistic devices Steve uses—putting thoughts in italics, and snappy dialogue"), the early Ray Bradbury (the horror and early fantasy material), and most especially Don Robertson, whom they would read to each other.

In the "Wanna Read" category, King told *Seventeen* that he enjoyed John D. MacDonald, Ed McBain, Shirley Jackson, collections of teleplays, Wilkie Collins, Ken Kesey, Tom Wolfe essays, Robert E. Howard, Andre Norton, Jack London, Agatha Christie, Margaret Mitchell's *Gone with the Wind,* and countless comic books.

In another magazine, *Scholastic Scope,* King cited his "favorite books . . . when he was a student." These included: *I Am Legend* (Richard

Matheson), *Hot Rod* (Henry G. Felsen), *Jude the Obscure* (Thomas Hardy), *Lord of the Flies* (William Golding), *The Collector* (John Fowles), *The Grapes of Wrath* (John Steinbeck), and *The End of Night* (John D. MacDonald).

Despite his exposure to popular and classic literature, the fiction King produced during this time drew heavily from earlier inspirations: TV shows like "Outer Limits" and "The Twilight Zone," and science-fiction and horror movies. As Chesley remembered, King wrote on the spur of the moment:

> He always wrote intuitively. He would say, "I'm going to write a story," and *that* would be the inspiration. He would sit down and put a piece of paper in the typewriter and he would write that first page. It sounds rather obvious to say, but that page would lead to the next. He wouldn't know where it was going; he would have ideas that he would be tossing and turning around in his mind, but beyond that, it was simply what came to him.

In 1963 Chesley and King self-published *People, Places, and Things—Volume I,* the earliest surviving example of King juvenilia, on David King's mimeograph machine. This "book," a collection of vignettes written over a three-year period, was published by the Triad Publishing Company in two printings: the first in 1960, the second in 1963. Of the eighteen stories, Chesley contributed nine, King eight, and they collaborated on one story.

According to Chesley, less than a dozen copies were ever printed. More than anything else, it was an opportunity for two young writers to see their work in print—self-publishing for its own sake, when they collaborated for the pure fun of it:

> I had gotten into the habit of visiting Steve, who liked to make up scary stories. I'd come over and contribute what I could, when I could. We'd have a good time, especially on hot August days, writing alternate paragraphs of stories about thunderstorms over big dark houses. We'd write on an old typewriter—one of the metal letters was broken. When you finished a page, you had to fill in the missing letters with a pencil.

In the uncredited "Forward" (foreword), the authors explained what to expect in the stories to follow:

> *People, Places, and Things* is an Extraordinary book. It is a book for people who would enjoy being pleasantly thrilled for a few moments.
>   For example: take Chris Chesley's bloodcurdling story, GONE. The last moments of a person left alone in an atomic-doomed world.

Let Steve King's I'M FALLING transport you into a world of dreams.

But if you have no imagination, stop right here. This book is not for you.

If you have an imagination, let it run free.

We warn you . . . the next time you lie in bed and hear an unreasonable creak or thump, you can try to explain it away . . . . but try Steve King's and Chris Chesley's explanation: *People, Places, and Things.*

Because all of the stories were vignettes—a half to a full page, at most—and because they are understandably derivative and early attempts at horror, science fiction, suspense, or fantasy, there is no point in examining them too closely; they were, after all, never intended for such scrutiny.

King's stories—some suggestively titled—were "Hotel at the End of the Road," "I've Got to Get Away!" "The Dimension Warp," "The Thing at the Bottom of the Well," "The Stranger," "I'm Falling," "The Cursed Expedition," and "The Other Side of the Fog."

Chesley's stories—similarly suggestive—were "Genius, 3," "Top Forty, News, Weather, and Sports," "Bloody Child," "Reward," "A Most Unusual Thing," "Gone," "They've Come," "Scared," and "Curiousity [*sic*] Kills the Cat."

King and Chesley collaborated on the last story in the book, "Never Look Behind You."

As Chesley remembered, King's stories grew in length as his storytelling abilities required larger canvases: "What I remember is a progression. When we started hanging out together, he was writing short stories; then they got longer and turned into novellas, and then the novellas turned into novels. It was a very gradual process."

The process could be seen in King's next literary effort, published a year later. *The Star Invaders*—one of several self-published, mimeographed "books"—was in fact only a short story in length (less than three thousand words), but the two-part tale was clearly designed to look like a book. Published in June 1964 by Triad and Gaslight Books under the "AA Gaslight Book" imprint, *The Star Invaders* survives today in one copy owned by King, accidentally discovered in a box of family papers dating back to the Durham days.

From the half-page to full-page vignettes in *People, Places, and Things* to this more ambitious effort, *The Star Invaders* owes much to the science-fiction films of the fifties, with its anxieties about nuclear holocaust, malevolent and bug-eyed monsters that traveled at light speed across the galaxy to plunder Earth, ripe for conquest. As *Earth vs. the Flying Saucers* reminded us: "Look to your skies . . . a warning will come from your skies . . . look to your skies. . . ."

In *The Shorter Works of Stephen King,* Michael R. Collings summarized *The Star Invaders*:

> In Part I, Jerry Hiken, one of the last defenders of the Earth, has been captured by the Star Invaders and tortured to force him to reveal the location of Jed Pierce, the brilliant mind behind the Counter Weapon. When Hiken resists, they use psychological torture; he breaks, telling everything he knows, then kills himself [by smashing his head against the floor]. Part II shifts to Pierce's hideout, where work on the Weapon is nearly finished. The Invaders attack. Pierce destroys ship after ship, ignoring the increasing danger as machinery overheats. When the last ship is destroyed, Pierce races to the atomic pile and single-handedly averts a meltdown. The Weapon works; Earth now has a defense against the Invaders.

A year later, in 1965, King published "I Was a Teenage Grave Robber," a short story notable for being his first work of fiction that was not self-published. Published in a fan magazine, *Comics Review,* "I Was a Teenage Grave Robber" obviously drew its title from the spate of fifties monster movies with titles like *I Was a Teenage Werewolf* and *I Was a Teenage Frankenstein.* (In 1966, King's story was reprinted by Marv Wolfman in his fanzine, *Stories of Suspense,* under the title "In a Half-World of Terror," drawn from the story itself.)

Unlike H. P. Lovecraft whose life and writing career were handicapped by his involvement with fanzines—amateur publications done for fun and not profit—the young Stephen King, early in his career, wisely avoided organized fandom. "I Was a Teenage Grave Robber" was his only early contribution to the fanzines of his time. As King said, "I was never part of a fan network. I never had that kind of a support system."

Nearly twice the length of *The Star Invaders,* "I Was a Teenage Grave Robber" owes much to the horror movies of the fifties, but in imagery and the use of the first person narrative, this story showcased King's storytelling abilities at any early age. Despite its flaws, this story was proof positive that, if nothing else, King could spin a yarn—an innate talent that can be developed but not taught.

In *The Shorter Works of Stephen King,* Michael Collings described its plot: "An orphaned teenager accepts a job as a grave robber for a scientist who, with all the flair of the 1950s 'mad scientist' stereotype, experiments with radioactivity and in the process creates monsters from the maggots inhabiting the corpses. The young man must rescue his girlfriend and destroy the monsters."

For all its flaws, the story still offers a brisk narrative and vivid imagery, with King's characteristically cinematic style making the story come alive:

> A huge, white maggot twisted on the garage floor, holding Weinbaum with long suckers, raising him towards its dripping, pink mouth from which horrid mewling sounds came. Veins, red and pulsing, showed under its slimy flesh and millions of squirming tiny maggots in the blood vessels, in the skin, even forming a huge eye that stared out at me. A huge maggot, made up of hundreds of millions of maggots, the feasters on the dead flesh that Weinbaum had used so freely.

King, who went for the gross-out in this story, has never allowed it to be reprinted. Although it is clearly juvenilia, King need not be apologetic about its relentless storytelling. It's a tale that reads easily, with a cinematic imagery that lingers long afterward.

The Aftermath, a fifty-thousand-word novel, is by far the most ambitious work of juvenilia King completed during his high school years. Although a handwritten note on the original manuscript indicates that it was written in 1963 when King was sixteen, when one considers the progression in story length and the maturity of the work, *The Aftermath* is more likely a later work; Douglas Winter, in *The Art of Darkness,* puts its writing at 1965 or 1966.

An apocalyptic novel—life after the atomic bomb is dropped—*The Aftermath* draws heavily on the rampant paranoia of that time, when it was feared that the Russians would start lobbing ICBMs into American backyards. No wonder the bomb shelter was a favorite home improvement project—perfectly understandable, too, for in 1962 the world held its collective breath for a week as President Kennedy and Premier Khrushchev engaged in a test of wills. Satellite photography had revealed the presence of Russian missiles in Cuba, capable of a first strike against the U.S. Although the Russians backed down, the point was clearly made. Suddenly, the ominous message in movies like *Earth vs. the Flying Saucers* didn't sound like science fiction at all. Instead, it simply sounded like the prudent thing to do. "Look to your skies . . . a warning will come from your skies . . . look to your skies. . . ."

In *The Star Invaders,* written in 1964, King wrote about external evil—invaders from another planet. In *The Aftermath,* King wrote about internal evil—destroyers from this planet. There was no need, King realized, to look for an intergalactic boogeyman—cosmic tommyknockers. As Walt Kelly reminded us in his most famous "Pogo" cartoon strip, we have met the enemy, and he is us.

"They don't call that stuff 'juvenilia' for nothing, friends 'n neighbors," King would write years later in the foreword to Harlan Ellison's *Stalking the Nightmare*. But, as King realized, " . . . there comes a day when you say to yourself, *Good God! If I was this bad, how did I ever get any better?*" The answer, of course, is that King, like any other writer, got better by learning how to write by writing; these early works, admittedly embarrassments to King, proved that even as a teenager, King's storytelling skills were firmly in place, providing a firm foundation for the work to follow. If you can tell a story, you may eventually make your living by writing fiction; but if you can't—if that narrative engine just isn't moving the story—no writing techniques can ever compensate.

Looking back on his high school days, King is not nostalgic. "My high school career was totally undistinguished. I was not at the top of my class, nor at the bottom. I had friends, but none of them were the big jocks or the student council guys or anything like that."

Chris Chesley echoed King's comments: "I've always assumed that he didn't have a wonderful high school experience, that it wasn't that great a time for him in his life."

The summer after graduation King began but did not finish what would be his first mature piece of work, *Getting It On,* which drew its title from the T. Rex song "Bang a Gong (Get It On)." A psychological study—the story of a high school boy who holds his classmates hostage—*Getting It On* tapped into King's childhood fears of not fitting in.

In an interview King once explained that one of his childhood fears was of "not being able to interact, to get along and establish lines of communication. It's the fear I had, the fear of not being able to make friends, the fear of being afraid and not being able to tell anyone you're afraid . . . . There's a constant fear that *I am alone.*"

A major departure from the derivative stories that he wrote during the four previous years, *Getting It On* marked a turning point in King's career. From this point on King's work would principally draw on a wellspring of fears common to all, in stories replete with American iconography. The monsters, King discovered, could be found on Maple Street, USA, and their most frightening aspect was that they looked pretty ordinary, just like Todd Bowden, the human monster King described in "Apt Pupil":

He looked like the total all-American kid as he pedaled his twenty-six-inch Schwinn with the apehanger handlebars up the residential suburban street, and that's just what he was: Todd Bowden, thirteen years old, five-feet-eight and a healthy one hundred and forty pounds, hair the color of ripe corn, blue eyes, white even teeth, lightly tanned skin marred by not even the first shadow of adolescent acne.

According to Douglas Winter, King had originally applied to Drew University in New Jersey, but "his family finances were insufficient to enable him to attend. . . ." Instead, King chose to attend the University of Maine at Orono, where he had obtained a scholarship, like his brother David.

2

The College Years

In the fall of 1966 King began his freshman year at the University of Maine at Orono, a college town with a population of approximately ten thousand.

Like other freshmen, King felt decidedly out of place, as he later wrote in his column for the campus newspaper:

> There I was, all alone in Room 203 of Gannett Hall, clean-shaven, neatly dressed, and as green as apples in August. Outside on the grass between Gannett and Androscoggin Hall there were more people playing football than there were in my home town. My few belongings looked pitifully un-collegiate. The room looked mass-produced. I was quite sure my roommate would turn out to be some kind of a freako, or even worse, hopelessly more With It than I. I propped my girl's picture on my desk where I could look at it in the dismal days ahead, and wondered where the bathroom was.

The "dismal days ahead" would be in stark contrast to the conservatism of the postwar fifties. Like his contemporaries, King would be swept up in the turbulence of the times, a decade dominated by political and social unrest: the Vietnam War and the civil rights movement.

Against this backdrop, King, who in his high school graduation picture looked clean-cut and all-American, would undergo radical changes: idealism would yield to a sense of realism; conservatism would be replaced by mild radicalism as a prelude to liberalism; a limited worldview would swell into a much larger worldview; and, perhaps most important, King would receive professional encouragement for his writing efforts and, on his own, find his fictional voice.

David Bright, a schoolmate, remembered King as being "rather shy but brilliant," which is probably a fair assessment. Years later King, writing about his freshman year, recalled that although he'd "swagger around" back home, on campus he would "promptly shrink back to three feet tall again." Wrote King, it was a time of mixed innocence—and fear, but most of all a time of discovery: college food wasn't so bad (or was it?), frat men carried bottles of booze in their pockets and rubbers in the wallet (or so King supposed), and then there was the nervousness when dating "your first Sophisticated College Girl." As King recalled, he "shaved three times in twenty minutes, and that was just to call her up and ask her."

King concluded: "And you never—I repeat, never—removed your beanie in public, because all upperclassmen could read FRESHMAN written all over your face through some mystic talent . . . and if they caught you in the Den without your beanie you would probably be lynched from the Memorial Union flagpole while the Campus Mayor led a justice-hungry crowd in three choruses of 'The Maine Stein Song.' "

In his first two semesters, King took general courses in geology, history, physical education, sociology, and public speaking. But it was his freshman composition class where he stood out. His professor, Jim Bishop, recognized and encouraged King's early writing efforts. Burton Hatlen, who taught King later, acknowledged that "Jim Bishop was the first person Steve King met on campus who was responsive to his work."

In "The Student King" Sanford Phippen recounted Jim Bishop's recollections of King as a freshman:

> Jim Bishop . . . remembers, "Steve's big physical presence" and how King was "religious about writing." He also remembers that King always had a paperback in his pocket, and knew all these authors that nobody else ever heard of.
>
> "Steve was a nice kid, a good student, but never had a lot of social confidence," Bishop says. "Even then, though, he saw himself as a famous writer and thought he could make money at it. Steve was writing continuously, industriously, and diligently. He was amiable, resilient, and created his own world."

In the summer of 1967 King completed a short story, "The Glass Floor." It was the kind of story he felt might be right for Robert A. W. Lowndes, who edited a line of pulp magazines—mostly short fiction and mostly reprinted material. For whatever reason, King didn't submit it immediately; in the last two years his submissions to Lowndes always came back, so what was the hurry?

As for book-length fiction, King turned his attention to completing *The Long Walk,* his first full-fledged novel. "I thought of it while hitchhiking home from college one night when I was a freshman," King later recalled in a 1985 letter to Michael R. Collings. The novel took its inspiration from President John F. Kennedy's endorsement of walkathons. As Kennedy had urged the public in 1962, "I would encourage every American to walk as often as possible. It's more than healthy; it's fun."

Taking that idea to the extreme, *The Long Walk* is the story of a group of boys who must walk from northern Maine, heading south, until only one survivor remains. To King, the story is perhaps a metaphor of life.

In the fall of 1967 King approached Burton Hatlen, who taught him American literature, with the finished manuscript. Years later Hatlen recalled what happened afterward: "I brought it home and laid it on the dining room table. My ex-wife picked it up and started reading it and couldn't stop—that was also my experience. The narrative grabbed you and carried you forward. That was what was most striking about *The Long Walk:* King had a fully developed sense of narrative and pace. It was there already. It was quite amazing to see that."

The novel then made the rounds in the English department. Edward Holmes, who taught creative writing, recalled reading *The Long Walk* and then told Hatlen enthusiastically that they had a writer on their hands. Jim Bishop read the novel, as did Carroll Terrell, who recounted in *Stephen King: Man and Artist* his first encounter with King. "Professor Hatlen said I should give this to you to read. It's a novel. I wrote it," explained King, who handed Terrell "a thick manuscript which suggested an MA thesis." As Terrell recalled:

> It was called *The Long Walk* and posed certain technical problems which would require more practice for him to solve. The design of the book made the action repetitive and got him into a kind of "another Indian bit the dust" trap. The solution to that might be a more extensive use of flashback to flesh out the characters.
>
> Steve's reaction to this was precise and (as I eventually came to see) correct. He said, in effect, that the sameness and routine were deliberate and part of the point. On the road to life few people become distinguished from the mass; they just stagger along until they conk out.

Terrell concluded, "I am conscious now that I thought *The Long Walk* was a first novel. But I should have known that it could have been no such thing: No one could have written such a balanced and designed book without a lot of practice; not just aimless practice, but conscious and designed practice."

Encouraged by the enthusiasm within the English department, King was satisfied that the novel was publishable and submitted it to a first-novel competition. The book, however, was rejected with a form letter and, discouraged, King put the book aside. "I was too crushed to show that book to any publisher in New York," King later wrote in an article, "On Becoming a Brand Name."

About that time King submitted "The Glass Floor" to Robert A. W. Lowndes and finally broke into print with his first professional sale. Published in the fall 1967 issue of *Startling Mystery Stories,* King's short story was prefaced with an editorial comment: "Stephen King has been sending us stories for some time, and we returned one of them most reluctantly, since it would be far too long before we could use it, due to its length. But patience may yet bring him due reward on that tale ["The Night of the Tiger"]; meanwhile, here is a chiller whose length allowed us to get it into print much sooner."

That first published story, according to King, was "the product of an unformed storyteller's mind," written so he could "*see better.*" The $35 sale was a harbinger of things to come. After collecting dozens of rejection slips since 1962, he could now say he was a professional writer. As King wrote years later, "I've cashed many bigger [checks] since then, but none gave me more satisfaction; someone had finally paid me some real money for something I had found in my head!"

In the next issue of *Startling Mystery Stories,* in a reader's poll King's story had tied for fifth place. Not bad, all things considered. Success, clearly, would not be overnight; a long walk still lay ahead.

During that sophomore year, in addition to Hatlen's American literature class, King took classes in English, American, and twentieth-century literature; second-year and advanced composition classes; and a creative writing class. King supplemented those with psychology courses, a sociology course on rural life, a course in play production, and a teaching course, The American School.

The contemporary American literature course, taught by Burton Hatlen, exposed King to John Steinbeck, William Faulkner, William Carlos Williams, and other writers. Years later Hatlen recalled:

> We read Steinbeck's *In Dubious Battle,* and I remember him being very struck with that. He might have started reading Steinbeck before the class—I don't want to take credit. I believe Steinbeck has been a major influence on him. We also read Faulkner in that class—*Light in August,* though I don't think Faulkner has been as strong a force as Steinbeck on him. We read William Carlos Williams—he was very excited by *Paterson.*

The creative writing class, in contrast, had a negative influence on him. King would later say that it was a constipating experience. An intuitive writer who even as a teenager had an instinctive understanding of plotting and narrative pace—the key elements in storytelling—King found that the overanalytical environment of the class inhibited his own efforts. As King said years later, "The creative writing courses at the college level are very important, but I don't think they're necessary. It's a supportive experience . . . . The best thing about it was that the art of writing was taken seriously, and that's an awfully good thing."

A self-taught writer, King was on a quest to find his own fictional voice, the path less traveled. Because of it, his fiction would stand out in comparison to that of his contemporaries, especially when published in *Ubris,* the college literary magazine.

In the spring 1968 issue of *Ubris* King published two short stories: "Here There Be Tygers," a readable but minor story about a boy in the third grade who finds a tiger in his school's bathroom, and "Cain Rose Up," the kind of story that showcased King's writing talent.

The idea for "Cain Rose Up" came from a real-life sniping incident that took place on August 1, 1966, when Charles Whitman—a former marine, a student with a heavy academic courseload, and a part-timer after school—took a firing position atop the twenty-seven-story tower at the University of Texas in Austin and began shooting. The result: he killed a dozen people and wounded thirty-three others. "University officials were at a loss to explain Whitman's actions. They said he had never been treated at the student health center for psychiatric disorder and had no record of being disciplined."

King, though, understood the pressures Whitman had been experiencing. A year later, in his May 1969 column for the campus newspaper, King wrote: "Maybe you get loaded on Thursday afternoon. You might develop a decided hostility in class. You might drop out. You might even start looking at the Stevens Hall tower and wondering—just *wondering,* mind you—how nice it might be to climb up here and pick a few people off."

It was an idea that had fascinated King for some time; *Getting It On,* half completed, told of a high school student who snapped under pressure, with disastrous consequences. In "Cain Rose Up," Garrish, a college student, takes up a firing position in his dorm room and, wielding a .352 Magnum with a telescopic sight, starts blowing students away.

A stark contrast to the other stories in *Ubris,* "Cain Rose Up" heralded a new literary talent on campus, one that couldn't be ignored. This wasn't imitative, self-indulgent pap from a student who wanted to write in a literary style; it was a raw, visceral kind of writing that had the effect of a knockout punch.

In the fall of 1968 King published in *Ubris* a short story, "Strawberry Spring," which he wrote in less than two hours on napkins in the campus cafeteria. Again, like "Cain Rose Up," this story pulled no punches. With that "false spring, a lying spring" comes "Springheel Jack," a killer that stalks the campus in the mist that accompanies the strawberry spring.

Also that fall, Burton Hatlen and Jim Bishop came up with the idea of holding a seminar on contemporary poetry, limited to an enrollment of a dozen students, who had to apply for the class, then be interviewed by Hatlen or Bishop. Hatlen recalled, "It was a very dynamic experience for a lot of people. Many of them started writing poetry as a result of it. As a result of the course, a poetry workshop grew out of it."

King remembered having written "about forty to fifty poems" during what he termed a "tremendously exciting experience," but noted that "nothing came of it. It was like being on a long drunk. But, on the other hand, I wasn't typical. For a lot of people, good did come from it."

Jim Bishop, in an introduction to a 1970 issue of *Moth*, elaborated:

> From that seminar . . . came a half dozen or so energetic and highly individual young poets who have been rapping in the hallways, in coffee shops, in front of Stevens Hall, or wherever any two of them chance to meet, ever since, and that original group has grown this year to a dozen, sometimes as many as twenty, who meet every other Friday in an informal workshop to read their poetry, alternatively to read and reassemble one another, and hopefully to emerge with a better understanding of themselves, their world, and their work.

In addition to the poetry class, King took courses in Shakespeare and twentieth-century British literature; an introductory course to radio and television; a debate class; and an education class, Growth Learning Process.

By spring 1969 King, then a junior, had become a campus institution, frequently sighted on campus, not unlike the northern Sasquatch. As Tabitha King later recalled, during one such sighting when he was pointed out to her, she saw an "enormous, shambling person in cut-off gum rubbers."

In the January 15, 1969, issue of *The Maine Campus* King appeared on the cover. A schoolmate of King's, Frank Kadi, shot a riveting photograph of him: long-haired, wearing a leather jacket and wielding a double-barreled shotgun aimed at the viewer, and with a decidedly maniacal gleam in his eye, King looked a lot like Charles Manson. The caption read: "STUDY DAMMIT!"

It showed a side of King that most people suspected—a broad sense of humor, the kind that was necessary to offset the pressures of January midterms.

The next month the readers of *The Maine Campus* encountered King again, this time on a more permanent basis. King rolled out with a regular column, "King's Garbage Truck," that debuted in its February 20, 1969, issue.

David Bright, a journalism major and editor of the paper, recalled when King initially approached him. "Steve came into the campus office and said he wanted to write a column. We were there to let students write, so he just did whatever he wanted to do. I said, 'Steve, you're more than welcome to write a column. My rules are that it's got to be here Tuesday at noon, and it has to fit the space.' Then King would show up and type it."

As editor, Bright never had to blue-pencil King's work. "The guy is very prolific; he likes to write and is excellent at it. He'd come in and bang those pieces out. They'd be letter-perfect and he'd lay them on the desk."

According to another staffer, "King was always late. We would be pulling our hair out at deadline. With five minutes or so to go, Steve would come in and sit down at the typewriter and produce two flawless pages of copy. He carries stories in his head the way most people carry change in their pockets."

The first installment, approximately seven hundred words, reviewed a program put on by students from a Vermont college, and a movie, *Hush, Hush, Sweet Charlotte.* The installments to follow would be characteristically King: informal and chatty, straight off the shoulder and direct, with personal commentary on campus activities, on the ongoing Vietnam War, and on controversial subjects like birth control. On the lighter side, King wrote book, movie, and record reviews, and rambling discourses on such topics as baseball, girl-watching, and popular culture. In short, King would write about virtually anything; you couldn't tell what King, like a garbage truck, would collect on his weekly rounds, or unload.

Turning to fiction, King published his fourth *Ubris* story in its spring 1969 issue. "Night Surf," a moody piece set on a beach where teenagers muse about life and death after a Superflu ravages the world. And in the spring 1969 issue of *Startling Mystery Stories,* Lowndes published a second story by King, "Reaper's Image," which earned him another $35.

In the spring of 1969, English courses were the bulk of King's academic load: The American Novel, Modern Grammar, British Drama, and—necessary for teaching certification—Teaching in Secondary School.

At that time the college was going through a period of self-appraisal; meetings were held with the students and faculty to assess the curriculum. King, a vocal critic of the English department because of its traditional approach to teaching literature, stood out, drawing attention to himself because of his oft-spoken views.

Burton Hatlen recalled that as an undergraduate "King was so different from most students. He had such a clearly defined identity and a sense of purpose. I think that's quite unusual."

The best evidence of this was King's stand on popular culture and literature. Hatlen explained:

> I remember a meeting in which the students and faculty got together to talk about the curriculum of the English department. Several people have a memory of Steve standing up at this meeting and denouncing the department because he had never been able to read a Shirley Jackson novel in any of the courses he had taken.
>
> He criticized the curriculum and insisted on the value and importance of popular culture and mass culture, and people listened to him. It was an important moment. King wanted to conduct a special seminar on popular American fiction, which produced a crisis. Here was an undergraduate proposing to teach a course.

With Graham Adams, a teacher in the English department, as the front man, King taught the seminar, Popular Literature and Culture. It was perhaps the first and only time in the history of the University of Maine that an undergraduate had taught his fellow students. Equally impressive: the subject matter was not picked up in the classroom; instead, he had learned it on his own, *outside* the classroom.

In the fall of 1969—the first semester of his senior year—his classes were divided into teaching courses (The Teaching Process, and Teaching Reading in Secondary School) and English courses (Poetry of the Romantic Movement, and The Earlier English Novel). Under Edward Holmes, King took Directed Writing.

Holmes remembered King's writing as "highly imaginative and he had a pretty good organization. There was no question about his getting anything less than an excellent grade. I enjoyed reading his work and giving him criticism."

Diane McPherson—one of the dozen who attended the first special seminar on contemporary poetry with King—had also taken Directed Writing under Holmes with King. "We wrote independently but then got together once a week and it was great fun, often hilarious. I was the ideal audience for Steve's wild inventive fantasies. My thing then was to cut all the extraneous adverbs and adjectives. Steve was pretty pop. He was writing exciting stories, but with no control," as McPherson later told Phippen in "The Student King."

Outside the classroom King continued work on a novel he had begun writing the year before. *Sword in the Darkness,* heavily influenced by John Farris's "Harrison High" novels, is the story of Arnie Kalowski, a teenager at Harding High School, set against the backdrop of a race riot. A naturalistic novel, *Sword in the Darkness* reflected the turbulent times in which it was written, a time when the civil rights movement came to the forefront.

Carroll Terrell, who was given an early, incomplete draft of the novel, recalled King's early efforts in getting it published:

> After he'd finished about half of it, he asked me if it would be a good idea to send it to a publisher to get an advance. At the time, I knew nothing of his serious financial difficulties. I told him it would do no harm, but it wouldn't do any good. I thought the book was potentially marketable, but not something in 1969 that a publisher would give an advance on. So I told him they'd read it, tell him it showed great promise, and invite him to send the completed version, but they wouldn't give an unknown either an advance or a contract. A few weeks later, he handed me a letter from a publisher and said something like: "At least you hit the nail on the head."

On April 30, 1970, King completed *Sword in the Darkness,* his most ambitious work to date. At 150,000 words, it was also his longest fictional effort. Through one of his professors, King was able to get a literary agent to shop it around New York. Patricia Schartle Myrer of McIntosh and Otis submitted the manuscript to a dozen publishers, including Doubleday, but the work found no takers. Years later King would call the book "a badly busted flush," a book so bad that "I can't even like it when I'm drunk."

In the second semester of his senior year in early 1970, King continued to take Directed Writing under Holmes; in addition, he took a modern literature course, Educational Sociology, and Man and His Environment. King also student-taught at Hampden Academy in Hampden, south of Bangor. As the story goes, King, a long-haired freak like many of his classmates, was told to get a haircut before beginning his student teaching.

It was a sensitive subject to King. He had unloaded his thoughts on the subject in the February 12, 1970, issue of *The Maine Campus.* He had, he began, "a few hard words to say about clothes, hair, and the general state of the young." King then lashed out at "a few of the things I'm sick of," starting with criticism against long hair. "Can you imagine a country supposedly based on freedom of expression telling people that they can't grow hair on their head or their face? Since when have we descended to the point where we care more about what people look like than what they think like?" King then facetiously suggested that we should "fall down and worship the real heroes—clean-cut fellows like James Earl Ray, Lee Harvey Oswald, Eichmann, and George Lincoln Rockwell. Idiocy! How can anyone be stupid?"

It was a time when it was hard *not* to be angry. As King explained to an interviewer years later:

> When I was in school, Vietnam was going up in flames, and Watts was going up in flames, and Bobby Kennedy and Martin Luther King had been shot, and these little dollies were bopping into their eight o'clock classes with nine pounds of makeup on and their hair processed to perfection, and the high heels and everything, because they wanted husbands, and they wanted jobs, and they wanted all the things their mothers wanted, and they wanted to get into a big sorority. Big deal.

Outside the classroom students marched and demonstrated against the war, rallied for free speech, and protested against university policies.

It was, as King later recalled, a time when horror fiction seemed especially appropriate as a metaphor, a time when parents saw their children change into monsters, symbolized by Linda Blair in *The Exorcist*:

> At that time, college campuses were in revolt—utter revolt. It's hard for a lot of us to remember—even me, and I was *in* it at the time; a lot of my friends were *in* it at the time; we had eggs thrown at us, we were gassed, this sort of thing. We went home and our parents said, "You going to get a haircut pretty soon?" And we said, "No, I don't think so. Want a joint, dad?" We didn't say that; I didn't say that. My point is, simply, there was a youthquake, a youth revolution, a kind of civil war between parents and children; and with all this as a backdrop, comes a movie about a wonderful, beautiful suburban girl who turns into a foul-talking, stringy-haired, ugly monstrosity who is saying these ugly words, these terrible obscenities, vomiting pea soup at people. Parents are looking at this and they're feeling horror . . . and a sigh of relief, saying, "*That's* what's happened to Susie. She went to college and the devil got her." In a way, it's a powerful parable for what parents saw. *The Exorcist* was able to reach out to older people and grasp something that made them very uneasy, that made

them heartsick, in a way the kids at the time couldn't understand certainly; and to translate it into a symbolic proposition.

To King, horror fiction seemed to be the best vehicle for those troubled times. Today horror seems even more appropriate. As King later wrote:

> They are unreal symbols of very real fears. I don't think that horror fiction works—I don't think it's possible to scare a person, particularly in a novel—unless you are talking in two voices: on one level, in a very loud voice, you are screaming at your audience. You are screaming about ghosts, you are screaming about werewolves, you are screaming about shape-changers, vampires, whatever. But in another, very low voice—a whisper—you are talking about *real* fears, so that in the best cases, you are trying to achieve that nightmare feeling that we've all had; that we know it's not real, but that doesn't matter anymore. When I can get that, I know I've got people right where I want them.

During that tumultuous time, King, like many of his contemporaries, was swept up in the momentum of the moment; he *had* to take a stand. King, once a registered Republican in his hometown, became a card-carrying Independent and metamorphosed into what he self-termed "a scummy radical bastard."

To King, being a scummy radical bastard meant that he was proud to be an American who believed in the "Declaration of Independence, the Constitution, and even the Articles of Confederation."

It was during his senior year while working at the university library that King met his wife-to-be, Tabitha Jane Spruce, a poet and a writer, majoring in history. Around that time, several reams of odd-sized, brightly colored paper mysteriously showed up in the library; King took a ream of "bright green" paper, Tabitha Spruce took a ream of "robin's egg blue" paper, and David Lyons—"the fellow she was going with back then," wrote King—took the "Roadrunner yellow" ream.

Putting his ream to good use, King—"living in a scuzzy riverside cabin not far from the University . . . living all by myself"—sat in front of his "office-model Underwood," presumably the same typewriter he had used during those Durham days. Using his two-finger typing technique, he tapped out the opening line to a new story: "The man in black fled across the desert and the gunslinger followed."

Later, when King was home from school at his childhood home in

Durham, Chesley came over and sat next to King in the kitchen. "He was sitting by the stove," recalled Chesley, "and I asked, 'What are you writing?' He held up these sheets—about ten of them—titled *The Dark Tower.* I read them and then said, 'Steve, this is the most amazing thing you've ever written. What are you going to do with it?' "

For the moment, however, King did nothing with the story. Graduation was imminent and job hunting would become the priority. Writing must wait.

On May 18, 1970, shots rang out that were heard around the world. At Kent State an antiwar rally turned ugly. Ohio National Guardsmen, headed back home from the duty of protecting truckers from sniper fire on the interstate, were rerouted to the campus at the request of university officials. In battle gear—fatigues, flak jacket, web gear with ammunition clips, and helmet—the guardsmen marched with rifles in hand in riot-control formation toward the students.

Then the unthinkable happened. Backed against the wall, pelted by rocks from the students, some of the enlisted men thought they heard the order to fire . . . and opened fire. The tragic result: two men and two women were killed; eight others were wounded—victims of peace, casualties of the supposedly peaceful war fought on the homefront.

The 1970 *Prism,* the UMO yearbook, recorded in words and pictures the reactions of the stunned student body at Orono:

> One morning, one sunshine morning, Kent State was a phrase, a rumor of four tragic deaths on the campus of a university noted more for athletics than for education.
>
> And then in twenty-four hours, it was a nationwide funeral.
>
> "See, then, if you can wipe out grief as you painted away idealism!" For very real was the anger of students. Not students as a body politic, but students as individuals.
>
> Students who had to make, for themselves, the decisions about their education. The knot that tied the [three-day] education moratorium to the national strike; a Council of Colleges jammed up against the wall, seven hundred students confronting President Libby. Academic freedom!
>
> Individuals.
>
> Deciding for themselves what stood highest and where. Whether to forsake school for something more important. Whether school was more important than ending a bloody war.

They held the candles; walked on the mall the night of May 7. Walked. Not marched. It was not a military ceremony. Indeed, it was not even a protest against the military. That would come later.

It was people. One thousand, solemn, singular persons. Some with tears in their eyes. Some with anger; the kind of vicious, hurting, destroying anger that eats and burns, like a bullet in the belly. So that no one forgot it! So that everyone knew.

In the yearbook, pictures showed the rest of the story: students, gathered together, reflecting individually; a coed tying a black armband on a long-haired male student, just another "scummy radical bastard"; students at a sit-in, confronted by a member of the administration armed with a megaphone; a river of students, grim-faced and somber, moving slowly across campus; students gathered in a chapel, and on a nearby stained-glass window, the simple words "Do Not Forget"; students gathered, sitting quietly, on an indoor stage, as four candles burned brightly against the darkness; a blonde coed looking into the flames of a candle, illuminating a pensive face; and, finally, a photograph of a single candle, its wax drops beaded around its base, nearly extinguished . . . now flickering . . . a candle in the wind.

As Crosby, Stills, Nash & Young reminded a stunned generation in their song "Find the Cost of Freedom," those four students had found— and paid—the ultimate cost of freedom: four lay dead in Ohio.

In the May 7, 1970, installment of "King's Garbage Truck," King wrote that "in a few weeks . . . I can march along with the rest of the Class of '70 into the Outside World, shining of eye (as long as I'm not hung over), noble of countenance, a smile on my lips, joy in my heart, and a cigarette cough in my lungs."

In the next installment, the forty-seventh, "King's Garbage Truck" made its last stop. On May 21, 1970, King's column was headlined: "A BLESSED (?) EVENT ANNOUNCED TO THE UNIVERSITY OF MAINE AT ORONO." Hailing his birth, King marked his date into the real world as June 5, 1970, at age twenty-two; six feet, three inches; and 207 pounds. King wrote that future prospects were "hazy, although either nuclear annihilation or environmental strangulation seem to be definite possibilities."

Assessing himself—a stark contrast to the bright-eyed, idealistic, registered Republican who attended freshman orientation some four years ago—King wrote:

This boy has shown evidences of some talent, although at this point it is impossible to tell if he is just a flash in the pan or if he has real possibilities. It seems obvious that he has learned a great deal at the University of Maine at Orono, although a great deal has contributed to a lessening of idealistic fervor rather than a heightening of that characteristic. If a speaker at his birth into the real world mentions "changing the world with the bright-eyed vigor of youth" this young man is apt to flip him the bird and walk out, as he does not feel very bright-eyed by this time: in fact, he feels about two thousand years old.

On June 5, 1970, Stephen King graduated from college, with a "Bachelor of Science degree in English and a Speech minor with a side interest in Drama," and his teacher's certification for secondary school.

3

The Long Walk

After graduation King moved into what he styled a "sleazy Orono, Maine, apartment" and continued work on *The Dark Tower* as it began to shape up in his mind—a long, heroic epic about a gunslinger.

That summer, in *The Maine Campus*, King published "Slade," a humorous western tale that recalled the Breckinridge Elkins tales by Robert F. Howard. Running sixty-five hundred words, and serialized in eight installments from June 11 to August 6, 1970, "Slade" would in some ways be a trial cut for the gunslinger tale that had preoccupied King's energies. "Slade" begins:

> It was almost dark when Slade rode into Dead Steer Springs. He was tall in the saddle, a grim-faced man dressed all in black. Even the handles of his two sinister .45s, which rode low on his hips, were black. Ever since the early 1870s, when the name of Slade had begun to strike fear into the stoutest of Western hearts, there had been many whispers about his dress. . . . [S]ome said he wore black because Slade was the Grim Reaper's agent in the American Southwest—the devil's handyman. And then there were some who thought he was queerer than a three-dollar bill. No one, however, advanced this last idea to his face.

With "Slade," King did ride off into the sunset insofar as his contributions to *The Maine Campus* were concerned, as it was a nonpaying market and King found himself—along with his contemporaries—with the grim prospect of trying to find a teaching position at a time when there were too many newly minted teachers on the marketplace but too few available positions.

First jobs are rarely auspicious; King's was no exception. King took a job pumping gas at a station in nearby Brewer. Gas was nineteen cents a gallon; if you got a fill-up, you'd get a free loaf of bread; and if you got your oil checked, you'd get a free Flintstone glass. The job paid $1.25 an hour.

When King had an opportunity to change jobs, he seized it. As a

51

laborer at the New Franklin Laundry in Bangor, King's income jumped to $1.60 an hour, $60.00 a week. In addition, King moonlighted as a freelance writer, submitting to men's magazines, which paid on publication, not acceptance.

"Almost all of the men's magazines are excellent markets for the beginning horror freelancer," King later wrote in an essay, "The Horror Writer and the Ten Bears." King continued: "They need lots of material, and most of them could care less if you're an unknown. If your story is good, and if you pick the right market, you can make a sale." One of the best such magazines, King wrote, was *Adam*. "If your story has sex interest and is still quality, I'd say send to *Adam* first."

It was good advice. King, in fact, practiced what he preached. Earlier that spring while still in college, King had made a sale to *Adam*. "The Float" is a story about college students from Horlicks University who seek sex and fun in the sun on a raft on a deserted lake, where they are trapped by a lake creature that attacks them.

The story behind the sale of "The Float"—later detailed by King in an afterword to *Skeleton Crew*—was the stuff of fiction, a real-life Stephen King story: In Orono, shortly after midnight, while driving home in his car with a rotting tailpipe, King ran over traffic cones at a traffic intersection and knocked off his muffler. Enraged, King drove around town and began collecting traffic cones with the intention of leaving them in front of the local police station.

A local policeman, however, saved him the effort. As King remembered, the cop asked: "Son, are those traffic cones yours?"

King represented himself in court—and lost. He faced a $250 fine without the financial wherewithal to pay and thus confronted the dismal prospect of a month in jail.

Out of the blue, however, came a $250 check for King's story, "The Float," from *Adam*. Since that company routinely paid on publication, one assumes the story was published. Oddly, however, King never received a copy from the publisher, nor could he find it on the stands.

That fall King made his first sale to *Cavalier* magazine, where a well-told tale would sell on its own merits. Unlike some of the men's magazines, this one didn't require that the story have gratuitous sex. In "The Horror Writer and the Ten Bears" King wrote:

> I have a particular warmth for *Cavalier,* because they published my own first marketable horror stories. Both Doug Allen and Nye

Willden are warm and helpful, and if your story is good, they'll publish it. They report in four to six weeks and pay from $200 to $300 depending on length and previous numbers of stories published. The best length is around 4,000 words.

In its October 1970 issue, *Cavalier* published "Graveyard Shift," for which King earned $250. It was drawn from his firsthand experiences after high school and in the summers at a textile mill in the Lisbon Falls area. Its genesis, like that of many of his stories, was sparked by his asking "What if?" As King recalled:

> I wrote most of "Graveyard Shift" in the office of *The Maine Campus.* I had this idea for a story: Wouldn't it be funny if these people cleaned out the basement of the mill—which is a job I had at one time—and found all these big rats? Wouldn't that be gross?
>
> Think of all the things you could do with that. So I wrote the story.

The story: Pressed into service by an overbearing foreman, a college student descends with coworkers into the basement of a mill to clean it out. In its depths, they discover a world where man is the intruder, where mutated rats grow to monstrous size.

An intuitive writer who doesn't work from outlines, King simply started writing the story. As the pages rolled out of the typewriter, a friend read them and said, "Oh, more! I think he ought to go around ripping the heads off rats and eating them!"

Though the premise is on the surface humorous, it was "the ultimate labor versus management story," according to King. Transmuting reality into fiction, the story had a serious message that transcended its pulpish plot:

> The real impetus to write this particular story was the mill I worked in. It was a non-union shop, and when they had vacation week, the people who had "tenure" got a paid vacation; the rest of us also got the week off—without pay, unless you wanted to work the clean-up crew, which was going to go down in the basement.
>
> I worked in the bagging area. They'd blow fabric up into these huge bins and we would bag it. Between the times you were waiting for your bin to fill up, you'd throw cans at the rats, because the rats were everywhere. They were big guys, too; some of them would sit right up and beg for it like dogs, which stuck in my mind. So when I was asked to join the clean-up crew, I said, "No, I can't do that. I'm going to beg off. You guys have a good time."

Afterward, a friend of his who worked in the dye house told King that he should have been there. According to his friend, "some of them were as big as puppies." It was this same friend who told King that for recreation, they'd "put the rats in the dye bins and see how fast they would run when they started to roll the drums."

When King got a copy of *Cavalier* with his story, he sent his mother a photocopy after he "blocked out all the ads for glossy photos and films" of young women in highly suggestive poses.

It was a difficult time in King's life. In fact, the only bright spot, it seemed, was Tabitha Spruce, with whom King had worked at the college library. Since his senior year, his relationship with her had become serious, serious enough that, at the end of the year, on Christmas Eve in 1970, they filed marriage intentions. King's address at the time was 112 North Main Street in Orono. On December 29, 1970, they were issued a marriage license.

Years later King wrote: "The only important thing I ever did in my life for a conscious reason was to ask Tabitha Spruce, the college co-ed I was seeing, if she would marry me. The reason was that I was deeply in love with her. The joke is that love itself is an irrational and indefinable emotion."

On January 2, 1971, Stephen Edwin King and Tabitha Jane Spruce were married in Old Town, just north of Orono. Because Tabitha was raised as a Roman Catholic, the ceremony was held at a Catholic church. Clergyman John M. Anderson performed the ceremony. Because Stephen was raised as a Methodist, the reception was held at a Methodist church.

That month also marked the publication of a new short story by King in the January 1971 issue of *Onan,* the literary magazine at King's alma mater; *Onan* published "The Blue Air Compressor." Owing much to "The Tell-tale Heart" by Edgar Allan Poe—whom King had read but not admired—King's story was also inspired in part by the horror comics of the fifties, especially Bill Gaines's E.C. line, which despite the lurid covers and graphic art often had a strong moral message, consistent with King's Methodist upbringing—the righteous prevailed, but sinners would suffer. (Back in the Durham days, Stephen and David King attended the Methodist Youth Fellowship "on Thursday nights in a hall that had a poster on the wall that said, 'Methodists say: No thank you,' " King recalled.)

King's childhood home in Durham, Maine. (1990, photo by GB)

Behind King's childhood home in Durham, the loft area was designated by Stephen King "the 249 Club." There, Stephen, David King, and their friends met to play cards, read magazines, and tell stories. Transmuted into fiction, the 249 Club would reappear as a brownstone in New York City, where its members met to tell stories. Its custodian: Stevens. (See "The Breathing Method" in *Different Seasons*.)

The view out of Stephen King's bedroom window in Durham, Maine, looking to the left of the house, with the West Durham United Methodist Church to the left. (1990, photo by GB)

The view across the road from King's childhood home in Durham, Maine. (1990, photo by GB)

The West Durham United Methodist Church where the Kings attended church services in Durham, Maine. (1990, photo by GB)

The one-room schoolhouse (now a private residence) where King went to grammar school. (1990, photo by GB)

The Shiloh Chapel (mentioned in "The Body" and, guesses David Lowell, perhaps an inspiration for the Marsten House in *'Salem's Lot*). (1990, photo by GB)

The Harmony Grove Cemetery in Durham, Maine, which appeared as Harmony Hill Cemetery in *'Salem's Lot.* (1990, photo by GB)

Chris Chesley standing in front of Runaround Pond in Durham, Maine, where the dead body was discovered. (1990, photo by GB)

Lisbon High School in Lisbon Falls, Maine, where King attended high school. (1990, photo by GB)

Stephen King at an antiwar rally at UMO, from the college yearbook, *Prism*.

Burton Hatlen, Bangor,
Maine. (1990, photo by GB)

Edward "Ted" Holmes, one of
King's college professors at
UMO, in Winterport, Maine.
(1990, photo by GB)

Carroll F. Terrell at home in Orono, Maine (note the King books in the background). (1990, photo by GB)

Hampden Academy in Hampden, Maine. (1990, photo by GB)

Stephen King in the Hampden Academy yearbook,
Hampden, Maine.

Stephen King, a teacher at Hampden Academy, shows his boogeyman pose.

Stephen King after *Carrie* was sold. (Photo courtesy of the *Bangor Daily News.*)

Stephen King signs a copy of *Pet Sematary* for Peter Bruder of New Jersey,
December 3, 1983. (Photo courtesy of the Portland *Press Herald*,
a Guy Gannett Publishing Company.)

Stephen King receives the key to the city from the mayor of Truth or Consequences, New Mexico. (Photo courtesy of *The Herald.*)

In March 1971 King published his second story in *Cavalier,* a science-fiction/horror tale, "I Am the Doorway." Though King had an early diet of science-fiction films and stories, his inability to write what was commonly called "hard" science fiction—the kind Robert A. Heinlein wrote—meant that King would have to write fantasy or horror instead. In this story, the setting is science fiction, but the story is pure horror. A spaceman returns to earth from Venus and brings back an alien affliction: eyes grow on his hands, which take on a life of their own, seeking to kill. Horrified, he burns his hands, but the deadly eyes grow back, on his chest.

Early on, King's fiction reflected a basic tenet of fantasy, which gave King the leeway to write pretty much anything he wanted: If the tale is well told, readers won't question the premise, as King learned as a youth from the Seuss story *The 500 Hats of Bartholomew Cubbins.*

In May 1971 Tabitha King graduated with a B.A. degree in history from the University of Maine at Orono. Like her husband, she was unable to find suitable employment after graduation. Tabitha eventually found employment as a waitress at one of two Dunkin' Donuts in Bangor.

Money was tight in the King household. Stephen and Tabitha King's combined income—supplemented with the occasional story that paid on publication—was simply not enough to live on, especially with the addition of their firstborn, Naomi.

Encouraged by his short-story sales, and thinking to get ahead with the sale of a book, Stephen King finished *Getting It On* and decided to submit it to Doubleday, since it had published Loren Singer's *The Parallax View,* which King felt was similar enough that it might be favorably received.

King now knew, having learned from his premature submission of *Sword in the Darkness,* an incomplete manuscript, that the only way to sell *Getting It On* would be to submit a finished manuscript.

King also knew, even though he had only recently begun publishing short fiction professionally, that he should not submit it through what the publishers called the "slush pile," the unsolicited manuscripts that came in across the transom. So King sent a query letter to Doubleday, addressed to the editor of *The Parallax View,* who—unknown to King—had left Doubleday. The query letter ended up at William G. Thompson's desk, where it received a cordial response. Send it in, Thompson wrote back, and King did. A sale would mean that he could quit his job at the laundry and finally write fiction full time.

Thompson later wrote that *Getting It On* "was a masterful study in character and suspense, but it was quiet, deliberately claustrophobic and it proved a tough sell within the house. I'd asked Stephen—for by now we were on a first name basis—for changes which he willingly and promptly made, but even so I couldn't glean sufficient support and reluctantly returned it."

The rejection hit King hard. His hope to write fiction for a living must temporarily be put on hold, but for how long? As King wrote: "Doubleday declined, a painful blow for me, because I had been allowed to entertain some hope for an extraordinarily long time, and had rewritten the book a third time, trying to bring it into line with what Doubleday's publishing board would accept."

When a position for an English teacher became available at nearby Hampden Academy, where King had student-taught in his senior year of college, King took the position. The job paid $6,400 a year.

As King later wrote, it was not the best of times; in fact, it was the worst of times. "There I was, unpublished, living in a trailer, with barely enough money to get by and an increasing sense of doubt in my abilities as a writer, and this kid was crying and bawling every night."

The one bright spot was his school life. A natural teacher, King was well liked by his students and also held in high regard by the administration. Years later, Robert W. Rowe, the principal at Hampden Academy, recalled: "King was a promising teacher."

Even at school, though, everyone could see he was serious as a writer. As Rowe recalled, "It was hard to catch him without a book under his arm; if he had the spare time, he'd be reading a book. But he always took the time to write; he was disciplined in his writing, consistent in sitting down and doing the work."

A former student, Brenda Willey, remembered King as "a good teacher who had seven classes a day and a study hall. He told us that he liked to write, and I think he wanted us to write. He was fun and had a pretty good sense of humor." (The school yearbooks, in fact, showed King's humorous side: In one photo, King spread his arms out in a boogeyman pose; in another, he's reading, not a textbook or a serious English text, but—*Mad* magazine.)

Living in a rented double-wide mobile home on top of a hill in nearby Hermon, Maine, off Route 2, Stephen King soon discovered that as a teacher, he'd have to take the work home; consequently, his evenings were spent preparing for classes and grading papers, which cut sharply into the available time for writing. Still, for up to two hours a night, King made the time to write; he would sit in the tiny furnace room of the trailer where he hammered out stories on his wife's portable Olivetti typewriter, hoping to make another sale, hoping somehow to get through another month with Tabitha skillfully juggling the bills.

In the winter of 1971 King decided to try his hand at another novel, *The Running Man,* a futuristic version of the short story "The Most Dangerous Game." In King's tale a man, unable to provide for his wife and child, becomes a contestant in a deadly game show and stands to make a fortune—if he survives.

In some ways, the novel can be seen as a parallel to King's life at that time. For King, though, the gamble would be in taking the time to write a novel as fast as he could, since it would have to be written during the school's winter vacation.

The Running Man, as King wrote, "was written during a period of seventy-two hours," and for him it was "a fantastic, white-hot experience." Like the protagonist in the story, King ran a race and gambled that his efforts would pay off.

King submitted the partial book to Thompson, who reluctantly rejected it—King's third rejection in a row at Doubleday, after *Blaze,* then *Getting It On.* In Thompson's words, "it still wasn't magic time." King then submitted the book to Donald A. Wolheim at Ace Books. King recalled:

> Three weeks after submission, I received my material back in the SASE with a note which was both cordial and frosty. "We are not interested in science fiction which deals with negative utopias," the letter said. "They do not sell." I muttered a few words to my wife— something to the effect that George Orwell and Jonathan Swift had done quite well with negative utopias—and tossed the book in a drawer, where it stayed for eight or nine years.

The book joined *Blaze* and *Getting It On* in King's writer's trunk.

The situation had not improved by early 1972. In fact, with the addition of a second child, Joseph, on June 4, the family budget, already strained, had to be stretched further.

In one respect, at least, things were looking up. Nye Willden, then an editor at *Cavalier,* recognized King as a talented writer. "I was very impressed, sensing that there was something very out of the ordinary about [King's] writing." Willden recalled that, on occasion, when King was really strapped, he'd call to ask for a check prior to publication, and Willden accommodated him. "He was having a difficult time financially," remembered Willden.

That year King made four short-story sales to *Cavalier:* "Suffer the Little Children," published in February; "The Fifth Quarter" under the pen name of John Swithen, published in April; "Battleground," published in September; and "The Mangler," published in December. Of those stories, one was atypical for King—the Swithen tale, a crime story. The others bore King's distinctive brand of short fiction: a kind of fantasy-horror that owed much to the early Ray Bradbury, the early Robert Bloch, Charles Beaumont, Jack Finney, and Richard Matheson.

King, the most recent explorer in the literary field of suburban horror on Main Street, USA, realized that horror could be found everywhere, if you had a little imagination: "It was like the horror could be in the 7–11 down the block . . . just up the street something terrible could be going on."

Willden recalled that King was paid up to $300 a story, more than the usual rates. Still, King couldn't make a living writing short fiction because it not only didn't pay enough, but couldn't build an audience—only a string of successful novels would do that.

Overworked and stressful, King began "drinking too much," as he later wrote. There wasn't enough money, so they had their phone taken out; adding to their troubles, their seven-year-old car started acting up—expensive repair bills loomed.

Worst of all, there was no time to write anything beyond the occasional short story, since preparation for classes consumed most evenings of the school year. Understandably, King went through what appears to be a writer's block; his writing machinery simply froze. As King wrote, "I began to have long talks with myself at night about whether or not I was chasing a fool's dream."

Chris Chesley remembered that year as being a time of considerable family stress. "Tabitha was home with the kids—Joe was a baby at that time, so she couldn't get out of the house that much. During the day she took care of the kids while Steve taught."

Timing, it's said, is everything; but for King, another adage seems more appropriate: Chance favors the prepared man. In the publishing world, the shock waves of interest in supernatural fiction were duly noted by book publishers, always eager to capitalize on a new genre.

The wave had begun with the publication of Ira Levin's 1967 novel, *Rosemary's Baby,* followed by two 1971 novels: *The Exorcist* by William Peter Blatty and *The Other* by Thomas Tyron. Horror fiction, the publishers decided, was shaping up as a New Publishing Trend.

Toward the end of 1972 King, after observing what had been happening in the book publishing industry and looking at what he had written, came to a realization. As he later wrote, ". . . it had never crossed my mind to write a horror novel. It's odd because I had never actually sold anything *but* horror stories."

The previous summer King had begun a straightforward Cinderella story with a twist—*The Catcher in the Rye* with a supernatural element. After an abortive effort, King threw the first few pages into the kitchen trashcan; Tabitha, however, fished them out and encouraged him to continue, which he did.

"Steve trusts Tabitha's opinion," Chesley explained. "She can give him an accurate opinion of his work. She didn't skew what she said. Because she cared for him, she told the truth—she doesn't pussyfoot around. To me, it's one of her more endearing qualities."

Unsure himself but encouraged by Tabitha's reaction, Stephen King doggedly continued writing, although it became clear that he wasn't going to have another *Cavalier* story; the character of Carrie had taken over the story, and the story grew, and grew.

"I persisted," King later wrote, "because I was dry and had no better ideas."

When King finished, he had a novella on his hands, a 25,000-word story—too long to be a short story, but too short to be a short novel. Adopting a technique John Dos Passos used in his trilogy, *USA,* King added bogus documentation from real-world publications to increase the wordage and give the novel verisimilitude.

By the end of 1972 King had a finished manuscript on hand, ready for submission. "My considered opinion," King concluded, "was that I had written the world's all-time loser."

4

The Doubleday Days

In January 1973 King sent *Carrie* to William Thompson at Doubleday. After reading it carefully, Thompson requested a rewrite to strengthen the last portion of the book, and King complied. Afterward both editor and author were in complete agreement; the rewrite strengthened the manuscript. Finally, in Thompson's words, "it was magic time."

"Thompson's ideas worked so well that it was almost dreamlike. It was as if he had seen the corner of a treasure chest protruding from the sand and unerringly driven stakes at the probable boundaries of the buried mass," King later wrote.

Thompson elaborated: "Basically, the editorial process means understanding what the author wants to do and helping him get there. With *Carrie,* I don't think at any time before or after, have I as editor been so in tune with the author's concept of a book."

Carrie passed the editorial hurdle, the first of several. Now it was up to Thompson to sell the book to "the profit-center types—sales, publicity, subsidiary rights." *Carrie* was probably not an easy sell, as would be true for any first novel; after all, the author and the book are unknown, so the only thing going for the author is his story. Fortunately for King and Thompson, *Carrie* was one hell of a story.

The next month King took a Greyhound bus to New York to meet Thompson for a publisher's lunch, to discuss the book. In an essay, "On Becoming a Brand Name," King recounted the hilarious misadventures of his odyssey, a comedy of errors: the appointment was for noon, but King arrived in town eight hours early. At six, after killing two hours in the bus terminal, King walked to the Doubleday offices some blocks away; his feet, however, blistered because he wore brand-new shoes.

Like most first-time out-of-towners, King gawked at the tall buildings; consequently, his neck hurt. Then, at the lunch itself, King drank two gin-and-tonics on an empty stomach and, as he put it, was "almost immediately struck drunk," a condition aggravated by his lack of sleep on the long bus ride from Maine. Finally, he ordered a pasta dish, portions of which decorated his beard.

Hedging his bets, Thompson, who kept in mind King's previous submissions and subsequent rejections, didn't want to give the nervous author false hope; Thompson said that the chances looked good, but there was still no guarantee. After all, the manuscript was still making its rounds in-house, and Thompson would have to get a green light right down the line in order to buy it. After lunch King took the Greyhound back to Maine, leaving behind the glamour world of publishing.

Teaching by day and writing by night, King finished *Blaze* on February 15, 1973. The tale was a psychological suspense novel of twenty chapters and 50,000 words, and was dedicated to King's mother. A literary bounce off Steinbeck's 1937 novel *Of Mice and Men, Blaze* was a ghost story of sorts, the story of an infant kidnaping, inspired perhaps by the real-world 1932 kidnaping of Charles A. Lindbergh, Jr.

The next month King began *Second Coming,* a novel that had its genesis in a conversation he had with Tabitha and Chris Chesley, who roomed with them at the time and commuted to Orono to attend classes at the University of Maine. King, who was teaching *Dracula* in his Fantasy and Science Fiction class at Hampden Academy, popped the question: If the famous Victorian count came to small-town Maine, what would happen? Wouldn't he be easily caught by the authorities?

Tabitha and Chris disagreed, stating that in some of these small towns, why, you could just lose yourself, couldn't you? And nobody would *ever* know, would he?

Although he wrote in the furnace room with the kids underfoot, King's concentration was total. Oblivious to everything around him, he wrote about vampires in small-town Maine, a subject for him of therapeutic value: it transported from the real world into a fantasy world where, at least for the moment, he could escape from the relentless financial pressures that haunted him. When you're down and out in Hermon, Maine, nobody—as a King character might say—gave a tinker's damn. Writing, King knew, was his only ticket out, a one-way ticket away from the past and its everyday horrors, and away from the misery of life in Hermon.

Meanwhile, in New York *Carrie* had cleared the final hurdle. As Thompson recalled, "When the rights director's eyes lit up and, when the advertising manager called it a 'cooker,' I knew we were home free."

The original advance, said Thompson, was $1,500—not too bad in those days. But Thompson got it upped to $2,500, payable in full on the signing of the contract.

In March 1973 Tabitha King received a telegram from Doubleday: " 'Carrie' Officially A Doubleday Book. $2,500 Advance Against Royalties. Congrats, Kid—The Future Lies Ahead. Bill."

Thompson would have preferred to call, but some time earlier the Kings decided to have the phone disconnected; they simply couldn't afford the additional expense.

Chesley recalled what happened later that day when he returned from his classes:

> After I hitchhiked home, I came down the little dirt road his house was on. I had just gotten in the yard when Tabby ran out of the front door. Waving a telegram, she said, "Look, look at this!" I took it, and Tabby jumped and shouted, I jumped and shouted, and when Steve got home later that day, I got out of the way. They just hugged each other and cried. It was one of the best days that I have ever had.

Shortly afterward, the standard Doubleday contract with (presumably) boilerplate clauses arrived in the mail. Drinking beers in the living room, King and Chesley went over the contract, clause by clause. King's persistence finally paid off.

After the contract was signed and the advance money arrived, the Kings used some of it to buy "a new blue Pinto" and moved out of their trailer and into an apartment on Sanford Street in Bangor. A second-story walkup, the new apartment was a step up from their quarters in Hermon, but it was still modest digs, as King recalled. At least they could afford to have the phone reconnected.

In early May King finished the first of several drafts of *Second Coming,* but the real news came on Mother's Day, May 12, when Thompson called King at home with the news that Doubleday had sold the paperback rights to *Carrie* to New American Library, which would publish it under its Signet imprint. The book, said Thompson, sold for $400,000; King would get half of that as his share.

King's reaction to the deal: "To say that Tabby and I were flabbergasted by this news would be to understate the case; there may be no word in English capable of stating our reactions exactly." To mark the event, "I went out to buy something nice for Tabby. I left and looked around and finally ended up buying her a $16.95 hairdryer from a drugstore."

King had no way of knowing that, at that time, he had made an indelible impression on Elaine Geiger (now Elaine Koster) at NAL. Years later King enlarged on the hardback and paperback sale of *Carrie*:

> When *Carrie* was bought by Doubleday, my editor was Bill Thompson, and Doubleday—not known as a truly princely and generous publisher at that time; in fact, they were sort of the Uncle Scrooge of publishing—bought that book for $2,500. And there was a woman whose name was Elaine Geiger, who worked at NAL, who read that book and was taken by it—taken by it enough to want to make an offer that seemed like a [princely] sum to a young man of twenty-four or twenty-five who was teaching on a salary of $6,400 a year.
>
> Elaine Geiger made an appointment with the subrights director of Doubleday, a man who has now died, named Robert Banker; if he wasn't dead, I think probably I would strangle him because she made this appointment to make a deal for this book for a huge sum of money, and Bob Banker stood her up. Can you believe that? Eventually, they got together and NAL made a deal for that book.

For King, the money meant that for the first time in his life he had the freedom to write without distractions. However, teaching—especially working with the kids—had its own rewards. Write or teach? King was on the horns of a dilemma.

David Bright, then a reporter for the local paper, the *Bangor Daily News,* conducted the first-ever interview with King, published in its May 25, 1973, issue:

> Steve King can't quite make up his mind whether or not he should retire. For King, the book marks his first hit after three strikeouts in trying to break into the novel business. That the book is about Maine high school life is no coincidence for King wrote his first book while in high school himself. His first rejection, along with a letter that perhaps he should try another field of endeavor, came that same year. King says teaching often takes up time he'd rather spend at writing.
>
> Five of his students at Hampden Academy have asked his advice on novels they are writing and he is encouraging them as best he can, which is one of the reasons he hasn't decided to quit teaching despite his new-found fortune.

In the end, King made the only decision he could make: he left teaching behind, with some regrets. The "promising teacher," as Hampden Academy principal Rowe recalled, "worked next door, he worked down here, he went to the college up the road—nothing unique, except when he sits down at the typewriter . . . *then* it becomes unique."

For King, it meant that for the first time in his life he could call himself a "freelance writer," even putting it down as his occupation on credit applications. But King would never forget what lay behind him—the "shit work," as King remembered, the poor-paying, no-future part-time and full-time jobs that he had taken to make ends meet: janitor, bagger, dyer and sewer in a mill, baseball coach, library shelver and stacker, industrial washroom worker, gas station attendant, and a worker in a laundry.

Years later, in a *Playboy* interview, King reminisced about that heady first sale. "It was a great feeling of liberation, because at last I was free to quit teaching and fulfill what I believe is my only function in life: to write books. Good, bad, or indifferent books, that's for others to decide; it's enough to *write*."

After only two years at Hampden Academy, King left secondary school teaching behind permanently. Still, he would never forget the friends he had made—fellow teachers like Charlotte Littlefield and G. Everett "Mac" McCutcheon—who knew him when, in the words of one of his former students, "He wasn't *Stephen King* the famous writer then; he was just a good teacher who taught different English courses."

After the school year finished, the Kings moved from Bangor to North Windham, a small town east of Sebago Lake located northwest of Portland. The mail would be collected at a post office box in town. Unlike Hermon, North Windham was the perfect place to write without distraction.

In June, with *Carrie* in the works, King followed up on a previous phone conversation with Thompson and sent in *Second Coming,* a logical choice in view of the supernatural subject matter of the first book. The only problem, insofar as Thompson could see, was his concern that King might be typecast as a horror writer, a concern not shared by King. "My own response was that reputation follows function as much as form does; I would write the things I had in me to write and leave it to the critics to figure out labels."

For the remainder of 1973 King reworked a third draft of *Second Coming* according to Thompson's editorial changes. Meanwhile, *Carrie,* to be published in hardback, was scheduled for publication the following spring.

As 1973 came to a close, tragedy struck the King household. Nellie Ruth King, diagnosed with cancer in the summer of the previous year, died on December 18 in Mexico, Maine. She was only sixty years of age.

In the aftermath of the tragedy Stephen King began a new novel, *Roadwork*. An attempt to write a serious novel, the book served a cathartic purpose as well. Years later King wrote:

I think it was an effort to make some sense of my mother's painful death the year before—a lingering cancer had taken her off inch by painful inch. Following this death I was left both grieving and shaken by the apparent senselessness of it all. . . . *Roadwork* . . . tries so hard to be good and to find some answers to the conundrum of human pain.

Roadwork, the story of Barton George Dawes, was an echo of King's life. Dawes worked at an industrial laundry, as King had. Set in the winter of 1973, the story deals with the senseless death of his son by cancer—an encroachment upon every part of Dawes's life, an unstoppable growth.

It had been a heady year, a transition period. King had continued to publish short fiction at *Cavalier* (three stories: "The Boogeyman" in March, "Trucks" in June, and "Gray Matter" in October). But more significant, he had also sold his first novel; he left teaching and also put Hermon behind him. Ironically, the one person who had always encouraged him, always found the money for stamps for the early submissions, never lived long enough to see her son's first novel published. The world had moved on, and now both of King's parents were part of his past.

In January 1974 King completed *Roadwork.* Meanwhile, in New York Thompson began the prepublication push on *Carrie,* beginning with an advance reading copy—an unusual commitment for a first novel—and a form letter laid inside that went out to booksellers nationwide:

Doubleday is pleased to present you with this special edition of *Carrie,* by Stephen King. We feel it may be *the* novel of the year—a headlong narrative with the drive and relentless power of *The Exorcist,* with the high voltage shock of *Rosemary's Baby.* More than that, it is part of a rare breed in today's fiction market—a good story. Don't start it unless the evening in front of you is free of appointments; this one is a cooker.

Carrie is the story of a girl who has been the odd one all her life, the misfit, the born loser. Torn between her fanatic mother who sees sin everywhere—in the nudity of a girl's shower room, in any friend-ship Carrie might develop with girls her own age, and especially in dating—and her own pathetic wish to become part of the world that shuns and attracts her, Carrie becomes the butt of every cruel joke, the object of any malicious prank. But Carrie is different, more than a victim of forces she cannot understand, she possesses a strange and frightening power which she can hardly control. And when one final prank is played, the unleashing of Carrie's power proves as spellbinding as it is devastating.

We hope that *Carrie* will excite you as much as it has us. A tremendously readable ESP novel, it is also a quietly brilliant character sketch of a young and unusual girl trying to find her way out of a very personal hell. We think *Carrie* and Stephen King have a bright future, and we welcome this chance to share both of them with you.

Carrie, set for publication on April 5, 1974, had already begun working its magic on advance reviewers. *School Library Journal* called it "a terrifying treat for both horror and parapsychology fans." *Publishers Weekly* called it ". . . [A] fine, eerie, haunting tale . . . . The result is sheer horror for all concerned. Not the least Mr. King's talent lies in his making Carrie always more pitiable than evil."

The dissenting review, from *Library Journal,* made no bones about its dislike: "This first novel is a contender for the bloodiest book of the year—menstrual blood, blood of childbirth, and miscarriage, blood of a whole town dying, and finally the lifeblood of the heroine draining away . . . . *Carrie* will provide a vicarious thrill for some, but cannot honestly be recommended."

The most penetrating review came from King's mentor at his alma mater, Burton Hatlen, who reviewed *Carrie* for the spring issue of *Alumnus.* As Hatlen pointed out—just in case anyone assumed King was an overnight success—by his count, *Carrie* was King's *sixth,* not first, novel. Remarking that King discovered "not the American Dream but the American Nightmare," Hatlen wrote that King "knows the desolation of rural Maine—the dreams gone sour, the bodies and souls twisted by lives of deprivation. And he knows the emotion which rules these lives is neither envy nor longing, but hate—a hate which, if it is ever unleashed, will bring all the dream castles crashing down on our heads."

Hatlen cited some weaknesses in the novel, but added that "we should not be surprised to find such weaknesses in a novel by a 25-year-old writer." He continued: "More important than these minor weaknesses is the power of Steve King's vision itself. Few of our writers have such a clear sense of the demons that lurk within the American psyche. And if Steve's ability to project this vision continues to develop, he has every promise of becoming a major American writer."

Like Thompson, Hatlen seems to have had a touch of prescience. Both could see the latent talent and potential in this promising young writer who made it largely on his own, without the traditional financial crutches—endowments, grants, and fellowships—used to support budding writers.

Carrie hit the bookstores in April 1974 with a first printing of 30,000 copies, according to Doubleday. A cheap-looking, poorly bound hardback, the $5.95 book of 199 pages sported an odd cover by Alex Gotfryd depicting a young woman who looked more like a New York fashion model than the pitiable figure King described as Carrie. Worse, the hyperbolic ad copy on the back cover did little to convey the sense of the story. "Stephen King's story will stun your sensibilities, jangle your nerve endings, and make you wonder even more. . . ."

It's doubtful that the book stunned and jangled readers, or made them wonder even more, but *Carrie* did have much going for it. In many ways it's J. D. Salinger's *The Catcher in the Rye* with a supernatural twist. Still, as King recalled, "It didn't get within hailing distance of anyone's bestseller list, it wasn't announced with trumpet flourishes from the first three pages of any critical magazine, and as far as *Playboy, The New Yorker, The Saturday Review, Time,* and *Newsweek* were concerned, it didn't exist at all. Ditto book clubs."

Also in April 1974 Thompson made the decision to publish *Second Coming,* which had been rewritten three times and by now sported a new title, *Jerusalem's Lot,* named after the town where the story takes place. Later, it would be shortened to its abbreviated title, *'Salem's Lot.*

Almost immediately, *'Salem's Lot* sold to NAL for $500,000. As with *Carrie,* King earned half the income of that sale. NAL, as King recalled, was happy with its investment:

> *'Salem's Lot* had been read at NAL with a great deal of enthusiasm,
> much of it undoubtedly because they recognized a brand name
> potential beginning to shape up. Horror was big in those days . . .
> and I showed no signs with my second book of exchanging my fright
> wig and Lon Chaney makeup for a pipe and tweed jacket and writing
> something Deep and Meaningful.

In late summer 1974 the Kings rented a house at 330 South Fortysecond Street in Boulder, Colorado. King explained the temporary move:

> I had written *Carrie* and *'Salem's Lot,* and they were both set in Maine,
> because that's where I'm from. I said to my wife, "I think it's time to

set a book somewhere else. This looks like it's going to be a career and not a hobby."

She said, "Where do you want to go?"

"I don't know—just someplace where I can see something else and get a feel for some other part of the landscape," I said.

So she got out the *Rand McNally Road Atlas* and opened it to the map of the United States. "Come over here," she said.

"What are you going to do?" I said.

She put a handkerchief over my eyes and said, "Point."

I pointed and it was Colorado; the finger was somewhere close to Boulder, so that's where we went.

Colorado, "a spooky state with mountains and high passes and the wind howling and the wolves," as King remembered, was ideally suited as a locale for another horror novel. Curiously, that's not what he found himself writing. Instead, he began writing *The House on Value Street,* a novel inspired by the real-world kidnaping by the Symbionese Liberation Army of nineteen-year-old Patty Hearst, daughter of California-based publishing mogul Randolph Hearst. As King recalled, "the story just wasn't marching. I went on nuzzling it apathetically for the next few weeks. . . ."

King set it aside temporarily and turned his attention to a novel idea that had its genesis in 1962. *Darkshine*—inspired by Ray Bradbury's classic short story "The Veldt"—would explore the idea of dreams turning into reality, just like Bradbury's story of a child's playroom gone awry.

"The idea came to me while I was in the shower, washing my hair. I opened my eyes wide, and both of them filled up with Prell . . . but the idea stuck," King wrote later.

Unfortunately, the idea became unstuck as King wrestled with an untenable problem of where to site the story. As he explained:

> I was wondering what would happen if you had a little boy who was sort of a psychic receptor, or maybe even a psychic amplifier. And I wanted to take a little kid with his family and put them someplace, cut off, where spooky things would happen.
>
> I sort of wanted it to be Disney World—Goofy's coming to kill you . . . . Anyway, I could never make it work. The thing is, you can't really cut a family off in an amusement park; they'll go next door and say, "We've got some problems here."

Like *The House on Value Street, Darkshine* went on the backburner. Unlike the former, though, the latter came to life again, in October, when Stephen and Tabitha King got away for a weekend by themselves. Having asked locals for a recommendation on where to stay, the Kings headed for the recommended Stanley Hotel in nearby Estes Park.

Driving up the winding mountain roads to the isolated hotel on October 30, 1974, the Kings passed a sign that read: "Roads May Be Closed After October 15."

When they arrived at the hotel, they were surprised to discover that it was clearing out fast. It was the last day of the season and the hotel was preparing to hibernate for the winter, when the roads would be virtually impassable; a sudden snowstorm could blanket the area and utterly isolate the hotel and its occupants.

As it turned out, the Kings were almost unable to check in, for the hotel had already sent its blank credit-card slips to their main office in Denver—all, apparently, except one receipt for an American Express card. Fortunately, Stephen King carried an American Express card—he doesn't leave home without it—and was able to check into the hotel, an eerie aerie.

As they headed to their room, 217, they walked down long corridors with fire hoses neatly rolled up on the walls and King's imagination went into maximum overdrive. He imagined the fire hoses coming alive, thumping against the carpet. "By then," King recalled, "whatever it is that makes you want to make things up . . . was turned on. I was scared, but I loved it."

That night, the Kings had dinner at the hotel's Colorado Restaurant. On a normal night a band would play; tonight there was no band, only taped music piped in through loudspeakers. On a normal night the room would be filled with people; tonight the room was almost empty—most of the tables and chairs were turned up. On a normal night the varied menu had something for everyone; tonight the choices were limited. The waiter, who resembled Lurch from the television show "The Munsters," asked them in a sepulchral voice, "What would you like? We have one choice. You may have Colorado beef or you may have nothing."

They took the beef.

After dinner Tabitha went to bed, but Stephen, restless, went to the bar and had a drink, served to him by a bartender named Grady. Heading back to his room, King got lost in the maze of corridors. When finally in his room, he went into the bathroom, looked at the claw-foot tub with a pink curtain drawn across it, and thought, "What if somebody died here? At that moment, I knew that I had a book."

For the remainder of 1974 King worked on *The Shine*. Renting a room in downtown Boulder, King took the original idea from *Darkshine* of the boy as a psychic receptor and transplanted him in the fictional Overlook Hotel. The boy, Danny Torrance, had an unwanted precognitive gift—the shine, the ability to "see" the paranormal world. A luxury hotel "built against the roof of the sky . . . looking out over the last rising jagged peaks of the Rockies," the Overlook bore a resemblance to the real-world Stanley Hotel, also surrounded by the Rockies. King, however, dissociated the two with a disclaimer: "Some of the most beautiful resort hotels in the world are located in Colorado, but the hotel in these pages is based on none of them. The Overlook and the people associated with it exist wholly within the author's imagination."

Sometimes, in writing *The Shine,* it seemed that the fantasy world exerted a pull that was a bit *too* real. Writing about Jack Torrance—who slowly goes crazy in this story, isolated from everything and everyone around him—King found that the character took him back to a time he would rather forget. "I seemed to be back in the trailer in Hermon, Maine, with no company but the buzzing sound of the snowmobiles and my own fears. . . ."

Some of those fears tapped into his concerns about parenting. "I was able to invest a lot of my unhappy aggressive impulses in Jack Torrance, and it was safe," King recalled. For King, the novel explored a dark side of his psyche, "the idea that parents are not always good." He explained:

> This was a revelation to me in a way, because I grew up without a father. I didn't have any experience in my own home, so when I got married and had kids, I had to fall back on the real role model of young American men, which is television.
>
> I thought I knew what a dad was. Fathers on TV were always cool. They had it together. Dad even wore a tie to the dinner table.
>
> The first time I realized that parents are not always good was when the kid wouldn't stop crying in the middle of the night. I was getting up to get the kid a bottle, and somewhere in the back of my mind, in some sewer back there, an alligator stirs . . . *Make it stop crying. You know how to do it—use the pillow.*
>
> These were shocking, unpleasant emotions for me to discover in myself. Because of the way I was brought up, I wasn't prepared for that. I was brought face-to-face with the idea that I was not always good in my motivations.

In January 1975 King met Thompson in New York. Together they went over the copyediting for *'Salem's Lot,* scheduled for publication later that year, in October. During that trip, King "spilled the plot of *The Shine* over roughly 2,000 beers in a pleasant little hamburger place called Jaspers."

According to King, Thompson "wasn't terribly enthusiastic" about *The Shine,* because of its similarity to Robert Marasco's *Burnt Offerings,* a 1973 novel scheduled for release as a full-length motion picture in 1976.

Stripped to their bare-bones plots—a family takes up temporary residence in an archetypal Bad Place—both King's and Marasco's novels have similarities. But as they say, it's all in the writing.

Thompson voiced another concern. "First the telekinetic girl, then the vampires, now the haunted hotel and the telepathic kid. You're gonna get typed," Thompson said.

King concluded that he "could be in worse company" and cited others in the field whose work he enjoyed: "Lovecraft, Clark Ashton Smith, Frank Belknap Long, Fritz Leiber, Robert Bloch, Richard Matheson, and Shirley Jackson (yes; even she was typed as a spook writer)." Thompson was probably unpersuaded.

When King returned home to Colorado, he finished the first draft of *The Shine.* A month later he began work, again, on *The House on Value Street.* As King later wrote:

> It was going to be a *roman à clef* about the kidnapping of Patty Hearst, her brainwashing . . . her participation in the bank robbery, the shootout at the SLA hideout in Los Angeles—in my book, the hideout was on Value Street, natch—the fugitive run across the country, the whole ball of wax. . . . Well, I never wrote that book.

For six weeks, King recalled, nothing worked. He couldn't get into the story, no matter what writing tricks he used to try to jump-start it. King reluctantly put it aside.

During those six weeks King was haunted by "a news story I had read about, an accidental CBW [chemical-biological warfare] spill in Utah. All the bad nasty bugs got out of their canister and killed a bunch of sheep. But, the news article stated, if the wind had been blowing the other way, the good people of Salt Lake City might have gotten a very nasty surprise."

That, to King, carried the germ of a good story, an idea he had previously explored in "Night Surf," with its virulent Superflu "Captain Trips," which destroys the world's population. ("Night Surf," originally published in *Ubris* in 1969, had been heavily revised for its August 1974 appearance in *Cavalier.*) Back then King had wanted to write a longer work exploring the Superflu, but the time wasn't right; and he knew from experience that it was better not to push it. At the right time the random elements linked through the magic of creativity and became *The Stand:* "Night Surf," the abortive attempt at *The House on Value Street,* the CBW accident, George Stewart's *Earth Abides,* and a preacher whom King heard on the radio who spoke of a generational plague.

The Stand would haunt King for the next two years. The seemingly endless novel became, as King put it, "my own little Vietnam, because I kept telling myself that in another hundred pages or so I would begin to see the light at the end of the tunnel."

The Stand—King's opportunity to lay waste the world and begin fresh, a theme he initially explored in *The Aftermath* while still a teenager— mirrored the huge changes the United States had been going through in the midseventies. Later, in *Danse Macabre,* King wrote:

> Its writing came during a troubled period for the world in general and America in particular; we were suffering from our first gas pains in history, we had just witnessed the sorry end of the Nixon administration and the first presidential resignation in history, we had been resoundingly defeated in Southeast Asia, and we were grappling with a host of domestic problems, from the troubling question of abortion-on-demand to an inflation rate that was beginning to spiral upward in a positively scary way.

The Stand was, in short, a fear fable for the times, as well as King's first attempt to move away from the trappings of traditional horror to explore a larger literary world. The story's epic scope and its imaginative fusion of science fiction, fantasy, and horror would, when finished, be his largest canvas to date: a twelve-pound, 1,200-page manuscript.

In April 1975 *Carrie* was published in paperback by New American Library under its Signet imprint. Its "rather puzzling cover," as King recalled, lacked his name and the book title. A double cover, the second page had a two-page spread of a small town in flames. In trying to come up with an arresting, fancy cover, the publisher encountered a printing problem that made it impossible to go with the original concept: trimming the front cover on the right edge, so it would reveal—vertically, on the second cover—the title and the author's name.

The first printing was 700,000 copies. In the next nine months, *Carrie* would sell 1.33 million copies—a far cry from the first-year sale of *Carrie* in hardback: 13,000 copies, according to King.

That summer, the Kings moved back to Maine. Boulder, alive with students and aspiring yuppies, just didn't have the kind of down-home, down-to-earth folk that they preferred.

In the fall the Kings bought their first home, located at RFD 2 on Kansas Road in Bridgton, Maine. Located on the west side of Long Lake, Bridgton seemed like the perfect place: far from the madding crowd, a scenic and seemingly idyllic place where they could enjoy their privacy; and if they wanted the benefits of a larger city, they could drive to Portland, forty miles away.

Even with only one published book available in the stores, King found himself the subject of unwanted attention from readers who would write and, sometimes, show up to ask locals where he lived, invariably resulting in "the sudden silence of country people on their guard."

In his new home, King continued working on the first draft of *The Stand* while awaiting the publication of *'Salem's Lot,* scheduled for an October release.

Near Halloween *'Salem's Lot* went to press with a first printing of 20,000 copies. In comparison to *Carrie,* a $5.95 hardback of 199 pages, *'Salem's Lot* in hardback was only $7.95 and over twice as long.

A rich, complex book that draws from a number of sources, *'Salem's Lot* is most obviously influenced by Bram Stoker's *Dracula;* similarly, in the depiction of the Marsten house, the novel recalls the archetypal Bad Place, especially Shirley Jackson's classic *The Haunting of Hill House,* which provided King with the book's epigram.

What gave *'Salem's Lot* its power, though, was more than its evocation of traditional horror trappings. King also drew from popular and contemporary literature as well as his own remembrances of growing up in Durham. The result: a rich, deeply textured novel that, along with *Carrie,* showed a remarkable writing talent in the making. *'Salem's Lot* recalls Grace Metalious's *Peyton Place* and Don Robertson's two-volume *Paradise Falls;* the flavor of King's novel, however, came from Thornton Wilder's *Our Town,* which King had taught at Hampden Academy. "I was moved by what he had to say about the town. The town is something that doesn't change. People come and go but the town remains. I could really identify with the nature of a very small town."

'Salem's Lot is a long, satisfying read, the perfect summer book, and it's easy to see how Thompson had "lost one entirely sunny summer weekend with Ben Mears, Susan Norton and company in the town of Jerusalem's Lot, Maine."

Unlike *Carrie, 'Salem's Lot* mightily influenced writers in the horror genre, who saw in it a world of possibilities in which horror had the potential to break out and appeal to the large, mainstream audience.

King, in short, virtually invented a new kind of writing with the storytelling appeal of genre writing and fused it with mainstream writing techniques; in short, a kind of writing that combined the best of two possible worlds.

Al Sarrantonio, speaking for others in the horror genre, summed up the impact of *'Salem's Lot*:

> While *Rosemary's Baby* and *The Exorcist* mined supernatural niches in the bestseller list, I would argue that *'Salem's Lot,* because of its genuineness, its verve, its originality, its willingness to reflect, expand and *celebrate* its sources, and most importantly, its establishment of Stephen King, after the sincere but *unseminal Carrie,* not as an interloper but as a pioneer in a field ripe for re-invention, was *germinal* and *originative* of the entire boom in horror fiction we find ourselves in the middle of—with no culmination in sight.

Notwithstanding the homage, King was not the first pioneer. Richard Matheson and many others had been there first, as King readily admitted. "When people talk about the genre, I guess they mention my name first, but without Richard Matheson, I wouldn't be around," King wrote.

Like Matheson—who jump-started the genre after the demise of *Weird Tales*—King infused the field in the midseventies with much needed new blood, a transfusion that revived the genre.

In early spring 1976 principal photography began on the film *Carrie.* Like the book on which it was based and its author, those involved in the movie project were unknowns. Behind the camera was Brian de Palma, who had previously directed *Phantom of the Paradise* in 1974; in front of the camera were Amy Irving, Nancy Allen, William Katt, John Travolta, and Sissy Spacek, in the title role as Carietta White. Only Piper Laurie, who abandoned retirement to enact Carrie's mother, had name recognition.

Lawrence Cohen's script stripped the story to its bones: the Ugly Duckling/Cinderella story of Carrie herself—perfect for young teenagers, the core moviegoing audience. Scheduled for release in November, it would face stiff competition, including the film adaptation of Marasco's *Burnt Offerings*.

Life for King in Bridgton seemed idyllic, at least on the surface, to the public, which saw only what it wanted to see, the trappings of King's "overnight" success: two hardback books, six-figure paperback deals, and

movie deals in the wings. To be sure, life had improved from the days
when King resided in North Windham—he now owned a $150,000 home
and had a Cadillac in the driveway—but few people knew he was still
getting low advances from Doubleday for each new book, despite the
sizable paperback income his publisher shared with him on a fifty-fifty
basis.

Even at that early stage in his career, King discovered that the price of
fame had its drawbacks. Mel Allen, who interviewed King at that time,
wrote:

> One of the newest pressures is the demand from reporters, schools,
> clubs, service organizations and the like for interviews and appear-
> ances. These have risen as fast as his meteoric climb to the top of the
> best seller lists.
>
> He's starting to say no for the first time. But he feels torn. "On
> the one hand I want to accommodate people, on the other I need time
> for myself. Yet every time I say no, I hear them thinking, 'That stuck-
> up bigshot writer.' . . ."

What King discovered was that he couldn't please all the people all the
time. Like moths drawn to a flame, the fans intruded on his life on a
regular basis:

> . . . [H]e's had his phone number changed, and the local operator
> tells countless people every day, "No, I'm sorry, we are not permitted
> to disclose that number," because strangers call from all parts of the
> country to ask for money, interviews, help in finding a publisher for
> the 800-page novel they've written about werewolves, or advice on
> how to do away with the demonic neighbor who has caused their
> vegetables to succumb to root rot.

King's response to all this unsolicited attention was simple: he'd write
his books, and *that* took priority; nothing else really mattered. With that in
mind, he finished the first draft of *The Stand*. In the process of writing it,
though, he had creatively drained himself. He would need to recharge his
batteries before tackling another major project.

For the remainder of that year, King's fictional efforts never caught
fire. *Welcome to Clearwater*—a bust. *The Corner*—another bust. An early
draft of *The Dead Zone*—still another bust. An attempt at writing *Firestarter*
didn't catch fire either, complicated by his concern that he was imitating
himself and merely rewriting *Carrie*.

By the latter part of the year, however, things were beginning to look up,
at least on the sales end. In August 1976 NAL released the paperback edi-

tion of *'Salem's Lot,* which quickly sold a million copies. The book, however, got a real boost when *Carrie* hit screens nationwide in November, bringing King's name to the attention of the moviegoing audience. Goosed by the movie, *'Salem's Lot* went on to sell 2.25 million copies in its first six months.

Clearly, a brand name was shaping up, and NAL couldn't be happier. The ricochet effect that would make King a bestseller—hardback, paperback sale, major subsidiary sale—had worked its magic on *Carrie* and now *'Salem's Lot.* Would it also work for *The Shining?*

It was also time for King to consider representation by a professional agency. He didn't need to sell the books himself. In fact, it would be better for him to stick to the writing and leave the selling to a hard-nosed agent who would invariably cut a better deal.

Though he had represented himself in the sale of his books to Doubleday, King probably signed boilerplate contracts, which always favored the publisher, especially in control over subsidiary sale income and film rights. Consequently, he signed away a small fortune or two.

Years later, in an article for writers, King offered this sage advice:

> And remember Stephen King's First Rule of Writers and Agents, learned by bitter personal experience: You don't need one until you're making enough for someone to steal . . . and if you're making that much, you'll be able to take your pick of good agents.

Which is precisely what happened to King. In 1976 at a New York literary party where James Baldwin was present, Stephen and Tabitha King met Kirby McCauley, a thirty-four-year-old transplanted literary agent from Minneapolis who represented several writers in the science-fiction and fantasy field. As McCauley recalled:

> I had heard of Steve, but frankly, when I went to the party I had only read one thing by Steve. Before the party, I went out and got a copy of *'Salem's Lot* and I was blown away by it. I loved it. So I went to the party and said to Steve, "I love that book, but to be honest, I haven't read anything else by you." So we started to talk about writers in general and the field of horror and science fiction. As it turned out, Steve's interests and my interests were very much alike. He was more interested in talking about relatively unknown writers like Frank Belknap Long and Clifford Simak and people whom I knew or represented, than he was in staying in the corner and talking with James Baldwin.

In *'Salem's Lot,* Benjaman Mears speaks of his chance meeting with Susan Norton: "Of such inconsequential beginnings dynasties are begun."

Such would be the case with King's meeting McCauley, who years later would admit that "I partly saw his success growing. I saw that he was going to get bigger and bigger. But . . . I can't say I foresaw Steve being the literary phenomenon of the last half of the 20th century."

After the party King and McCauley began corresponding. Soon thereafter McCauley had made up his mind: "Naturally, I wanted Steve to consider having me represent him." But King had yet to make up his mind.

In January 1977 King added a third book to his publishing credits: *The Shining*—originally titled *The Shine*—was published by Doubleday as an $8.95 hardback. At 447 pages, *The Shining* exceeded *'Salem's Lot* in length; but if Doubleday had retained its prologue ("Before the Play") and its original epilogue ("After the Play"), *The Shining* would have been even longer, a 500-page novel by King's estimate.

As with his two earlier books, *The Shining* sold to NAL; because *'Salem's Lot* was bought by it for $500,000—$100,000 more than *Carrie*—it's likely that the rights for *The Shining* sold for at least $500,000, perhaps $600,000, of which King got half.

The first King book to hit the *Times* bestseller list, *The Shining*, according to its flap copy, had been written by "the undisputed master of the modern horror story." That assertion and the catchy title had an unforeseen side effect. Hoping to ride what was perceived as a horror bonanza, other publishers began issuing similar-sounding titles. As King said, "I won't mention any by name. But I see a lot of books that must have been inspired by some of the stuff I'm doing. For one thing, those 'horror' novels that have gerund endings are just everywhere: *The Piercing, The Burning, The Searing*—the *this*-ing and the *that*-ing."

The Piercing, in fact, owed much—a hell of a lot, as it turned out—to *The Shining*. The tale was written by Yvonne McManus, and her publisher made no apologies for its likeness to King's novel, even trumpeting its similarities, according to Ray Walters:

> "Bridgewater was such a lovely place to live, a quiet place where nothing ever happened . . . Until little Emma Winthrop invented a playmate named Abigail . . . Until Abigail taught Emma how to make strange things happen with her mind . . . Until Emma learned how to move objects, arrest heartbeats and create grisly fires . . . Until blood flowed like water and people began to die. . . . A masterpiece of modern horror in the tradition of Stephen King's *Carrie*."

Thus Pinnacle Books advertises . . . a novel it is stuffing into the mass-market racks this week. Similar descriptions are being offered by a dozen other publishers for three dozen books they're releasing this summer, paperbacks bearing such titles as *Hobgoblin, Nightmare Country, Don't Talk to Strangers* and *Creepshow.*

Like *'Salem's Lot, The Shining* attracted immediate attention. Peter Straub, after reading it, wrote that "it was obviously a masterpiece, probably the best supernatural novel in a hundred years." Straub elaborated: "In its uniting of an almost bruising literary power, a deep sensitivity to individual experience, and its operatic convictions, it is a very significant work of art."

Stanley Kubrick—the celebrated British director whose credits included *Dr. Strangelove* and *A Clockwork Orange*—thought so too, and decided he would direct *the* ultimate horror film and his vehicle would be *The Shining,* just as he felt his *2001: A Space Odyssey* was *the* ultimate science-fiction film.

In hardback, *The Shining* would sell 50,000 copies in its first year; in paperback, however, it would rack up an impressive 2.3 million copies.

Doubleday, no doubt pleased with the sales figures, had much to celebrate: *The Shining* would soon be followed by *The Stand,* King's most ambitious novel to date.

In the interim, the publisher was willing to take a chance and publish a collection of King's short fiction, a privilege customarily reserved only for authors whose novels have created a built-in audience, since such collections typically sell far fewer copies than a novel. *Night Shift,* with an introductory essay by John D. MacDonald and a long introduction by King, would collect his short fiction, most of which had appeared in *Cavalier* magazine, which owned all rights but reverted them to King on request.

By that time, King probably had a sense of growing disenchantment with Doubleday, for several reasons, as *Newsweek* later reported. First, advance money: ". . . [A]fter he started raking in millions for Doubleday, his publisher still continued to dole out paltry advances." For the five books, King received $77,500—an average of $15,500 per book. Second, King's treatment at Doubleday: "Every time he came to the office, I'd have to introduce him all over again to the executives," Bill Thompson was quoted as saying. Third, concerns about *The Stand:* King wanted to publish a limited edition, "but Doubleday balked at that, claiming it was impossible because of previous licensing arrangements with book clubs."

"The Doubleday policy on paperback money is a 50–50 split, a policy that is non-negotiable," said King, citing the deal breaker. According to King, that policy "finally led to our parting of the ways. . . ."

In the spring, in a move engineered by King's new literary agent Kirby McCauley—who had gained King's confidence by selling several short stories, some to major markets—King signed on with New American Library, which by then had in print 2.9 million copies of *Carrie* and 2.2 million copies of *'Salem's Lot.* The three-book deal, negotiated by McCauley, fetched $2.5 million, dwarfing the small advances King had got at Doubleday when he acted as his own agent. "A writer who is his own agent has a fool for a client," King concluded later, and this new deal seemed to prove it.

For McCauley, the deal represented a major change in his status too. "It put me in a whole different league. Not just income, but now that of a major agent."

The three books included *The Dead Zone* and *Firestarter,* which had already seen first drafts, and a third novel to follow, yet unnamed.

That deal, as King recalled, marked "the widening trend of writers signing directly with paperback publishers." By doing so, King increased his income immensely. NAL could elect to publish King in hardback and paperback, or sell the hardback rights separately while retaining the paperback rights. No matter what NAL did, King would come out a winner; no longer would he share the lucrative paperback income with the hardback publisher. Clearly, the paperback, not the hardback, publishers had the economic clout. As King wrote, ". . . the paperback industry is now the giant of the publishing world," and he was right.

With a new agent, a new contract, and a new publisher, King—finally—had clout. In the beginning, King needed the publishers; now the publishers needed him. Still, though with a new publisher, King had two books at Doubleday awaiting publication: *Night Shift* and *The Stand.*

When *Publishers Weekly* in its July 1977 issue trumpeted the news to the industry of King's three-book deal, everyone took notice. But virtually no one noticed two months later when NAL published a $1.50 mass-market paperback curiously titled *Rage,* and authored by Richard Bachman, whose real identity was Stephen King.

Originally titled *Getting It On, Rage* was the first of several Bachman novels. "The Bachman novels were 'just plain books,' paperbacks to fill the drugstore and bus-stations of America. This was at my request; I wanted Bachman to keep a low profile. So, in that sense, the poor guy had the dice loaded against him from the start," King wrote later.

In one of the few reviews *Rage* received, *Publishers Weekly* clearly perceived it to be the first published novel of a fledgling writer:

> Even a lesson in Latin grammar would have been more involving than what goes on in the Maine classroom in which psychopath Charlie Decker holds fellow students hostage. Charlie is in a rage, but it's never clear why, other than that he's got a grudge against both his father and the high school authorities who put him on probation for assaulting a teacher. Now Charlie has killed two teachers, set a fire in the school and taken over his classroom at gunpoint. When the other kids begin to act like clones of Charlie, playing mean-spirited games on one another, they too turn out to be merely rebels without a cause, but apparently the author considers their violence sufficient to engage our interest.

To keep Bachman's low profile, his true identity was revealed on a "need to know" basis at NAL, which included Elaine Koster (then Elaine Geiger), King's book editor, and an attorney in the legal department who handled the contract, Reportedly, not even NAL's chief executive officer, Robert Diforio, knew of Bachman's true identity.

When the copyright was filed at the Library of Congress, the paperwork bore King's, not Bachman's, name as copyright holder. Presumably an error of the publisher, it went unnoticed, like the publication of the book itself.

In fall 1977 the Kings put their Bridgton home on the market and headed to England, planning to stay one year. Just as King had moved to Colorado for one year to get a change of scenery and explore a new locale for a new book, King now elected to visit England so he could write a book "with an English setting. When the novel is finished . . . it will be set back in a fictitious place, although it will be based on Fleet," reported *Fleet News,* an English newspaper, in which the Kings put an advertisement which simply read: "Wanted, a draughty Victorian house in the country with dark attic and creaking floorboards, preferably haunted."

The house they rented at Mourlands, 87 Aldershot Road, Fleet Hants, wasn't haunted, though it was large enough for the King family, now larger with a third child, son Owen, born earlier that year.

Naomi and Joseph were enrolled at St. Nicholas School in Fleet; Owen, seven months old, according to the *Fleet News,* was "already getting his teeth into dad's books—literally."

Back in the States, NAL issued a press release, stating that King had temporarily moved to England to write an English novel. "With its history of eerie writers and its penchant for mystery, England should help Stephen

King produce a novel even more bloodcurdling than his previous ones—a novel that will only go to prove his title of 'Master of the Modern Horror Novel.' "

As for the English novel King had intended to write, like the ghost they wanted in their rented house, it never materialized. The third book in King's three-book deal would not be a ghost story at all. Instead, it would be set in Maine, and it would be about a rabid Saint Bernard that terrorizes and holds at bay a mother and her son in a disabled Ford Pinto.

The idea came from an article in a Portland, Maine, newspaper. "This little kid was savaged by a Saint Bernard and killed," King recalled. That idea cross-pollinated with a real-life experience King had a year or two earlier when he got his motorcycle out of the garage "and it wasn't running right." Asking around, King was told "there's a place about seven miles away, kind of isolated," where the guy who owned the shop had a funny way of doing business; he'd tell you what he'd charge, and then charge you that amount.

Nursing his motorcycle, running on one cylinder, King found the place, located on the outskirts of the town. As King recalled:

> I drove into the house driveway, and the bike died. I put it on the kick-stand and got up. Then I hear this noise that sounds like a motorboat, and coming out on the other side of the road was the biggest Saint Bernard that I ever saw in my life. He started to walk across the road. His head was down, his tail was down, he wasn't wagging his tail; and he knew what he wanted—he wanted *me.*
>
> The guy who ran the place came out of the rusty, corrugated garage and walked across the road. "Don't worry," he said. "That's just Joe. He *always* does that."

As King recalled, the dog coiled down on its haunches and started to growl. Its owner, wielding an adjustable socket wrench, brought it down on the dog's rump. "It sounded like a woman beating a rug with a carpet beater," remembered King.

The owner looked at King and simply said, "Joe must not like you."

After that incident, *Cujo* clicked. King asked himself: *What would happen if you put people in that situation and there was nobody to get the dog?*

King began writing a first draft of *Cujo,* a grim and relentless novel that exposed the raw side of life in Maine, a dark side locals live with, and tourists—the summer people—never see.

A month later, in mid-October, the King family had dinner with Peter Straub and his wife at Straub's home in Crouch End, a suburb of London. After dinner the two writers kicked around the notion of writing a novel together and decided they would collaborate. However, both were tied up contractually for several years, so the idea went onto the back burner.

King's trip to Crouch End did yield literary fruit, however; he wrote "Crouch End," a short story inspired by Lovecraft's Cthulhu Mythos.

By year's end the first draft of *Cujo* had been completed. Things hadn't turned out quite the way King had planned—the English horror novel was never written, and the one-year stay in England was truncated to three months. The Kings then headed back to Maine, where they purchased a house in Center Lovell, located in the Lakes area.

In February 1978 King published his first collection of short fiction. *Night Shift,* an $8.95 hardback, included an introduction by John D. MacDonald, a lengthy essay by King on the nature of writing supernatural fiction, and twenty short stories originally published in magazines: eleven stories from *Cavalier;* two from *Penthouse;* one each from *Gallery, Cosmopolitan,* and *Maine;* and four that appeared in print for the first time, in this collection: "Jerusalem's Lot," "Quitters, Inc.," "The Last Rung on the Ladder," and "The Woman in the Room."

Very cinematic, all the stories—except "Jerusalem's Lot," an epistolary story—would eventually be optioned for television or movie adaptations. "The books are visual," King explained. "I see them almost as movies in my head. When I sign a copy of *Night Shift,* if I'm not pressed for time, what I usually sign is, 'I hope you've enjoyed these one-reel movies,' which is essentially what they are."

Night Shift sold 24,000 copies in hardback in its first year, excellent for a short collection, but still approximately half the number of copies sold of *The Shining.*

In September 1978 the Kings moved to Orrington, a small town southwest of Bangor. Renting a house that flanked the main road that cut through the town—a major truck route leading to Bangor—King commuted to Orono to teach two creative writing courses at his alma mater. Explaining King's appointment, Burton Hatlen recalled:

When "Ted" Holmes was forced to retire in 1975 at age sixty-five, we had the question of what to do with a creative writing position. The English department decided that instead of bringing in a permanent creative writing teacher, we would invite writers for relatively short periods.

We invited Stephen King on the understanding that it was for one year. We tried to talk him into extending it, but he didn't want to. I think he wanted to come back and be at the university in the English department as a member of the faculty.

For King—who had taught at UMO as an undergraduate, and taught at the high school level—this was an opportunity to teach again, with a different emphasis. "I'm looking forward to teaching on a college level because we can focus more on creativity than grammar," King said. The teaching stint also had a side benefit—an office King could call his own: "This is great. I've never had a real office before. Now I can say to my wife, 'Dear, I'm going to the office.' "

That fall semester King taught two literature courses and two creative writing seminars: one in fiction, the other in poetry. After school King worked on the final draft of *Firestarter.*

September also marked the publication of King's fifth Doubleday book, *The Stand,* a $12.95 hardback with 823 pages. His longest and most ambitious tale to date, the book received generally positive reviews, especially from *Publishers Weekly,* which said that King "outdoes himself in this spine-chilling moral fantasy where gritty realism forms the basis for boldly imaginative raids upon the bizarre . . . . King's message is simple, but his characters are compellingly real, his complex, nightmare scenario is so skillfully done one almost believes it."

At that time, however, nobody knew that King had cut the book by one-fifth of its published length—the equivalent of a short novel. The cuts rankled King, who reportedly made a promise to himself to restore the text and one day reissue the book as he originally intended.

With *The Stand* behind him, King also put Doubleday behind him. So did Bill Thompson, who had edited all his books there. King went to NAL, and Thompson went to Everest House as its senior editor.

5

America's Literary Boogeyman

In early November 1978 Bill Thompson telephoned King and suggested he write a nonfiction survey of the horror field. "Why don't you do a book about the entire horror phenomenon as you see it? Books, movies, radio, TV, the whole thing."

It was the right idea at the right time, for King was then working on a syllabus for a literature class, Themes in Horror and the Supernatural. After giving it careful consideration, King felt that "writing a book on the subject would complete the circle."

In the interim a family incident sparked King's imagination. On Thanksgiving Day Naomi King's cat Smucky was run over by a passing vehicle on Route 15, which flanked the Kings' house. "Naomi was really upset," recalled King. "I just wanted to tell her, 'Gee, I haven't seen the cat for a while.' But my wife said that we should tell her, because she's got to find out about death sometime."

Smucky was buried in a local pet graveyard started by neighborhood children, which they had designated "Pets Sematary," a child's spelling. Smucky was gone, but the incident haunted King. Soon thereafter, as he was walking across a street in town, an idea came to him: "On one side of the road, I wondered what would happen if that cat could come back to life. By the time I got to the other side, I wondered what would happen if a human came back to life."

To answer that question, King, for the first time, would have to grapple with the nature of death. He would touch the shape under the sheet:

> Death is it. The one thing we all have to face. Two hundred years from now there won't be any of us up walking around and taking nourishment. That's it. Sooner or later, God points at you and says, "It's time to hang up your jock, the game is over, it's time to take a shower. It's the end." But the point is, this is something that every creature on the face of the Earth goes through, but so far as we know, we're the only creatures on earth that have an extended sense of

futurity. We are the only people who can look ahead and say, "Yes, that's right, it's going to happen. And how am I going to deal with the idea of my own conclusion?"

Well, if you stop and think about it, and you stop to realize how clearly we grasp the concept, the answer should be, "We can't cope with it; it'll drive us crazy." For me, the fact that it doesn't is one of the really marvelous things in human existence, and probably also one of the true signs of God's grace on the face of this earth. The ability to go on, day after day, to build meaningful lives, to prepare children in the face of all that, is akin to the act where they talk about a man pulling himself up by his bootstraps. At the same time, we have to prepare for it in some way; we have to experience all the possibilities. And so, for a lot of us, one of the ways we do it is take a worst-case analysis. You say to yourself, *Okay, let's go see a horror movie and see how bad it can be, and then if I die in bed it won't be so awful.* You try to experience that in as many different ways that you can.

For a long time, death has been one of the great unmentionables in our society, along with sex and how much money you make. It's generally something you try to keep from the kids.

In *Pet Sematary* King confronted what he has repeatedly told interviewers over the years is his and every other parent's worst nightmare: the death of one's child, which King could too easily imagine, especially when Owen ran out toward Route 15 one day, the same road that continually resupplied Pets Sematary.

Pet Sematary would be a difficult book for King to write, particularly since he felt the need to write it without compromise. (In *Cujo*, Tad Trenton dies because the internal logic of the story demanded it.) "If you are going to use real people in a story, you ought to play fair," King explained. "I think characters dictate events; I don't think events dictate characters. You have to let the characters do what they have to do."

Putting *Pet Sematary* and teaching aside, King left with the family for a winter vacation at Saint Thomas in the U.S. Virgin Islands. Foremost in his mind: the forthcoming spring semester and, perhaps, *Danse Macabre*—the two being inextricably linked, as the classroom would provide an opportunity to discuss the substance of the book; afterward King could collect his final thoughts in the book.

In January 1979 the spring semester commenced, and King began teaching a literature class, course number EH-90, to 100 students. Occasionally, guest lecturers came in—Burton Hatlen, for instance, lectured on *Dracula*—and films were used too. As King explained, "We are having a film series for this course. We've seen *Psycho, The Exorcist, Night of the Living Dead, The Haunting of Hell House, Invasion of the Body Snatchers.* Couldn't get hold of *Carrie*—isn't that funny?"

Teaching by day and writing by night, King worked on *Danse Macabre,* finding the process to be completely unlike writing a novel, for which you simply make everything up as you go along. As King wrote: "With nonfiction, there's all that bothersome business of making sure your facts are straight, that the dates jibe, that the names are spelled right . . . and worst of all, it meant being out front. . . . The writer of nonfiction is all too visible." Unlike fiction, where the story is king, in *Danse Macabre* King was in a real sense the story—his perceptions of the field, his opinions, and his conclusions would shape and inform the book.

In May 1979 the first draft of *Pet Sematary* was finished, but King had no intention of publishing it. It's too gritty, too realistic, too frightening, thought King, and *Pet Sematary* was put aside.

That month also marked the end of the semester and of his teaching stint at UMO as the writer-in-residence. King declined the invitation to teach a second consecutive year. King, a working writer, probably felt that his time was best spent writing, not teaching. Besides, there were other writers, graduates of the university, who would welcome the opportunity to go back and teach writing (later, Sanford Phippen, class of '64, returned to teach).

The Kings headed back to Center Lovell, Maine, where King could concentrate on writing *Danse Macabre,* the experiences of the classroom still fresh in his mind.

That summer King published two books: in July the second Richard Bachman novel, *The Long Walk;* and in August his first Viking novel, *The Dead Zone.*

An NAL mass-market paperback under its Signet imprint with a $1.95 cover price, *The Long Walk,* like *Rage,* went virtually unnoticed.

Clearly a different fictional voice from the one King employed in his more recent novels, *The Long Walk* revealed a side of King that has been eclipsed by the more popular horror material.

Hatlen gave the novel good marks: "I still think *The Long Walk* is a first-rate book. I think it was the best thing he wrote as an undergraduate, and the best thing he wrote until *'Salem's Lot.* I think it's a better book than *Carrie.*" King, however, viewed those first two published Bachman books much less kindly:

Both *The Long Walk* and *Rage* are full of windy psychological preach-ments (both textual and subtexual), but there's a lot of story in those novels—ultimately the reader will be better equipped than the writer to decide if the story is enough to surmount all the failures of percep-tion and motivation.

Also in summer 1979 King turned his attention to "The Mist," a story idea that had its genesis during a shopping trip to the grocery store. King explained:

> I got the idea doing one of these dull chores where your wife says to you, "Will you go to the market?" and hands you a list. I went to the market and got all this stuff, and I'm rolling up and down the aisle. And if you're a writer, you suddenly realize that in the daytime, between nine and five, the world belongs to the women, but that's another story. People are looking at you and saying, *What's wrong with you, turkey? You on welfare?*
>
> I was totally bored and I was walking down an aisle that was lined with canned goods, and I thought: *Wouldn't it be funny if a ptero-dactyl just came flapping up this aisle and starting knocking over Ragu and Hunts and all this other stuff?* The image delighted me, and I started writing this story around this one little irritant. I don't know if you'd call this story a pearl, but it's there, anyway, and it began with that. The story is nice, and it's nice to be paid for the story, but it's just as good to have had that freedom from boredom.

When King's agent Kirby McCauley began soliciting contributions for *Dark Forces,* McCauley's second horror anthology—a followup to *Frights*—McCauley, hoping for a short story, solicited a contribution from King, and was offered "The Mist." Afterward McCauley received a series of phone calls from King, explaining that the story grew on him.

According to McCauley, the story went from seventy manuscript pages to eighty-five, then to "over a hundred," and finally "145 manu-script pages, or about forty thousand words!" McCauley wrote that he "expected an ordinary-length story and ended up with a short novel by the most popular author of supernatural horror stories in the world."

"You're supposed to visualize that entire story in a sort of grainy black-and-white," King said about "The Mist," recalling the science-fiction and horror movies of the fifties.

"The Mist," one of King's best works, a continuing exploration of technohorror, would be one of the fictional bookends in *Dark Forces,* which Viking would publish later that year.

In June the long-awaited adaptation by Stanley Kubrick of *The Shining* opened in theaters nationwide, and to mixed reviews. Putting things in perspective, King said, " *The Shining* cost roughly $19 million to produce as a film; it cost roughly $24.00 to produce as a novel—the cost of paper, typewriter ribbons, and postage."

Depending on your viewpoint—whether you are a Kubrick fan, or a King fan—the film either satisfies or disappoints. "I went with Steve to see *The Shining,*" Chris Chesley recalled. "I could tell from sitting there beside him and watching him that although he didn't say so in so many words, he liked what the director had done, but the supernatural side of it had been excised—it wasn't his vision at all. That's what he said when we left the theater. It wasn't his book—it was Kubrick's movie."

Anticipated widely as a fusion of Kubrick's skills as a moviemaker and King's powerful imagination, *The Shining* struck King, and many of his readers, as "a beautiful film. It's like this great big gorgeous car with no engine in it—that's all."

Unlike *Carrie*—a winsome story that lent itself to film adaptation— *The Shining,* despite its brand-name director and monstrous budget, showed the inherent difficulties in adapting King's material faithfully to the screen.

Afterward King remained philosophical about the entire process of seeing his books translated to the screen:

> When you sell something to the movies—and I love the movies, and it's immensely flattering to have somebody want to turn a book into a movie—there are two ways to go about it: one is to get involved, all the way or part of the way, and stand up there and take the blame or criticism for everyone else; and the other is to say, "I'm going to sell it; I'm going to take the money."
>
> You know what John Updike used to say about it: It's the best of all possible worlds when they pay you a lot of money and *don't* make the movie.
>
> But when you don't get involved, you are in a no-lose situation, when you can say, "If it's good, that's based on my work." And if it's bad, you can say, "I didn't have anything to do with that."

As for *The Shining,* King had nothing to do with it; from the beginning, it was clearly a Kubrick construct, and clearly not *the* ultimate horror film that Kubrick had originally envisioned.

By early fall King had presumably completed the first drafts of *Danse Macabre, Christine,* and his first screenplay, *Creepshow.*

Christine, an idea King had in summer 1978, was originally a short story, but like some of his other stories, it grew into book length. As King recalled, *Christine* had its genesis as a short story idea:

> It all began with me walking home one day and thinking about my car, which was falling apart. I thought, *Wouldn't it be funny if the little numbers on the odometer started to run backwards, and that when they ran backwards, the car would get younger?* And I thought: *This would make a funny little short story. At the end of the story the car will just fall apart, because it would get back to zero, and it would go back to its component parts.* It didn't quite come out like that; it came out as this great big long novel.
>
> But everything else aside, the fun was walking along the road and thinking, "What if?" because it frees you, it untethers you from the world, and you're not worrying about your insurance payment, nuclear war, or Reagan; you're worried about whether or not the car's going to fall apart when it gets back to zero.

The story of a boy and his car—Arnie Cunningham and a 1958 Plymouth Fury—*Christine* amplified a theme that King had originally explored in "The Mangler" and "Trucks," short stories collected in *Night Shift* that explored the idea of technohorror: malevolent machines brought to life, usurping the natural order by terrorizing people.

Creepshow, an original screenplay, drew its inspiration from the fifties horror comics; William Gaines's E.C. comic line comes to mind. For the anthology film, which comprised five unrelated stories, King used the comic-book format as the script's framing device. *Creepshow* would mark the beginning of King's long-standing personal and professional relationship with Philadelphia director George Romero, best known in the field for his visceral exploration of modern-day zombies that stalked people in *Night of the Living Dead. Creepshow* would also mark King's initial professional involvement with the film community. Many projects would follow.

In August 1979 Viking published its first King novel. *The Dead Zone* went to press with a first printing of 80,000 copies. An $11.95 novel of 426 pages, *The Dead Zone* would be the first indication that King could potentially reach larger audiences; in fact, all indications pointed to the possibility that King, a paperback bestseller, would become a bestselling author in hardback too. Toward that end, Viking set King up for an author's tour of seven major cities in six days—a whirlwind tour, as King recalled:

> If you've ever done the tour, at the end of that period it feels like
> you've been in a pillow fight where all the pillows have been treated

with a low-grade poison gas. You're totally disconnected from your time and your place. And I finished my last gig on this tour, which was in Cleveland, which is also known as the mistake on the lake, and I was scheduled on a flight back, a Delta plane that made a number of different stops, before it got to my little town, which is Bangor, Maine.

I got on the plane in Cleveland and I was just feeling that sort of out-in-the-ozone sensation, and I was in first class and I did the seat belt and the plane pulled away from the jetway, and it started to turn, and then it started to go back, and I went, *Oh, geez, we've got some kind of motor problem; this is just what I need.* But it wasn't. It was a late platform. They pulled back to the gate, the door opened, and Ronald McDonald got on the plane. It was Ronald McDonald with the tufts of orange hair—this character later *did* show up in a book I wrote—with the big nose, and the big floppy orange shoes, and the buttons down the front, and I thought to myself, *I know where this sonofabitch is going to sit.* And he did. Ronald sat down in first class in the aisle next to me and ordered a gin-and-tonic from the stewardess. It was ten o'clock in the morning. He drank it and said, "I hate these little whistle-stop tours. I just hate this. I almost *missed* this plane." And I'm going, *Uh-huh, right.* And the plane took off and when the no-smoking light went out—this was back in those old days when you could still actually smoke on an airplane—Ronald took out a pack of cancer. And there I sat, after seven days on the road, next to Ronald McDonald who is drinking a gin-and-tonic and smoking a Kent. And I said the only thing I could think of, which was, "Where did you come from?" And he said, "McDonaldland." And it was years later that I found there is such a place in Chicago which is sort of McDonald's clown central. That was the end of my first real tour.

Viking undoubtedly boosted sales by designing book jackets that had much in common with the design techniques used by mass-market paperback publishers. King's reaction: "I like the jacket pretty well. I think that, in a large measure, it's been responsible for some of the book's success because it's a very high contrast type, something I think Viking might have lifted from the paperback houses."

King explained the different looks in packaging between his former and new publisher:

I like books that are nicely made, and with the exception of *'Salem's Lot* and *Night Shift,* none of the Doubleday books were especially well made. They have a ragged, machine-produced look to them, as though they were built to fall apart. *The Stand* is worse that way: it looks like a brick. It's this little, tiny squatty thing that looks much bigger than it is. *The Dead Zone* is really nicely put together. It's got a nice cloth binding, and it's just a nice product.

A book with mainstream appeal, *The Dead Zone* would eclipse the sales of King's most recent Doubleday novel, *The Stand,* which sold 50,000 in its first year. *The Dead Zone* would sell 175,000 copies in its first year, due in part to what some considered to be more aggressive marketing and, unquestionably, more attractive books as product. *The Dead Zone,* particularly, had an appealing cover design for its jacket, the work of One + One Studio.

Over the Halloween 1979 weekend King was feted as the guest of honor at a convention, the World Fantasy Con, held in Providence, Rhode Island. The gathering place for aficionados of fantasy and horror, the World Fantasy Con featured guest speakers, panels, an elaborate art show, and a dealer's room where collectibles could be purchased; in short, heaven on earth for those whose tastes run a little on the hellish side.

At that World Fantasy Con, King was approached by Christopher Zavisa, a specialty publisher from Michigan, to write "a story which would run in twelve monthly installments of vignette length," with illustrations by horror artist Berni Wrightson. The text and art would then be published as a calendar.

For Zavisa the World Fantasy Con was the perfect time to approach King, who was awash with guilt at the success he had achieved, dwarfing that of other, less financially successful writers who were in attendance. As King later wrote: "I was, after all, rubbing elbows with writers I had idolized as a kid, writers who had taught me much of what I knew about my craft—guys like Robert Bloch . . . Fritz Leiber . . . Frank Belknap Long . . . . They had labored long and honorably in the pulp jungles; I came bopping along twenty years after the demise of *Weird Tales* . . . and simply reaped the bountiful harvest they had sown in that jungle."

King agreed to write the calendar copy, writing "the *only* something which fits so neatly into the format Zavisa was suggesting. That something, of course, was the werewolf myth."

King's original plan was to write one vignette a day and complete the assignment in less than two weeks. Unfortunately, that didn't happen. Instead, work on *Cycle of the Werewolf* came to a halt after he wrote the first three vignettes. Something was seriously wrong, but King didn't know what. "Every now and then," King wrote, "I would look guiltily at the thin sheaf of pages gathering dust beside the typewriter, but look was all I did. It was a cold meal. Nobody likes to eat a cold meal unless he has to."

Cycle of the Werewolf, as King wrote, was a "stillbirth." For the remainder of the year King would do no more work on the book.

In November 1979 King's first "made-for-TV" adaptation appeared. 'Salem's Lot aired on November 17 and 24. Directed by Tobe Hooper—best known for Texas Chainsaw Massacre, a cult favorite, and Poltergeist—'Salem's Lot was originally optioned for a full-length feature film, but the richness and complexity of the novel could not be shoehorned into a ninety-minute feature; after several early scripts were rejected, Paul Monash's script was accepted, "a 200- or 225-page script—a four-hour mini-series script," recalled Hooper.

Budgeted at $4 million and shot in the small northern California town of Ferndale, 'Salem's Lot was King's first encounter with the network's restrictive Standards and Practices guidelines, which made it difficult to show horror on TV in an explicit manner. "Considering the medium," King said, "they did a real good job. TV is death to horror. When it went to TV a lot of people moaned and I was one of the moaners."

In downtown Bangor, Maine, a 31-foot, 3,700-pound statue of Paul Bunyan recalls the late 1800s when Bangor was "the lumber capital of the world," when lumber was king. Summer 1980, however, marked the arrival of another King—Stephen King—who would be a testament to its future, one in which entrepreneurial spirit makes all the difference.

Finding a home for sale in Bangor's Historic District, the Kings paid $135,000 for what was known locally as the William Arnold house, an Italianate villa originally built in 1856 at a cost of $6,000.

At this point in King's career, moving to Bangor simply made good sense, beyond the original impetus to move. "For five years I've wanted to write a book set in a fictional Maine city," King said.

Bangor, a city latticed with canals and waterways, and flanked by the Penobscot, would be transmuted into Derry, Maine. In "A Novelist's Perspective on Bangor," King wrote: "I had a very long book in mind, a book which I hoped would deal with the way myths and dreams and stories—stories, most of all—become a part of the everyday life of a small American city . . . . Oh, my Lord, my Lord, the stories you hear about this town—the streets fairly clang with them. The problem isn't finding them or ferreting them out; the problem is that old boozer's problem of knowing when to stop."

Derry, which would be retitled *IT,* would be King's longest novel to date. An ambitious book set in the late 1950s—the first half of the book would tell the story of the children who confront a monster in the sewer and wound it; and the second half, set in the mideighties, would conclude the story with the kids, now adults, confronting It for the last time.

More than just a locale for another book, Bangor—unlike Center Lovell and Bridgton, his previous addresses—offered several amenities to King: a major airport, close proximity to a major university with all its resources, an excellent library—one of the finest in New England—and a number of bookstores, as well as a new eight-in-one cineplex near the Bangor mall.

Characterized by King as a "hard-drinking, working man's town," Bangor *felt* right to King, who eschews designer clothes for jeans and a work shirt, the typical "uniform" around town. "I think a place is yours when you know where the roads go. They talk my language here; I talk theirs. I think like them; they know me. It feels right to be here," King said.

As the Kings made plans to settle down in their winter home in Bangor—Center Lovell would be their summer residence—King's growing pile of manuscripts finally found a permanent home too. That summer King donated "six boxloads of manuscript papers" to the Special Collections of the Fogler Library at his alma mater, the University of Maine at Orono. The donation was the culmination of years of effort by Eric Flower, then the Special Collections librarian, who had written to King back on November 20, 1975, reminding King of his intentions to deposit *Carrie.*

When King confirmed that he'd bring *Carrie,* Flower asked about *'Salem's Lot,* citing its importance to "future researchers of Maine literature," to which King replied that he didn't feel there was much "Maineness" in his work.

King subsequently deposited at the Special Collections drafts, proofs, and galleys for numerous books, including *Carrie, Jerusalem's Lot, The Dead Zone, The Stand,* and *The Shining.* Additionally, King turned over to Collections short fiction and nonfiction—published and unpublished—and, more important, several early King novels, all unpublished: *The Aftermath, Blaze, Second Coming* (the first of three drafts of *'Salem's Lot*), and *Sword in the Darkness.*

In later years, King would make additional deposits, including *Night Shift, Firestarter, Cujo, Pet Sematary, Christine, Skeleton Crew,* and *The Talisman.*

In fall 1980 the Kings made the move to their new house in the Historic District. As King began work on *IT,* Viking published its third

King novel, in September; *Firestarter,* issued in a first printing of 100,000 copies, would sell 285,000 copies in its first year—110,000 copies more than *The Dead Zone* the previous year.

Dedicated to Shirley Jackson—whose fictional voice, King wrote, never needed to be raised—*Firestarter* amplifies the telekinetic theme he initially explored in *Carrie.* Charlie McGee's psychic talent, however, was more deadly; pyrokinetic, she possessed the ability mentally to trigger spontaneous combustion.

The subtext that runs throughout the novel is the pervasive effect of the government in our lives, a theme directly addressed in the afterword to the paperback edition of *Firestarter.* In it King wrote, "The U.S. government, or agencies thereof, has indeed administered potentially dangerous drugs to unwitting subjects on more than one occasion."

King's speculations raise disturbing questions about the extent to which the government has in the name of national security used its own citizens as human guinea pigs. The world, King concluded, "is still full of odd dark corners and unsettling nooks and crannies."

Firestarter was also issued in a limited edition by Alex Berman's Phantasia Press, which issued 725 copies, signed and dated by King, with 26 lettered copies bound in asbestos (the special edition of Ray Bradbury's *Fahrenheit 451* was similarly bound). Sporting a full-color wraparound cover by Michael Whelan, the limited edition of *Firestarter* would mark the beginning of King's involvement with the specialty market, which catered to the science-fiction, fantasy, and horror fans, the same ones who in October 1980 voted to give King the World Fantasy Award—a small bust of H. P. Lovecraft—for "special contributions to the field."

At year's end King had reportedly begun work on the first draft of *IT,* a novel that would take four years, off and on, of writing.

In January 1981 Chris Zavisa called King, asking for a progress report on *The Cycle of the Werewolf.* The artist, Berni Wrightson, had already begun the artwork. "Guilt rushed over me anew," King wrote. "Lying through my teeth, I told Chris it was coming along real well."

In February King and family left for Puerto Rico for a vacation. Mindful of his outstanding obligation, King took the manuscript with him, intending to finish it, but it became apparent to him that he simply couldn't continue beyond June. "The vignette form was killing me," King wrote. An intuitive writer who usually does not write fiction to order—preferring, rather, to let the story assume whatever length is required for the telling—King switched gears and began writing it as a short story.

Then the story unreeled in his mind's eye. After writing three more vignettes covering July through September, King called Zavisa and informed him that they didn't have a story calendar on their hands anymore—they had a short book.

Zavisa, wrote King, responded "with such enthusiasm" that King "wondered if it wasn't what he had sort of wanted all along, but had been, maybe, a little to shy to pitch." Zavisa, however, hadn't been too shy to pitch a book; he had originally conceived the notion of a calendar, but when King offered the opportunity of a book, Zavisa realized it was simply a more marketable idea and, perhaps, should have pitched that in the first place.

Unlike *Firestarter,* which had a limited edition, *The Cycle of the Werewolf* would be unique: there would be no trade edition issued in the bookstores. Fantasy fans who subscribed to specialty magazines like *Locus* would know of its publication, but the King audience at large—the ones that snapped up each new novel in record numbers—would not even know of its publication.

In April 1981 Everest House published *Danse Macabre* in hardback, with a first printing of 60,000 copies in its trade edition ($13.95) and 250 numbered copies in its limited edition ($65), signed by King. It would later be reprinted by Berkley, which had bought the paperback rights for $585,000. King's first and to date only nonfiction book, *Danse Macabre* surveyed the horror field from the fifties to the eighties. The jacket copy made it clear that King had carved out a niche for himself in the horror field:

> Stephen King's stunning success as a novelist just may be unrivalled in publishing history. Other writers in their early twenties have been acclaimed, but few have reached sales figures of over 25 million books a decade later, and none save King has staked a solid claim as undisputed master of a very special literary genre—the horror story. *Carrie, The Shining, The Dead Zone, Firestarter* have led to a worldwide curiosity about Stephen King and his intuitive affinity for the spine-chilling tale.

Appropriately, *Danse Macabre*'s dedication included writers who opened the way for King and his contemporaries: Robert Bloch (best known for his psychological suspense thrillers like *Psycho*), Jorge Luis Borges (a South American fantasist who wrote what is called magic realism), Ray Bradbury (whose early horror stories influenced King, and who went on to write *The Martian Chronicles* and *Fahrenheit 451*), Frank Belknap Long (a member of the original H. P. Lovecraft circle), Donald Wandrei (who, along with August Derleth, started Arkham House, a specialty press initially formed to issue the works of Lovecraft in hardback), and Manly Wade Wellman (a North Carolina writer, best known for his fantasy stories about John the Balladeer, who wielded a silver-stringed guitar).

A stark contrast to literary criticism written for an elevated audience, *Danse Macabre* was what King called a "user-friendly" overview of the field, an approach readers and reviewers found irresistible and compulsively readable, just like his fiction.

"Knowledgeable and engaging, King is a perfect tour guide," said *Publishers Weekly*. "King's narrative style is refreshingly informal . . . . Yet such informality can and does lead to an annoying amount of digression. Nevertheless, King's account is perceptive and remarkably inclusive. A solid history both for those who are King's fans and for those who aren't."

In late May 1981 George Romero began shooting *Creepshow*, an anthology film backed by United Film Distributors. Budgeted at $8 million—a far cry from the $127,000 budget Romero had when shooting *Night of the Living Dead*—*Creepshow* could afford top talent: Tom Savini and Cletus Anderson for its special effects, as well as veteran actors and actresses like Adrienne Barbeau, Ted Danson, Hal Holbrook, E. G. Marshall, and Leslie Nielsen.

Creepshow would also mark King's first acting debut, as a hayseed Mainer in "The Lonesome Death of Jordy Verrill."

Based on Stephen King's original screenplay, *Creepshow* was shot entirely in Philadelphia, except for one story. As King explained:

Richard P. Rubinstein, the producer, was real interested in filming "Something to Tide You Over" in Maine. He sent a production scout to Ogunquit, Maine, where the beach was right. The story had to do with a guy who's buried below the high tide line up to his neck, and the high tide comes in. They went to the town manager and said, *Listen, we want to film on the beach, and here's what we need; and of course we'll have to block off a little part of this beach every day.*

And the town manager replied, "Oh, no, you can't do that. Nossir. You can't do that. You can't block off this beach."

"I don't think you understand. It's really just this small section of this beach. We can't have people walking around the background, because this is about a murder, and this guy's buried up to his neck. If people are walking around the background, it'll destroy that window of credibility."

"Golly, I understand that, but you can't do that," replied the town manager.

"Why not?"

"Because nobody ever has."

The segment was subsequently filmed in New Jersey, but the incident rankled King, for two reasons: because most of his stories were set in Maine, it simply made artistic sense to film the adaptations in Maine too. In addition, bringing the film community to Maine—virgin territory for Hollywood—would also bring an influx of much needed money into a state that relies too heavily on the tourist trade in the summer. If the story from *Creepshow* had been filmed in October, the off-season, it would have been like manna from heaven to the local community.

King did not win that battle, but it got him thinking about Maine and the film community, especially with all the other stories under option.

Set for a Halloween 1982 release, *Creepshow* would have a book tie-in too. Berni Wrightson, the best macabre artist in the comic-book field, agreed on short notice to adapt illustratively the film to the comic book format in a full-color graphic album. King would provide the continuity, the panel-by-panel breakdown for the five stories.

While on the set of *Creepshow,* King put his free time to good use and began writing *Cannibals,* a novel written in longhand, similar in plot to J. G. Ballard's *High-Rise* in which "the inhabitants of a massive multistory apartment block gradually revert to savagery as the amenities of civilisation, which form a restrictive veneer around their lives, break down." *Cannibals,* as King told Winter, is "all about these people who are trapped in an apartment building. Worst thing I could think of. And I thought, wouldn't it be funny if they all ended up eating each other? It's very, very bizarre because it's all on one note."

Cannibals sounded like nothing so much as *High-Rise* and *Lord of the Flies* crossed with Romero's *Night of the Living Dead.*

In October 1981 Viking published *Cujo,* a $13.95 hardback with a first printing of 350,000 copies—a far cry from the 50,000 copies sold in the first year by Doubleday of *The Shining* and *The Stand.* Clearly, with each new book, King converted some of his paperback readers to hardback buyers—proof positive that King as storyteller was delivering what his audience wanted. *Cujo,* set in Castle Rock, Maine, was another chapter in King's continuing exploration of the Maine myth. It is also quintessential King, characters trying to find the American dream but, instead, realizing the American nightmare—a major motif in King's work, as Burton Hatlen pointed out in his 1974 book review of *Carrie* in *Alumnus*.

Unlike the supernatural trappings that marked his early novels, *Cujo* draws much of its strength from the horror that is present in everyday life. Cujo, a rabid Saint Bernard, is relentless in his attacks against Donna and Tad Trenton, who find themselves in a broken-down Ford Pinto at Joe Camber's garage. There Donna Trenton makes her last stand, as Cujo lays siege.

A naturalistic novel, *Cujo* highlights King's ability to invoke terror— the highest level of achievement, as King pointed out, followed by horror and the gross-out—within the world of the ordinary. "With a master's sure feel for the power of the plausible to terrify as much or more than the uncanny, King builds a riveting novel out of the lives of some very ordinary and believable people in a small Maine town, and an unfortunate 200 lb. St. Bernard," said *Publishers Weekly*.

Ironically, just as *Cujo* drew attention to its author because of its first printing and its unrelenting realism, *Roadwork*—no less relentless in its realism, a naturalistic novel that used cancer as its metaphor—went virtually unnoticed, with a shelf life approximating milk's. Perceived as just another cheap-rack paperback, *Roadwork* had a serious subtext, as King explained:

> Cancer is everywhere; cancer is one of the things that frightens almost everybody. It's an invader that comes into your system, takes a foothold, begins to spread. Sometimes its growth can be retarded, sometimes it can be stopped, but a lot of times it kills.
>
> People are very frightened by this. They are frightened of the interloper in their system. And more and more, the news that we get is that *everything* you do causes cancer: If you smoke, you'll get lung cancer; but even if you don't smoke and you work in an asbestos mill, you'll get lung cancer. And if you eat too much beef, you might get intestinal cancer; but if you eat too much fish, you might get mercury poisoning—and that can cause lymphatic cancer.
>
> There are all sorts of possibilities here: paraquad, Agent Orange . . . . Cancer appears to be floating around—it's *everywhere*. There's this great cloud of cancer just waiting to rain down on us all.

In November 1981 King published "Do the Dead Sing?" in *Yankee* magazine. King's poignant story about Stella Flanders—regional writing at its best, and a work of American literature in its own right—made it clear that King was a writer worth taking seriously. The tale showcased his writing talent, a talent that would begin to receive considerable attention outside the field, even as it had within the field.

The previous month King received the Career Alumni Award from the University of Maine at Orono. At thirty-four King was its youngest recipient. And within the fantasy field, for contributions to the field, King received the British Fantasy Award, and had two stories nominated for awards: "The Mist" for a World Fantasy Award, and "The Way Station" for a Nebula Award.

For King, fame had its rewards in other ways too. In a newspaper roundup for Christmas, King told the *Bangor Daily News* that he wanted "some new bread pans," since he enjoyed baking bread, and then added, "I know what I want, but I'm not going to get it. I want a jukebox. I think some of the old ones are really beautiful things."

Tabitha King got him the bread pans, but he also got the jukebox, from an unexpected source. Edward Ames said, "I read in the paper that Stephen King wanted a jukebox but never thought he'd get it. I thought, 'Gee, that's too bad. I have one right here.' It worked the last time I played it."

Around noon on Christmas, a gift fit for a king was delivered to King's Bangor residence. King's "eyes grew wide in surprise—then softened in obviously pleasure," reported the *News.* "Far out. Holy cow. That's incredible. Amazing. I'll be a son of a gun," King said. "Where did you find it?"

In spring 1982, working from a lengthy outline they had written the previous year, King and Peter Straub began writing the first draft of *The Talisman.* To avoid the jarring narrative effect of two distinct prose styles telling the same story—King's bodacious style contrasting with Straub's deliberate, measured prose—they made the decision to tell the story through a blend of both voices, creating a third voice, making it impossible for readers to discern who wrote what.

Using a modem, King transmitted text files through the phone lines from his Wang word processor at his home office in Bangor to Straub's IBM Displaywriter in Connecticut. Straub, in turn, would pick up where King left off in the story, write until he wanted to stop, and then send his installment to King.

The story bounced back and forth between them for the rest of the year. For King, *The Talisman* was his first successful attempt to write a novel-length work since the first draft of *IT,* which drained him creatively as *The Stand* had done earlier.

In 1981 King published several books, but none was a full-length novel of recent vintage.

King published in May 1981 his fourth Richard Bachman novel, *The Running Man,* which he felt "may be the best of them because it's nothing but story—it moves with the goofy speed of a silent movie, and anything which is *not* story is cheerfully thrown over the side." Like the previous Bachman volumes, it was generally ignored by reviewers, though the story was sufficiently strong to attract a film option.

In July 1981 *Stephen King's Creepshow,* the graphic album illustrated by Berni Wrightson, appeared as an oversized trade paperback. In full color, the $6.95 book sported a cover by E.C. artist Jack Kamen. A teenage boy is reading a *Creepshow* comic book in bed late at night. On the wall behind him are movie posters of *Dawn of the Dead, The Shining,* and *Carrie.* Outside the window a skeletal figure peers in.

In August 1981 Viking published *Different Seasons.* Unlike *Night Shift,* a collection of predominantly reprinted material, *Different Seasons* consisted of four previously unpublished novellas. According to Douglas E. Winter:

> Somewhat contrary to the recollection reflected in the "Afterword" to *Different Seasons,* it now appears that the four novellas were written by King in the following sequence: "The Body" upon completing the first draft of *'Salem's Lot;* "Apt Pupil" upon finishing the first draft of *The Shining;* "Rita Hayworth and Shawshank Redemption" after the first draft of *The Stand;* and "The Breathing Method" following the first draft of *Cujo.*

Precisely because fiction collections don't sell as well as full-length novels—much as anthology movies don't draw as well as full-length movies—*Different Seasons* had initially been greeted by its Viking editor with muted enthusiasm. King wrote:

> "Novellas," Alan says. He is being a good sport, but his voice says some of the joy may have just gone out of his day; his voice says he feels he has just won two tickets to some dubious little banana republic on Revolucion Airways. "Long stories, you mean."

King's editor needn't have worried. In its first year *Different Seasons* sold 140,000 copies, according to King.

Comprising four novellas, *Different Seasons* highlighted King's strength with the novella—arguably the literary form that best displays his strengths because of the necessity for concision. *Different Seasons* also highlighted King's ability to write nonhorrific material to great effect.

In his introduction to King's *Night Shift,* a 1978 collection, John D. MacDonald wrote that "at the risk of being an iconoclast I will say that I do not give a diddly-whoop what Stephen King chooses as an area in which to write. The fact that he presently enjoys writing in the field of spooks and spells and slitherings in the cellar is to me the least important and useful fact about the man anyone can relate. . . . Stephen King is not going to restrict himself to his present field of intense interest."

MacDonald was correct. Since *Night Shift,* King's fiction has increasingly drawn from a horror pool with widening ripples; the comic-bookish vampires, the werewolves, and the ghosts have been relegated to the past. The element of horror is still present, but it has been transmuted, made more powerful, more *real,* as King has explored horror in everyday America—seen in the parasitic relationship between Todd Bowden and Kurt Dussander in "Apt Pupil," one of the novellas in *Different Seasons.* According to King, that hit a raw nerve with his publisher:

> I got a really strong reaction to the "Apt Pupil" story . . . . My publisher called and protested. I said, "Well, do you think it's anti-Semitic?" Because it's about a Nazi war criminal, and he begins to spout all the old bullshit, once the kid in the story gets him going. But that wasn't the problem. It was too real. If the same story had been in outer space, it would have been okay, because then you'd have that comforting layer of "This is just make-believe, so we can dismiss it."
>
> So they were very disturbed by the piece, and I thought to myself, "Gee, I've done it again. I've written something that has really gotten under someone's skin." And I do like that. I like the feeling that I reached right between somebody's legs . . . like that. There has always been that primitive impulse as part of my writing."

Different Seasons also offers "The Body," a coming-of-age story that is clearly one of King's best works, and that leans on several incidents from his life. According to King, the original inspiration came from a story George McLeod, a college roommate and writer, told him about a dog being struck by a train. According to King, McLeod was going to write the story but never did. Five years later King told him, "I took your idea and I wrote a story about these kids who walk down a railroad track to find the body of a boy."

But an idea is not a story, so, said King, "I took a lot of things that I had felt when I was a kid and put them in [Gordon Lachance]." One such incident went back to when King was four years old, living in Stratford, Connecticut. One day he returned home from playing with a friend. King, in shock, had witnessed a horrible accident. "The kid I had been playing with had been run over by a freight train. . . ." Another incident, from his Durham, Maine, days, was a boating accident at Runaround Pond, down the road from Chris Chesley's house. As Chesley recalled:

> A friend of mine said to me and Steve, "Do you want to see a dead body?" "Why not?" we said. "It'd be great! No problem there!" When we got to Runaround Pond, they had dragged the body up, with lights shining on it. They had not covered up the corpse yet.
>
> It was an educational experience for all of us. It wasn't a pleasant sight.

Also, many of the names in "The Body" were drawn from the *New England Telephone* directory for that area, according to Maine writer David Lowell. From the 1970 directory the names of several characters can be found: Lachance (the story's protagonist), Merrill (the bully that terrorized Lachance and his friends), Hogan (the protagonist of the story within the story, "Lard Ass Hogan," which is also the name of a bowling alley in nearby Lisbon Falls), Desjardins, Doughterty, Thomas, Cote, Gamache, Charbonneau, Cormier, Duchamp (Ducharme in the directory), and Tessio (Tessier in the directory).

Similarly, several places mentioned in the story are real places in the Durham area: the Hillcrest Chicken Farm, the Royal River, Shiloh Church, and WLAM (WALM in the story).

The two stories-within-the-story, purportedly by Gordon Lachance, were in fact written by King and published in literary magazines during his college days. "Stud City" appeared in the fall 1969 issue of *Ubris,* and "The Revenge of Lard Ass Hogan" appeared in the July 1975 issue of *Maine Review.*

In "The Body" Gordon Lachance writes—in words that just as well spoke for Stephen King—about "Stud City":

> It ought to have THIS IS A PRODUCT OF AN UNDERGRADU-ATE CREATIVE WRITING WORKSHOP stamped on every page . . . because that's just what it was, at least up to a certain point. . . . And yet it was the first story I ever wrote that felt like *my* story—the first one that really felt *whole,* after five years of trying. . . . Even now when I read it . . . I can see the true face of Gordon Lachance lurking just behind the lines of print, a Gordon Lachance younger than the one living and writing now, one certainly more idealistic than the best-selling novelist who is more apt to have his paperback contracts reviewed than his books . . . .

Similarly, the fourth story in *Different Seasons,* "The Breathing Method," recalls King's Durham days. The fictional brownstone in New York at 249B East Thirty-fifth Street, better known as The Club, where old men meet to tell tales, had its origin in the loft behind King's house, according to Chesley—the 249 Club where the kids met to trade yarns.

In the fictional brownstone, over the oversized fireplace, is a keystone, on which is inscribed this legend, "IT IS THE TALE, NOT HE WHO TELLS IT." Its seemingly ageless custodian, Stevens, explains that in this building there are many rooms, endless rooms and corridors. "Here, sir, there are *always* more tales," he tells an inquisitive club member.

Different Seasons found an enthusiastic audience, especially among those who felt like John D. MacDonald that King could clearly write fiction that did not require the traditional trappings of horror to capture and hold the reader's attention. *Publishers Weekly* called the stories "some of his best work," and *Book World* echoed, "The important thing to acknowledge in King's immense popularity, and in the Niagara of words he produces, is the simple fact that he can write. He can write without cheapening or trivializing himself or his audience."

Even King's hard-to-please correspondents, the die-hard horror fans, found that by trusting the storyteller, the kind of story was secondary to its telling. "I don't remember a single correspondent . . . who scolded me for writing something that wasn't horror," wrote King.

While King felt confident that his mainstay readers would enjoy *Different Seasons,* he felt less confident that they would embrace *The Dark Tower: The Gunslinger,* which collected five stories originally published in *F&SF* in 1980 and 1981.

Its publisher, Donald M. Grant, made it clear that no matter what you thought of King's fiction, these stories were like nothing you've ever read, by King or anyone else:

> Written over a period of twelve years, *The Dark Tower: The Gunslinger* is the first cycle of stories in a remarkable epic, the strangest and most frightening work that Stephen King has ever written. It is the book of Roland, the last gunslinger, and his quest for the Dark Tower in a world in which time has no bearing.
>
> Against the weird background of a devastated and dying planet—with curious ties to our own world—the last gunslinger pursues the man in black. It is a time when man's thirst for knowledge has been lost, and the haunted, chilling land harbors strange beings: the Slow Mutants, less-than-human troglodytes dwelling in darkness; a Speaking Demon, laired beneath a forgotten way station; and a nameless vampiric presence, held captive in an ancient circle of altar stones.
>
> Herein lies a tale of science-fantasy that is unlike anything best-selling author Stephen King has ever written; indeed, it is unlike anything anyone has ever written. And it is a volume that begs for illustrations! *The Dark Tower: The Gunslinger* is a joining of the foremost

author and artist in the field of science fiction and fantasy. Complementing Stephen King in this most unusual of books is artist Michael Whelan, recipient of both "Howard" and "Hugo" awards as best artist in the genre.

With five full-color illustrations, color endleaves, and numerous black and white designs and devices.

Published in an edition of only 10,000 hardback copies at $20 and a $60 limited edition of 500 numbered copies signed by King and Whelan, *The Dark Tower: The Gunslinger* was intended for sale only within the fantasy circles. King explained his rationale: "I didn't think anybody would want to read it. It wasn't like the other books. The first volume didn't have any firm grounding in our world, in reality; it was more like a Tolkien fantasy of some other world. The other reason was that it wasn't done; it wasn't complete."

For King, it was also a way to keep his rocketing career in perspective. "To issue such a book, of course, is one of the few ways I have left of saying that I am not entirely for sale—that I'm still in this business for the joy of it, and that I have not been entirely subsumed by the commercial juggernaut I have cheerfully fueled and set in motion."

The Dark Tower: The Gunslinger went out of print almost immediately, with almost no distribution to the trade bookstores. The book then began an upward spiral in price, to the surprise of King and his publisher. "The book was published at twenty dollars, and I was a little bit horrified by what happened. The price jumped and it became a collector's item, and that hadn't been my intention at all, to see these books climb from $20 to $50 to $70, to whatever," King observed.

A fan at heart, King published *Cycle of the Werewolf* and *The Dark Tower: The Gunslinger* because he wanted to give something back to the fantasy community that nurtured and sustained him. King's participation in a small press typically brought a guarantee that virtually no other author in the field could match: a King project inevitably sold out—no-risk publishing.

As *Whispers* publisher Stuart David Schiff wrote in his editorial to his special King issue:

> I am certain that there is not a single person reading this who needs an introduction to Stephen King. His meteoric rise to the top of the book-publishing field is one of the incredible stories of the past decade. Despite his new and lofty position, Steve has kept his roots. His support of small presses and authors who have not been as successful as himself is ample evidence of this. Without Steve wanting *Whispers*

to share in his success, this issue simply would not have been possible.

A commercial success outside the field, King is *the* favorite within the field. In September 1982, at the world science-fiction convention, King won a Hugo Award for *Danse Macabre,* the best nonfiction book of the previous year. In October, at the World Fantasy Con, King won an award in the short-fiction category for "Do the Dead Sing?"

Ironically, because of his fame, King had a sweet-sour relationship with the fans at conventions. A prisoner of his own success, King found that he was a magnet to them, regardless of whether he was there as a guest of honor or as an attendee. He explained:

> I'm still a fan at heart and one of the things which is real rough is not being able to go to a convention and go into the huckster's room and look around, maybe pick up some copies of *Weird Tales* or other pulps without having people come for autographs, or to talk about something they've written, or you've written. They're hitting on you all the time.

In its convention report of the World Fantasy Con, *Locus*—the trade journal for the field—reported that "Stephen King spent a lot of time in his suite, because he was mobbed wherever he went." King's response: "I love conventions, but may have to give them up if this continues."

Unfortunately, for King as well as his fans, the mob scenes continued and King reluctantly left the convention scene; the fans had driven him away permanently. The conventions, King explained, were "no longer any fun."

King's fame, though, was not restricted to the fan world. In the public eye his visibility took a giant leap when a flattered King agreed to appear in a television ad promoting American Express as part of its "celebrity" ads.

Things had certainly changed from the time when his application for a Diner's Club card had been declined on the grounds that he was a freelance writer.

Produced by Ogilvy & Mather, an ad agency based in New York, the thirty-second ad shows King hamming it up. Dressed in an after-dinner jacket, he slinks through a haunted mansion on a stormy night and rhetorically asks:

> Do you know me? It's frightening how many novels of suspense I've written. But still, when I'm not recognized, it just kills me. So instead of saying, "I wrote *Carrie,*" I carry the American Express card. Without it, isn't life a little scary?
> The American Express card—*don't leave home without it.*

Back on the homefront King would find privacy an increasingly scarce commodity. As word went out that King had permanently settled in Bangor, the King house became the focus of attention, especially on Halloween. Stephen King, who once enjoyed Halloween, soon found it a bloody nuisance. Years later, when asked by a reporter if he would be at his Bangor home on Halloween, King replied, "God, no! I'll be far away!" King elaborated: "I hate Halloween. I've turned into America's giant pumpkin and I can't relate to that."

October 1982 also marked the release of the movie *Creepshow* from Warner Brothers. Expectations ran high among those who had worked on the movie. And King, who wrote the script and starred in one story, had high hopes too. He hoped it would be a terrifying moviegoing experience—his kind of movie:

> My idea of a perfect horror film would be one where you'd have to have nurses and doctors on duty with crash wagons because people would have heart attacks. People would crawl out with large wet spots on their trousers. It would be that kind of experience. They'd say, "What the hell are you doing with me?" The answer: "What *you* wanted. We're scaring you."

Creepshow wasn't the perfect horror film, for it failed to terrify or horrify and went strictly for the gross-out. Still, *Creepshow* gave King valuable on-camera experience as an actor that would give him much needed insights into the acting profession. It also gave him a firsthand look at *how* movies were made.

As the year drew to a close, two specialty publishers issued the first of several books about Stephen King. Underwood–Miller published a collection of essays about King's work, *Fear Itself: The Horror Fiction of Stephen King;* and Starmont issued *Stephen King* by Douglas E. Winter, who in his foreword wrote, "It is the first book-length study of King's fiction, but it certainly will not be the last."

The year ended with the publication of *The Plant* by Stephen King, from his own publishing company, Philtrum Press. Designed by Michael Alpert, *The Plant* had a limited circulation: 200 copies were sent only to those on the family Christmas list. King explained:

> It's sort of an epistolary novel-in-progress. A couple of years ago I got thinking about Christmas cards and how mass-produced they were.

You buy them from the Girl Scouts and it says, "Best Wishes," and inside in red print it says "The Andersons."

It didn't seem like a sincere, personal thing. So I thought, "Well, I'll do this little book every year and print it, and send it out to friends."

In a few short years, from 1979 to 1982, so much in King's life had come full circle. He had gone back to his alma mater as a teacher and a celebrated alumnus. He wrote *Danse Macabre,* which firmly established his credentials and helped make him the spokesman for the field. He saw his novels at Viking reaching a larger audience that, with each successive book, grew even larger. He moved to Bangor in grand style, geographically close to Hermon where it all began, but where success was light years away. He began to be noticed favorably by the book-reviewing media for writing mainstream fiction like "Do the Dead Sing?" and the novellas in *Different Seasons,* depite his firmly entrenched reputation as a horror novelist. He saw books *about* him being written, the beginnings of that cottage industry. And after the American Express commercial aired, he became *the* brand-name horror writer perfectly positioned for becoming *the* bestselling author in our time. King now was unquestionably, as he put it, "America's literary boogeyman."

6

Bestsellasaurus Rex

At his home in Center Lovell, Maine, King began work on a new novel. It was January 1983, and for the past several months he had been toying with a book idea, which finally jelled.

"It was the perfect time and place," King wrote, "to start such a story: I was alone in the house, there was a screaming northeaster blowing snow across the frozen lake outside, and I was sitting in front of the woodstove with a yellow legal pad in my hand and a cold beer on the table." King wrote thirteen pages that night and put them aside.

The Napkins was King's attempt to reach out to his daughter Naomi, who had "read little of my work, and quite simply put, I wanted to please her and reach her." Before the end of the year *The Napkins* would see completion and King would give it to Naomi, hoping she'd read it and like it. As King explained, "Although I had written thirteen novels by the time my daughter had attained an equal number of years, she hadn't read any of them. She's made it clear that she loves *me,* but has very little interest in my vampires, ghoulies, and slushy crawling things."

Three months later King published *Christine.* " . . . I *love* my haunted car, and I think it's going to make a lot of people nervous about crossing busy streets after dark," King wrote. A $16.95 hardback, *Christine* had been sold to Viking for a $1.00 advance. King reasoned:

> I wanted not to be taking a lot of cash which I didn't need, and it ties up money other writers could get for advances. We took a lot of money on *The Dead Zone, Firestarter,* and *Cujo,* and [the publishers] are ahead of me right now. They paid out the advance in yearly installments—lots of money. Before they had finished paying the advance in five or six staggered payments, the books had earned into the black, but they're not required to pay royalties until they're finished paying the advance.
>
> On *Christine,* the first time they sell a book they're in the black, I'm in the black. There are no staggered payments—it's hard to stagger a dollar!

Christine rolled out into the bookstores nationwide and would sell 303,000 copies within a year of its publication. A dark *American Graffiti*, *Christine* is, according to King, "a monster story. But it's also a story about cars and girls and guys and how cars become girls in America. It's an American phenomenon in that sense. *Christine* is a freeway horror story. It couldn't exist without a teenage culture that views the car as an integral part of that step from adolescence to adulthood. The car is the way that journey is made."

Publishers Weekly praised *Christine* because it "contains some of the best writing King has ever done; his teenage characters are superbly drawn and their dilemma is truly gripping. However, Christine, we soon realize, is just a car, a finally inanimate machine that does not quite live up to the expectations King's human characterizations have engendered."

At the same time the book was published, the movie had begun principal photography in California—an atypical schedule, possible only because Richard Kobritz, who produced *'Salem's Lot* for television, had been given a copy of the manuscript a year earlier.

Kobritz, who had read several other King manuscripts but didn't feel they were right for him, had read *Christine* in three days and knew it was perfect for him. "This one just seemed very, very special to me. It was teenagers, it was rock 'n roll, it was taking America's love affair with the automobile and turning that into a horror story. King has a great ability to render familiar objects scary, and when he can do that with a car, that's special. And it was a fun book, as opposed to *The Shining*, which is the serious side of King."

Kobritz optioned the book for $500,000; its 550 pages were condensed into a two-hour screenplay by Bill Phillips.

The difficulty *Publishers Weekly* pointed out—the emphasis on Christine, which is overshadowed by the human characters—would be a difficulty that faced Kobritz and his director, John Carpenter, in translating the book to film.

Though the sales of Viking's *Christine* were impressive, they would be dwarfed by those of Doubleday's *Pet Sematary*, published later that year, in November. Mindful of the success of *Christine*, Doubleday ambitiously announced a first printing of 500,000 copies for *Pet Sematary*, though it was in fact 335,000 copies. Nobody, however, predicted the book would take off as it did. *Pet Sematary* would sell 657,000 copies in its first year, all the more impressive because King did virtually no promotion or publicity in behalf of the book. *Pet Sematary*, a book King never intended to publish, was an unexpected bonanza for Doubleday—and for King. As *The Writer's Home Companion* pointed out, *Pet Sematary* finally freed up reserve money that King had earned on his early books but, contractually, couldn't get until now:

> A number of publishing houses, such as McGraw–Hill and World Publishing, initiated a royalty payout plan for a few of their successful authors. The arrangements varied, but all were done to help the author defer taxes on earned royalty.
>
> Doubleday was among these publishers, and they had two plans: one a boilerplate clause available to every author, and another slightly different plan offered to only a few of their most successful authors. Both arrangements allowed Doubleday to pay a fixed yearly amount, which was selected by the author, no matter what the royalty earnings were, with the balance to be invested by the publisher.
>
> The young Stephen King was offered this plan and opted for an annual payment of $50,000, seemingly a princely sum, but his kitty soon swelled to over $3 million. Realizing that, at $50,000 a year his Doubleday income would outlast him . . . King, no longer a Doubleday author, asked to have the agreements ended and a lump sum payment made. Doubleday refused, saying that if it ended the agreement without a "due consideration," the IRS would conclude that all such agreements could be easily terminated. Doubleday wanted something of value in exchange and asked for two books from the author. Instead, he delivered one novel, *Pet Sematary* . . . and with that King was out of his contract.

Despite King's misgivings about the book, the reviewers saw the book for what it was: an unflinching, hard look at a subject by a writer who, in writing it, pulled no punches. The *Sunday Portsmouth Herald* said, "At 36, [King] is not only far from running out of steam but becoming a better novelist. His new one, *Pet Sematary,* is a work of such skill and quality that it transcends the horror genre to become an unforgettable piece of literature about death and bereavement."

Publishers Weekly echoed the *Herald*'s comments: "King's newest novel is a wonderful family portrait that is also the most frightening novel he has ever written. . . . [T]he last 50 pages are so terrifying, one might try to make it through them without a breath—but what is most astonishing here is how much besides horror is here. . . . Witty, wise, observant, King has never been a more humane artist than he is here."

Pet Sematary, the first of King's monstrous-selling books, also attracted attention for another reason. In the front part of the book, a list of other

works by King included "*The Dark Tower* (1982)." King, who had inno-
cently listed the book, inadvertently placed himself at the center of controversy with his fans. How, they asked, could he publish a book they not only
didn't know about but never had the opportunity to buy?

The *Dark Tower* listing immediately triggered an explosion in the value
of the Grant edition; the price zoomed rapidly. Letters from King's faithful
readers—many of whom haunted the bookstores for each new King release—poured in to King, his publishers, and book dealers nationwide.

King, who did not foresee a trade edition of the book in the near
future, talked to Donald M. Grant about the matter:

> I wanted to do something about it, and Don [Grant] wanted to do
> something about it. He was upset. We talked on the phone one night
> and I said, "What if you publish another 500 or 5,000?" There was a
> long sigh. And I said, "That would be like pissing on a forest fire,
> wouldn't it?" He said, "Yeah."

Plans were made to go back to press for a second printing, holding
back copies for King's readership that wrote in. The second printing was
set at 10,000 copies. Unfortunately, it was like pissing on a forest fire . . .
this one, burning out of control.

What *Pet Sematary* readers didn't know was that *another* limited-edition
book by King had been published—*Cycle of the Werewolf*. Like Grant's
edition of *The Dark Tower: The Gunslinger, Cycle of the Werewolf* went virtually unnoticed, because it was sold principally in the specialty market
and, unlike *The Dark Tower*, not listed along with his other books in
Christine. An oversized nine-by-twelve-inch book with a retail price of
$38.50, the Zavisa edition was limited to 7,500 copies for its trade edition.
Even though beautifully illustrated by Berni Wrightson, *Cycle of the Werewolf* struck many as being overpriced, including King, who according to
one reviewer wrote that "King himself has expressed discomfort with the
high price tag."

Like *The Dark Tower, Cycle of the Werewolf* was conceived as a limited-
edition book. Explained King, "I had not intended that it should be
reprinted—one of the ways I've tried to keep my own career in perspective
is to try, from time to time, to find alternative ways to publish, to get out
from under the sheer weight of the numbers."

The numbers had grown huge indeed. As King wrote:

> I started out as a writer and nothing more. I became a popular writer
> and have discovered that, in the scale-model landscape of the book
> business, at least, I have grown into a Bestsellasaurus Rex—a big,

stumbling book-beast that is loved when it shits money and hated when it tramples houses. I look back on that sentence and feel an urge to change it because it sounds so self-pitying; I cannot change it because it also conveys my real sense of perplexity and surprise at this absurd turn of events. I started out as a storyteller; along the way I became an economic force, as well.

Just as King had become impossible to avoid in the bookstores, with a new novel out every fall, moviegoers found a number of King film adaptations on the screen in 1983. In fact, it was too much of a good thing. With three movies released within a six-month period, King took criticism from reviewers who made light of what they called the Stephen-King-Movie-of-the-Month, though he obviously had no control over their release dates.

Cujo, released in June by Warner Brothers, was shot on a $5 million budget and returned $9.8 million in domestic rentals. Directed by Lewis Teague and filmed in northern California during an eight-week shoot, *Cujo* differed from the book in one critical point: in the book the little boy, Tad Trenton, dies; but in the movie Trenton *lives*—an affirmation that Teague felt was essential.

Four months later, in October, *Dead Zone* was released by Paramount. Shot on a $10 million budget in Niagara-on-the-Lake—a small town near director David Cronenberg's hometown of Toronto—*Dead Zone* returned $8.1 million in rentals.

Two months later, in December, *Christine* was released by Columbia Pictures and returned $9.3 million in rentals.

A "bestsellasaurus rex," King found himself, more than ever, the center of attention—sometimes a dubious honor. In a *Playboy* interview King recalled his early days when life was a continual struggle for economic survival. "We were living in a trailer on top of a bleak, snow-swept hillside in Hermon, Maine," King told *Playboy*. Then, in his characteristically candid manner, he made a derogatory comment about Hermon.

When the town manager of Hermon read the interview, he wrote to *Playboy* and announced that they were canceling plans for Stephen King Day; furthermore, plans for the "King Museum, originally sited upon his old trailer pad, are terminated."

King, in a letter to his hometown newspaper, wrote that Hermon was never one of his "favorite places," recalling the misery of those early days: hassles from his landlord, an eviction, and memories of carrying his wounded dog to the field behind the house, after someone had gratuitously shot the poor animal.

Fortunately, his "reception" at Hermon was the exception. More typical was his welcome at the Billerica Library in Massachusetts and at the public library in Truth or Consequences, New Mexico, that year.

When Carolyn Beane, the public relations director at the Billerica Library, invited King to speak on the occasion of National Library Week, King accepted the invitation and suggested his visit be used as a fund-raiser. On April 22, 1983, King spoke to an estimated crowd of three hundred. The "Evening with Stephen King" raised approximately $1,200 through the sale of library memberships, membership tickets to the event itself, buttons, and posters. Most in demand, however, were the 400 copies of King's books, including 100 copies of *Christine*. For two hours King entertained the crowd, reading from one of his stories ("Here There Be Tygers"), followed by a general talk, a question-and-answer period, and a book signing—fortified by cigarettes and Heineken beer, King signed copies of his books for two hours.

On November 19, 1983, King made another public appearance, in Truth or Consequences, New Mexico. Unlike the Billerica visit, this one was sparked by a conversation early in the year between one of the library patrons and a librarian at the public library. Lois Chesley, wife of Chris Chesley, walked into the library and wanted to check out a copy of *Different Seasons* because, after all, "King didn't send us one."

"How'd you get on his mailing list?" asked Ellanie Sampson.

Lois said that her husband, who grew up with King, was still good friends with him.

"The next time you talk to him, ask if he'd come out and give us a talk," said Sampson.

Chris Chesley subsequently talked to King, who agreed to come and speak for expenses only (hotel lodging and plane fare). Immediately, El-lanie Sampson, the architect of King's visit, worked closely with local businesses to ensure that it would be special indeed.

The day King arrived he was presented with the key to the city by Mayor Elmer Darr, who proclaimed that day as Stephen King Day. From there King went to the Convention Center, where he signed books for almost two hours, then rode in a caravan of vehicles to the Damsite Restaurant, where he attended a barbecue luncheon in his honor, spon-sored by a local civic group, the Chamiza Cowbelles. Afterward, at the Middle School, he gave a talk to an estimated eight hundred people—mostly out-of-towners—and attended a reception that evening in his hon-or at the Geronimo Springs Museum. There he signed more autographs, until his writing hand blistered. He stepped outside in thirty-degree weather and announced that it was physically impossible for him to sign any more books. Some fans had stood outside for hours and were understandably upset. However, King had no choice.

Back home in Bangor matters awaited his attention. Atlhough King enjoyed being king for the day, thriving on the interaction with and feedback from his readers that such public appearances provide, his business obligations and responsibilities, temporarily postponed, had to be addressed: finding a new secretary and overseeing a recent real estate investment.

His secretary, sister-in-law Stephanie Leonard, was scheduled for a six-month leave of absence due to pregnancy, and he needed to interview a replacement. Stephanie Leonard, who had worked with Shirley Sonderegger at a local bank, recommended her to King. The interview was brief. King dictated a letter, which she took in shorthand. He interviewed her, then hired her on the spot.

The other matter was more complicated. At the urging of his New York business manager, attorney Arthur B. Greene, King had recently invested in real estate in his hometown because he didn't want to be an absentee owner. When the opportunity arose, King bought from Acton Corporation a 5,000-watt AM station—an opportunity to do his part in keeping rock music alive on the AM band. In one sense, King explained, it was a sound investment: "I didn't do it to make money; if I had, I'd have to count the venture as a failure. I did it because the cutting edge of rock and roll has grown dangerously blunt in these latter days."

WZON, operated by King's new corporation, the Zone Corporation, offered a side benefit. As owner, King, who writes to loud rock music, could turn to WZON and know it would be playing his kind of music. Said King, "When I write, I just crank the music. I inundate myself in rock and roll, and it kind of poisons the atmosphere around me so that people don't approach me, unless they really, really want to get close. . . ."

As 1983 drew to a close, King published the second installment of *The Plant,* increasing distribution by twenty-six lettered copies, a print run totaling 226. King also completed first drafts of *The Talisman, Napkins* (retitled *The Eyes of the Dragon*), and a long novel, *The Tommyknockers.*

The winter is the "preferred time" for writing a novel because, as King reasoned, unless you are into winter sports, "you have to find something to keep yourself amused or you go insane . . . . So I get up around seven o'clock, make myself a cup of tea, go upstairs and fall into this world for three hours."

In early winter 1984 King had finished *Gypsy Pie,* a new Bachman novel. On January 14, 1984, Douglas Winter and King were "huddled before a woodstove fire, watching in silence as a terrifying blizzard descended upon Bangor, Maine," as Winter recalled. King then handed Winter a manuscript, *Gypsy Pie,* by Richard Bachman, which would later be retitled *Thinner.*

That spring, over the Memorial Day weekend at the Annual Booksellers Convention, NAL gave away thousands of advance reading copies of *Thinner,* scheduled for release in November as an NAL hardback at $12.95; optimistic, NAL announced a first printing of 50,000 copies. Most booksellers, however, were more interested in *The Talisman,* the King–Straub collaboration that looked to be the fall's blockbuster. *Thinner,* perceived by booksellers as NAL's attempt to publish a breakout book for an unknown author, simply didn't have the brand-name appeal, though NAL beat the drums in a letter enclosed with the advance copy, which simply read: "Richard Bachman is an incredibly talented writer, and *Thinner* is a riveting novel that gives a new meaning to the world 'horror.' Read it and enjoy."

Meanwhile, the second printing of *The Dark Tower: The Gunslinger* drew more attention than *Thinner.* But this "piss-on-the-forest-fire-edition" of 10,000 copies had virtually no effect in stemming the firestorm of controversy surrounding the book, although a large part of the run had been held back specifically for concerned readers who wrote to King and his publishers asking how to obtain the book. The $20 hardback would sell out within months of publication, with no plans by King to issue a trade edition. The prices for the first and second editions continued to climb, with no ceiling in sight.

As King fans waited impatiently for *The Talisman,* the summer heated up with the release of two King movies: *Stephen King's Children of the Corn* in June, followed by *Firestarter* in October.

Children of the Corn, based on the short story of the same name, is a horrific tale that would have been perfect for a story in an anthology film. Unfortunately, blown up to a full-length picture, the story suffered and was universally panned by reviewers. Even its author came out and trashed it. In "Lists That Matter (Number 8)," King cited ten films that, if they weren't the worst movies of all time, were certainly "right up there":

Here is another horror movie, and to me the most horrible thing about it is that it was based on one of my stories. Not very closely— just closely enough so the producers could call it *Stephen King's Children of the Corn,* which it really wasn't. . . . I understand this gobbler made money, but so far I haven't seen any of it, and I'm not sure I want to. It might have corn-borers in it.

Four months later, in October, a Dino DeLaurentiis production was released through Universal Pictures. *Firestarter* had all the makings of a sure-fire hit: a strong storyline, spectacular special effects, and brand-name actors like George C. Scott, Martin Sheen, and Art Carney. Moreover, director Mark Lester generally followed the book faithfully, which other directors had not always done in their King movies.

Unfortunately, the burden for the success of the movie ultimately depended on child actress Drew Barrymore, who simply was not convincing in her portrayal of Charlie McGee, a frightened eleven-year-old girl on the run from the authorities. Alone, Barrymore couldn't carry the movie.

Firestarter, with its $15 million budget, returned only $7.5 million in domestic film rentals. While it didn't catch fire at the box office, Stephen King's incendiary remarks about the film—"the worst of the bunch" in film adaptations from his work, as King put it—lighted a fire under the film's director, Mark Lester, who took umbrage at what he perceived as two-faced behavior by King. As Lester told interviewer Gary Wood:

When you make a film, you try your best. You hope it succeeds with the public, and I think [*Firestarter*] did. It's enough in show business that we have critics that write about our pictures, sometimes rightly, sometimes wrongly. But to have a person so intimately involved, who actually approved the script and loved the movie, and collaborated every step of the way in the making of the film, come out and attack the movie, to me is sickening . . . . I've wanted to say this for years because he's attacked me so many times in print.

After reading Lester's comments in *Cinefantastique,* King fired off a letter, expressing his point of view:

I see that Mark Lester has finally revealed my dark secret; I'm a two-faced son of a bitch, a liar, and an all-around *eevil* guy. Actually, I'm none of those things, and neither is Mark; he's just another director who ended up with his scalp dangling from a pole outside the lodge of Chief Dino DeLaurentiis. . . . Mark's assertion that I saw the movie and loved it is erroneous. I saw *part* of an early rough cut. When I saw the final cut . . . I was extremely depressed . . . . There were $3 million worth of special effects and another $3 million of Academy Award–winning talent up there on the screen, and none of it was working. Watching that happen was an incredible, unreal, and painful experience.

While the many King movies were making the rounds that year, King was working on a new novel, begun in summer. *Misery,* a short novel of psychological suspense, as Tabitha King later wrote, explored "[t]he very connection that exists . . . between the writer and the reader" which "inevitably draws those most in need of connection with anyone, anything, as well as those for whom the connection is life-enriching. I hope we are all honest enough to admit that there are fans whose devotion is unhealthy and unbalanced."

For those fans it's not enough to read the book; they want in some way to get the attention of the author, personified in the character of Annie Wilkes in *Misery.* As King explained in an interview with David Streitfeld of the *Washington Post,* "I love these people. I don't hate them. I get very few crazy letters. I do autographs because the fans support me and I owe a debt." Still, insofar as King is concerned, a line must be drawn, a line that separates his personal from his professional life. He owes his fans "[s]omething to read. It's a 50-50 trade-off. I want you to read my book; you want to read my book. We get off even. They don't have a right to my life, but they take pieces of it just the same. When I went to look for videotapes this afternoon, there were a bunch [of fans] outside my house." He continued: "I've had a lot of my life amputated already. It's like you're a Delco battery and someone's got a pair of jumpers on you all the time."

Even with all that, as Streitfeld wrote, "[King] doesn't worry about a deranged, passionate fan coming after him."

On October 8, 1984, shipped from nine warehouses nationwide, an estimated half-million copies of *Talisman* hit the bookstores in one wave—the largest first printing of any King novel, in the wake of the 657,000 copies sold of *Pet Sematary.* Unlike some of the authors' earlier books, this one would *not* be offered through the book clubs; King and Straub, through their agents, were looking for a $700,000 offer and rejected a $400,000 offer from Literary Guild. They cited as their reason the reduced royalties earned on book-club editions.

An altogether different reading experience for King fans expecting another *Christine* or *Pet Sematary, The Talisman*'s measured pace recalled Straub's, not King's, narrative momentum.

For mainstream reviewers, here was the opportunity to take pot shots and bag two birds with one stone. *People* magazine's "Picks & Pans" concluded its review of *The Talisman* thus: "In horror fiction, two heads are better than one only if they're on the same body." *Esquire,* styling King and Straub "Shockmeisters," attempted to put both authors in their place, in the ghetto of horror literature:

> King, whose own style is American yahoo—big, brassy, and boda-cious—has always expressed admiration for Straub's cooler, less emo-tional diction, and Straub in turn has praised the grand, "operatic" quality of King's work. Their collaboration is both cool and oper-atic—and very, very scary. It's a horrific work of art. But is it really art? Probably not. We are talking about mass-market books and popular movies here. People consume horror in order to be scared, not *arted.*

More balanced in its appraisal, *Publishers Weekly* said the book was "infused with warmth, vivid characterization and dramatic intensity" and "surpasses the expectations created by their separate work. . . ."

A literary experiment, *The Talisman* was "a definite departure from [King's] previous ventures into the supernatural," according to *Booklist.* "As Casey Stengel used to say, you've got to put an asterisk by it," King told interviewer Douglas Winter.

In November 1984 *Thinner* hit the bookstores, though in a much smaller wave than did *The Talisman.* A $12.95 hardback that went to press with a first printing of 26,000 copies, *Thinner* was dedicated "To my wife, Claudia Inez Bachman." It sported on the dust jacket a photo of a middle-aged, balding man; the caption read, "Richard Bachman lives and works in New Hampshire." The photo was credited to Claudia Bachman.

The publication of *Thinner* brought Bachman—purportedly a dairy farmer who wrote on the side—much unwanted attention, including scru-tiny from careful King readers who saw in *Thinner* King's inimitable prose style. This was one book they couldn't judge by the cover. The earlier Bachman books had been early works, but this was a recent work, with dozens of connecting points to other, recent King novels.

By early winter 1984, cracks had appeared in the Bachman facade. In the fantasy field, two major book dealers of impeccable reputation, Robert Weinberg and L. W. Currey, declared that Stephen King was in fact Bachman. (Weinberg, especially, was adamant because he had incontro-vertible written proof.)

Meanwhile, in Colorado, Mark Graham, a teacher and a King reader who had reviewed several King novels for the local newspaper, offered specific reasons why he felt King was Bachman. In a review sluglined "THINNER by Richard Bachman (Stephen King?)," Graham cited the NAL connection (*Thinner*, a hardback, and King's paperbacks were all from NAL), the similarities between the authors (both from New England, with the story itself set in Maine), the L. W. Currey catalogue citation, and the book's "off-the-wall" premise that only King could have pulled off.

Graham concluded, "If you are still not convinced that this book was written by the No. 1 writer in the genre of the strange and the supernatural, wait until the last page. If King didn't write the end of this little narrative, his doppelganger did—which of course would be only appropriate."

Within the fantasy community the true authorship of *Thinner* became an open secret, but in the larger world beyond the confines of fandom, readers accepted the book at face value; after all, the photo of Bachman clearly wasn't King. Still, how could they miss the little in-joke on page 111 in which Dr. Houston tells the protagonist: "You were starting to sound a little like a Stephen King novel for a while there. . . ."

The same month *Thinner* was released as an NAL hardback, Douglas Winter's revised Starmont study on King was reissued in an expanded and revised hardback edition. *Stephen King: The Art of Darkness*, the first and best book on King, was written with his consent and full cooperation. Winter, obviously in the know, understandably made no reference to the Bachman connection, although the index indicated that on page 200 Bachman was mentioned. (The index was in error: it should have listed page 201, where Winter wrote, "*The Long Walk* by Richard Bachman . . . owes much to Stephen King.")

In December 1984 King self-published *The Eyes of the Dragon*, a limited-edition book issued from King's Philtrum Press, which he termed "a very humble storefront in a world dominated by a few great glassy shopping malls." Its print run—250 red-numbered copies for private distribution, and 1,000 black-numbered copies for sale—and its associational value with King would make it a special book indeed.

Designed by Michael Alpert and illustrated by Kenny Ray Linkous (under his pen name, Kenneth R. Linkhauser), *The Eyes of the Dragon* was sold by lottery. Three ads in *Fantasy Newsletter, Locus*, and *F&SF* stated that the book would cost $120; those interested should send in their names, but if more than a thousand were received, a lottery would be held.

Two thousand names came in, and after the lottery was held, confirmation letters were sent out by Stephanie Leonard. For $120 (plus $7 postage), what buyers got was what King defined as a true limited edition—a book not available in any other form—and a work of art. Opposed to what he termed "autographs masquerading as books"—so-called limited editions that by virtue of a limitation sheet numbered and signed by its author claim to be unique, when in fact they are little more than autographed trade editions—King made sure his edition was distinctive.

The Philtrum Press edition was special indeed. The large format (roughly 8½ by 13 inches) and oversized, handset type made the reading a pleasure and a private reading experience, just as designer Michael Alpert had intended. The acid-free paper with a linen napkin texture has a distinctive weight and substantial feel to it, further enhancing the presentation. The illustrations by Linkous, printed in separate runs from the type, served as proper illustrations and not merely visual filler. Protecting the book, encasing the text and art, the quality binding and slipcase ensured that this tale for all ages could last for ages. "With good care," wrote Alpert, "*The Eyes of the Dragon* will stay in fine condition for centuries."

Like *The Dark Tower: The Gunslinger* and *The Cycle of the Werewolf, The Eyes of the Dragon* served a purpose apart from the rolling gross of King's trade editions, sold and marketed not as books but as product. Limited editions, in King's mind, recalled the nineteenth century when "books were viewed as things of great value, and were jealously guarded." As King explained:

> A real limited edition, far from being an expensive autogaph stapled to a novel, is a treasure. And like all treasures do, it transforms the responsible owner into a caretaker, and being a caretaker of something as fragile and easily destroyed as ideas and images is not a bad thing but a good one . . . and so is the re-evaluation of what books are and what they do that necessarily follows.

In January 1985 *Castle Rock,* the official Stephen King newsletter, began publication out of Bangor, Maine. In its premiere issue—a modest letter-sized, eight-page newsletter—the *Rock* (as it came to be called) took its name from King's fictional Maine town Castle Rock, which King in turn had got from Golding's *Lord of the Flies.*

"Our goal is to keep you up-to-date on the work of this prolific writer," wrote its editor and publisher, Stephanie Leonard, who as King's personal secretary was in the ideal position to provide advance notification of major King projects, movies, and personal appearances.

Castle Rock was, as Leonard told interviewer Stephen Spignesi, a way to cope with the flood of mail—averaging 500 pieces a week, of which 450 required a reply—and it would also "serve as a vehicle for communication between the fans. So *Castle Rock* was born with Stephen's blessing, and on the condition that he would have nothing to do with it."

The newsletter had a modest print run of 500 copies for its first few issues, but its subscription base soon began to mushroom dramatically after full-page ads for subscriptions ran in all of King's paperback editions from NAL.

In the second issue Leonard hinted that there would be "a secret revealed at long last. . . ."

Richard Bachman—born in 1942, a graduate of the University of New Hampshire, a Vietnam veteran, window washer, commercial fisherman, private security guard, and most recently a dairy farmer and part-time writer—died a sudden death of what King termed "cancer of the pseudonym" on January 9, 1985. Stephen Brown, a bookstore clerk in Washington, D.C., wrote to King and enclosed a copy of the copyright registration to *Rage,* bearing King's name; all the other Bachman books had copyrights registered to Richard Bachman.

Confronted with the evidence, King called Brown to discuss the discovery. King had planned to announce his authorship of the Bachman books in the March issue of *Castle Rock,* but Brown had blown it prematurely—but not by much.

Originally an open secret only within the fantasy circles, the Bachman pen name was by now a matter of open speculation in the media, fueled by *Entertainment Tonight'*s story on Bachman in late January.

The crack in the facade broke wide open on February 9, 1985, when Joan H. Smith of the *Bangor Daily News* ran the story "Pseudonym Kept Five King Novels a Mystery." As she told King, with or without his consent, the story would run. His cover completely blown, King admitted to Smith, "You know how when you're carrying home some groceries in the rain and the whole bag just kind of falls apart? Well, that's how it's been with Bachman lately."

Fan reaction was predominantly positive, since it meant that here were five "new" King novels. But after fans discovered that only two were in print—the recently published *Thinner* and *The Running Man*—some reacted in bitter disappointment; one reader wrote to King's hometown newspaper and complained about his deliberately publishing five books but not letting his fans know. "That is so mean. Cruel, too," asserted the Minnesota reader.

As the Bachman revelation made news nationwide, there was a run at the bookstores as his fans snapped up the few remaining copies of *Thinner'*s first edition and the paperback of *The Running Man.*

In the wake of the revelation, King's hometown newspaper made factual errors in its followup story. Consequently, King wrote a letter to the editor of his hometown newspaper, which was published in the March 5, 1985, issue, setting the record straight. First, King did not try to time the release of the information to benefit two Bachman books optioned for the movies—they had sold on their own, before the revelation came to light. Second, he had confirmed the pen name a month earlier to Stephen Brown, who had originally planned to break the story in the *Washington Post* two weeks before Joan Smith's story ran. Third, he had no choice but to confirm Smith's inquiry, since the story would have run regardless and, all things considered, further denials were useless. Fourth, he took exception to the readers who wrote to complain about his use of a pen name. King pointed out that they confused "enjoyment with ownership."

On April 9, 1985, Brown's story ran in the *Washington Post,* providing the story behind the story. One month later *Thinner* hit number one on *Publishers Weekly*'s hardcover bestseller list.

Before the announcement, there had been only two printings of the book: the initial printing, and a second printing of 5,000 copies. But after the revelation *Thinner* went back to press for a third and a fourth printing of 50,000 each, followed by a fifth printing of 100,000 copies—a total of 231,000 copies.

King later wrote that when he was Bachman the sales were 28,000. But when Bachman was confirmed as King, the sales were 280,000, which "might tell you something . . ."

It told King's publishers in unmistakable terms that his readership couldn't be satiated; they would buy any new King book, no matter how frequently he published. Plans were then made to accelerate the publication of King's hardbacks, and NAL, in response to King's fans' demands, made plans to reissue the first four Bachman books in an ominibus edition in October later that year.

The Bachman incident also showed King that being a brand name, a bestsellasaurus rex, meant that he could harbor no secrets; too many readers were out there watching his every move. In the wake of the Bachman disclosure, King in a candid moment told an interviewer:

> I was pissed. It's like you can't have anything. You're not allowed to because you are a celebrity. What does it matter? Why should anyone care? It's like they can't wait to find stuff out, particularly if it's something you don't want people to know. That's the best. That's the juice. It makes me think about that Don Henley song, "Dirty Laundry." Hell, give it to them.

In the wake of the Bachman revelation rumors were rampant about other pen names King might have used. In truth, King had used only one other pen name: John Swithen, for "The Fifth Quarter," a story published in *Cavalier* magazine in April 1972. Stephanie Leonard, in the April 1985 issue of *Castle Rock,* reassured the readership: "As to whether or not he has any other pseudonyms, except for using the name John Swithen . . . he has never used any other pseudonyms. Really . . . Trust me. . . ."

Still, rumors persisted, at least in the fantasy circles. *Invasion,* a paperback original from Laser Books and edited by Roger Elwood, was thought to be a King book, since its foreword made it clear that Aaron Wolfe was a pen name. Set in Maine, *Invasion* certainly sounded like a King story: a rural family attacked by aliens. But its author was Dean R. Koontz, not King.

Then there was *Love Lessons,* reviewed in *Fantasy Review* as a porn novel purportedly written by King while in college. It was "published" by Beeline Books and was "available" in a limited-edition reprint in hardback. Unlike *Invasion, Love Lessons* was in fact a fictitious book, a hoax perpetrated by Charles Platt, with editor Neil Barron in the know. Conceived as a marketing tool to test the "pull" of *Fantasy Review, Love Lessons* proved to be a lesson only for its publisher, Robert Collins, who received letters from both King and his attorney setting the record straight and posing the prospect of litigation.

Although there was no lawsuit, the point was clearly made: King, who valued his name and reputation, would not hesitate to use all available legal means to protect his best interests.

The fallout from *Thinner* accelerated the publication of King's books for 1986 and 1987, with four books scheduled for publication in hardback over a fourteen-month period: in October 1986 *IT;* and in 1987 *The Eyes of the Dragon, Misery,* and *The Tommyknockers.* The last two were sold by King's agent Kirby McCauley for $5 million each, with *Misery* going to Viking and, as a favor to King's former Viking editor, Alan Williams, *The Tommyknockers* to G.P. Putnam's Sons. It would be, as NAL's Elaine Koster termed it, "a Stephen King firestorm." King's assessment: "Some critics will want to dismiss it as a grandstand act, but most, I hope, will view it as a remarkable feat."

In the interim, however, King would go to press with four books in 1985 alone: *Cycle of the Werewolf* in two separate editions; a second collection of short fiction, *Skeleton Crew* (originally titled *Night Moves* after the Bob Seeger song); and *The Bachman Books.*

In April NAL published *Cycle of the Werewolf* in trade paperback, resetting (and correcting) the type from the Zavisa edition, and retaining the Wrightson illustrations. At $8.95, though, it was a thin book for the price, as King observed; later it was reissued as *Silver Bullet,* a tie-in edition to the movie, and a much better buy. At $9.95 the new incarnation offered the complete text of *Cycle of the Werewolf,* supplemented with a lengthy foreword explaining the story behind the story, King's final draft of the screenplay for *Silver Bullet,* and an eight-page photo section with movie stills.

In June G.P. Putnam's Sons went to press with an impressive 500,000 copies of *Skeleton Crew,* a very healthy first printing for a collection. Unlike *Night Shift,* an earlier collection, this one offered a broader range of material: poetry, short stories, and a short novel. Only the most dedicated King fan would have read them all, as it collected stories from mainstream magazines like *Redbook* and *Yankee,* from men's magazines like *Gallery* and *Playboy,* from genre magazines like *Twilight Zone, Weird Tales, Startling Mystery Stories,* and the *Magazine of Fantasy and Science Fiction (F&SF),* from anthologies like *Dark Forces, Shadows, Shadows 4, Terror,* and *New Terrors 2,* and from *Ubris,* the literary magazine at UMO. In addition, *Skeleton Crew* collected two stories from an abortive attempt at a novel, *Milkman.*

A remarkably eclectic collection of early and recent work, *Skeleton Crew* exhibited the work of a more mature writer, especially with "The Reach" (originally published as "Do the Dead Sing?") and "The Mist," quintessential King. *Library Journal* called the collection "a showcase for his enormous talent and range," stating that King was "equally home with horror, science fiction, fantasy, and the classic ghost story. . . ."

Publishers Weekly agreed, concluding that this "hefty sampler from all stages of his career . . . demonstrates the range of his abilities."

Skeleton Crew, published as a 512-page hardback at $18.95, would in its first year sell 600,000 copies.

In October NAL published *The Bachman Books: Four Early Novels by Stephen King.* A 692-page hardback, the $19.95 omnibus edition collected *Rage, The Long Walk, Roadwork,* and *The Running Man,* along with an introduction by King, "Why I was Bachman."

In Mercer Island, Washington, Ted Dikty, publisher of Starmont House—a specialty publisher of literary criticism for the fantasy and science-fiction fans—took note of the publishing activity surrounding King and announced an ambitious publishing program specializing in King titles. Winter's study, *Stephen King,* was its bestselling title to date. Now, to follow up on that success, it announced,

Seven books about Stephen King for readers of his proliferating series of bestselling novels and story collections. Starmont's in-depth program of studies on this remarkable literary phenomenon will provide a wealth of insights on his work and life.

What is there in his stories that draws readers to him in ever-increasing numbers? When even his pseudonymous work reaches the bestseller lists, it is evident that here is a major American literary talent—a writer who has tuned in to the American psyche to a degree never before achieved.

Starmont's program of literary criticism zeroes in on Stephen King in all respects—his novels, his shorter works, his pseudonymous material, his films, his life. It explores the entire extraordinary achievement that is known as Stephen King.

Starmont wasted no time in going to press with four King books in 1985: a collection of essays on King, *Discovering Stephen King,* edited by Darrell Schweitzer, and three books by Dr. Michael Collings, a Pepperdine University professor—*The Many Facets of Stephen King, The Shorter Works of Stephen King* (with David Engebretson, one of his students), and *Stephen King as Richard Bachman.*

Collings encapsuled King's books and movies, coining the epithet "the Stephen King Phenomenon." King, he believed, had positioned himself as a one-person entertainment industry, especially in light of his increasing involvement with the movie industry.

Early in the year, King had written a screenplay, "Trucks," based on his short story of the same name, collected in *Night Shift.* Castle Rock reported that he "hopes to direct this one." As he finished up the screenplay for "Trucks," *Cat's Eye* was released in April 1985. Based on King's screenplay, the movie was shot on a $6 million budget. The ninety-four-minute film was composed of three nonrelated stories: "Quitters, Inc.," from the *Night Shift* collection, "The Ledge" (again, from *Night Shift*), and "The General," a new story.

Although King's previous anthology film *Creepshow* had earned $10 million in domestic rentals, this anthology film—a Dino DeLaurentiis production—earned less than $4 million in domestic rentals.

In summer 1985 two King movies began principal photography. On the West Coast, in Eugene, Oregon, Rob Reiner's Castle Rock Entertainment began in June filming "The Body," to be adapted for the screen as *Stand by Me.* A gentle, nonhorrific story, its adaptation to film would be a significant departure from what King's moviegoing audience expected from him. Reiner, admittedly not a horror fan, optioned the story because it struck a responsive chord in him. A babyboomer close in age to King, Reiner felt that the story, a universal and timeless coming-of-age tale, evoked his childhood too.

The next month, July, principal photography began on *Overdrive,* under the auspices of Dino DeLaurentiis's film company in Wilmington, North Carolina. King, who had written several screenplays—including *Creepshow* and *Cat's Eye*—and had appeared in front of the camera in a starring role in a segment for *Creepshow,* now found himself behind the camera as director.

In a promotional trailer prior to its release, King said, "A lot of people have made movies out of my stories . . . but I thought it was time I took a crack at doing Stephen King . . . . After all, if you want it done right, you have to do it yourself."

As Michael Collings suggested, *Maximum Overdrive* could be a success, or disaster:

> With King working as both screenwriter and director, *Overdrive* has become an intriguing project. For the first time, King will have a substantial effect on the final product, although DeLaurentiis retains control over the final cut. This is, of course, a double-edged sword. *Overdrive* will clearly reflect King's individual vision in ways that *Creepshow, Cat's Eye,* and *Silver Bullet* could not; what will emerge should be a clearer definition of Stephen King as filmmaker.
>
> On the other hand, however, his dual role (triple-role, if one counts his having written the original property on which the screenplay is based) gives *Overdrive* a notoriety that may work against it. King realizes that his name on the film as director provides a "built-in draw; the idea that people will come to see the film the way they come to see the two-headed cow." More seriously, *Overdrive* will represent Stephen King brought to the screen exactly the way Stephen King would wish it. If the film does not succeed, there will be no one to lay blame on—no idiosyncratic directors, eccentric screenplays, etc.

From July to early October of 1985, King's life centered around Wilmington, North Carolina, where the $10 million production was based. King's work routine, six days a week, included getting up at six, riding to work on his Honda motorcycle, stopping off at McDonald's for a quick $2.38 breakfast, shooting all day in the North Carolina summer heat and humidity with a small army of people waiting for him to make things happen, and reviewing the dailies after that day's shoot. Then he'd stop off at the Zip-Mart for beer and pick up dinner at a local fast-food restaurant, and ride back to his rented house around eight-thirty. There he would drink beer, wolf down his dinner, then work on revisions to *IT* for two hours.

As King explained, "I got paid $70,000 to direct this thing, and as far as I'm concerned it was disaster pay. This whole [moviemaking] business is so . . . unreal." When asked how he enjoyed directing as opposed to writing, King replied, "I didn't. I didn't care for it at all. I had to work. I wasn't used to working. I hadn't worked in 12 years."

During the time he spent in North Carolina orchestrating a cast and crew, King could have spent the same time in writing another novel for $5 million. Clearly, it wasn't the money that attracted him, but the opportunity to try something he hadn't done before.

That summer North Carolina passed what King called an "anti-porn statute" in July, and overnight "the Porn Fairy" made the *Playboy* and *Penthouse* magazines disappear, as well as X-rated videotapes and some R-rated videotapes in the local rental stores. After seeing a policeman in Waldenbooks screening cheesecake calendars in search of "topless," King observed, "In North Carolina, bare breasts and cocaine are both crimes. I think that's the real obscenity."

Given the choice of deciding for oneself what to read or letting someone *else* decide what one should read, King concluded that "it's our responsibility. Pass a law like this, and the question of what's obscene passes out of your hands once and for all; you've given up your freedom to judge for yourself, which is one of the things America is supposed to stand for—or so we teach our children in school. Get rid of the hard-core and what goes next?"

Back home in Maine the question about what was obscene and what was not became a subject of discussion, with the Reverend Jack Wyman of the Christian Civic League fanning the flames.

While King was finishing production on *Maximum Overdrive,* another Dino DeLaurentiis production hit the theaters nationwide. *Silver Bullet,* a $7 million movie, was released in October through Paramount Pictures. Returning $5.4 million in domestic rentals, the film struck moviegoers as a formulaic story with stereotyped characters. Even with King's script, something was missing: the essence of the story, which was present in the original story, *Cycle of the Werewolf,* but conspicuously absent in the film adaptation.

As the year ended, King's Philtrum Press published the third install-ment of *The Plant*. Though its last page promised that the story would be continued, the story ended—at least temporarily—when King realized after seeing the remake of *The Little Shop of Horrors* that both *The Plant* and the movie shared a similar plot. In fact, the similarity was sufficiently close that King later told an interviewer that he had no intention of finishing the epistolary novel-in-progress.

A year earlier the Maine Christian Civic League conducted a poll and concluded that the public "favored restrictions on pornography." Encour-aged by its "findings," the League subsequently obtained the requisite number of signatures from Maine's registered voters to force the issue to a statewide referendum. Though the League's intent was to force it on the November 1985 ballot, the referendum was moved to the June 1986 pri-mary ballot.

In spring 1986, at the second regular session of the 112th Maine Legislature, document number 2092 was introduced: "In the Year of Our Lord/Nineteen Hundred and Eighty-Six/AN ACT to Prohibit the Promo-tion and Wholesale Promotion of Pornographic Material in the State of Maine." Its statement of fact read: "The purpose of this bill is to make it a crime to make, sell, give for value, or otherwise promote obscene material in Maine."

Rallying around their slogan—"Do It for the Children"—Rev. Jack Wyman of the Christian Civic League and his Christian soldiers marched onward, their ranks swelled by the Guardians for Education for Maine, the Pro-Life Education Association, the Maine chapter of the Eagle Forum, and the Women's Christian Temperance Union.

The battle line drawn, opponents of the referendum, rallying around their slogan—"Don't Make Freedom a Dirty Word"—included the Maine Civil Liberties Union, the Maine chapter of the National Organization for Women (NOW), the Maine Teacher's Association, the Maine Library Association, magazine and book distributors in Maine, the Maine Women's Lobby, the Maine Citizens Against Government Censorship, and, accord-ing to the *Civic League Record,* "the leadership of the state's homosexual community."

The Christian Civic League, having marshaled its forces, launched a vigorous, spirited campaign to spread the gospel: 1,500 churches in Maine received informational packets; petition signers were contacted and urged to contribute money to the self-financed campaign by joining the mem-bership of the Christian Civic League. Besides speaking to churches statewide, Wyman debated the issue on radio and television stations, supplemented by a television ad campaign costing $100,000, with two ads "stressing the link between pornography and child sexual abuse."

In "Another Viewpoint," an op-ed piece in the *Bangor Daily News* headlined "Hard-core, Violent Pornography Debases and Destroys," Wyman expressed his opinion:

> Hard-core and violent pornography debases and destroys lives, families and marriages. It is a cultural, social and moral blight. It lowers the entire tone of civility upon which a free public depends. It exploits and threatens innocent women and children. The statewide law we have advanced will not totally eliminate pornography in Maine nor will it end rape and child abuse, both of which have been linked to pornography. This law, however, will help control the extreme manifestations of this cultural disaster. Those charged with enforcing and interpreting the anti-obscenity law will, we believe, do so fairly, reasonably and with intelligent discernment.

Fighting fire with fire, Stephen King lent his support to the opponents of the referendum. He appeared in a television commercial that began, "Want to hear something *really* scary?"

In "Say 'No' to the Enforcers," an article that appeared in a Maine newspaper, King wrote: "I think the idea of making it a crime to sell obscene material is a bad one, because it takes the responsibility of saying 'no' out of the hands of the citizens and puts it into those of the police and the courts. I think it's a bad idea because it's undemocratic, high-handed, and frighteningly diffuse. I urge you to vote on June 10, and I urge you to vote 'NO.' "

In "Another Viewpoint," and under the title "An Obscenity Law Is Obscene," Joseph King echoed his fathers concerns. "There are a few holes in the idea of an obscenity law. Unfortunately, these holes are big enough to drive Mack trucks through."

Opponents of the referendum appealed to the emotions of the viewers with a followup ad, inflammatory but very effective. It showed a leather-jacketed man setting fire to books by John Steinbeck, Alice Walker, and Jean Auel. The voice-over of the narrator concluded, "If the censorship referendum passes, your freedom could go up in smoke. Vote 'No' on the censorship referendum.' "

After seeing the ad, Stephen King admitted, "I hate that ad. I mean, the guy in it looks like a Nazi . . . . But you know, once you start down that road [to censorship], it might not be that far off. . . ."

On June 6 Stephen King debated Rev. Jack Wyman on a local radio station. Christopher Spruce, in *Castle Rock,* explained King's position during the debate:

> Stephen King, who has had his books banned from some school libraries, said he didn't know what the law might result in. "Jack," he told Wyman during the radio debate, "you can sit there and say you know what [the law] will do, but you don't. No one does. And that's why I'm against it. I'm against what I don't know about."

On June 10, 1986, the referendum was resoundingly voted down by Maine voters; 72 percent said no to the proposed bill. Although the Christian Civic League maintained from the beginning that the opposition's linking of obscenity and censorship was misleading, and that the anti-obscenity law passed in North Carolina was improperly used as ammunition, a spokesman for the League finally admitted defeat:

> We fought the good fight. Our cause was noble. We can be proud of our accomplishments. While our opponents waged a shameful campaign, we can only acknowledge their cleverness and appreciate their success. I wish we could have won.
>
> I of course wish we could have won for our children . . . . God surely has His purposes, even in dealing us this defeat. We will come back stronger, with His help, I assure you.

King and other opponents of the referendum won that battle, but King lost on another front. *Maximum Overdrive* initially received the kiss of death from the Motion Picture Association of America's review board, an X rating. As King wrote in an article, "The Dreaded X," "Ratings can sell tickets or destroy movies." The X rating would mean that most newspapers would not accept advertising for the film. The $10 million movie, scheduled to open in a thousand theaters nationwide in August, had to go for the R rating. After editing out several objectionable scenes, including a child being run over by a steamroller, the movie finally earned an R.

"For the record, I don't think the picture is going to review badly," King predicted before the movie's release. Unfortunately, not only did the movie review badly, but reviewers seemed to take a special glee in trashing King's first directorial effort.

Even King's hometown newspaper, the *Bangor Daily News,* found nothing to recommend in this film. Critic Robert H. Newall wrote, "As I left, I felt the urgent need of a hot bath . . . . I wanted to scrape off the grime of a scurrilous, mindless film . . . . It lacks in short taste, grace, civilization and, above all, humanity." And according to the *New York Times,* King "has taken a promising notion—our dependence on machines—and turned it into one long car-crunch movie, wheezing from setups to crackups." The *Boston Globe* added, "Stephen King's latest movie . . . is a factory reject. . . . King makes his debut as director of his own material, and his treatment of horror is boneheadedly banal."

After earning approximately less than $4 million in rentals, the movie left the screens and went to video within four months. *Maximum Overdrive* had run out of gas.

Years later, when asked if he planned to direct again, King replied, "I don't have any plans to direct, but sooner or later I would like to do it again . . . in Maine. The nice thing about directing is that you control everything; and the terrible thing about directing—the real drawback—is that you control everything."

Total freedom, King discovered, implied total responsibility.

In the wake of *Cat's Eye, Children of the Corn, Firestarter, Silver Bullet,* and now *Maximum Overdrive,* the Stephen King name didn't quite have the cachet in Hollywood or with the moviegoing audience that it had secured with his book audience. Rob Cohen explained the difference to interviewer Gary Wood:

> Hollywood is always looking for some way to *market* films, more than they're looking for a good story. They're looking for marketable hooks. If you can create a marketable hook for a movie, you've got a much better chance of getting it sold, even if the script is inferior. You can say, "I have a *Stephen King* picture!" So [producers] flocked, in the early part of the Stephen King–Hollywood romance; they flocked because they thought, "My God! We have a trademark!" That didn't work. The trademark alone is not enough to make a successful picture.

The next month, when Rob Reiner's *Stand by Me* opened to a handful of theaters nationwide, the King connection was deliberately downplayed. The hope was that positive word of mouth would slowly build an audience, enabling the film to get distributed to several hundred theaters. If, however, the reviews were bad, the distributor could pull it on short notice, cutting the losses early. At stake was an $8 million investment, the cost of bringing *Stand by Me* to the screens.

Unfortunately, the plot of *Stand by Me*—too easily summarized—did nothing to convey the sense of the story, which is what attracted Reiner in the first place, a story that would have to find its own audience. *USA Today* capsuled the film: "A boy and his buddies set out on a hike to find a dead body."

Stand by Me opened in only sixteen theaters nationwide, but a funny thing happened: the film turned into the surprise hit of the season, a "sleeper," as the film trade called it. Typically, people reacted initially with denials, then surprise, followed by amazement, and finally a begrudging admiration when they realized it *was* a King story. By focusing on the story—a timeless, poignant tale about four boys who pass from adolescence to the beginnings of adulthood—Reiner showed that not only could a King film be profitable, but King could be translated effectively to the screen; the essence of a King story could be adapted to film intact. Reiner explained to interviewer Gary Wood:

> When you read [King's] books, and because so many people have seen his films, people assume that Stephen King is just a schlocky kind of horror writer; but if you read his books, [you'll discover] he is a brilliant, brilliant writer. His characters are very well drawn, his dialogue excellent, his references great. He really is a very good writer.
>
> I think one of the reasons he is popular is because he has the horror aspect, the supernatural aspect to his work. People like those kinds of things. But if you take all of that out and just look at characters—the way he draws his characters—he's really good. That's what attracted me more than [the horror aspect], because I'm not a big horror fan. . . . That's what attracted me to "The Body." . . . [T]o me, it wasn't really a horror piece. It was a character piece about four boys who go through a rite of passage.

Insight's David Brooks wrote, "Who could have predicted that a movie, let alone a good movie, could be made from a story about four 12-year-olds hiking to find a dead boy?" Brooks concluded that the movie was a "stunning accomplishment" and a "powerful, affecting and completely original movie." Another reviewer, mindful of King's most recent release, wrote:

> Considering what a disaster Stephen King's *Maximum Overdrive* is, directed by the best-selling horror novelist himself, it's a pleasure to report that *Stand by Me,* based on his novella "The Body," is an almost unqualified success . . . . [O]ne of the extremely rare films ever to convey a sense of what it is truly like to be a 12-year-old boy in rural America. Ignore the stupefying title and go see *Stand by Me,* which at its best has overtones of Mark Twain and Faulkner.

Stand by Me went on to earn $22 million in domestic film rentals, compared to the $4 million of *Maximum Overdrive.* The key differences were in the story—and the director.

On October 6, 1985, King was the cover subject of *Time* magazine. The cover—suggesting that reading a King novel was literally a hair-raising experience—made it clear that *Time* considered him the "King of Horror." The profile of King was complemented by an overview of the horror tradition and photographs. "The Master of Pop Dread," as *Time* anointed King, had become a part of American culture.

King was undoubtedly flattered by *Time*'s coverage, but "the apotheosis of my public life," as he explained, was not the cover story but a chance encounter with a fan. King recounted the story:

> I had dinner with Bruce Springsteen—the Boss himself—just before they all went on the "Born in the USA" tour, and his career exploded to a different level. I'd used a number of quotes from his songs in my books. I think he was sort of curious about me, and I was a big fan of his, so we went out to a little East Side Irish bar and restaurant; a guy tried to sell us cocaine as we went in the door, so we knew we looked like regular guys.
>
> And we sat down and we had a meal. And about halfway through this meal, I looked across the room and there was a girl sitting there, who was obviously with her parents. She was about fourteen years old, blonde hair, black velvet bow in her hair, and she looked around and [did] a double-take, and stars went off in her eyes, whole novas and rockets; and she got up, left her parents sitting at this table, didn't even look at them or say where she was going, and she did not walk across this room—she drifted toward [our] table. Bruce Springsteen reached into his pocket and took out the pen, but she never even looked at the guy. She [looked at me and] said, "Aren't you Stephen King? I've read everything you ever wrote!"

That October the first of the four books in the "firestorm" was published by Viking. *IT,* four years in the writing, marked King's end to writing about children and traditional monsters. King explained:

> I knew *IT* would be long since I was trying to focus and understand all the things I had written before. You see, my preoccupation with monsters and horror has puzzled me, too. So, I put in every monster I could think of and I took every childhood incident I had ever written of before and tried to integrate the two. And *IT* grew and grew and grew . . . .

At 1,138 pages, *IT* drew attention because of its length, which King expected—an old concern, as it turned out. In 1980, in *Adelina,* King wrote about the dangers of writing long novels:

[T]here was an age—it ended around 1950, I should judge—when the long novel was accepted on its own terms and judged upon matters other than its length; there was a time before that when the long novel was the rule rather than the exception. Since 1950 . . . the novel has been more and more discriminated against on the grounds of length alone. Many critics seem to take a novel of more than 400 pages as a personal affront.

King, who had sent Michael Collings a photocopy of the manuscript before publication, was understandably relieved when Collings sent King a copy of his review of *IT,* concluding that "*IT* literally transcends itself, to stand as the most powerful novel King has written." King, echoing his *Adelina* comments, wrote back to Collings:

Thank you for your kind letter and the accompanying essay. I'm pleased that you liked the book so well. Actually, I like it pretty well myself, but when I saw that ludicrous stack of manuscript pages [a foot high], I immediately fell into a defensive crouch. I think the days when any novel as long as this gets much of a critical reading are gone. I suspect part of my defensiveness comes from the expectation of poor reviews, partly from my own feeling that that book really is too long.

King had anticipated the reviews correctly. In cases where *IT* garnered favorable comments, they reinforced what everyone already knew: King is a consummate writer when evoking what it is like to be a child growing up. As one reviewer wrote: "The exciting and absorbing parts of *IT* are not the mechanical showdowns and shockeroos—but the simple scenes in which King evokes childhood in the 1950s. If—fat chance—he ever takes a vow of poverty and tries for true literary sainthood, this intensely imagined world would be a good place to begin his pilgrimage."

Other reviewers, after finishing the 550,000-word novel, saw *IT* as an exercise in literary self-indulgence, the kind that only a bestselling writer could get away with. In *Twilight Zone* E. F. Bleiler writes that King, "who is in many ways the Thomas Wolfe of our times . . . has never met the Maxwell Perkins that he needs and deserves."

The comparison seems apropos, particularly since King later wrote in *Nightmares in the Sky*:

I am a writer who exists more on nerve-endings than the process of intellectual thought and logic. When someone asked Maxwell Perkins if Thomas Wolfe, whose books Perkins edited, had been a great writer, Perkins snorted, "Hell, no! Tom was a divine wind-chime. No more

than that." . . . I'm claiming to be the Thomas Wolfe of my generation no more than I am claiming any artistic merit for my work . . . ;
I'm only saying that what I write comes from the gut instead of my
head, from intuition rather than intellect. In that sense, I am also
more wind-chime than writer.

Whether King was a wind-chime or not, the critics didn't care for *IT*'s
symphony of words; there were too many notes, they complained. In the
New York Times Book Review, Walter Wagner wrote, "Where did Stephen
King, the most experienced crown prince of darkness, go wrong with *IT*?
Almost everywhere. Casting aside discipline, which is as important to a
writer as imagination and style, he has piled just about everything he
could think of into this book and too much of each thing as well."

Even *Publishers Weekly,* which generally gave King's books positive
reviews, didn't take *IT* to heart. "Get *IT.* Buy *IT.* Everyone's reading *IT.*
The catchy sales pitches are innumerable. But how about forget *IT*? . . .
Overpopulated and under-characterized, bloated by lazy thought-out phi-
losophizing and theologizing, *IT* is all too slowly drowned by King's
unrestrained pen . . . . [T]here is simply too much of *IT.*"

And so *IT* goes.

Still, nothing could stop *IT.* The $22.95 book went to press with a
million copies. King fans couldn't care less about what the critics said
because his fans are legion. One of them, entertainer Whoopi Goldberg,
reviewed *IT* for the *Los Angeles Times* and expressed their collective viewpoint: "I wait for each new King novel as an alcoholic waits for that next
drink. I am addicted."

Just as *IT* marked the beginning of the firestorm, books *about* King
became a cottage industry, with four books in 1986 alone: *The Films of
Stephen King* by Michael Collings (a Starmont book), *Stephen King at the
Movies* by Jessie Horsting, *The Annotated Guide to Stephen King* by Collings,
and a second collection of essays from Underwood–Miller, *Kingdom of
Fear,* edited by Tim Underwood and Chuck Miller.

Another Underwood–Miller book, *Bare Bones,* created considerable
confusion in the book trade when a Bowker reference book, *Forthcoming
Books,* listed it as being a book *by* King, when in fact it was a collection of
interviews *with* King. It probably never crossed King's mind that all the
interviews he had freely given would be compiled for such a collection.

For most of early 1987 King concentrated on finishing *The Tommyknockers,* which saw completion on May 19. Creatively exhausted, King

would spend the next year in a writer's block. As King recalled, "I would do stuff and it would fall apart like wet tissue paper. I don't know how to describe it, except that it's the most impotent, nasty, awful feeling . . . . You feel like a batter in a batting slump."

Under pressure to produce books on a regular schedule, besieged by the media for requests for interviews, pressured by fans who wrote hundreds of letters a week—70 percent of them requesting replies—King found himself in the eye of the storm . . . and unable to write.

Tabitha King, a writer in her own right, knew what her husband was going through. In an interview she explained the importance of writing in both their lives:

> All I know is, if I don't do it, I go crazy. Steve used to say he'd commit suicide if he couldn't write, which has always pissed me off. I'd tell him if he pulled an Ernest Hemingway on me, I'd kick his body into the street and dance on it! Whether Steve really believes that he'd kill himself or not, I do understand how devastating it would be not to be able to write anymore.

When *Castle Rock* broke the bad news that Stephen King was taking a break from publishing, it sent shock waves of concern through its four thousand subscribers, die-hard fans who constantly needed their King fix. Outside the inner circle, however, King's writer's block went virtually unnoticed; after all, the King firestorm was in full flame, with *Eyes of the Dragon, Misery,* and *The Tommyknockers* scheduled for release in 1987.

In addition, three King movies were scheduled for release: *Pet Sematary, Creepshow 2,* and *The Running Man.*

There were even three new books *about* King: *The Gothic World of Stephen King, Stephen King Goes to Hollywood,* and *The Stephen King Phenomenon.*

It didn't look like a dearth of King material at all, but because King was not writing, no new King novel would grace the bookstores come fall 1988.

In February 1987 *The Eyes of the Dragon* was published by Viking as an $18.95 hardback, with new illustrations by David Palladini. Concerned that it would be perceived as a children's book, King stressed: "It is—or if it succeeds—a tale, and a tale is something that can be read profitably by any who have the wit to do so."

Even though *The Eyes of the Dragon* sold 525,000 copies in its first year, it undoubtedly suffered in sales from King readers who expected only horror books from King, and who had grave reservations if King strayed from the path. Margi Washburn, in a letter to *Castle Rock,* disclosed that she had reserved a copy of the book but after reading the flap copy on a display copy at a bookstore canceled the reservation. "Why? Because Mr. King had written for a thirteen-year-old, and not for me. I am thirty-four."

When Washburn finally gave the book a chance—after getting an enthusiastic recommendation from a local librarian, in whose library forty-four copies circulated as 110 people crowded the waiting list to read them—she discovered her preconceptions had prejudiced her against the book. After giving the book a chance, she wrote: "It took me three days to finish this treasure. . . . I laughed and cried and prayed it would not end."

That reaction was shared by King's own daughter, Naomi, for whom the book had originally been written. Stephen King, noting her reaction, wrote that she had taken the manuscript "with a marked lack of enthusiasm," which changed into "rapt interest as the story kidnapped her." When she finished, she told her father that "the only thing wrong with it was that she didn't want it to end."

"That, my friends, is a writer's favorite song, I think," concluded King.

For King readers raised on a steady diet of his more horrific work, *The Eyes of the Dragon* surely came as a surprise, even as many were surprised to discover that *Stand by Me* was based on a King story. Both instances, I think, show King's tremendous range as a writer—rare enough in these times when some bestselling authors are content to rewrite the one book they have in them.

In June 1987 *Misery* appeared from Viking as a short novel. It had 310 pages, and was published at $18.95 in a print run of 900,000 copies. King's horrific interpretation of John Fowles's *The Collector, Misery* struck a raw nerve in King, as well as his readership, prompting Tabitha King to write an article for *Castle Rock,* "Co-miser-a-ting with Stephen King," which she began:

> I have read several pained, angry, and offended letters from fans who
> mistakenly believe that Steve was recording his true feelings about
> his readers in *Misery*. . . . [I]ts exploration of the worst aspects of the
> celebrity-fan connection is obvious and real.

In a later interview Tabitha elaborated: "The public is frequently possessive and unforgiving, without seeming to understand that what they are attempting to exercise is a kind of emotional slavery." She continued, "Money and fame attract the self-seeking, who are willing to do anything . . . even if it hurts or kills you. . . ."

Like *Pet Sematary,* praised for its unflinching look at a subject most people prefer not even to discuss, *Misery* was a psychological thriller. It was King's best novel in years—a short, tightly written story made tighter by editorial suggestions that King heeded.

King explained that *Misery* was more than simply an entertaining tale; it was an exploration of his writer's psyche:

> I thought it would be about escape, pure and simple. About halfway or three-quarters through, I found out I was actually talking about something as opposed to just telling a story. I thought to myself, you're talking about *The Thousand and One Nights,* and you're talking about what you do. The more I wrote, the more I was forced to examine what I was doing in the act of creating make-believe; why I was doing it and why I was successful at it; whether or not I was hurting other people by doing it and whether or not I was hurting myself.

Certainly King's faithful readers—the ones who had avoided *The Eyes of the Dragon* because it wasn't horror—saw themselves lampooned in *Misery,* and didn't find it funny at all. In *Misery,* Paul Sheldon, a romance novelist, is "forced" by his readers, encouraged by his publisher, to give them what they want: stories about Misery Chastain, and nothing else:

> They wanted Misery, Misery, Misery. Each time he had taken a year or two off to write one of the other novels—what he thought of as his "serious" work with what was at first certainty and then hope and finally a species of grim desperation—he had received a flood of protesting letters from these women, many of whom signed themselves "your number-one fan."

To a writer, that situation *is* misery, personified by the character Annie Wilkes, who forces Sheldon to write another Misery Chastain novel against his will. The literary work initially holds the writer captive, then the reader, but in *Misery* the order is perverted, with the reader holding the writer captive—the writer, literally, a prisoner of his own success.

"People really like what I do," said King, though he admitted that "some of them are quite crackers. I don't think I have met Annie Wilkes yet, but I've met all sorts of people who call themselves my 'number-one fan' and, boy, some of [them] don't have six cans in a six-pack."

In the wake of what critics considered midrange King (*Firestarter* and *Christine*) and ambitious but fundamentally flawed novels (*The Talisman* and *IT*), *Misery* stood out. In the dedication to his personal secretary and publisher-editor of *Castle Rock* and her husband, King wrote, "This is for Stephanie and Jim Leonard, who know why. Boy, *do* they."

Reviewers were virtually universal in their praise. *Publishers Weekly* was typical: "King's new novel, about a writer held hostage by his self-proclaimed 'number-one fan,' is unadulteratedly terrifying. . . . The best parts of this novel demand that we take King seriously as a writer with a deeply felt understanding of human psychology."

Over the years King has told the story about the time when he was accosted by Mark Chapman, the man who shot and killed John Lennon. King remembered having left the headquarters of a major TV network in New York, where a Mark Chapman approached him for a photograph. Afterward, Chapman insisted King autograph the Polaroid with a special marking pen.

It almost sounds like something from a Stephen King story: a real-life incident too fantastic to be true, which appears to be the case. David Streitfeld, in the *Washington Post,* wrote that at the time King recollects the event took place, "[Chapman] was living in Hawaii, and his constrained financial circumstances made it unlikely he had come to New York." Streitfeld wrote that King remembers signing an autograph for *a* Mark Chapman, but King himself wasn't sure it was *the* Mark Chapman.

In November 1987 King published *The Tommyknockers,* a sprawling novel of 558 pages, with a cover price of $19.95 and a first printing of 1.2 million copies. Unlike *Misery*—a riveting, fast read—*The Tommyknockers* suffered from self-indulgence, as King admitted in an interview:

> At this point, nobody can make me change anything . . . . [W]here does a 10,000-pound gorilla sit? The answer is, any place he wants. That's why it becomes more and more important that I listen carefully to what people say, and if what they say seems to make sense, I have to make those changes even when I don't want to, because it's too easy to hang yourself. You get all this freedom—it can lead to self-indulgence. I've been down that road, probably most notably with *The Tommyknockers.* But with a book like *Misery,* where I did listen, the results were good.

The story of the inhabitants of Haven, Maine, who are in the process of "becoming" less human and more alien because of the ill effects of an alien spaceship buried in the ground, *The Tommyknockers* took its knocks. *Library Journal* said it was "not one of King's more original novels," and *Booklist* made fun of its characters and King's readership, saying that "we smugly tell ourselves that no one could be as stupid as the people in this book. But then, considering the seriousness with which fans take these works, some recalculations may be necessary."

Just as *Publishers Weekly* praised *Misery,* it found much to fault in King's latest book:

> *The Tommyknockers* is consumed by the rambling prose of its author. Taking a whole town as his canvas, King uses too-broad strokes, adding cartoonlike characters and unlikely catastrophes like so many logs on a fire; ultimately, he loses all semblance of style, carefully structured plot or resonant meaning, the hallmarks of his best writing. It is clear from this latest work that King himself has "become" a writing machine . . . .

A sharp contrast to *The Tommyknockers* with its 1.2 million copies in print, *The Dark Tower II: The Drawing of the Three,* published earlier that year, in May, was issued in a small run: 30,000 copies in its "trade" edition, at $35; and 850 copies, of which 800 were for sale, in its $100 "deluxe" edition, numbered, and signed by King and artist Phil Hale.

Whereas the first *Dark Tower* book was a collection of five stories, the second was clearly a novel in its own right, and a part of a large mosaic that, according to King, was beginning to come into focus. Dedicating the book to his publisher, King acknowledged that Grant had "taken a chance on these *novels,* one by one."

In an afterword to the second book in the series—projected then to comprise seven books—King wrote, "This work seems to be my own Tower, you know; these people haunt me, Roland most of all . . . . All I know is that the tale has called to me again and again over a period of seventeen years . . . . And the Tower is closer."

Like the first *Dark Tower* book, this one was a true limited edition, available in no other form, a distinction shared with *Cycle of the Werewolf* and *The Eyes of the Dragon,* both subsequently reprinted by King's trade publishers.

Throughout 1987, however, King's agent, Kirby McCauley, was negotiating with NAL to issue trade editions of the *Dark Tower* to satisfy King's readership, which wouldn't take no for an answer. It became clear to King's publisher and, presumably, King himself that the fans wanted the opportunity to make a buying decision, and not have others—including the author—make the decision for them.

In August 1987 King's own specialty press, Philtrum Press, issued its first work of fiction by an author other than King. Don Robertson's *The Ideal, Genuine Man* appeared in a small edition of 2,700 copies, of which

500 were numbered, and signed by both King and the author. A handsome example of bookmaking, *The Ideal, Genuine Man* was designed by Michael Alpert, who shepherded the previous Philtrum Press titles through production.

In explaining why he published the book, King, who has drawn much from Robertson's narrative style, wrote: "Publishing this book is no thank-you note, but a simple necessity. To not publish when I have the means to do so would be an irresponsible act." Placing Robertson as the "latest . . . in a brawny bunch of American story-tellers who wrote naturalistic fiction," King observed that Robertson follows a long tradition of writing, "from Mark Twain to Stephen Crane to Frank Norris to Theodore Dreiser to James Jones and Hubert Selby, Jr." King concluded that *The Ideal, Genuine Man* "is, quite simply, a great book by an ideal, genuine writer."

It's not hard to see why King is so enthusiastic about Robertson or, indeed, the naturalist writers. King, after all, is one of them, even though he certainly belongs with—in King's own terms, which he applied to Bradbury—the "American naturalists of a dark persuasion. . . ."

Although King's fans buy each new book with the hope that it will satisfy their reading expectations, they had come to be less hopeful of King's film adaptations, especially after *Maximum Overdrive* the previous year, a movie that even King admitted was "a critical and financial flop." Even though it was followed by *Stand by Me*, there was little reassurance that King's horror material would translate effectively to the screen.

In May 1987 *Creepshow 2* appeared and it was a letdown—far inferior to the original *Creepshow*, which had earned $10 million in domestic rentals. *Creepshow 2* in comparison took in only $4.9 million in domestic rentals, principally because the movie's success hinged on the quality of the stories, of which two were tepid fare: "Chief Woodenhead" and "The Hitchhiker." That left "The Raft" to carry the weight of the movie.

The movie itself offered nothing new to King's oeuvre, though it was the first time a Maine locale had been used in any King film. "The Hitchhiker" was shot in the Bangor–Brewer area and pumped an estimated $750,000 into the local economy. Maine, as film-maker William Dunn maintained, *was* King country, so why not film there?

In 1987 the purported sequel to *'Salem's Lot*, initially made for theatrical release, never made it to the screen. Instead, it went directly to video, after advance screenings in California made it clear that it was a King movie in name only.

One California King fan who attended a screening, and who was also a *Castle Rock* subscriber, noted in a letter to its editor: "It was undoubtedly one of the worst films I have ever seen . . . . I urge all Stephen King's fans to stay away from this poor excuse of a movie. BEWARE! *Return to 'Salem's Lot* is not an adaptation of any King work at all. It is just a rip-off of Stephen King's name and reputation."

King, who had nothing to do with the film, didn't think much of the sequel either. "It's actually gotten some good reviews, but I think it's dreadful. Apparently, this was something where Warner Brothers had the rights to do a sequel after their TV movie . . . . It was *made* for theatrical [release], it's just not released. If you look at it, you'll know why [King laughs]."

The best King movie of 1987, released by Taft Entertainment in November, was *The Running Man,* loosely based on the Bachman book. With Arnold ("I'll be back!") Schwarzenegger as Ben Richards, the movie was a vehicle more for Arnold as a one-man killing machine—a role he had perfected in *The Terminator, Commando,* and *Predator I*—than for King's essentially tragic story. Though *The Running Man* earned domestic receipts of $16 million, its prohibitively high cost—estimated as high as $27 million—made it nearly impossible for the film to make a profit.

In 1988, from January to May, King remained blocked. "Finally, I wrote a little story called 'Rainy Season' and all at once, everything opened up and flooded out. I've been writing horror since then," King explained.

Although the writer's block was over, Viking still would have no new King novel for the fall. Viking attempted to plug the king-sized hole with *Nightmares in the Sky,* a collection of photos originally titled *Gargoyles,* with a 10,000-word essay by King in the front of the book.

In the *Washington Post Book World,* David Streitfeld wrote that Viking published 250,000 copies of the oversized $24.95 photo album. Unfortunately, the book proved to be a nightmare, with a reported 100,000 copies returned to its publisher. Viking got the message: King fans wanted original fiction, not photo-illustrated essays.

In July NAL issued a four-cassette, unabridged reading of *The Dark Tower: The Gunslinger,* read by King himself. NAL's Robert Diforio declared that King was "as mesmerizing in audio as he is in print. [King] has an incredibly seductive quality that just draws you in. He's clearly not a professional actor or reader, but it doesn't matter, because what you get is Stephen King himself. I think his fans will be thrilled."

King felt strongly that his unabridged reading had much to offer. "I thought that even though I don't have a professional voice, I know what the story means to me, which is a great deal. It seems built to be heard around a fire. A lot of fantasy is that way."

Two months later, in September 1988, NAL under its Plume imprint finally published its trade paperback edition of the *The Dark Tower: The Gunslinger,* very reasonably priced at $10.95. With that publication, all of King's major books were now available to King's general readership.

Strange though it may seem, more books *about* King were published in 1988 than books *by* King. In addition to two scholarly examinations of King's work (*Landscape of Fear* and *Stephen King: The First Decade*), Underwood–Miller issued its third collection of essays (*Reign of Fear*) and *Bare Bones,* its first collection of interviews with King.

The fall and winter of 1988 marked a transitional period for King. In August *Castle Rock* announced that Stephanie Leonard was stepping down as publisher-editor. She would be replaced by long-time *Castle Rock* staffer and her brother, Christopher Spruce, who doubled as the general manager at WZON, King's radio station.

WZON, in fact, was undergoing its own changes. Earlier in the year it appeared that the station would go up for sale. In October, however, King decided to keep the station and change its programming. As King explained, "All the change means is that Z-62 will offer its programming commercial-free. That means more music and no commercial interruptions. Commercial AM rock 'n' roll is nearly dead. Resurrecting the Z as a non-commercial rocker may be one way of keeping the format alive on AM."

The biggest change, however, was King's change in literary representation. In the September issue of *Castle Rock,* Stephanie Leonard confirmed what had already appeared in the trade journals in the field. "A recent article in *Fantasy Newsletter* mentioned a shake-up at the Kirby McCauley agency. It is true that Stephen King is no longer represented by Kirby McCauley, as the article implied. At this time he has not signed with any other representatives."

Neither King nor McCauley went on record explaining the change in representation. Consequently, we can only speculate as to the reasons why.

As it turned out, King subsequently vested control in his business manager, Arthur B. Greene, who in December negotiated King's next contract.

In February 1989 *Castle Rock* broke the news in a front-page cover story: "Happy New Year: SK Inks Four Book Contract." NAL's Robert Diforio said, "This is simply wonderful to report. We enjoy being King's publisher and we're happy that we'll be continuing that relationship."

For King, his writer's nightmare was over; his writer's block was history. Spruce reported: "After that time off from writing . . . the ideas and creativity started up again and resulted in much of the work that is part of the new publishing contract."

From fall 1989 through 1992, four new King books would be issued. The first, *The Dark Half,* was nearly finished and scheduled for a November 1989 publication date, only nine months away. Speaking about *The Dark Half,* Douglas Winter said:

> It is a strange thing. It's a peculiar beast. You've taken a life outside
> of yourself. And that's what Steve's *The Dark Half* is really all about—
> the horror that is fame, the way it creates a persona that is not you,
> but may well take over if you don't watch out. Peter Straub, for all his
> success, has always told me how happy he was that he's avoided all
> that. And I can understand why. I have rarely been in a place with
> Steve, for example—and this even goes back a number of years—
> where he wasn't recognized.

The remaining books would be *Four Past Midnight* (a collection of novellas), *Needful Things* (the last Castle Rock story, a novel), and *Dolores Claiborne* (a novel).

At the same time, Book-of-the-Month Club—with its 1.5 million copies of King books sold to its membership—announced that it paid a mid-seven-figure sum for book-club rights to the four books, along with arrangements made to issue eighteen previous King books in a uniform edition for a new subscription series, the Stephen King Library. Each book would cost $14.95.

Spring 1989 was a busy period for King. In March King finished *The Dark Half.* And that month NAL published in trade paperback *The Dark Tower II: The Drawing of the Three,* a facsimile reprint edition—retaining typesetting, design, and artwork—of the Grant edition, at $12.95.

In short fiction, King's 7,000-word story "Rainy Season" appeared in a special Stephen King issue of *Midnight Graffiti. Dolan's Cadillac,* a 20,000-

word tale that had appeared only in a serialization in *Castle Rock,* appeared as a separate book from Lord John Press. This jewel of a book was limited to 1,000 copies, of which 250 made up the deluxe edition (at $250), and the remainder the limited edition (at $100). As usual, *Dolan's Cadillac* was out of print before publication.

Even at those prices *Dolan's Cadillac* was affordable in comparison to the $2,200 for *My Pretty Pony,* a 9,000-word short story published by the Whitney Museum as the sixth book in its Artists and Writers Series. Its publication coordinated by May Castleberry, *My Pretty Pony* was limited to 280 copies and signed by King. Barbara Kruger, a graphics artist and designer, illustrated the book; however, her work was not generally well received by the fan community.

In the fall the Whitney Museum would co-publish a trade edition with Knopf, limited to 15,000 copies, with a retail price of $50.

In April *Pet Sematary*—the first King screenplay for a King novel, and the first major King novel to be filmed entirely in Maine, at King's directive—was released nationwide. At the world premiere in Bangor, King observed the reactions of the audience and said, "I think that they responded the way that we hoped that they would, the way we dreamed they would—at all the correct places. And I think everybody got a kick out of seeing a lot of locations they know from life. What scares me most, though, is what the [general] audience's reaction is going to be."

King needn't have worried, for *Pet Sematary* went on to become a critical and financial success. It was the movie that *Maximum Overdrive* should have been but wasn't. *Pet Sematary* would go on to earn in domestic rentals $26 million.

Part of the success, perhaps, was King's insistence that *Pet Sematary* be filmed in Maine—"King country," according to William Dunn, who scouted out locations for the film. To King, for both financial and aesthetic reasons, the movie *had* to be filmed in Maine, a nonnegotiable point in the contract:

> Because *Pet Sematary* of all my novels was the one that I thought would
> be the most difficult to film, I just simply made it an unbreakable
> part of the deal that whoever was going to do it, would have to do it in
> Maine. And Laurel came along, and Bill Dunn came along and said,
> "Yeah, OK, we'll make it in Maine."
>
> And, again, why not? You've got production facilities, lab facili-
> ties, and an acting pool to draw on here in New England. And if you
> need to go to Boston and New York, they're 600 miles down the road,
> and they're closer than, say, San Francisco is to Los Angeles.

We've got stuff up here that nobody's seen; [Maine's] supposed to be Vacationland. And ideally, what should happen is that people should look at the movies and say, "We'd like to go there." And they should come there and say, "Gee, this is as great as we saw it."

In other words, a movie like *Pet Sematary* . . . should serve as [a] commercial for the state, as much as all the movies made in California, Los Angeles, New York have served as commercials for those places.

Considering the subject matter of the film, one will not likely conclude that *Pet Sematary* will greatly enhance Maine's reputation as the vacation state—as Maine's license plates proclaim. But the movie did pump millions of dollars into the state's economy, giving the newly formed Maine Film Commission a shot in the arm.

Even though King pushed for *Pet Sematary* to be filmed in Maine, it wouldn't be prudent to do it for every film, no matter how desirable. Still, it was a start, and King, who had been instrumental in pushing for the formation of the Maine Film Commission, made it clear that the way was paved for more movies in Maine:

If you're going to tell about Maine, why not come here? People like Bill [Dunn] have helped to blaze the way for that, to create a precedent for it, so I think it'll happen more. I think that one thing you can count on is that I will try as hard as I can to get film production up into this particular area. I can do it to some degree with my own work—it's not going to become my life's crusade with me—but nonetheless, the more film that comes up here, the stronger the Film Commission gets.

At the local level King also had a financial impact. Later that year, in winter, at the Milton Academy in Massachusetts, the Kings made a "hefty donation" to finance its $6 million arts and music center; its theater was named after Stephen King's late mother, Ruth King, a talented pianist who also had a gift for public speaking. At the ceremony naming the new center, King said, "As children, we need to have our dreams encouraged and nurtured. My mother did that for me."

Closer to home, in nearby Old Town where Tabitha had grown up, the Kings pledged half of the $1.5 million needed for a 6,000-square-foot addition to the public library. The addition would be designated the Tabitha Spruce King Wing.

The winter also marked a major change at the King residence, which had become *the* local tourist trap, especially around Halloween when the

King residence took on special significance. After years of operating out of his home office, King moved his secretarial staff to a nearby office building in the Bangor–Brewer area, which made King's home his castle, appropriately surrounded by a wrought-iron fence.

The office—its location and phone number well-kept secrets—is headed by Shirley Sonderegger, who supervises two part-time secretaries. At the office King gives interviews, talks to the media, coordinates his activities with his staff, signs letters and copies of books from fans, and reviews necessary paperwork—all afternoon work. The morning is always reserved for the writing itself.

David Lowell, a Maine writer who has visited King's office, said that it is across from Sonderegger's office and is the smaller of the two, though large enough for his purposes:

> Steve's office, where he writes personal letters and answers mail, is equipped with a large desk facing the wall, a stereo in the corner, and a comfortable-looking blue chair that swivels.
>
> On his desk is an electric typewriter, a calculator, and numerous books and gifts sent by fans.
>
> On the walls: a UMO pennant, a Boston Red Sox shirt and pennant, a gold album with Steve pictured in the center disc, an original Michael Whelan painting, original art from *The Dark Tower: The Gunslinger,* drawings of Steve's face sent in by fans, a photo of him as the minister in *Pet Sematary,* and a poster of Michael J. Fox holding a copy of *Skeleton Crew* which says "READ" at the very top.
>
> There is a poster of *IT* on Steve's office door, and a bulletin board near his desk, plastered with all kinds of photos and notes. Over the stereo is a framed *New York Times* list that has *Pet Sematary* in the #1 slot; Steve has circled it in red.
>
> There are also numerous small shelves in the offices, with mostly his novels.

In November *The Dark Half,* a 431-page novel with a retail price of $21.95, hit the stores just in time for Christmas. The announced first printing was 1.2 million copies, the same as for *The Tommyknockers.*

An exploration of the writer's psyche, *The Dark Half* was originally to have been published as a "collaboration" by Stephen King and Richard Bachman—especially appropriate, since the story concerns a writer's pen name that comes back to life with a vengeance. As King and Thad Beaumont (the novel's protagonist) found out, sometimes they come back.

Publishers Weekly called "the new King thriller . . . so wondrously frightening that mesmerized readers won't be able to fault the master for reusing a premise that puts both *Misery* and *The Dark Half* among the best of his voluminous work."

As the year drew to a close, so did *Castle Rock,* which ceased publication with its fifty-fifth issue, cover-dated December 1989. From its first few issues with an estimated 300 subscribers, *Castle Rock,* which had 5,000 subscribers during its heyday, ended its successful run with a circulation of 1,500 subscribers, the hard-core fans who had shelled out $20 every year for a subscription.

As editor-publisher Christopher Spruce explained, part of the reason for shutting down *Castle Rock* was his perception that, like the Gunslinger in *The Dark Tower,* the world had moved on. For Spruce, it meant going back to school, to the University of Maine at Orono, to get his master's degree. Spruce also felt that Stephen King's feelings about *Castle Rock* had to be considered:

> I'm not sure he has ever been entirely comfortable with the idea of a newsletter devoted to "Stephen King." After all, he is yet a tried-and-true Yankee possessed of that sometimes endearing quality of self-effacement who just might be a little embarrassed by all the fuss. At the same time, he understands his faithful fans need both a source of information about him and an outlet for their comments about their favorite writer.

The late Ray Rexer, a hard *Rock*er who published *Castle Schlock*—a hilarious parody of *Castle Rock,* which at times with its sycophantic reviews was a ripe target for lampooning—said it all in his poem, an ode to the original *Rock*:

> It's been around for five full years
> with stories and reviews,
> and screaming editorials
> and horrifying news.
> For five full years it crammed me full
> of Stephen King-ish stuff,
> then Mr. Spruce, The Editor,
> proclaimed "Enough's enough!"

In 1990, as the decade came to a close, King neared the midpoint of his career and realized things in his life had come full circle. In an introduction to a story in *Four Past Midnight* he wrote, "I'm forty-two now, and as I look back over the last four years of my life I can see all sorts of cloture."

In April 1990 King's hometown newspaper reported that pending FCC approval WZON would be sold to dentist John Tozer of Bangor. Neither Tozer nor King would comment. The next month, however, Tozer filed with the FCC to buy the station, and subsequently bought it. On the day the music died, the *Bangor Daily News* reported that "the oldest radio station in Bangor" became "the city's newest station," and the hard rock was replaced by a talk-show format.

That month, May, Doubleday republished *The Stand,* twelve years after its original publication as a $12.95 hardback of 823 pages that in its first year sold an estimated 50,000 copies. The new edition, *The Stand: The Complete & Uncut Edition,* cost $24.95 in hardback at 1,153 pages, exceeding the page count of *IT.*

In part two of his preface to the new *Stand,* King wrote that "approximately four hundred pages of manuscript [100,000 words] were deleted from the final draft. The reason was not an editorial one; if that had been the case, I would be content to let the book live its life and die its eventual death as it was originally published."

According to King, "The cuts were made at the behest of the accounting department." But according to King's editor and publisher at Doubleday, there was more to the story, as reported by the *New York Times*:

> King's editor at that time, William G. Thompson, who is now with another publisher, says he edited the manuscript strictly for editorial reasons. "There was no pressure on me to cut it because it was too big," Thompson told *The New York Times.*
>
> However, Thompson left Doubleday before *The Stand* went into production, and according to King, Doubleday's publisher, Samuel S. Vaughan, told him that the book would have to be cut even more, to keep the retail price down.
>
> Vaughan, now a senior vp and editor at Random House, says, "Steve has always made me the heavy in the story. It's the book that was heavy. By trying to keep the price down so that it was not prohibitive, we were trying to build the career and sales of a young author."

Peter Schneider, then the marketing director of Doubleday for the new *Stand,* said that after everything had been said and done, the author and publisher closed ranks to bring out the new edition: " . . . [T]here was no damning of the old Doubleday, and there was no rancor. [King] just said it was a financial decision he didn't agree with, and that he made the cuts rather than have them made for him."

The new *Stand* had 150,000 additional words, a time frame updated from the eighties to the nineties, a new beginning and ending to the story itself, a dozen black-and-white illustrations by Berni Wrightson, and a two-part preface in which King explained that he had allowed the book to be reissued not for himself but "to serve a body of readers who have asked to have it."

To commemorate the event, Doubleday published a limited edition— 1,250 numbered copies, $325; and 52 lettered copies, not for sale—signed by author and artist. Imaginatively designed around the motif of the book as a "long tale of dark Christianity," the new *Stand* was sold only through Doubleday's sales representatives, each of whom had an allotment of thirty-three copies.

Although not his favorite novel, "[I]t is," said King, "the one people who like my books seem to like the most." For that reason the limited edition of *The Stand* became a "must" for King readers who wanted the best edition of their favorite book.

Doubleday, to its credit, spared no expense in the production of the limited edition. With elaborate gold-and-red-foil stamping on black leather boards, the limited edition resembled a family Bible. And rather than simply reuse the plates from the trade edition, Doubleday reset the type, then employed two-color printing (black for text, red for ornamental designs) on heavier paper stock than that used for the trade edition. Encased in a hand-finished, varnished wooden box lined in red silk and with a brass plate affixed to the cover, the limited edition could be extracted by a silk pull-ribbon.

Unfortunately, because only Doubleday accounts were offered the limited edition, the specialty dealers who normally stock and sell King limiteds found themselves unable to get more than a handful of copies—if they were lucky. (One dealer, who was promised three copies from the publisher, received several hundred phone calls and letters when he published news of their availability in his catalogue.)

Just as rare-book dealers were besieged with requests, Doubleday reportedly had to turn down offers of up to $1,250 from anxious fans who *had* to own a copy—price be damned, this edition was a needful thing.

In conjunction with *The Stand*'s release, Doubleday re-released newly designed editions of King's other Doubleday books—except *Pet Sematary*— with sturdier bindings, readable typefaces, and colorful dust jackets. Finally, the early King books were made available in handsome editions.

Beyond the hoopla surrounding *The Stand*'s publication, the important thing was that, as *Publishers Weekly* noted, the new edition remained the "same excellent tale" with the additional wordage making "King's best novel better still. A new beginning adds verisimilitude to an already

Ellanie Sampson and Stephen King in Truth or Consequences, New Mexico, November 19, 1983. (Photo courtesy of Ellanie Sampson.)

Stephen King signs copies of his books in Truth or Consequences,
New Mexico, November 19, 1983. (Photo courtesy of Ellanie Sampson.)

Stephen King talking to a student after class during his one-year stint
as Writer-in-Residence at UMO. (Photo courtesy of the Alumni Association
at UMO.)

The rented house flanking Route 15 in Orrington, when King was a Writer-in-
Residence at UMO; here, King wrote *Pet Sematary*. (1988, photo by GB)

A view past the house behind which the real pet cemetery was located. (The local children called it the "Pets Sematary," which they had painted on a sign, posted on the grounds.) (1988, photo by GB)

The Stephen King residence and a winter wonderland.
(February 12, 1984, photo courtesy of the Portland *Press Herald,* a Guy Gannett Publishing Company.)

The three-headed griffin that guards the King residence in Bangor, Maine. (1988, photo by GB)

The Paul Bunyan statue in Bangor, Maine. (1989, photo by GB)

A side view of the King residence in Bangor, Maine. (1988, photo by GB)

Stephen King's home office (IBM Selectric typewriter on the left, CPU for the computer in the middle, and the Wang keyboard and screen on the right). (Photo courtesy of the *Bangor Daily News*; date not known.)

Stephen King prepares to throw the ceremonial first pitch at the Maine Little League All-Star Championship game in Old Town, Maine, on August 5, 1989. (Photo courtesy of the *Bangor Daily News*.)

Stephen King at the Portland City Hall, March 6, 1990. (Photo by Gordon Chibroski, courtesy of the Portland *Press Herald,* a Guy Gannett Publishing Company.)

John Esposito (screenwriter), Bill Dunn (co-producer), and Stephen King at the press conference for *Graveyard Shift* at the Hoyt Cinema in Bangor, Maine, October 25, 1990. (Photo by GB.)

Stephen King at the Waterford Memorial School in Waterford, Maine.
(April 10, 1990, photo courtesy of the Portland *Press Herald,* a Guy Gannett
Publishing Company.)

Stephen King at the Virginia Beach Pavilion in Virginia Beach, Virginia, on September 22, 1986. King said: "I would just say to you as students who are supposed to be learning: as soon as that book is gone from the library, do not walk, *run to your nearest public library or bookseller and find out what your elders don't want you to know, because that's what you* need *to know*!" (1986, photo by GB)

Disc jockey playing the platters that matter at WZON in Bangor, Maine. (1988, photo by GB)

Christopher Spruce, editor-publisher of *Castle Rock,* prepares camera-ready copy at his office at the WZON radio station. (1988, photo by GB)

Stephen King's brother, David King, holding "Cujo." (1990, photo courtesy of David Lowell)

Douglas E. Winter, author of *Stephen King: The Art of Darkness,* in his home office in Alexandria, Virginia. (1988, photo by GB)

Tabitha King giving a reading at BookMarc's, a bookstore in downtown Bangor, Maine. (1991, photo courtesy of the *Bangor Daily News*)

Tabitha King in her home office in Bangor, Maine. (Photo courtesy of the *Bangor Daily News*; date not known.)

frighteningly believable story, while a new ending opens up possibilities for a sequel."

Though it's not likely King will write a sequel—he has steadfastly refused to write one—it's likely Randall Flagg, King's most enduring fictional creation, will reappear in another book, just as he did in *The Eyes of the Dragon*. To King, Flagg is the embodiment of pure evil:

> Randall Flagg to me is everything that I know of in the last twenty years that's really bad, or maybe even since Hitler. He's mostly Charlie Starkweather whom I was afraid of when I was a kid. I read the stories about Charlie Starkweather and his killing spree and I was really terrified by what he was doing. He's partially Charles Manson and he's partially Charles Whitman, the Texas tower killer, and Richard Speck and all these people.

Three months later, in August, *Four Past Midnight* went to press with a first printing of 1.2 million copies. A $22.95 hardback of 763 pages, this collection of short fiction marked a turning point in King's career. In his introductory note he wrote: "When this book is published, in 1990, I will have been sixteen years in the business of make-believe." Along the way, King wrote, "I had become, by some process I still do not fully understand, America's literary boogeyman. . . ."

The four stories in *Four Past Midnight*—unlike the previous novella collection, *Different Seasons*—showed King as a literary boogeyman. "The Langoliers" and "The Library Policeman" are, King described, "tales of horror." In "Secret Window, Secret Garden," King wrote his "last story about writers and writing and the strange no man's land which exists between what's real and what's make-believe." *Misery, The Dark Half,* and "Secret Window, Secret Garden" closed the circle of King's exploration of the writer's psyche. "The Sun Dog," the last story of the book, is the penultimate Castle Rock tale, a prelude, according to King, to *Needful Things,* scheduled for publication in October 1991.

Clearly, King could continue to write about Castle Rock for the rest of his career, but he has deliberately chosen not to do so, since he realized he must continue to break new ground instead of replowing too familiar fields:

> I'll never leave Maine behind, but Castle Rock became more and more real to me. It got to the point where I could draw maps of the place. On the one hand, it was a welcoming place to write about. But there is a downside to that. You become complacent; you begin to accept boundaries; the familiarity of the place discourages risks. So I

am burning my bridges and destroying the town. It's all gone—
kaput. It's sad but it had to be done.

Inevitably, comparisons were made between *Four Past Midnight* and
the earlier novella collection, *Different Seasons*. The reviews, though mixed,
were generally positive, citing King's storytelling abilities and fecund
imagination. *Playboy* hailed the collection: "More than just good yarns,
these are can't-tear-your-eyes-away stories that burn in your imagination
long after you close the book . . . . These are four wonderful pieces of dark
magic from a master conjurer who knows how to leave the crowd gasping
in amazement." *Book World* said this was King's best book since *Pet Sematary* and acknowledged King as "above all a master storyteller, and these
stories grab hold and will not let go . . . . King shapes his material with
the sure hand of a master woodworker, tossing off unexpected similes,
deftly using dreams to reveal character, subtly planting clues to coming
revelations, and skillfully managing the coincidences on which his stories
often hinge."

Between the late fall and early winter of 1990 King saw things come
full circle with his movie and television adaptations: King's first *Cavalier*
story, "Graveyard Shift," was released as a full-length feature film; *IT,*
King's final statement about children and traditional monsters, was released as a two-part miniseries on television; and a second Rob Reiner
film, *Misery,* proved once again that at the heart of every successful movie
is the story.

Like *Pet Sematary, Graveyard Shift* was shot entirely in Maine. The
movie pumped an estimated $3 million into the local economies, including
Bangor, Lewiston, and Lisbon Center. The Paramount film, budgeted at
$10.5 million, gave King the opportunity to work, again, with Bill Dunn
as its coproducer, as well as with newcomer John Esposito, who wrote the
screenplay. At a press conference at the world premiere of *Graveyard Shift* in
Bangor near Halloween, King shed light on the original short story and the
movie that resulted:

> *Graveyard Shift* was written by this 22-year-old kid who sold two pieces
> of fiction beforehand, both to specialty magazines. That kid was still
> in school when the story was written and rewritten. It's a very early
> piece of work. It is in fact the second earliest piece of fiction I've ever
> included in any of my published works.
>
> It was put together years later by people who are seasoned,

people who have worked in this field a long time, in any number of capacities.

In a way, John Esposito and I are the perfect team, in terms of him adapting my material, because we were both starting out, cutting our teeth. And you have advantages that balance off the disadvantages of being new—boundless enthusiasm, which John has, and the ability to go for it all, which is automatic when you're starting off.

Whether or not *Graveyard Shift* does the job in terms of art, I don't much care. It works in terms of sitting back and putting your feet up and watching the movie and having a good time. We'll let Martin Scorsese and those guys take care of themselves; they didn't make this movie—*this* movie was made by cannibals.

Unfortunately, *Graveyard Shift* recalled *Maximum Overdrive*. The flick, based on a short story, simply had too much on-screen time and far too little story. To make matters worse, the movie had been handicapped by a nearly impossible shooting schedule, presumably to take advantage of the favorable fallout from *Pet Sematary* and also to beat *Misery* to the theaters. Work began on May 14, 1990, with principal photography from June through August, and a release date set for October—one month before the release of *Misery*.

A grave disappointment for King fans, *Graveyard Shift,* as the *Washington Post* predicted, passed "quickly into that great video graveyard in the suburbs." About the movie, the *Post* said, "The acting and directing are substandard. Even the hackneyed plot is barely turned over . . . . Even the jaws of life couldn't extricate this film from the quick burial it deserves."

In a curious way, history repeated itself. As *Maximum Overdrive* was followed by Reiner's *Stand by Me,* so *Graveyard Shift* would be followed by Reiner's *Misery*. In both instances, the Reiner film emphasized story over scares, which in the end proved to be the right choice.

As the bittersweet story of *Stand by Me* recalled Reiner's youth, and in doing so recalled our youths, so *Misery*—a story in which one's creative craft collides with the public's expectations—recalled Reiner's early adulthood, when he was overprinted with the identity of Mike Stivic from the television show "All in the Family." As Reiner left behind his career as an actor in front of the camera and began a career as director behind the camera, the public at large still perceived him as Mike Stivic. (Similarly, director Ron Howard couldn't shed his identity as Opie from his television days on "The Andy Griffith Show.")

Misery, then, is the story of every creative person who is trapped in the hell of the demands and expectations of fandom, which usually wants more of the same. The curse of expectations was symbolized in *Misery* by Paul Sheldon, romance novelist whose most enduring character, Misery Chastain, is reluctantly resurrected by its author after his number-one fan holds him captive . . . and *demands* another Misery novel, much as Stephen King's number-one fans demand he write more horror novels.

In an interview with Gary Wood, Reiner explained his interest in *Misery*:

> The thing that drew me to the book was not that it was a suspense thriller genre. That's not what I was interested in doing next. What I was drawn to was the theme; the artist's dilemma of attaining a certain success doing something, and the fear of breaking away from that in an attempt to grow and change, the fear that you'll lose your audience.

For Kathy Bates, the Broadway actress who played Annie Wilkes in the role of Sheldon's number-one fan, *Misery* underscored the problem she knew she'd have if the movie became a success. For most of her life, wannabe comedians predictably connected her name to Norman Bates of *Psycho*. "It's an old, tired joke. I leave my name at a restaurant or the dentist and someone says, 'Oh, like in Norman Bates—a relative of yours?' "

Ironically, Bates, who realizes she will forever be associated with Annie Wilkes, is not a horror fan per se:

> I've admired King's work over the years, but I'm not a horror devotee. I read metaphysics and Jung and occasionally Clive Barker. I'm an eclectic reader . . . . After this film, it'll start again. More Norman Bates references, and *People* magazine will refer to me as Kathy "Misery" Bates. Everybody wants to type you. There's a human urge to pigeonhole. It's just rampant in Hollywood.

Not unlike book publishing either, wherein there's Stephen King—you know, the *horror* writer . . .

Things had come full circle. *Carrie,* King's first movie, was a critical and financial success. Actress Piper Laurie (as Carrie's mother) received an Oscar nomination, and Sissy Spacek (as Carrie) received an Academy Award nomination. Similarly, *Misery* was a critical and financial success, and actress Kathy Bates received both a Golden Globe Award and an Academy Award for her riveting performance as the deranged nurse-fan Annie Wilkes.

For Reiner, *Misery* solidly cemented his reputation among King fans as being *the* director of choice for King's movies. As with *Stand by Me*, *Misery* earned almost universal praise. *USA Today* wrote, "Though *Pet Sematary* and *Graveyard Shift* have inspired countless moviegoer moratoriums on Stephen King adaptations, even non-fans might consider giving *Misery* a shot."

Misery loves company, and on television that month, on November 18 and 20, *IT* aired on ABC-TV. Haunted by memories of the 1979 miniseries *'Salem's Lot*—a somewhat successful adaptation, though it fell far short of the power inherent in the original novel—fans, concerned about shoehorning a 1,138-page novel into a four-hour television feature, expected the worst. But what they got was a visual treat, a $12 million production directed by Tommy Lee Wallace, proof positive that horror can be convincingly done for television, even within the restrictions of the network censors.

The first episode of *IT* told the story of the children who encounter It. In the second episode *IT* focused on the children, now adults, as they band together to confront It for the last time. The all-star cast gave an excellent performance—Tim Curry as It, John Ritter, Tim Reid, Harry Anderson, Annette O'Toole, Richard Masur, Richard Thomas, and Dennis Christopher—but the second segment lacked the power of the first segment with its evocation of childhood. As the *Virginian-Pilot and Ledger-Star* pointed out:

> The film seems best when it centers on the children. Indeed, the cast
> of young actors is superior to their adult counterparts mainly because
> the script is more interesting, and palpable, when it deals with the
> horrors of childhood. . . . [King] should write more often about
> children because he's got a touch for reaching this level of innocence.

For King, *IT* was King's last exploration of the world of childhood. To go back would be, at this point in his career, pure misery. King had said everything he wanted to say about children, so why repeat himself? He had other books to write. The world moves on.

In December 1990 King found a ghost from his past returning to haunt him—the specter of "King's Garbage Truck." Like Spike Milligan's truck that came out of nowhere to follow Rocky and Leo in King's "Big Wheels: A Tale of the Laundry Game," "King's Garbage Truck" suddenly reappeared twenty years later. *The Maine Campus,* preparing a collection of alumni writings, made plans to reprint the columns in toto.

Running 35,000 words, "King's Garbage Truck" is impossible to find in any form. If reprinted in an affordable edition, the complete text of the columns would certainly enhance the sales of any collection.

Upon hearing of the book's impending publication, Arthur B. Greene—an attorney, and King's business manager and literary agent—fired off a letter to Steven M. Pappas, the editor of the anthology in the works. Wrote Greene: "[King] feels embarrassed by these early columns and considers them juvenilia . . . [he] has a faithful readership which expects the high caliber of literary materials customarily handcrafted by him . . . the material you want to reprint is not up to this standard."

In response, *The Maine Campus* immediately retained an attorney in Portland, Maine, to protect its interests, and to look into the copyright question: Did King or the newspaper own publication rights? Its attorney said, "My general understanding is, if you write a column for a newspaper, it belongs to the newspaper. This looks like it will be a lot of fun."

The press got wind of this brouhaha, and the matter wasn't fun for anyone. The result: the day after the original story ran, *Maine Campus* editor Doug Vanderweide, after talking with King, decided to drop the issue. Said Vanderweide, "We just don't have the kind of funds to take on protracted litigation . . . . We don't want to cause him any professional discomfort . . . . I think it's best to be fair to the man, and the way to be fair to him is just to let this issue slide."

The brouhaha soon became history, but not without commentary from another newspaper, which published an editorial by Douglas Rooks, the editor of the editorial pages of the *Kennebec Journal*. After reading a sampling of the columns, Rooks agreed that some of the writing was, as King noted, "juvenile." But Rooks didn't agree the work was "embarrassing" because he saw the serious intent behind the trappings of the humorously titled column. As Rooks explained: "For what is easy to see in King's writing is a growing awareness, a coming of age, common to college students of his generation . . . . The self-discovery that Stephen King made writing his 'juvenile' campus columns is an important one for everyone to make." Pointing his finger at King, Rooks concluded, "It's too bad that some people don't remember the lesson."

At the end of 1990 King saw himself the subject of media attention for his achievements as a one-man entertainment industry, now spanning nearly two decades. King, as he explained himself and the phenomenon that surrounded him, had started out as "a young man who knew no one in the publishing world and who had no literary agent [and] became what is known in that same publishing world as a 'brand name author.' "

In the fantasy field the most prestigious journal, the *Magazine of Fantasy & Science Fiction,* published in December 1990 its "Special Stephen King Issue." Within was a new short story ("The Moving Finger"), an excerpt from the beginning of *The Dark Tower III: The Wastelands* ("The Bear"), a critical overview of his career by A. J. Budrys, and a bibliography of primary and secondary works. Explaining the occasion for this honor—one of the magazine's few one-author issues—publisher-editor Edward L. Ferman simply stated in his editorial, "Stephen King is unique."

In the movie world film devotee Gary Wood surveyed the history of King's filmic adaptations in *Cinefantastique* (cover-dated February 1991 but distributed in November 1990). The subject of three books about his movies, King agreed to cooperate in this retrospective look because, as he explained to Wood, "The idea of doing a piece, an overview on why these films haven't worked, is really interesting to me."

Outside the specialty magazines King received considerable print coverage too. He was viewed not so much as a writer but as an entertainer—a superstar in his own right.

Entertainment Weekly ranked King seventy-ninth in a listing of "The 101 Most Powerful People in Entertainment." He was bracketed between Danielle Steel and Jean Auel, and Rob Reiner and Tom Clancy. And in its 1990 roundup, the weekly ranked King sixth, between M. C. Hammer and Sean Connery.

People Weekly selected King as one of the "20 Who Defined the Decade." The periodical explained, "Love them or loathe them, you couldn't have had the '80s without them," including King, about whom it wrote:

> Nothing is as unstoppable as one of King's furies, except perhaps King's word processor. In this decade alone he has spewed out 15 novels that have sold close to 15 million copies. And what of the unliftable? At 1,138 pages, *IT* weighed in at 3½ pounds.
>
> King's popularity reflects his uncanny ability to exploit the anxieties that swirl around the modern American family. His audience— and his victims—are baby boomers, a generation that has had to reconcile the buoyant fantasies of the '60s with the dismaying realities of the '80s. In King's novels, ordinary people suffer appallingly contemporary fates.

Even ABC-TV, on its news program "Prime Time Live," profiled

Stephen King in "King Fear," in which sales figures of his books figured prominently as the lead-in "factoid" for the story.

But perhaps the most telling—and most important—story ran in the *Publishers Weekly* roundup of "The Top 25 of the '80s: Fiction Bestsellers." Of them, Stephen King claimed seven out of twenty-five—almost one of every four. Ranked according to copies sold and shipped, King's titles were:

2. *The Dark Half,* 1989, at 1,550,000 copies.
3. *The Tommyknockers,* 1987, at 1,429,929 copies.
10. *IT,* 1986, at 1,115,000 copies.
15. *Misery,* 1987, 875,000 copies.
17. *The Talisman,* 1984, 830,000 copies.
22. *The Eyes of the Dragon,* 1987, 750,000 copies.
25. *Skeleton Crew,* 1985, 720,000 copies.

It appears that King will very likely dominate the '90s too. *Four Past Midnight,* after four months, had 1.7 million copies in print—a record.

Like the Gunslinger in the *Dark Tower* books, King moved on just as 1990 drew to an end; and with it, the end of the decade, though one with promise. As the jacket copy of *Four Past Midnight* observed, ". . . the 1980s saw him become America's bestselling writer of fiction. He's glad to be held over into the new decade."

7

The Wastelands—and Beyond

When Donald M. Grant ran announcements in specialty magazines of the forthcoming publication of the third *Dark Tower* book, speculation ran rampant about its cost and print run; rumors, like sparrows, began to fly. In Grant's full-page ad opposite the contents page of the Stephen King *F&SF* issue, Grant provided only enough information to whet the appetite:

> The publishers of the first two *Dark Tower* volumes and the collector's editions of *The Talisman* and *Christine,* are proud to announce the early 1991 publication of *The Dark Tower III: The Wastelands.* Please send us your name and address to get the full-color prospectus (now in preparation) . . . .

Mindful of the early sellouts of the previous *Dark Tower* books, concerned readers immediately contacted Grant, to confirm that they were on his mailing list. In March Grant mailed out a color flyer to his customers. He explained:

> We have been inundated with calls and letters concerning the long-awaited third book in Stephen King's *Dark Tower* series. We have even had to return premature deposit checks from collectors concerned about early sell-out. At this time—by way of assurance to those collectors who wish to confirm the fact that they will receive a copy of this eagerly-awaited hardcover book—*we are now accepting orders!*
> *The Dark Tower III: The Wastelands* is currently undergoing revision by Mr. King. This third book in the series . . . contains 12 full color illustrations, including 10 double-page spreads, by brilliant artist Ned Dameron. Available in a signed and numbered deluxe edition [1,200 copies, $120] as well as a trade edition [40,000, $38].

Predictably, demand for the limited edition, numbered and signed by author and artist, exceeded supply. Of that print run, 800 were reserved for those who had bought the limited edition of *Dark Tower II: The Drawing of the Three;* the remaining 400 copies went into a general lottery for anyone who wanted to take a chance.

In his introduction to "Secret Window, Secret Garden" in *Four Past Midnight,* King said that the act of writing is analogous to looking through "an almost forgotten window, a window which offers a common view from an entirely different angle . . . an angle which renders the common extraordinary. The writer's job is to gaze through that window and report on what he sees."

King continued, "But sometimes windows break. I think that, more than anything else, is the concern of this story: what happens to the wide-eyed observer when the window between reality and unreality breaks and the glass begins to fly?"

The story begins with the narrator confronted by a man on his doorstep who matter-of-factly tells him: "You stole my story and something's got to be done about it. Right is right and fair is fair and something has to be done."

Life imitated art as Anne Hiltner of Trenton, New Jersey, seemingly stepped from the pages of King's story into his life . . . and the glass began to fly.

In the April 18, 1991, edition of the *Daily Press* (Newport News, Virginia), a short news item headlined "Woman Sues King" told the story:

> A woman is suing author Stephen King claiming the horror novelist plagiarized from her writings and based a character in *Misery* on her.
>
> Anne Hiltner also claims King burglarized her home and stole manuscripts, including ones for his best-selling novel, *Misery.* King's attorney angrily denied the allegations.
>
> Hiltner, of Princeton, is seeking damages, a share in book profits, and its removal from store shelves.
>
> She claims King stole in 1986 or 1987 eight copyrighted manuscripts written either by her or her brother, James Hiltner.
>
> Hiltner charges the author incorporated parts of her unpublished works into *Misery.*

King's hometown newspaper, the *Bangor Daily News,* provided additional information about Anne Hiltner. John Ripley of the *News* staff wrote:

> Anne Hiltner is suing King in New Jersey courts, alleging that the Bangor author broke into her home and a rented storage facility to

steal her work. She also claims that King flew over her home in an airplane and eavesdropped with listening devices.

Hiltner, who has been sending letters to King for a decade, also alleges the Wilkes character in *Misery* is based on her life.

In an August 1990 letter to the NEWS, Hiltner claimed she was a "victim of five assaultive books by Stephen King, and over 150 burglaries by King in 1990 alone."

Hiltner said in the rambling, unpublished letter that she had filed criminal complaints against King last July with the Bangor Police Department, and that King had called her last August. She also complained of receiving little help from Bangor police.

The Bangor police department would not comment on the matter. The department was, understandably, more concerned about Erik Keene of San Antonio, Texas, who, according to the *Bangor Daily News,* had been haunting King's business office and King's residence in the Historic District. Keene "told police . . . he had planned to do something to gain publicity."

On April 18, 1991, Keene went to the Kings' business office. According to the *News,* "Marsha DeFilippo, who works in the office, said Keene wanted King to help him write a book. That's a fairly common request, but DeFilippo said it appeared that Keene was agitated and angry. Keene wanted King to buy him a pair of contact lenses, house him for a couple of months and keep him supplied with cigarettes and beer."

"He had become enough of a concern that I told a couple of people who work with me to call the police if he came back around," Stephen King told the *News* later.

Two days later Keene returned, but King wasn't around; he and one of his sons were in Philadelphia attending a basketball game. Feeling ill, Tabitha King elected to stay behind. She was home alone when, at 6:00 A.M., she "heard glass breaking in the kitchen." She thought "it was the glass cupboard over the sink and . . . the cat had gotten up there."

Instead of her cat, she saw Keene. "I didn't have time to be scared," Tabitha told the *News* later. "He moved away from me toward the TV room. I was just shocked. My body was already making the decision for me. I was already headed toward the door before he told me he had a bomb."

Dressed in pajamas, Tabitha fled the house and, from a neighbor's house, called the police. Sealing off the street, the police went in with a canine unit to sniff out Keene, who was discovered in the attic. The "hand-held detonator unit" Keene had was only some "cardboard and some electronic parts from a calculator."

"I wanted to get into that attic. I did exactly what I planned to do by going up to that room. I looked at it as compensation for all the effort I went to," Keene later told the *News,* who asked what he would have done if the police hadn't found him.

"I don't know what I would have done, but it's an amusing thing to contemplate, isn't it?" Keene mused.

According to the *News,* Keene was "on parole from Dallas County in Texas for theft." The *News* also reported that "the Texas man said he has been diagnosed as a schizophrenic and said he has spent years taking drugs prescribed by doctors who have treated him." As to motive, the *News* reported, "Keene said he wants to write a book with King. He said he is tired of being poor and said he has been discriminated against because he suffered from a mental handicap."

Charged with burglary and terrorizing, Keene was later arraigned and indicted for the incident in the Penobscot County Superior Court, where, according to the *News,* "he pleaded innocent to a burglary charge and innocent by reason of insanity to a terrorizing charge."

According to the *News,* "Keene said he has many troubles. He added he has a lot of things planned if he ever gets out of jail. He said if he gets out he will give King a present 'from the macabre.' He said the present was something his grandmother gave him before she died."

In the aftermath of the incident that Keene termed "my little episode of terror," Stephen King told the *News* that, "after all, we've lived here for 12 years and this is the first time somebody has tried to plant a bomb in the attic." Refusing to be a prisoner of his own success, King told the paper that he was rarely hassled by locals; it was always the "outsiders" that provided the serious harassment. "Usually those people write, but they don't show up," King said. "I don't want to live like Michael Jackson or like Elvis did at Graceland. That's gross. It was bad enough when we had to put up a fence. It was worse when we had to put up a gate. I hate to think I have to keep that gate locked."

After the incident, about which the Kings were understandably not keen, the *News* reported that "security at their house . . . will be increased."

Later that month, as reported in an Associated Press story, Stephen King appeared at the Landmark Theater in Syracuse, New York, and spoke to an estimated three thousand fans who had bought $35 tickets to his talk through Ticketron, which normally handles rock concerts—appropriate, since King, a rock and roll fan, is a superstar in his own right.

As King told the crowd—hundreds of which brought copies of books to be signed, though that opportunity did not present itself—he was "a lightning rod" for his fans. "I had one drop by to visit my wife last week."

King then read an excerpt from his forthcoming novel, *Needful Things*.

Although *Needful Things* is scheduled for release in October 1991, the $24.95 novel has already been selected as a Book-of-the-Month Club main selection (in September), with an unabridged, three-part audiotape in the works to be read by King himself (in November), and a movie adaptation by Rob Reiner's Castle Rock Entertainment to follow.

According to an Associated Press story, King "said Castle Rock had become something of a safe haven for him, a place where the people were well known to him and he could forget about the troubles of excessive fame."

But Castle Rock is no longer a haven. It is, as the book's subtitle indicates, "The Last Castle Rock Story," and the story is now told. With *The Dark Half* and "The Sun Dog," *Needful Things* completes what King called his "Castle Rock Trilogy—if you please—the *last* Castle Rock stories." Said King:

> *Needful Things* is about buying and selling American. I don't know how to put it any other way. I've written about Castle Rock a lot, this little town, and the idea of the book is simply that a new shop opens in town. The name of this new shop is Needful Things, and it's sort of like a curio shop, but not quite, and it's kind of like a used appliances and knickknack shop, but not quite, and the proprietor is Mr. Leland Gaunt from Akron, Ohio, who seems really nice, but not really. The upshot is that whatever you want most in the world to buy is in that shop—and you can have it, if you'll pay for it. So in that respect, I guess it has something in common with the Faust story. And I guess I'm interested in how much people will pay for the things . . . I'm not so interested in how much people will pay for the things they *need* as for the things they think they really *want*.

Precisely because King knew the town *too* well, he felt it was time to leave it behind:

> It's easy to dig yourself a rut and furnish it. I've done that a little bit in Castle Rock. Going back to Castle Rock for me has been like going

home and slipping into an old smoking jacket or an old pair of bluejeans and settling down. After a while, I started to feel excessively comfortable in Castle Rock—I don't think that's a good state for a novelist to be in, particularly if you're in my situation and you've sold a lot of books, if you're not going to be wary of bloat, your effective half-life is going to be very short indeed, because let's face it: When you become extremely popular and you command extremely big bucks, bloat sets in no matter what you do. I'm just trying to postpone it as long as possible . . . .

According to the publisher, the plot is in a sense King's version of Thornton Wilder's play *Our Town,* though clearly a walk on the wild side. In its fall 1991 book catalogue, Viking states:

> Castle Rock, Maine, where Polly Chalmers runs You Sew 'n' Sew and Sheriff Alan Pangborn is in charge of keeping the peace. It's a small town, and Stephen King fans might think they know its secrets pretty well: they've been here before.
>
> Leland Gaunt is a stranger—and he calls his shop Needful Things. Eleven-year-old Brian Rusk is his first customer, and Brian finds just what he wants most in all the world: a '56 Sandy Koufax baseball card. By the end of the week, Mr. Gaunt's business is fairly booming. At Needful Things, there's something for everyone.
>
> And, of course, for everyone there is a price. For Leland Gaunt, the pleasure of doing business lies chiefly in seeing how much people will pay for their most secret dreams and desires. And at Needful Things, the prices are high indeed.
>
> For Alan and Polly, this autumn week will be an awful test—a test of will, desire, and pain. Above all, it will be a true test of their ability to grasp the true nature of their enemy. They may have a chance. . . . But maybe not, because, as Mr. Gaunt knows, almost everything is for sale: love, hope, even the human soul.

A 639-page novel, the plot of *Needful Things*—as bookseller Grover DeLuca pointed out—is that of "The Distributor," a short story collected in Richard Matheson's *Collected Stories,* for which King had contributed a nonfiction piece.

Completed—according to King's note at novel's end—on January 28, 1991, *Needful Things* is King writing with a sureness that could only come from knowing Castle Rock as a long-time resident. In fact, it's especially appropriate in this case, since King as an unnamed fictional narrator addresses the reader directly in the preface to the novel—he sits himself down on the steps of the bandstand in the Town Common and points out the passersby of the town.

Recalling 'Salem's Lot, Needful Things is a rich and satisfying read told with an authoritative storytelling voice that is King's distinctive trademark. Fictionally, King has come full circle with this novel: he has thoroughly explored the Maine milieu, and it's time for him to move on.

While Needful Things may initially appear to be a metaphor for the price King has had to pay for success—an idea King emphatically rejects—it cannot be denied that King has, indeed, paid a high price for his writer's life free from financial worry: that price is a complete lack of privacy. As King told an interviewer recently:

> Probably the worst of it is that the phone rings all the time and people drive by the house and take pictures and there's a lot of mail to be answered. It seems like a lot of people want something. They want a piece of you . . . . You want to help as many people as you can, but you come to the awareness that if you do that, there won't be anything left for yourself . . . . The best part of all this is that I know I can do what I love doing for the rest of my life, or as long as I'm capable of doing it. At this point, unless something drastic happens, I won't have to worry about painting houses or throwing cases of Coke up on a Coca-Cola truck. I can write. Even if nobody reads it, I can write.

Comfortable with the notion of bringing out one major book a year through his trade publisher, King, it seems, is pacing himself like a runner in a marathon—not a race to the finish, but a race over the long haul.

But all the attention paid to King—as a writer, as a figure in the film community, as a celebrity (to his dismay) in his own right—means that books about him will continue to be written. Making his point clear in a letter to a specialty publisher, King wrote that insofar as books about him were concerned, his personal life and unpublished works should not be discussed; only the *published* works should be fair game.

King, on the surface an advocate of New Criticism, appears not to want what he perceives as intrusions into his life through book-length studies, especially when it means looking at him and not his work. In King's case, however, it's simply impossible to separate the man from his work, his life and values from the fiction.

In an interview, King once said, with emphasis, "What comes out of your fiction is what you live." In King's case, the life *is* the work, and the work *is* the life; consequently, New Criticism becomes a literary exercise in futility:

. . . New Criticism insisted on close reading of the text and awareness of verbal nuance and thematic (rather than narrative) organization, and was not concerned with the biographical or social backgrounds of works of art. The text existed as a text on a page, an object in itself, with its own structure, which should be explored in its own terms; inquiries into the writer's personality or motivation were considered largely illegimate or irrelevant.

Which brings us to the question about literary propriety and impropriety.

With the explosion in what *Newsweek* termed "the boom in trash biography," in the aftermath of Kitty Kelley's biography on former first lady Nancy Reagan, Stephen King is understandably concerned. After all, muses the public, what skeletons lurk in *his* closet?

J. R. R. Tolkien, the subject of unwanted attention and public scrutiny after *The Lord of the Rings* became a cult classic, knew the phenomenon all too well. As Lin Carter wrote:

[Tolkien] finds the attentions of his enthusiastic following rather embarrassing and his notoriety a bit of a bore. He particularly feels that studies of his work (such, I presume, as this one) to be an annoyance. He feels they are premature. When asked if he approved of this sort of intensive research, he replied: "I do not, while I am alive anyhow." He went on to say that he has read some of these studies, "and they are very bad, most of them; they are nearly all either psychological analyses or they try to go into the sources, and I think most of them rather vain efforts."

Justin Kaplan, author of *Mr. Clemens and Mark Twain,* and *Walt Whitman: A Life,* maintains that "no biographer, even the best disposed and admiring, who has any gumption and integrity can be altogether a friend to the person he or she is writing about. The subject sees a life one way, the writer sees it another."

Arguing a case for unauthorized biographies, he wrote: "I think there is something salutary even in carnival excess when it concerns people we know mainly through the work of spin doctors, damage controllers, speechwriters and stage managers of pseudo-events and photo ops. I'd guess that the more we are presented with public-relations figments the more likely we are to get into a feeding frenzy over inside stories. . . ."

In King's case—in which the public sees him at his best, agreeably signing books until his hand cramps up, speaking to enthusiastic audiences who pay up to $35 to see him for two hours, appearing in carefully managed interviews in the media—the image of the Maine-hick-turned-entertainment-industry has prompted an enormous curiosity about the man *behind* the work, on the assumption that there's got to be more to King.

In this instance, the readers questing for the "real" King are bound to be disappointed because King is as he appears to be. As several of his friends have pointed out in numerous interviews, King is the real McCoy: an ideal, genuine man who, despite his success, has kept his roots, and in the face of success that has warped other bestselling authors has managed to remain free from affectation. He's a hard-working writer who paid his dues and has done it largely on his own, a generous and gracious gentleman who has kept things in perspective, even as his fans—especially the more sycophantic—and his detractors have not. David Bright, a long-time King friend, wrote in *Castle Rock* that King "talks the same, looks the same, and generally conducts his life the same as he did back in the late 1960's. . . ."

There's King the writer, whom we "know" through the work. There's King the family man, whom we know not at all. And there's King the private man—driven by whatever demons haunt him—whom we rarely see: the man behind the growing body of Maine myth, the man who, as childhood friend Chris Chesley said, is the *real* story. As Chesley told Stephen Spignesi in an interview, "My thoughts are that the real Stephen King is much more interesting than the external myth that surrounds him now. To me, there are reasons why he's had the success that he has, and those reasons are much more interesting than any attempt to glamorize him—to attribute a 'luster' to him."

Ironically, said Chesley, King has a "sense of himself as being outside the mainstream, outside the American suburban middle class ethos," though he is clearly an embodiment of the middle-class American dream—he has become rich and famous, an appropriate subject for Robin Leach's television show, though it's very unlikely he would agree to be profiled.

Precisely because of his wealth and fame, King has necessarily barricaded himself in Bangor, where, he remarked, it's sufficiently far away from everything that you must really want to make the trip to see him—if he allows you to visit.

King even conducts much business off-screen, so to speak. When CBS executives were working on a 1991 made-for-TV adaptation of King's story "Sometimes They Come Back," Jonathan Levin, CBS vice president of drama development, told *USA Today:* "We do business with him like no one else. We don't talk direct, he doesn't come down, we get mysterious faxes from his lair in Maine."

Occasionally, though, King breaks the silence, as he did for a rare appearance at the annual bookseller's convention, held in 1991 in New York City over the Memorial Day weekend and the first four days of June. On June 2, King—in the company of southern writer Dr. Ferrol Sams and Gloria Steinem—dominated the author's breakfast held at the New York Hilton, where an estimated twenty-five hundred con attendees paid $35 to eat crepes and bacon, but mostly to hear King talk.

King was by far the most popular speaker, and his presence drew hundreds of fans who, before breakfast, went up to the head table for photographs, autographs (none given), and one-on-one conversation. Despite the mob scene, King appeared calm, relaxed, and except for giving autographs accommodating.

Following breakfast, King, in the company of Gloria Steinem, gave a short press conference, in which he talked about his own success, the things that really scared him, and commented on *American Psycho*.

A woman in the audience lamented that it's nearly impossible for a first-time author to get a book published, and asked King what could be done to increase the possibilities of first publication. King replied:

> I'm not sure what you do about it. [As to] my own success: I was lucky enough to have a book that was adapted into a film that was a success. I've always wondered but I don't wonder very deeply if *Carrie* the film had been a failure if I would be anywhere where I am today. I'd like to think so, but who knows? I think it's something of a crapshoot, but I'll tell you one thing I do believe is that talent almost always finds the light, even today; and I think if you need proof of that, all you need to do is look at Amy Tan [author of *The Joy Luck Club*], who's a fantastic success story and deserves every bit of it. I just wish as many people as know Amy Tan knew Katherine Dunn, who wrote *Geek Love*.

One reporter, presumably from the *New York Times*, asked King, "What do you read when you want to be frightened?" King looked her straight in the eye and, perhaps catching her name tag, said, "The *New York Times*," which brought a round of laughter from the audience.

Somewhat miffed, the reporter said, "Play it straight. Answer the question."

King played it straight and elaborated:

> The answer is the answer that I gave. I think that the things that scare me are reading about what's happening to the environment, the destruction of the rain forest. I still wish that I didn't know the statis-

tics about the constant rate at which it's disappearing and what's happening to the atmosphere of the planet as a result. And I think what's
worse is this sort of existential comedy of knowing we are denuding
these forests in order to make more grasslands to make more cows so
McDonalds can make more hamburgers, so Ronald McDonald can
ride on the plane next to me. We're destroying the Earth for Ronald
McDonald—think about it.

And they say *I* write horror.

Because King was seated next to Gloria Steinem, one reporter citing
their proximity asked him what, in light of the explosion of horror and
violence against women, was his reaction to *American Psycho*? King replied:

American Psycho is a disturbing book. It's disturbing because it's very
difficult for me to separate my feelings of revulsion about what's
going on in the book, and the violence that's not just directed toward
women—the violence in the book is directed toward the homeless,
toward men, toward women, toward animals, across an entire spec-
trum. It's hard for me to separate that from my pervasive feeling that
something is really going on in that book, that Bret Easton Ellis is
trying very hard to express an entire attitude of an entire alienated
culture. The people in the book are extremely nasty—all of them are
extremely nasty—yet there is a ring of reality in that book that can't
be denied. At the same time, whatever he did, I don't feel he succeeded at it very well, and I think that in order to find out what Bret
Easton Ellis was reaching for, you have to go back to some of the great
naturalistic Grove Press books in the late fifties and sixties. I'm
thinking of *City of Night* and *The Last Exit to Brooklyn*.

So my feelings about the book are ambivalent, but ambivalent on
the downside.

After the short press conference King went to the exhibition hall of the
convention and headed to the New American Library booth. As he made
his way, people gathered behind him, following him in a long, growing
train. Towering over most of the people, and wearing a white jacket, King
stood out. People in the crowd pointed to him and said, "Look! That's
Stephen King!"

It appeared that King wanted to make the rounds and see people from
NAL but found himself accommodating the fans who had suddenly arrived with books in hand. Cornered at a stand-up table, he patiently
signed promotional Castle Rock postcards, promotional *Cujo* facemasks,
and copies of books.

That evening King attended a closed party at Cafe Society. There, according to a *Washington Post* reporter, King took to the stage with John Cafferty and the Beaver Brown Band:

> At the jamboree for Stephen King, held in a downtown club with tighter security than a presidential candidate gets, the band was loud enough to jump start your heart. Around midnight came the moment: King, a frustrated rocker, got up, grabbed a guitar and played (passably) and sang (too softly) "Twist and Shout" and "Whole Lotta Shakin' Goin' On."

For King, the ABA convention seemed the appropriate place and time to reflect on his career. So much had changed from the early days when King finally made that first sale. As Joyce Meskis introduced him to the breakfast crowd:

> It was the first work of a man who in catering to a public's worst nightmares would become a publisher's dream. It was the start of a record-breaking career that would redefine a genre and would push publishing into numbers that movie producers dream about. The book was *Carrie* and the author was Stephen King.
>
> Seventeen years and a phenomenal thirty books later, Stephen King has over 150 million copies of his books sold, and [had] a record five books on the various *New York Times* bestseller lists simultaneously last winter.
>
> His catalog of novels reads like a "Who's Who" of the horror world: *It, Four Past Midnight, Misery, The Dark Half, The Stand*, and *Needful Things.*
>
> But how has King managed to grasp the minds and raise the blood pressure of the world's readers so consistently? How is he able to make us care about killer clowns, malevolent cars, pet cemeteries and their remains? Why is he so incredibly popular? It isn't just great writing, although he is a great writer; it is perhaps we tend to think of him as ours—America's Horror Writer Laureate. [King reacts—hits table with fist; silverware clatters.] Where he leads, we gleefully follow. And whatever he writes, no matter how outrageous, we believe it.

King had become America's literary boogeyman, as he once styled himself. The once invisible man had become very visible indeed. He observed:

> Writers, novelists in particular, are actually supposed to be secret agents. We're supposed to be observers, but not observed. We're

supposed to look around, record these things with our unblinking gimlet eyes, and take it back for the delectation of the rest—particularly a guy like me who lives with one foot in the twilight zone most of the time. And it used to be that way. I did not used to be a recognizable face.

But King's face and name are so recognizable that today he need not ask, as he did in the American Express commercial, "Do you know me?" Everyone, it seems, knows Stephen King.

For King, who realized the American dream by making the American nightmare a popular obsession worldwide, the success has, in the end, meant only one thing. As he told the booksellers at the convention: "You are the people who have allowed me to do for money what I would otherwise have done for free anyway."

Fame and fortune have their rewards, but in the end, to a genuine writer, only the work matters. King, who charted his own path to success, has never lost sight of what made it all possible: " . . . the writer's job is to write, and there are no brand names in the little room where the typewriter or the pen and notebook sit waiting. There are no stars or brand names in that place; only people who will try to create something out of nothing, and those who succeed and those who fail."

In the end, Stephen King, an ideal, genuine writer, stands alone.

8

Stephen King
in the Heart of Darkness

The Art of Writing

The novelist is, after all, God's liar, and if he does his job well, keeps his head and his courage, he can sometimes find the truth that lives at the center of the lie.
—Stephen King, Danse Macabre

If you watch an artist at work, surrounded by paints and brushes and the other tools of his trade, you would not presume that he without extensive and specialized training could create a painting worthy of hanging in a gallery. On the other hand, if you watch a writer at work, there is an almost universal presumption that because the tools of the trade are so commonplace—twenty-six letters and a handful of punctuation marks—the art of writing is a God-given talent, an innate skill. The result: magazine and book publishers are flooded with unsolicited, mostly unpublishable, manuscripts by wannabe writers; they think that if they can write a letter, they can write a publishable short story or a novel. Their most erroneous assumption, though, is that in fiction the *idea* is the story; that, they think, is all it takes.

Amy Tan, author of *The Joy Luck Club,* penned her experiences after the success of her first novel. In "Angst & the Second Novel" she wrote: "Thanks but no thanks to the five or six people who offered to let me write their complete life stories, 50/50 on the royalties since I was already a proven author." More typically, these people say: I'm not a writer like you, but I've got this *terrific* idea for a story, so I'll tell it to you. You can write it down, and we can split the profits, fifty-fifty!

An idea is not a story, as any professional writer will tell you. Besides, most writers have far too many stories to tell on their own. Writers simply don't need, or want, more ideas.

From the well intentioned and the curious, the question is frequently asked of writers: Where do you get your ideas? If you have to ask *that* question, you'll never be a writer. *Never.* King is frequently asked that question. Most often the query presupposes that ideas come from a specific place—a retail store catering to writers where ideas are sold like six-packs.

The question is meaningless because writers get their ideas from all over; everything is grist for the mill. In time and with luck, the irritating grain of an idea will, with the application of imagination, result in a pearl of a story.

When asked *the* question, King has in the past responded humorously ("I get them from the lord Satan"), sometimes even citing a specific location ("I get mine from Utica [New York]"). But when he answers honestly, he'll admit there is no easy, pat answer. In his essay "On the Shining and Other Perpetrations" he wrote: "Twenty different sexual encounters may result in twenty different children, and twenty different ideas may result in twenty different books, brothers and sisters, but each individual in itself. There is no idea-bin, no general case, so the writer is left groping, trying to answer an unanswerable question without looking too dumb."

As King explained, "A story or a novel is, after all, only a chain of coherent imaginative thoughts tied together with occasional bursts of that mysterious nerve-lightning we call creativity."

In King's case, some of his stories begin with a single image vividly imagined. King then takes that image and plays with it, until a story *explains* that image. For instance, in "The Langoliers," a novella in *Four Past Midnight,* King wrote, "With 'The Langoliers,' that image was of a woman pressing her hand over a crack in the wall of a commercial jet-liner. . . . It got so I could even smell that woman's perfume (it was L'Envoi), see her green eyes, and hear her rapid, frightened breathing."

From that image came a story of a jetliner that inadvertently found its way into the twilight zone, and the courageous airline captain who would guide the survivors out—if he could.

In other cases, King has asked himself this question, What if? Like most writers, King is a woolgatherer by nature and has generated many stories and novels by answering that question. For instance: What if vampires came to small-town Maine? (*'Salem's Lot*). What if a superflu ran rampant throughout the world? (*The Stand*). What if a car fell apart after its odometer ran backward? (*Christine*). As King explained *The Dark Half:* "For a while I started to think, 'Suppose Bachman wasn't dead?' And immediately the idea jumped to mind: What if a guy had a pen name that didn't want to stay dead and isn't that an interesting idea and how would that work out?"

As King informed *W•B,* a Waldenbooks store publication, being a writer means moving between two separate worlds: the real world and the imaginary world. Storytellers have two addresses; King's other address, as he has stated, is in the twilight zone:

> I took my daughter to see "Les Miserables" in New York and I was just transported by the play. But somewhere toward the end of the second act, I dropped out entirely . . . . I was hypnotized. I didn't want to be at the play anymore. I wanted to write all this stuff down. But usually it's not that hard to go back and forth because writers are fantasizers and daydreamers by nature and we slip in and out of that world fairly effortlessly. I wouldn't like to get caught in that world though.

Taking that idea and developing it into a story or novel is the art of writing. However, the art of fiction is taking that idea and making it a vivid reading experience with emotional content and the verisimilitude of life.

In the end, as Robert Bloch wrote in "Heritage of Horror," an essay about H. P. Lovecraft:

> "Sick" or healthy, all creative activity—including writing—is the product of individual imagination, colored by personal viewpoint, an attitude towards life. And it seems generated by an intense desire or need to communicate with others.

For King, the process of writing itself is not important. Peter Straub, who collaborated with King on *The Talisman,* said in a *Castle Rock* interview: "By now, I really am sick of questions about word processors, since that seems to me to focus on the least interesting aspect of writing fiction." Still, it's what people can grasp. It's much harder to divine the nature of creativity.

King, like most writers, has worked out his daily writer's routine. In the mornings he writes the serious work, the books under contract. Typically, after rising King takes a walk, comes back to the office in his home, drinks a tall glass of water, turns on the stereo with loud rock music, and slips into his fantasy world as effortlessly as one dons slippers. He'll write for two or three hours a day, producing six to eight typewritten, double-spaced pages—fifteen hundred or two thousand words in first draft. If King works steadily, this will produce an average of two long novels a year, King's average over the past eighteen years, if you total up the published books and the wordage of the uncollected fiction, nonfiction, and screen-plays.

Like Faulkner, King writes only when the spirit moves him, but it moves him almost every day. Moreover, the method of writing doesn't affect his output. King has written longhand in school notebooks while on airplanes and on one occasion on location at a movie set (*The Cannibals*). He has written novels on the typewriter (*Misery*). He has written novels on his Wang word processor. If bedridden, one suspects he would dictate his stories—the compulsion is so strong.

Typically, King does not outline, though he did with *The Talisman,* because of the collaborative effort. An intuitive writer by nature who trusts his ability to improvise as he goes along, King invents his fictional world on the fly. It recalls *Who Framed Roger Rabbit,* in which actor Bob Hoskins as a gumshoe drives toward Toontown; on the horizon a cartoon landscape forms out of nowhere, as he drives closer. Childhood friend and literary collaborator Chris Chesley said that when he watched King write, one page would naturally lead to the next.

King explained to Charles Platt, in a 1983 interview for *Dream Makers: Volume II,* that each novel is worked through several drafts:

> I like to write three drafts: a first, a second, and what I think of as the editorial draft, when I sit down and take an editor's criticism and work it through in my mind, and put the whole book through the typewriter again, and repolish the other stuff as well. But as the successes have mushroomed, it's been tougher and tougher for me to get my editors to give me the time to do that third draft. What I'm really afraid of now is that one of them will say, 'I think this is great,' just because it fits the publication schedule.

Another problem, King pointed out to Platt, is that with his economic success comes editorial clout, presenting a dilemma:

> I think that if there was any change suggested to me that I didn't want, all I would need to say would be, "No, I won't do that." And it would never be a question of their withdrawing my contract, would it? They'd just finally say, "Well, okay then, don't do it that way." Which means, in effect, that if I'm willing to be really intransigent, there'll be no editing at all."

King concluded: "It's a terrible position to be in. I think I just have to resolve to take editing, even if I think the changes are wrong. To do otherwise is to become a monster and claim that I'm doing it right, and I don't need any criticism, editorial help, or guidance. And I can't do that."

In looking at King's books, you can sometimes see the presence of the book editor. Doubleday's William Thompson did a commendable job in editing King's early novels. Both agreed that *Carrie* benefited from the necessary editorial touch. And on *The Shining,* which lost its lengthy prologue and epilogue, King wrote, "I agreed willingly enough, and . . . I don't regret the decision. . . ." Yet the cuts did have a detrimental effect. In the restored edition, *The Stand* became deeper, richer, and more complex, as reviewers have noted.

King's later books vary in quality. Notably, *Misery* and *The Tommyknockers* show the difference between listening to the editor (*Misery*) and not listening hard enough (*The Tommyknockers*). Even though the reader may not always notice the presence of the editor, the writer does; a good editor sees what the author has *tried* to do in the book, and helps him find the perfect words and perhaps improve the structure.

With King, as with any writer, sometimes the work comes easily, sometimes not. When the muse visits King, it's not the image most people have in mind. As he told *Time:*

> People think the muse is a literary character, some cute little pudgy devil who floats around the head of the creative person sprinkling fairy dust. Well, mine's a guy with a flattop in coveralls who looks like Jack Webb and says, "All right, you son of a bitch, time to get to work."

A short story is a snapshot in time. A novella is a short movie. And a novel, a long movie. All are slices in time. When the work comes easily to King, he sees the story on a continuum, with a history that precedes the story, the story itself, and its future history. *The Shining* is a good example, with "Before the Play" recounting the history of the hotel, and "After the Play" relating what happened after the story ends and the Overlook Hotel burned to the ground.

Sometimes, though, the work doesn't come easily. One example, as King explained in *Danse Macabre,* was his attempt to write *The House on Value Street,* an aborted novel:

> I gathered my research materials . . . and then I attacked the novel. I attacked it from one side and nothing happened. I tried it from another side and felt it was going pretty well until I discovered all my characters sounded as if they had just stepped whole and sweaty from the dance marathon in Horace McCoy's *They Shoot Horses, Don't They?*

I tried it *in medias res*. I tried to imagine it as a stage play, a trick that sometimes works for me when I'm badly stuck. It didn't work this time.

When King is not ready to tell the tale, the words don't come. But when he's ready, he finds the words, as he explained in the afterword to the first volume of his epic *The Dark Tower:* " . . . I'm never completely sure where I'm going, and in this story that is even more true than usual . . . . But what of the gunslinger's murky past? God, I know so little. The revolution that topples the gunslinger's 'world of light'? I don't know. . . . When it's time, those things—and their relevance to the gunslinger's quest—will roll out as naturally as tears or laughter."

That, I think, capsulates King's storytelling process. Although he may generally know his destination, the journey itself is one of discovery. In this case, it's particularly apt, since we can see King's journey as a storyteller not unlike that of Roland the Gunslinger, who has embarked on a journey toward an end he cannot foresee.

Ralph Vincinanza—King's foreign rights agent—assessed King's career in three phases, according to *Publishers Weekly:* phase one, the 1970s, when King was a paperback bestseller, when hardback sales capped at 50,000 with *The Shining* and *The Stand;* phase two, the early 1980s, when King began to gain momentum as a brand name in hardback, selling hundreds of thousands of copies, topping 657,000 with *Pet Sematary;* phase three, from 1983 on, when King began selling in record numbers, with *The Talisman* up through *Four Past Midnight,* which had 1.7 million copies in print within four months after initial release. (*Needful Things,* King's forthcoming book, will have a first printing of 1.5 million copies.)

Clearly, there is a need that King is satisfying with his fiction. Unlike other bestselling authors, King cuts a wide swath among his diverse and faithful readership: a cult audience, a mass audience, a growing academic audience made up of people of all ages. Part of it is surely that King's fiction offers something for everyone. To his cult audience, he offers the limited editions and esoteric material. To his mass audience, he offers a steady diet of compulsively readable fiction, book after book, averaging two a year. To his academic audience, he offers a rich vein for academic tapping. To teenagers, he offers a horripilating roller-coaster ride. And to those old enough to have forgotten what it is like to be a child, King's stories—like "The Body" and *IT*—re-create the sense of wonder of childhood with aching nostalgia.

Part of King's accessibility is that his fiction is not literary fiction. You don't have a sense that you are *reading* fiction; instead, there is a strong sense that you are *hearing* a tale. It is a kind of immediacy that recalls the oral, not written, tradition of storytelling. It is as if you were sitting around a campfire at night, with King spinning the yarn. (" 'What's this story?' Vern asked uneasily. 'It ain't a horror story, is it, Gordie? I don't think I want to hear no horror stories. I'm not up for that, man' "—from "The Body.")

More than anything else, King's commitment to the idea of story—the necessity to capture and hold the reader's attention—makes his tales compulsively readable. As King wrote in his foreword to *Night Shift:* "All my life as a writer I have been committed to the idea that in fiction the story value holds dominance over every other facet of the writer's craft; characterization, theme, mood, none of those things is anything if the story is dull."

No matter what King writes—in his conversational, informal style, which makes it easy for the reader to "fall" through the page—the narrative moves the story right along, much like a stripped car with a turbocharged engine. King employs a transparent writing style with a limitless range. He has a fictional voice capable of telling any kind of story.

Part of King's success is the honesty with which he approaches his craft. Inspired by the naturalist writers, King holds a mirror up to life and sees a world where bad things happen to good people, as one popular book suggests. It's a grim world, a dark but realistic vision that offers cold comfort. King explains:

> I'm not afraid of spiraling down into a very unpleasant conclusion.
> Partly because I think life sometimes does that, and also because I
> was really impressed by the American naturalists and the British
> naturalists when I was in high school and college. People like Thomas
> Hardy, Theodore Dreiser and Frank Norris. Even people like Ray-
> mond Chandler seemed very naturalistic to me. They all say the same
> thing: Things are not ever going to get any better, and if you want to
> see how things go, just think about what's going to happen to you.

Death, in the end, awaits us, as King well knows. How, then, can we become accustomed to our own mortality at the end of the road? The answer is simple, says King: "We're afraid of the body under the sheet. It's our body. And the great appeal of horror fiction through the ages is that it serves as a rehearsal for our own deaths."

In an interview for *Fangoria* King explained his own popularity as a matter of timing. When he came on the literary scene in the mid–seventies, the way had been paved by the success of *The Exorcist* (a 1971 novel published in hardback, and made into a movie in 1973). Said King:

> I think if I had been publishing twenty years ago, if I had started in the mid-sixties, I would have become a fairly popular writer. If I had been publishing in the mid-fifties, I would have been John D. Mac-Donald. I would have been somebody that twenty million working men knew about, and carried in their back pockets to work, or in their lunch pails to read on their lunch hour or their coffee break . . . . I don't think I could've gotten a hardcover house in hell to look at my stuff if it hadn't been for *The Exorcist* and some of those others.

Even without *The Exorcist,* I think that eventually someone would have recognized King's talent, notwithstanding his credentials as solely a paper-back novelist. As Dean Koontz, in "Breaking Through," observed, in a literary genre, the writing standards are lower because the readers' expec-tations are correspondingly lower. In the horror genre King was the writer who transcended, and permanently transformed, the shape and substance of the field:

> To have a broad sales potential, a book must have scope. It cannot be a simple genre novel of limited ambition. I'm always surprised at writers who produce 70,000-word novels, utilizing the age-old mate-rial of the genre, seeking only to spook or thrill, making no effort to convey a sense of their time and culture, with no clear idea of what they're trying to say—yet convinced that they are writing potential bestsellers if only the "dumb editors" would pay more attention . . . . But to have breakout potential, to reach the much larger pool of readers needed for a book at the top of a publisher's list, your novel must transcend its genre, contain a flame of originality, and bring the material to the reader from a fresh point of view.

As Koontz pointed out, it takes a king-sized talent to enlarge the definition of a genre. Appropriately, in the horror field Stephen King was that writer.

Following in the tradition of writers like the early Bradbury, the early Robert Bloch, Don Robertson, John D. MacDonald, Jack Finney, Charles Beaumont, and Richard Matheson, King brought horror to the suburbs, and in doing so popularized horror as a genre. As King told *Publishers Weekly,* "I have redefined the genre of horror-writing in this country. I'm not trying to say they're great books, mine, but for better or worse I have changed the genre."

Clive Barker echoed King's comments in an interview for *Grimoire:*

"One would have to . . . say that [King's] definition of horror is so broad and so populist that whether he's actually opened a market for the very hard-core horror writer is a moot point. I think his genius is to make horror acceptable, to make it acceptable to read on the train without covering it behind the cover of the new John Updike novel."

Indeed, King is so popular that reviews no longer have any effect on his sales. Although identified with the horror genre, King—as Harlan Ellison and A. J. Budrys have pointed out—has created his own genre, and he is its sole practitioner; nobody else writes material like his. As such, King stands alone. Said Budrys in his essay "Stephen King" in *F&SF*:

> Most of all, I think that trapped inside King is one of the finest writers of our time. I think he understands that, though he may be wrong about when and where that writer emerges, and he may or, more likely, may not, understand what he gave up in order to be a money-maker on this gigantic scale. Most of all, I think he has done an almost unthinkable thing; he has not narrowed down, but rather has expanded the definition of what he is as a writer, to the point where he can say, as no one else can, that he has tried everything and made it work in some sense.

King's range, more than anything else, has made critical assessment difficult, for each person approaches King with his own perspective. King is commonly termed a popular novelist. As such he is perceived in some circles as a writer of only pop literature. The academic community perceives him as a major figure in American horror literature, but not as a writer of note outside those muddied waters. The fan reviewers in the fantasy/science-fiction crowds who read nothing but King lack the background to critique his work; they write instead about their reactions to the work in question—celebrations, not cerebrations. And, predictably, the New York literary establishment sees him as a pop novelist, the shockmeister and schlockmeister of horror.

In the end, as Budrys suggests, King's greatest achievement is that "he is the first writer, ever, to have truly baffled the critics."

King's success, I think, is attributable to three factors. First, King never fails to *deliver;* he doesn't cheat the reader, and doesn't provide comforting escapist stories that divert you from reality. Instead, in many of his better books, he does just the opposite: he makes you face the issue; he makes you look within yourself to find the answers. (If you were Dr. Louis Creed in *Pet Sematary,* what would *you* have done? Let your son die, or try to bring him back to life—and suffer the consequences?)

Second, King is passionate about the craft of writing, and that shows up in the work. As he wrote about his stories in his foreword to *Night Shift,* "I didn't write them for money; I wrote them because it occurred to me to write them. I have a marketable obsession. . . . I am not a great artist, but I have always felt impelled to write."

Third, there is King's serious intent. He takes his work seriously, though he does not take himself too seriously. As King wrote in his introduction to "The Sun Dog":

> The fact is, almost all of the stuff I have written—and that includes a lot of the funny stuff—was written in a serious frame of mind . . . . I do what I do for the most serious reasons: love, money, and obsession. The tale of the irrational is the sanest way I know of expressing the world in which I live. These tales have served me as instruments of both metaphor and morality. . . . I am no one's National Book Award or Pulitzer Prize winner, but I'm serious, all right. If you don't believe anything else, believe this: when I take you by your hand and begin to talk, my friend, I believe every word I say.

As King has said before, he wants to achieve popular and critical success—every writer's dream. As *Publishers Weekly* noted:

> King says he always wanted to "build a bridge between wide popularity and a critical acceptance. But my taste is too low, there is a broad streak of the *vulgate,* not the 'vulgar,' in my stuff. But that is the limitations of my background, and one of my limitations as a writer. I've got a lot of great things out of a small amount of talent."

Out of King's "small amount of talent" have issued the "great things" associated with success. He is the highest paid writer in our time. He holds the record for the number of film and television adaptations of his work. His books generally review well, from the trade journals of the book field to the newspapers across the country. He has become, to his horror, a recognizable figure, a celebrity in his own right. He has freedom from editorial tampering—copyeditors wanting to rewrite his books their way. Most important, King can afford to write the stories he wants to write, knowing the readers will trust him and give each new book a try. Freed from the distractions of economic necessity, King can write unperturbedly—a writer's dream. As King explained to a *Bangor Daily News* reporter in a March 1976 profile piece, "Money is important to me . . . only as it gives me time to write."

There is much to suggest that King is seeking terra incognita. Though he could do what less talented bestselling authors have done—write the same book time and again—King has chosen the path less traveled, and in doing so is leaving the familiar landmarks behind. Lesser writers would continue to mine Castle Rock until it became a fictional cliché, but King destroyed it and moved on.

King, to be sure, doesn't need the money, so what's the incentive to write? For King, as for any writer who cares about the art of writing, the writing itself is its own reward, as he acknowledged in his introduction to *Skeleton Crew*:

> All the same, you don't do it for money, or you're a monkey. You don't think of the bottom line, or you're a monkey. You don't think of it in terms of hourly wage, yearly wage, even lifetime wage, or you're a monkey. In the end you don't even do it for love, although it would be nice to think so. You do it because to not do it is suicide.

"The only thing that matters is the story, not the person who writes it," King told an interviewer from *W●B*. It's the story, after all, that endures, long after the writer is gone.

Although the world moves on, as King has frequently pointed out, the writing of fiction has been the one constant in his life, and his only fear is every writer's nightmare. In the words of Gordon Lachance from "The Body," "These days I sometimes look at this typewriter and wonder when it's going to run out of good words. I don't want that to happen. I guess I can stay cool as long as I don't run out of good words, you know?"

So much has changed, but as King noted in *Four Past Midnight:* "One thing hasn't changed during those years—the major reason, I suppose, why it sometimes seems to me . . . that no time has passed at all. I'm still doing the same thing: writing stories."

"The act of writing is beyond currency," King wrote. In the end "the mouth can speak, but there is no tale unless there is a sympathetic ear to listen."

King has millions of readers worldwide who willingly listen, who come to King to experience what he termed the "restorative powers of fiction" and fiction's magical ability to take them away from the mundane world.

Most of all, his readers celebrate King's imaginative vision, wherein the heart and art of darkness finally intersect. It's King country, where above all else the story is king.

Afternote

Stephen King: An Anecdote

by Carroll F. Terrell

Money—that is, lots of it—can be a destructive force in one's life. Tales of horror abound about what big money has done to instant Hollywood or rock and roll stars. It's a test of character to maintain one's balance and keep an even temperament if one is burdened with enough of the stuff. First, a horde of con men will descend upon one to get their hands on some of it. Even worse are the appeals for help from the hundreds of poor people who need money and would use it well. And so on. Thus, reasons abound why the Rockefellers, Fords, and Carnegies set up foundations to deal with the problems.

Stephen King has weathered the storm well. While Saudis and rock stars buy a fleet of Porsches and Cadillac limos, and fit out their palaces with gold fixtures, Steve looks, acts, and dresses about the way he always did. And maintains the same modest residences he's had for years. His priority has been to ensure that he has time to write. That he does mostly from eight to noon, unless he's facing imminent deadlines or some other commitment.

In the early years of his fame he used to accept invitations to speak to certain student groups on campus. Over the years, I introduced him several times to audiences that seemed to grow larger. Always he was a good showman and talked mostly ad-lib, glancing at notes or a script only sparingly. Always, too, he'd leave time for questions, and the questions were always the same: "Where do you get your ideas for your books?" "What does [title of book] really mean?" And so on.

Steve's reactions varied. Sometimes he'd say he didn't know where his ideas came from. Or, if he ever knew, he had forgotten. Once he said he got them at some pawnshop in Bangor. To questions about whether his books were any good, he'd say, "That's for the public to decide," or, "Time may tell."

Over the years, he has continued to be an easygoing, unpretentious Mainer, a breed of people who are usually noncommittal and hard to pin down. For example:

QUESTION: Is it raining?
MAINIAC: 'Tain't snowin'.
QUESTION: Are you winning?
MAINIAC: Ain't losin'.

But one can get them cornered if he knows how:

QUESTION: How far is it to Bangor?
MAINIAC: Don't rightly know.
QUESTION: Twenty miles?
MAINIAC: 'Tain't that far.
QUESTION: Three miles?
MAINIAC: More 'n that.

Finally, you can get a good approximation: "Eight miles?" The answer here might likely be, "Wouldn't be surprised."

As a number of Steve King's books and characters show, people are very likely not to be what they seem. As the adages go, appearances can be deceiving, and first impressions can be wrong about character. So in judging people, the wise man listens to the unspoken words shadowing the words heard, and then watches the actions that follow. Only among a select few do actions that speak louder than words reflect exactly the verbal assertions consistently and over time.

I remember a story Steve once told to a campus group. It seems that when he and his family were driving along some highway in the south, he spotted a car beside the road that seemed to need help. At least the elderly driver standing by it was looking around vaguely as if he didn't know quite what to do. So Steve stopped to see if he could help. He could indeed. It turned out that one of the tires was flat and the driver had no inkling of what he should be doing. Said King, "May I?" Said the man, "Please do."

Thereupon, Steve got out the spare and in the time it would take to learn to say "Peter Piper picked a peck of pickled peppers" backward, the tire was changed and the car was ready to go. The man's attire in the car suggested that they had no need of money. Since Steve was already a millionaire, neither did he.

The experience occurred long after he had become the world's bestselling novelist. But he was dressed in sloppy jeans and sneakers and, as he quite often does, looked as if he could use the price of a good meal. So the driver not only thanked him for his assistance, but hauled out his wallet and came up with $5. Steve started to hold up his hand and say, "No thanks. Not at all necessary." But on second thought, he took the five with thanks. Why? Simple to a person with Steve's apperceptive mind. It would make the guy feel better about his own failure and allow him to make a magnanimous gesture.

Another nuance here is worth thinking about. The guy who spends much of his time in front of a personal computer screen pushing keys got the chance to do something useful to help someone. And that's a great feeling. As they say, it sort of "made his day."

But the final word here implies much more. This kind of attitude is and has always been a guiding beacon for Stephen King, the man and artist.

Orono, Maine
May 1991

Afterword

Quo Vadis, Bestsellasaurus Rex?

by Michael R. Collings

Scholarly writers occasionally run the risk of becoming proprietary about the authors they study. A scholar has often read much—frequently everything—the chosen author wrote. The scholar might spend months or years (sometimes a lifetime) immersed in the author's words and ideas and life. The scholar has engaged those words and ideas on levels of conscious thought that probably far surpasses most readers' involvement with most texts.

One danger of such a close relationship is that the interpreter may come to feel an odd sense of ownership. "So-and-so is my man. His books are fodder for *my* grist mill. His successes are, in some obscure sense, my successes. I am thrilled to see a new title on the shelf, or find someone reading one of my favorite books."

After a while, if the victim of choice is still alive and writing, the scholar-critic might try to second-guess the author.

It usually doesn't work.

Even when the author reveals bits and pieces of plot summary before publication of a novel—as King has done with *IT, The Dark Half, Misery, Needful Things,* and others—knowing what the author says the book will do rarely suggests the specific directions the book will take. Knowing, for example, that several children will meet again as adults to confront a monster in the sewers beneath Derry did not adequately suggest the complexity of *IT.* Knowing that a pseudonym comes murderously to life does not indicate the psychological twistings and turnings of *The Dark Half.*

Even when a writer such as King indicates in interviews or articles what topics he wants to write about, that means little. It means even less when a reader, no matter how enthusiastic, speculates on what a writer might tackle.

If may be more profitable (if any such exercise is profitable at all) to consider not what the author might do, but what one might *wish* him to do.

In this context King has provided some suggestions. He mentions the possibility of a baseball novel. He notes in an interview that he is considering or has considered writing about Jonestown, about "an evangelist, not necessarily an Elmer Gantry novel, but I'd like to write about religion"; a novel about Christ; a baseball novel that he noted was "closest to actually happening."

All of these are possibilities, of course. He may strike out in entirely new directions, although as he has demonstrated in everything he has written, each of his novels and stories already does that. It may even be that he might continue writing horror. He closed one stage of his development with *IT*, in which his children-under-threat confront the monster, as adults and as children, and finally, conclusively defeat it. He closed another with *Tommyknockers*, in which the monsters are long dead and threaten by indirection rather than by direct action. In the subsequent *Misery*, evil and horror and terror are exclusively human realms, just as the monster is uniquely human. He promises to close yet another in *Needful Things*, when he bids farewell to Castle Rock. Which might mean that—taking the lead of a writer such as Arthur C. Clarke, who has publicly retired from writing half a dozen times, only to produce yet another novel—King may simply decide that those earlier concerns are still the themes and the stories that he still needs to explore. King has not yet written a sequel to any of his novels, for example, but several seem to invite the possibility. There are, after all, King's published comments on *'Salem's Lot*.

Or it might mean that King may choose to move in entirely new directions. When the furor over the Bachman pseudonym reached its height a few years ago, it seemed likely (to me, at least) that King might simply continue writing novels of terror and horror . . . but that gradually, a new writer of mainstream fiction might emerge, one whose name was unfamiliar but whose verbal-visual imagination and intuitive grasp of the minutiae of late twentieth-century, technological American culture would rival King's own. Freed from the weight of expectation that his name has become encumbered with ("Fright King," "Horror King," "King" of this and "King" of that), a pseudonymous King might be able to return to the realism of the Bachman novels: the vision that resulted in the strengths of *The Long Walk* and *Roadwork* might be amplified by his subsequent development as a writer and released from the pressure imposed on him by his fans' expectations and by the consistent antagonism of mainstream criticism.

At this point, however, resorting to a pseudonym may not be necessary. There are those who are becoming aware that in the strictest senses, King is perhaps *not* a "horror writer" at all. His monsters, when they occur, often function more metaphorically than literally. Even if no one believes in haunted hotels or haunted cars or werewolves or vampires, one *must* believe—because the evidence is all around, on every street, in every newspaper, on every television news broadcast—in educational systems that destroy rather than build; in parents who, as Arnie Cunningham realized, destroy their children; in cancer, that insidious disease that systematically destroys living tissue; and in political negligence that destroys societies and culture and civility. In all but a few of King's works, these are the real monsters; and humans appear as their avatars.

In others, the distinction between "mainstream" and "horror" fiction is marginal at best. "The Reach" is a superlative story by any literary standards—restrained, moving, authentic, and humane. The horrors of *Misery* can be matched in their violence and brutality, if not indeed exceeded, by lead stories on most nightly news broadcasts. "The Body" and its film analogue, *Stand by Me,* have been justly praised by mainstream critics for their narrative power and their nostalgic evocation of a sublimely naive generation of American childhood. In these works and others like them, King need not hide behind a self-effacing public mask and his often repeated comparison of himself to a Big Mac and fries; in these—to explore the nutrition metaphor further—we are invited beyond fast-foods and greasy-spoon horrors to partake of repasts (a consciously archaic word) that require time and concentration and involvement, and that repay with fulfillment and growth.

As a reader of Stephen King's prose—as well as a fan and, at some levels at least, a critic—this is what I would like to see. King accepting and integrating his media-imposed role as General, and growing beyond it into a larger role as speaker for our times. King allowing himself to take himself seriously, rather than donning the public persona of disparagement (Big Mac and fries).

King doing what he does best.

Simply telling Stories.

And Stories.

And more Stories.

Thousand Oaks, California
March 1991

Appendices

Appendix 1

Recent and Forthcoming Projects

Note: The information provided herein is subject to change. Check with your local bookstore for current publication information.

Terms used: "Trade hardback" is a hardback edition issued for the general book-buying public from a major publisher; "trade paperback" is a quality, oversized paperback edition; and "paperback" is the smaller-sized reprint printed on pulp paper, known in the book trade as a mass-market paperback.

Before ordering, inquire about availability; some King material may go out-of-print very quickly. To ensure a reply, *always* enclose a self-addressed, stamped postcard, preferably one with a typed or printed return address, or a no. 10 envelope. Without an SASE, you may not get any response.

Foreign readers: Always inquire before ordering, since shipping is *not* included in the prices quoted herein. As any U.S. publisher will tell you, it's prohibitively expensive to ship anything overseas, with no guarantee of delivery, unless an air courier like Federal Express or UPS is used.

1. Books by King

The Dark Half, published by Viking as a $21.95 hardback in 1989, was reprinted as a $5.95 paperback in 1990 by NAL under its Signet imprint.

The Dark Tower III: The Wastelands was published by Donald M. Grant, Publisher, Inc., in August 1991 in two states: a trade edition of 40,000 copies ($38 plus $3 postage/handling) and a numbered edition of 1,200 copies ($125) signed by Stephen King and artist Ned Dameron. Though sold out, copies may be available through specialty booksellers (see the appendices in *The Stephen King Companion*).

New American Library (NAL) will be publishing the trade edition of *The Dark Tower III: The Wastelands* ($14.95) in January 1992. It will be a facsimile reprint of the Grant edition, retaining typesetting, design, and original artwork, including the full-color art.

Four Past Midnight, published in 1990 by Viking as a $22.95 trade hardback, will be reprinted in paperback by NAL under its Signet imprint. It will be 752 pages, $6.99, and be published in August 1992.

Needful Things was published in October 1991 by Viking as a 640-page, $24.95 trade hardback. The announced first printing is 1.5 million copies. It will be reprinted in paperback by NAL under its Signet imprint, probably in summer 1992. The book has a fictional introduction by King (beginning with the words, "You've Been Here Before"), and is divided into three parts: Part I: "Grand Opening Celebration"; Part II: "The Sale of the Century"; and Part III: "Everything Must Go."

The Stand: The Complete and Uncut Edition was published in 1990 by Doubleday as a $24.95 trade hardback and a limited edition ($325, out of print; numbered and signed by King and artist Berni Wrightson). It was reprinted by Quality Paperback Book Club (QPBC) in trade paperback at $12.95 for its membership only; NAL reprinted it in 1991 as a $6.99 paperback edition under its Signet imprint.

2. Announced Projects

In October 1991 NAL will be republishing *Carrie, 'Salem's Lot,* and *The Shining* as the initial offering in what it terms "a definitive collectors' series of the entire King canon." According to NAL, the books will feature "new covers, flaps, and the highest quality materials and design." Each book will also "contain a specially inserted plate of the original hardcover jacket art in full color."

The first printing of each title will be 50,000 copies each:

Carrie (introduction by Tabitha King), 160 pp., $12.95.
'Salem's Lot (introduction by Clive Barker), 400 pp., $14.95.
The Shining (introduction by Ken Follett), 432 pp., $14.95.

In September 1992 Viking will publish *Dolores Claiborne* (a novel) in trade hardback.

In an afterword to the second *Dark Tower* book, King announced the title of the fourth book in the projected seven-book series, *The Dark Tower IV: Wizard and Glass.* Said King, it "tells of an enchantment and a seduction but mostly of those things which befell Roland before his readers first met him upon the trail of the man in black." In other words, it's a "prequel" to the first book in the series, *The Dark Tower: The Gunslinger.*

If King follows suit, Donald M. Grant, Publisher, Inc., will issue the limited edition, followed by a trade paperback from NAL in a Plume edition.

At an October 1990 press conference in Bangor, Maine, King said that when he had enough stories on hand, he would be publishing a third collection of short fiction. (As you can see in Appendix 2, King has enough uncollected short fiction on hand to assemble such a collection. As to when he'll publish it, nobody knows.)

3. Books about King

There are more books *about* Stephen King than there are books *by* him. Thus, at this point it has become increasingly difficult to break new ground. A cottage industry catering mostly to those with specialized interests in King—hard-core fans, completists, academicians—has produced these books, which for the most part are not for the lay reader. Too, because they are generally issued from specialty publishers in small print runs, availability is frequently limited and, depending on the edition, expensive.

In recent years King has not actively participated in books about him, though he has sanctioned some of them. By and large, he prefers that books not be written; but if they are, he has said that they should be restricted to discussions of his *published* work and not his unpublished work or his life.

Dr. Seuss and the Two Faces of Fantasy (fall–winter 1991) is a book *by* Stephen King and *about* Stephen King. Northern Lights (493 College Avenue, Orono, ME 04473) will be issuing it in a first printing of 5,000 copies: 4,000 in trade paperback at under ten dollars; and 1,000 in hardback, numbered and signed by Carroll Terrell, $25. It will include the manuscript of the speech King *intended* to give at the Fifth Annual Swanncon in 1984, and a transcript of the actual speech, with commentary by Terrell. The book will be photo-illustrated, with a dozen photographs of King, culled from the files of the *Bangor Daily News.*

Feast of Fear is a second collection of interviews from Underwood–Miller. This collection was compiled by Don Herron, with Underwood–Miller credited as the series editors. Published in 1989 as a limited edition of 600 numbered copies, *Feast of Fear* is available at its in-print price of $75 from Underwood–Miller (*new* address: 708 Westover Drive, Lancaster, PA 94948).

Though a trade hardback edition was announced by McGraw–Hill—the publisher of the hardback edition of *Bare Bones,* its first collection of interviews—it subsequently canceled the title. No further editions of this book have been announced from any publisher.

Underwood–Miller has no plans to publish a third collection of interviews. Of the two collections, *Bare Bones*—the first collection—offers the better interviews; *Feast of Fear,* while informative, admittedly suffers from the inclusion of minor profile pieces and repetitious interviews.

A previously announced title, *Infinite Explorations* by Michael R. Collings, has been canceled by its publisher, Starmont House. According to Collings, the book is temporarily on the back burner, though he does intend to finish it for eventual publication.

In the Darkest Night: A Student's Guide to Stephen King is a bibliography compiled by Tim Murphy. According to its publisher, the book is tentatively scheduled for publication by late 1991. The trade paperback will be $11.95, the hardback $21.95. For information, write to: Starmont House Inc. (PO Box 851, Mercer Island, WA 98040).

The Moral Voyages of Stephen King is a scholarly examination of "several of [King's] paramount literary themes and philosophical concerns," according to Anthony Magistrale. The trade paperback is $11.95, the hardback $21.95. From Starmont House (see above).

Observations from the Terminator: Thoughts on Stephen King and Other Horrorists (*sic*) is by Tyson Blue. It is scheduled for publication by late 1991. The trade paperback will be $11.95, the hardback $21.95. From Starmont House.

The Shape Under the Sheet: The Complete Stephen King Encyclopedia is king-sized: at 780 pages, 8½ by 11 inches, this exhaustively researched book is in fact two books in one: a companion book with interviews, articles, profiles, photographs, and artwork; and a reference work with detailed, cross-indexed listings of King's books, short fiction, and audio, television, and movie adaptations.

Approximately half the book is its 400,000-word, 18,000-entry concordance of people, places, and things in King's fiction (published and unpublished), organized by the literary work itself.

The book does not include any material about King's nonfiction, which to date numbers nearly 200 pieces.

Available from Popular Culture, Ink. (PO Box 1839, Ann Arbor, MI 48106), the first printing is limited to 3,000 copies, at $110. A limited edition of 350 numbered copies ($175) to be signed by 30 contributors, should see publication by early fall of 1991. Write to Overlook Connection Press (PO Box 526, Woodstock, GA 30188).

Spignesi is currently in the process of developing and refining material from *The Shape Under the Sheet* for possible spinoff books.

The Shining Reader, edited by Anthony Magistrale, is a casebook—the first in a series—that collects critical essays about *The Shining.* The trade paperback is $11.95, the hardback $21.95. (Note: Unlike earlier Starmont books, this one is laser-typeset—a big improvement.) From Starmont House.

The Stephen King Bibliography, compiled by Douglas E. Winter, is still in the works. Its publisher will be Donald M. Grant, Inc. (PO Box 187, Hampton Falls, NH 03844).

Stephen King: Man and Artist is a study of King by Carroll F. Terrell, who taught King as an undergraduate at the University of Maine at Orono. An important associational title as well an illuminating study, this volume is profusely illustrated by Kenny Ray Linkous, a Maine artist who rendered the illustrations for the Philtrum Press edition of *The Eyes of the Dragon.* It is available in several states at varying prices, and its publisher is Northern Lights (493 College Avenue, Orono, ME 04473).

The Stephen King Quiz Book by Stephen Spignesi is for those King fans who want to be quizzed to death, with 100 "razor-keen quizzes and 1,500 tantalizing questions." Published by NAL under its Signet imprint, this $3.95 mass-market paperback was published in 1990.

The Stephen King Quiz Book: Volume Two by Spignesi takes up where the previous book left off, with all the fiction from *Four Past Midnight* to present. This mass-market paperback will be published by NAL under its Signet imprint in 1992.

The Stephen King Short Story Concordance by Chris Thompson is, according to the author, "a coded cross-reference for every significant person, place, and thing which is named in the King canon, as well as a brief description. This initial volume will deal only with the short fiction of Stephen King." No publication date has been set from its publisher, Starmont, but it's in production and may see publication in winter 1991.

The Work of Stephen King: An Annotated Bibliography & Guide by Michael R. Collings is an extensive revision and update of his earlier book for Starmont, *The Annotated Guide to Stephen King,* published in 1986. To be published by Borgo Press (PO Box 2845, San Bernardino, CA 92406), this book will be 400–500 pages and be published in both hardback and trade paperback. Tentatively scheduled for an October 1991 publication date, this bibliography promises to be especially useful for libraries. As Collings observed, bibliographies on popular authors do not conform to the bibliographic format preferred by libraries; this bibliography, however, will satisfy their requirements.

I have seen an advance copy and can recommend this book without reservation; hard-core fans, serious students and scholars, and libraries will want to add this to their collection.

The book includes a chronology, and a bibliography of primary and secondary material, domestic and foreign:

A. Books
B. Short Fiction
C. Poetry
D. Non-Fiction: Reviews, Articles, Notes
E. Screenplays
F. Speeches and Public Appearances
G. Screen Appearances
H. Non-Print Adaptations of King's Books: Film Versions and Audiocassettes

About the Author
I. Books
J. Newsletters
K. Profiles, Biographical Sketches
L. Interviews
M. Bibliographic Studies

4. Visual Adaptations

Although King has over the years consistently maintained that a book and its film adaptation are two separate entities, he admits: "Bad or good, movies nearly always have a strange diminishing effect on works of fantasy. . . . In the end," King wrote, works of fiction are best visualized by the reader who will see them "through the lens of imagination in a vivid and constantly changing way no camera can duplicate."

The recent success of *Misery* and the high ratings for *IT* have, predictably, renewed interest in King's film properties.

Explaining the crossover between the books and the movies, King told Gary Wood:

My guess would be that in a lot of cases, the people who read the books and the people who go to the movies are the same people. And [some of them] stay away because they know that whatever they read in the book, they're just not going to see on the screen. It can't be done. You can do stuff in a book that you simply can't do in a film without earning yourself an X rating for your troubles.

Admittedly, King's movie adaptations are a mixed bag, ranging from the execrable (*Children of the Corn*) to the embarrassingly bad (like *Maximum Overdrive*) to the masterful (like *Stand by Me, Carrie,* and *Misery*). Though King's works *can* be successfully translated to the screen, it's ofttimes a long and winding road.

An advocate of filming in Maine, King has pushed hard for getting his material shot in what William Dunn calls "King country," which makes artistic sense to King.

Even television, which he felt was the death of horror, has proven to be fertile ground for his works. The mini-series "IT," after all, had gotten good reviews and good ratings. The mini-series, in fact, gives King's stories room to breathe, as Richard P. Rubinstein, working on a new King mini-series, told *USA Today*: "Historically, Stephen has seen his material condensed for film and television, and he saw this as an opportunity not to have to cram it all into two hours."

With King's lifelong love of the media and his continuing involvement in adapting his works for television and the screen, he has grown in his understanding of how best to "translate" his fiction to film. For that reason, I am hopeful we will see better adaptations, including some from King himself.

An intriguing project, *Apt Pupil* will certainly not see completion in its current form, though it may be resurrected from scratch someday. Ricky Schroder played the part of Todd Bowden, the teenager obsessed with Nazis and their death camps, especially the "gooshy stuff," and Nicol Williamson enacted Kurt Dussander, an ex-Nazi camp commandant in hiding, recently discovered by Bowden. Of the work on hand, King said, "They shot for about ten weeks. I got a rough assemblage of about three quarters of the film. Then they ran out of money. And *that* was good! That sucker was *real* good!"

Creepshow 3 is forthcoming from Laurel Entertainment. Among the stories may be "Pinfall," an original King story which originally was slated to be in *Creepshow 2*. A cross between *Night of the Living Dead* and an E.C. comic story ("Foul Play"), "Pinfall" seems perfectly appropriate for this anthology series.

The Dark Half, filmed by George Romero in Pittsburgh for Orion Pictures, will star Timothy Hutton in a dual role as Thad Beaumont and George Stark, Amy Madigan as his wife Liz Beaumont, and Michael Rooker as sheriff Alan Pangborn. The release date is fall 1991. (It is not known whether the movie will end with a fire—in Hollywood, you know, they just love fires.)

A Feature from Stephen King's Nightshift Collection is a 1991 release in videocassette only. Running 40 minutes, this comprises two student films, only one of which can properly be referenced to *Night Shift.* Distributed by Simitar Entertainment, Inc., the videocassette offers *Night Waiter*—bearing no relationship to King—and *Disciples of the Crow,* based on King's short story "Children of the Corn." The recipient of a National Merit Award and a Gold Hugo Award (awarded by the Chicago Film Festival), *Disciples of the Crow* is worth viewing.

Stephen King's The Golden Years, a made-for-television miniseries for CBS, aired in summer 1991. An initial two-hour episode aired on July 16 followed by six one-hour episodes. Created by King, this miniseries would, he told *USA Today,* "fulfill my dream. . . . I'd like to do the equivalent of a novel for TV that tells a beginning, a middle and a middle and a middle."

As *TV Guide* explained, this series is:

> "Cocoon"—Stephen King style. King wrote the first five episodes of this seven-part thriller, which concerns 70-year-old Harlan Williams, a janitor at a forbidding Government-run "agricultural testing facility." But as Part 1 opens, Harlan might be on the way out—he has failed an eye test, and besides, his boss (Stephen Root) simply wants to get rid of him: "People get stale," he says. "Young blood is the key to success." Harlan's blood will soon get younger.

As its coexecutive producer Richard P. Rubinstein put it, "It's the fountain of youth, but in Stephen King's world that's not always the best thing. This fountain is a little sour."

Although King has a large readership, he realizes that success in this medium will mean capturing—and holding—an audience on a much larger scale. He explained the correlation, using this project as an example:

> For every person who reads novels in this country, there are hundreds, maybe thousands, of people who don't. Somebody brought up a statistic the other day to me that really amazed me. I wrote an extended TV show that's been chopped up into segments for a summer series, and they're going to sell it with my name, but the guy who's producing the series said, "Really, I don't want you to think that something's going to happen with this, or it's going to be a success, because if everybody who bought your last book tuned into this program on the first night, that would be one point that the networks count, and it needs like twenty-two points to have a chance, so that puts things in perspective." All at once, Stephen King, the Titan of Terror, looks like the midget of the entertainment world—it changes the perspective entirely.

The Lawnmower Man will be a full-length feature film from Allied Visions. It is "based" on King's short story of the same name, collected in *Night Shift*. According to Gary Wood, the screen treatment shares little, if anything, with the King story.

The Mangler will be a full-length feature film from Allied Visions. It is based on King's short story of the same name, collected in *Night Shift*.

Misery, 105 minutes, was released by Columbia Pictures in October 1990. Shot on location in Reno and Los Angeles, *Misery* was directed by Rob Reiner, produced by Reiner and Andrew Scheinman, from a screenplay by William Goldman, and based on the novel of the same name.

Starring Kathy Bates as Annie Wilkes, the "number-one fan" of writer Paul Sheldon (played by James Caan), *Misery* was a critical and financial success. (By May 9, 1991, *Misery* had domestic rentals of nearly $61 million—the most profitable King film to date. To put things in perspective: $100 million is considered a blockbuster, the equivalent of a number-one bestselling book.)

"The Moving Finger," a short story, is being adapted by Laurel Entertainment as a teleplay for "Monsters."

Needful Things, to be published in October 1991, will be a full-length feature film from Rob Reiner's Castle Rock Entertainment. To King's way of thinking, the novel presents Reiner with a real challenge, though he feels Reiner is up to the task:

> *Needful Things* will present the biggest problem in terms of adaptation of any of the things Rob Reiner has done of mine. I don't think it's any secret that I feel he's done the best adaptations of my work.

I've been adapted to film a ridiculous number of times, and Rob has done a couple of really good adaptations that have, I think, to do with two factors: the first is that he's picked material that's fairly limited: *Misery* is a short novel, and he did *Stand by Me* which is based on "The Body," from *Different Seasons,* which my kids used to call *Different Sneezes.* And the other factor is that Reiner hasn't been afraid of the humor involved. My theory has always been that if you want to scare people, you have to let them laugh because that is their most common action to relieve that feeling of mounting terror. If you don't give them a place where you want them to laugh, they'll laugh where you *don't* want them to laugh, and Rob knows that and he's used it, and it's paid off very well.

Needful Things is, I think, in some ways an extremely funny book. It's an extremely gruesome book in places, which is a real departure for me. But it's funny in a lot of places, and it's also very long and it's got a lot of characters, which is something Reiner hasn't dealt with before, but the first step that he took was a good one: He hired a guy named Larry Cohen to adapt it, who is the guy who adapted *Carrie* for Brian de Palma and "IT" the miniseries.

"The Night Flier," a short story published in Douglas E. Winter's anthology, *Prime Evil,* will be adapted for television by Laurel Entertainment.

Sleepwalkers, an original screenplay by King, will be a full-length feature film from New World.

"Sometimes They Come Back" aired on CBS on May 7, 1991. It was based on the short story of the same name and collected in *Night Shift.* Tim Matheson played the title role of Jim Norman, a high school teacher. *USA Today* concluded that although it "chokes on its hokeyness . . . in its own modest way, it tells a fairly good campfire ghost story."

The Stand is under development at Richard P. Rubinstein's Laurel Entertainment, and is based on a script by Rospo Pallenberg. It may be released through Warner Brothers. King's most popular novel, *The Stand* has been in development for a decade. After King wrote five drafts and gave up, Pallenberg's three-hour script met with approval at Warner Brothers. Pallenberg later revised his script to two hours. In an interview with Gary Wood, Rubinstein remarked on the essential difference between King's drafts and Pallenberg's:

> The point is, I think Rospo was successful where Steve wasn't in terms of being able to get some distance on the material and make those decisions that needed to be made, in terms of what stays in the movie and what gets left out. . . . Basically what I'm looking to do, and I think Rospo has been successful in doing, is not being literal in the translation but reproducing the *feel.*

Stephen King's Graveyard Shift, an 86-minute film, was released by Paramount in October 1990. It was shot on location in Maine, directed by Ralph S. Singleton, produced by William J. Dunn and Singleton, from a screenplay by

John Esposito, and based on the King short story of the same name, collected in *Night Shift*. (After five weeks it dropped off *Variety* magazine's weekly lists; the last listing was on December 3, 1990, with rentals of a little over $11 million.)

At a press conference for *Graveyard Shift* in Bangor in October 1990, King revealed his concerns about selling his work to the movies, and his enthusiasm for William Dunn, with whom he had previously worked on *Pet Sematary*:

> All the concerns come before the decision is made to sell.
>
> If a movie is not a good movie, it doesn't reflect back upon the book or the writer; but if a movie turns out to be a really good piece of work, sometimes it does reflect back. You can't lose. Nonetheless, it's good to be involved with people who are honest, who have a certain amount of integrity—personal and artistic—and in terms of this production, my decision to go with Bill Dunn and with the people that he put together should speak for itself. I have a world of respect for his ability to put together people on a production side that are valuable and useful, on his refusal to compromise on some of his artistic visions; like them or dislike them, when you see the film, they are part of Bill's view of this particular work. He didn't compromise what was going into the picture or where the picture was going to be made. That's the sort of thing I look for.
>
> I have a tendency to look for a real east coast sensibility. In that sense, Bill is probably the second-most understandable person I've ever talked to, because he comes from Down East, he comes from Maine. Dino DeLaurentiis came from Italy, and that's *way* [over there]. When it comes to people from west of the Mississippi, I run into communications problems, until you get to California where they are talking what seems to be English, but doesn't make a whole lot of sense. They talk about synergy, windows of opportunity, taking meetings, that sort of thing.

Stephen King's "IT," a two-part miniseries aired on ABC on November 18 and 20, 1990. Including commercials, each installment ran two hours. The first installment told the story of the children; the second told the story of the children as adults. Directed by Tommy Lee Wallace from a teleplay by Lawrence Cohen (part one) and Wallace and Cohen (part two), the miniseries got good ratings and, overall, was well received by the critics.

Tales from the Darkside: The Movie, a 93-minute film, was released in May 1990 by Paramount. It was directed by John Harrison, and produced by Richard Rubinstein and Mitchell Galin. One of the stories of this anthology film is "Cat from Hell," based on a King short story. The screenplay for that tale was written by George Romero.

The Talisman has been in "development limbo" for several years, according to Gary Wood. It is currently planned as a full-length feature film, and Steven Spielberg's Amblin Entertainment is developing the project for Universal.

Thinner, in development at Warner Brothers, will be a full-length film. The screenplay is by Michael McDowell.

5. Audiocassette Adaptations

Books on tape—both abridged readings and unabridged readings—have become so popular that virtually all the major books are preceded by the release of its audio adaptation. King's books are no exception.

By far the closest to the books, readings—preferably unabridged, and read by the author—reinforce the notion that in the beginning storytelling was an *oral,* not written, tradition. A good reading, unadorned by distracting sound effects, is the next best thing to being around the proverbial campfire with the storyteller, hearing the tale unfold, and seeing it in the mind's eye.

The Dark Tower III: The Wastelands will be released in audiotape in January 1992 (on sale in December 1991). As before, King is the reader for this unabridged reading (10 cassettes, 15 hours, $34.95).

Four Past Midnight is available in unabridged audiotape recordings from Penguin USA and HighBridge Audio. The set includes: "The Langoliers" (6 cassettes, 9 hours, $29.95), read by Willem Dafoe; "Secret Window, Secret Garden" (4 cassettes, 6 hours, $23.95), read by James Woods; "The Library Policeman" (6 cassettes, 8 hours, $29.95), read by Ken Howard; and "The Sun Dog" (4 cassettes, 6 hours, $23.95), read by Tim Sample.

Of the first tape in the series *Publishers Weekly* said, "Given King's reputation as a phenomenal bestseller in the bookstore, if this title can't get consumers interested in the unabridged format, nothing can. King is a great storyteller, and the nine-hour presentation never seems ponderous."

Needful Things—read by King—will be released in unabridged audiotape readings by the author in November. Part One (6 tapes, 9 hours, $29.95), Part Two (6 tapes, 9 hours, $29.95), Part Three (6 tapes, 9 hours, $29.95); or a boxed set of all three parts (27 hours, $89.85).

Note: Random House Audiobooks has reissued some of the unabridged readings originally published and distributed by Waldenbooks under its Waldentapes label. These include: "Gramma" (1 cassette, 100 minutes, $9.95), read by Gale Garnett; "The Monkey" (1 cassette, 100 minutes, $9.95); and "Mrs. Todd's Shortcut" (1 cassette, 100 minutes, $9.95), read by David Purdham.

6. Periodicals of Interest

For anyone with a more than casual interest in the making of fantasy films, *Cinefantastique* does an excellent job covering forthcoming films. Stephen King's movies are frequently covered in its pages. Of special interest is its February 1991 issue, with a cover story on King. Gary Wood, who interviewed King at length, wrote several articles examining why some of King's movie adaptations have succeeded—and failed. The result is a perceptive and provocative overview that, if you have any interest in the story behind the filmmaking of King's movies, is required reading.

Write to Cinefantastique (PO Box 270, Oak Park, IL 60303) for its flyer on back issues, which include several other issues with cover stories on King.

Gauntlet magazine, Barry Hoffman's book/magazine that is on the cutting edge of the censorship issue, is worth getting for its cross-sectional, in-depth, ongoing coverage of censorship in this country. King readers, however, will find their March 1991 issue, *Gauntlet #2,* to be of special interest, for it is Hoffman's "Stephen King Special." The issue reprints a long essay by King on film censorship ("The Dreaded X") and his 1990 update, and also offers a potpourri of articles about King: Howard Wornom writes about King and censorship, Michael Collings compares and contrasts the two versions of *The Stand,* Stephen Spignesi provides outtakes from interviews he conducted for his book *The Shape Under the Sheet,* and there's also a guide to buying King collectibles, as well as an art portfolio, a horror gallery of King art. Now in its second printing, *Gauntlet #2* costs $8.95, plus $2 for postage. Write to Gauntlet (309 Powell Road, Springfield, PA 19064).

A limited edition of Gauntlet—500 numbered copies, signed by numerous contributors, *including Stephen King*—is available for $78 from Borderlands Press (PO Box 32333, Baltimore, MD 21208). This may well be sold out by now, so write before ordering.

The Magazine of Fantasy and Science Fiction (or *F&SF,* as it's commonly called in the field) published in December 1990 one of its rare, one-author issues—this one, on Stephen King. With a new short story ("The Moving Finger"), an essay by A. J. Budrys (thought-provoking, though at times irritating), an excerpt from *The Dark Tower III: The Wastelands,* and a bibliography (incomplete), the King issue is worth your attention. For information on availability and cost, write to F&SF (PO Box 56, Cornwall, CT 06753).

Stephen King called *Midnight Graffiti* the horror field's version of *Spy* magazine, and it is. Slick, irreverent, and just plain fun, *Midnight Graffiti* is one of those magazines you can't browse without buying. Of special interest: *MG #3* with "Rainy Season," a King short story that has not been collected in book form. For information on availability, write to Midnight Graffiti (13101 Sudan Road, Poway, CA 92064). By the way, that is also the preferred address for ordering *Stephen King/Clive Barker: Masters of the Macabre* by James Van Hise; an updated version of his earlier books on King, this edition is 146 pages and costs $14.95.

Weird Tales #298 (fall 1990, $4.95) reprints "The Glass Floor," King's first professionally published story. For this appearance, King has written introductory comments that put the piece in perspective. For information on availability, write to Terminus Publishing Company (PO Box 13418, Philadelphia, PA 19101).

7. Miscellaneous

Michael Whelan's cover artwork from NAL/Plume edition of *The Dark Tower: The Gunslinger* is now available as a 17-by-23-inch photoprint with a double matte, at $100. His work sells very fast, so I recommend your writing immediately if you're interested in obtaining one. Write to Glass Onion Graphics (PO Box 88, Brookfield, CT 06804).

Glimmer Graphics has recently published a portfolio by Berni Wrightson of the art from the restored version of *The Stand*. The trade edition consists of 12 plates, reproduced the same size as the originals, at $20. The limited edition of 1,200 sets signed by artist Berni Wrightson, with one bonus plate of Randall Flagg, consists of 13 plates, at $40. This is likely to sell out quickly. Write to Glimmer Graphics (137 Fulton Street, Trenton, NJ 08611) for information on availability.

Horrorfest, a professionally run convention by Ken Morgan, has now found a home permanently in Chicago. Originally conceived as a gathering hole for Stephen King fans, the convention has branched out to include horror in general, and in doing so has been attracting larger crowds every year. For information on upcoming conventions, write to con organizer Ken Morgan at Horrorfest (PO Box 277652, Chicago, IL 60627).

A limited-edition broadside of "Letters from Hell" ($130) by Stephen King is still available from Lord John Press (19073 Los Alimos Street, Northridge, CA 91326). A hilarious essay about the fan mail King receives and the questions he's most frequently asked ("Ever et raw meat?" writes one correspondent), this broadside has hand-set type with three-color printing, and is limited to 500 copies—*signed by Stephen King.*

Over the last few years David Hinchberger has changed the format of his book catalogue and has now gone to a magazine format. This is the most "user-friendly" of the catalogues in the field. Hinchberger's company, Overlook Connection (PO Box 526, Woodstock, GA 30188), offers virtually everything in the horror field—King, naturally, but also Koontz, Robert McCammon, Straub, and other writers you've probably never heard of, but should sample.

The current catalogue is 208 pages (on newsprint, 8½ × 11 inches) and costs $3, credited toward your first order. (If you prefer, you may use a push-button phone with Touch-tone service and, guided by the menu, get a current update on new and forthcoming books. Call 404/926-1762. The company can also take a fax transmission at that number; just listen to the voice message and, when prompted, press 2222, wait for the tone, and send your fax.)

Dave's chatty, informal writeups are compulsively readable. If you like Dave's brand of irrepressible enthusiasm—and I do—you'll want to get, and stay, on his mailing list.

Appendix 2

Annotated Checklist of Fiction

With several excellent reference sources in print and Collings' definitive bibliography soon forthcoming, I see no value in contributing yet another detailed bibliographic listing of primary and secondary material, fiction and nonfiction, and adaptations. Still, I do feel that since this book focuses on King's fiction, a checklist of all his fiction is appropriate, along with annotations, including King's comments where applicable.

Unless there is a notation indicating the work is unpublished, unfinished, or forthcoming, the work was published.

A black box (■) indicates the work is unpublished, unfinished, or aborted.

If you need more information, there are several fine books available:

Begin with the first and best book on the subject, *Stephen King: The Art of Darkness* by Douglas E. Winter, which is in print from New American Library under its Signet imprint as an affordable mass-market paperback. It was revised and expanded, making it current through 1986.

The Annotated Guide to Stephen King by Michael R. Collings from Starmont is still available. When it's updated and available in the Borgo Press edition, you'll want to add the updated edition to your collection.

The Shape Under the Sheet: The Complete Stephen King Encyclopedia by Stephen J. Spignesi.

1. Books

❏ **The Bachman Books: Four Early Novels by Stephen King** (NAL Books, 1985) is an omnibus edition collecting **Rage** (originally titled **Getting It On**), **The Long Walk**, **Roadwork**, and **The Running Man**. In "Why I Was Bachman," the introduction to the book, King wrote: "Are they good novels? I don't know. Are they honest novels? Yes, I think so."

Three of the four books bore dedications to people King knew early in his career; **The Running Man** bore no dedication.

Rage was "For Susan Artz and WGT [William G. Thompson]."

The Long Walk was dedicated to three of his college professors at UMO who read the book in manuscript form and encouraged his writing talent: "This is for Jim Bishop and Burt Hatlen and Ted Holmes."

Roadwork was dedicated to a teacher in the English department at Hampden Academy when King taught there: "In memory of Charlotte Littlefield. *Proverbs* 31:10–28." (*The Art of Darkness* sheds light on Littlefield and her importance to King, who told Winter that he "loved [her] almost as much as I loved my mother," and because of her death within a year after writing **Pet Sematary**, the book is "a *real* cemetery." Before Littlefield died she left a request that King read from Proverbs; presumably, King read the passage cited in the dedication. Though an experienced speaker, King was emotionally overcome during the reading and "almost lost it.")

■ **Blaze**, an unpublished novel of approximately 50,000 words, is King's supernatural version of John Steinbeck's *Of Mice and Men*. After its completion on February 15, 1973, the double-spaced, 173-page manuscript underwent a partial rewrite, totaling 106 double-spaced pages. The first draft shows editorial notes, though—from what I can tell—not in King's hand. The dedication: "This book is for my mother, Ruth Pillsbury King."

Both the original manuscript and the rewrite were deposited at the Special Collections of the Fogler Library at the University of Maine at Orono.

Over the years King has expressed his opinion that *Blaze* is not very good, although at one time he deemed it publishable. In his afterword to **Different Seasons**, King wrote that he submitted it and **Second Coming** (later published as **'Salem's Lot**) to Thompson at Doubleday for publication consideration.

This novel will likely remain unpublished.

■ **The Cannibals** is an unpublished novel that in plot recalls "Survivor Type," published in **Skeleton Crew**. Originally begun in 1977, it was then titled **Under the Dome**; in 1982, when King wrote the 450-page novel, it was retitled **The Cannibals**. The novel was reportedly written in longhand when King was in Philadelphia, working with George Romero on **Creepshow** (I).

The novel also recalls J. G. Ballard's novel with the same theme, *High-Rise*—a case of concurrent inspiration. For that reason King may never publish this novel. My best guess: it will remain unpublished or, if published, will be done only in a limited edition.

❑ **Carrie** (Doubleday & Company, 1974) is the kind of book that can, and did, launch a literary career. Published in the wake of enormous public interest in supernatural phenomena, **Carrie**—originally set in Massachusetts, not Maine—was first conceived not as a novel but as a short story, which, like many a King story, grew. Padded to novel length by the inclusion of bogus documentation, **Carrie** is one of the few King books that have translated effectively to the screen.

In a 1989 interview with *W•B* (Waldenbooks' consumer magazine) King, when asked about **Carrie**, said that he had never gone back to reread it, then added: "But my oldest son, who has just written a novel himself and who has read eight or nine of my books, went back and read that book and said, 'Not bad, dad—for a first novel.' He said that from the heights of his 17-year-old literary critical experience, of course."

Later, in a 1991 interview with *Publishers Weekly,* Bill Goldstein wrote:

> **Carrie** probably lies lowest in King's estimation of his works. "I remember once years ago seeing the author of *The Third World War* . . . on a television chat show in England. And when the interviewer asked John Hackett about his book, the first thing he said was, 'Oh yes, it's just some old trash I put together.' I do think of **Carrie** that way.' " (Maryann Palumbo, vice-president of marketing at NAL, King's publisher, said, "I'm glad we thought otherwise," when she heard of King's self-criticism.)

❏ **Christine** (Viking, 1983) is admittedly midrange King. It brings to mind several antecedents: Theodore Sturgeon's "Killdozer," a story about a bulldozer that comes to life and attacks its construction crew; the movie *The Car*; and King's short stories "The Mangler" and "Trucks."

In book-length material, **Christine** recalls **Carrie** in its evocation of adolescent life and **Sword in the Darkness**'s Arnie Kalowski for the character of Arnie Cunningham.

One of the few King novels told in the first person, which King employs more typically in shorter fiction, the novel shifts to third person in its middle portion, disrupting narrative flow. When asked about this, King explained to Randy L'Officier in *Twilight Zone* magazine that he "got in a box. That's really the only reason. It almost killed the book."

In **Four Past Midnight** King wrote that "when most of the reviews of **Christine** suggested it was a really dreadful piece of work, I came to the reluctant decision that it probably *wasn't* as good as I had hoped (that, however, did not stop me from cashing the royalty checks)." Checks that were big indeed, since King had taken only a $1 advance on the book!

A limited edition was published by Donald M. Grant, Publisher, Inc., with beautiful work by Stephen Gervais, who later published a separate portfolio of the artwork.

King once told an interviewer that **Christine** was "Happy Days" gone mad, which sums up the book nicely, especially with its emphasis on rock and roll—the book's headings are from fifties rock and rollers . . . car tunes.

■ **The Corner** is an aborted novel from 1976. In *Art of Darkness* King tells Winter that that year was a particularly bad one for his writing.

❏ **Creepshow** (Plume, 1982) is, insofar as King's books are concerned, an oddity—"illustrated fiction" it's styled on the back cover. In the comic-book field **Creepshow** would be called a graphic album. Illustrated by Berni Wrightson—the premier macabre illustrator in our time—**Creepshow** looks and reads and feels like nothing so much as an E.C. comic book, which is also the "feel" of the movie.

King, who adapted the stories to the graphic album format, has rarely written continuity for comics. However, he can do so easily. As Marv Wolfman has attested, in "King of the Comics?" an essay in *Reign of Fear: Fiction and Film of Stephen King*:

> King, too, has written comics—for a special Stephen King magazine published by Marvel Magazines [*Heroes for Hire,* a benefit comic book; his story was illustrated by Berni Wrightson], and his comics work was crisp and clean and showed a strong understanding of the medium. I point that out because not all prose writers have been able to write comics.

☐ **Cujo** (Viking, 1981), a Castle Rock story, is part of King's continuing exploration of the Maine myth. With its archetypal characters—especially Joe Camber—**Cujo** is the perfect example of what Burton Hatlen has pointed out is the American dream turning into an American nightmare.

☐ **Cycle of the Werewolf** (Land of Enchantment, 1983; Signet, 1985) is minor but enjoyable King. The tale represents one of the few occasions in which King, in a fashion, wrote to order. It was also King's first opportunity to work with Berni Wrightson.

The difficulty in writing about such traditional monsters, as he told Bill Munster in an interview for *Footsteps*, is that the subject matter is traditionally "overworked and threadbare." King added, "I tried a werewolf novel set on a college campus, but had to abandon it. Just couldn't breathe life into it."

☐ **Danse Macabre** (Everest House, 1981) is King's only published nonfiction book, though material deposited at the Special Collections at UMO indicates that, some years earlier, King had begun work on a collection of essays.

Danse Macabre, especially with its autobiographical chapter, suggests strongly that King ought to put together a collection of his nonfiction pieces. Interestingly, King stresses that the book is "not an autobiography of yours truly. The autobiography of a father, writer, and ex-high school teacher would make dull reading indeed. I am a writer by trade, which means that the most interesting things that have happened to me have happened in my dreams."

Danse Macabre was published in 1981, early in the decade that would mark him as its bestselling author. A decade later, in 1991, his career come full circle, King told *Publishers Weekly*: ". . . I've redefined the genre of horror-writing in this country. I'm not trying to say they're great books, mine, but for better or worse I have changed the genre."

More than that, King has fundamentally changed the shape and substance of popular fiction in his attempt to "build a bridge between wide popularity and a critical acceptance. But my taste is too low, there is a broad streak of the *vulgate,* not the 'vulgar,' in my stuff. But that is the limitations of my background, and one of my limitations as a writer. I've got a lot of great things out of a small amount of talent."

Interestingly, King doesn't see himself as *the* bridge between popularity and critical acclaim, as he told *Publishers Weekly*:

> I'd like to win the National Book Award, the Pulitzer Prize, the Nobel Prize; I'd like to have someone write a *New York Times Book Review* piece that says, "Hey, wait a minute guys, we made a mistake—this guy is one of the greatest writers of the 20th century." But it's not going to happen, for two reasons. One is I'm not the greatest writer of the 20th century, and the other is that once you sell a certain number of books, the people who think about "literature" stop thinking about you and assume that any writer who is popular across a wide spectrum has nothing to say.

❑ **The Dark Half** (Viking, 1989), along with "The Sun Dog" from **Four Past Midnight** and **Needful Things**, forms what King termed his Castle Rock Trilogy. Originally submitted to the publisher as a "collaboration" between King and Richard Bachman, **The Dark Half** was initially described as "a kind of riff on the Frankenstein theme," though **Pet Sematary**—with its overtones of tampering with the unknown, with the restoration of life—seems to fit his description better than **Dark Half**. To me the tale is something of a riff on Stevenson's *Dr. Jekyll and Mr. Hyde,* one of three novels (along with *Dracula* and, yes, *Frankenstein*) King discussed at length in an essay for an NAL omnibus edition of those three literary classics.

In that essay about *Dr. Jekyll and Mr. Hyde,* King wrote: "The evil of Mr. Hyde . . . is an evil that proceeds from the human mind." That neatly capsulizes **The Dark Half**.

According to King, the genesis of **The Dark Half** began with his musings after his pen name had been uncovered:

> For a while I started to think, "Suppose Bachman wasn't dead?" And immediately the idea jumped to mind: What if a guy had a pen name that didn't want to stay dead and isn't that an interesting idea and how would that work out? It just stayed like that for a while and didn't get written. Then the thought that finally drove me to start writing was the idea: Suppose Bachman collaborated on a book with me? And so originally, *The Dark Half* was submitted as a collaboration by Stephen King and Richard Bachman. But Viking didn't like the idea. They thought it was confusing and that people would think it was a collaboration like *The Talisman.*

King said that **The Dark Half** was the bridge to **Needful Things**: ". . . [E]very now and then something will shine through that's pure creation and you'll be inspired—literally touched with fire—and you'll be able to do something that you didn't expect to do. It happened with me halfway through **The Dark Half** when I realized that I wasn't done with Alan Pangborn, who's the sheriff."

In an author's note in **The Dark Half** King wrote: "I'm indebted to the late Richard Bachman for his help and inspiration. This novel could not have been written without him."

☐ **The Dark Tower** [I]: **The Gunslinger** (Donald M. Grant, Publisher, Inc. 1982) collects five stories originally published in the *Magazine of Fantasy and Science Fiction*. King dedicated the book "To Ed Ferman who took a chance on these stories, one by one." That and their serialization were enough to put the idea in a number of critics that this book was *not* a novel proper but a collection of interrelated short fiction. King, it appears, did not have that intention in mind, for in his dedication in the second **Dark Tower** book he emphatically reminds us that these are "*novels*" as opposed to stories—stories only in the larger sense of the word.

Dark Tower draws its inspiration from a Robert Browning poem, "Child Roland to the Dark Tower Came." King's life as a writer can perhaps be seen as a quest not unlike Child Roland's.

The Oxford Companion to English Literature explains the Browning poem:

> A knight errant crossed a nightmare landscape in search of the Dark Tower (or has been deceived into doing so; it is not clear which); he eventually reaches the Tower and blows his horn defiantly at its foot. The poem ends with the title phrase, and there is no indication of what happened next. Because the story is told by the knight himself, the poem's form raises insoluble problems of interpretation, and the poem is both profoundly satisfying as a dream narrative and profoundly disturbing as an impenetrable allegory— of life, of art, or of both. Browning consistently refused to explain the poem, saying simply that it had come upon him as a dream.

Originally published at the suggestion of Donald M. Grant, **The Dark Tower: The Gunslinger** was the first of what King has termed the "true" limited editions. In other words, here's a book that was not available in any other form. As King in an interview explained to Janet Beaulieu in *Castle Rock*:

> It wasn't like the other books. The first volume didn't have any firm grounding in our world, in reality; it was more like a Tolkien fantasy of some other world. The other reason was that it wasn't done; it wasn't complete. I had a volume of work, and it was "peg-legged"; it was there, inside its covers, it made a certain amount of sense, but there was all this stuff that I wasn't talking about that went on before the book opens, and when the book ends,

there's all this stuff to be resolved, including: What is this all about? What is this tower? Why does this guy need to get there?

King's concerns about reactions from his readers—those who expected only horror from him—came to the forefront after a public speech in 1989. During the question and answer period that followed, a reader asked whether the Bachman books and the **Dark Tower** books were "like a vacation" because they didn't "seem to quite fit in with your horror." King, resignation in his voice, replied: "All I can say is, I'm a horror writer if you *want* me to be. You can call me anything you want to—I don't care. We have this thing in America where everybody's got to have a brand name. You've got your generic game-show host; you've got your generic western writer; you've got your generic bad-guy actor; you've got your generic horror writer. I just write stories, but I *tend* to write [horror]."

In writing something like the **Dark Tower** books, King didn't fulfill his reader's expectations—he exceeded them and himself, requiring them to stretch with him.

In this series, King explores one of his frequent themes: our world has moved on, like the Gunslinger's world. "I want to talk about the way things fall apart." King elaborated:

> I think that we will come to a world, if things go on the way they are, where you have degenerate people who worship gas pumps, that sort of thing. . . . Everybody in **The Gunslinger** kind of shrugs and says, "Well, the world's moved on." But the point is that if nobody tries to stop the world from moving on, inertia will take care of all of our problems. The whales will all be gone, the ozone layer will be depleted. There'll be a degeneration where technology continues to progress and there's no morality to keep it in check, as though machines would somehow solve all of our problems.

Magnificently illustrated by Michael Whelan, the book showcases—as do all of Grant's books—the creativity that is possible in book design and production, and thereby recalls the turn-of-the-century illustrated books of fiction, all but gone today.

In his afterword to the book King anticipated questions from the reader. An intuitive writer, he admitted that he knew at times no more than the reader; but when the stories were ready to be told, they'd come to him and would "roll out as naturally as tears or laughter."

❏ **The Dark Tower II: The Drawing of the Three** (Donald M. Grant, Publisher, Inc., 1987) picks up where the first book left off, seven hours later. Clearly a novel—as opposed to interrelated short stories—this book, written several years after the last installment of the story ran in *F&SF*, shows a stronger, more mature fictional voice.

Whelan was approached to illustrate this edition but declined because his work schedule would not permit it. Instead, Phil Hale, a relative newcomer to the field—he had illustrated a plate in Grant's limited edition of **The Talisman**—was approached and rendered a unique set of illustrations, well suited for this second volume. (Whereas Whelan's depiction of Roland the Gunslinger is romanticized, Hale's depiction is more gritty: Hale sees Roland the Gunslinger as tall, lean, and hard, as if he had actor Rutger Hauer in mind.)

As in the afterword in the first book, the afterword in the second book tantalizes and provides hints but reveals little, whetting the appetite.

❏ **The Dark Tower III: The Wastelands** (Donald M. Grant, Publisher, Inc., August 1991) "details half of the quest of Roland, Eddie, and Susannah to reach the Tower," wrote King in his afterword to the second book in the series. A longer book than the second, this third volume is 512 pages.

According to the publisher, artist Ned Dameron provides "12 full-color illustrations, including 10 double-page spreads." The $38 trade edition is limited to 40,000 copies; the numbered edition of 1,200 copies ($120) is signed by King and Dameron.

■ **The Dark Tower IV: Wizard and Glass**, forthcoming novel, yet to be written.

❏ **The Dead Zone** (Viking, 1979), set in Castle Rock, Maine, is one of King's favorite novels for writing and, especially, plot.

❏ **Different Seasons** (Viking, 1982) collects four novellas, with an afterword that tells a little about the genesis of each piece. In **Four Past Midnight** King wrote about the earlier collection and its critical reception: "The critics, by and large, also liked **Different Seasons**. Almost all of them would napalm one particular novella, but since each of them picked a different story to scorch, I felt I could disregard them all with impunity . . . and I did."

In his afterword to **Different Seasons** King wrote of his novels: "Most of them have been plain fiction for plain folks, the literary equivalent of a Big Mac and a large fries from McDonald's." Food for thought, the statement is to me more a comment on the accessibility of his prose than anything else. When King explores the waters of mainstream fiction, as he does in "Apt Pupil" and "The Body," he patently has waded out beyond the boundaries of the horror genre, in which critics seem determined to place him.

If anything, King has *broadened* the boundaries of the genre, feeding into the mainstream.

❏ **Dolan's Cadillac** (Lord John Press, 1989) was out of print before publication. That was its only appearance apart from serialization in the early issues of *Castle Rock* (issues 2 through 6 in 1985). It will very likely be reprinted in King's next short-fiction collection, if he decides to bring it out.

The use of a Cadillac in the story is not accidental. For one thing, the Cadillac is built like a tank, which is important to the integrity of the story. For another, a Cadillac is a symbol of wealth, again important to the integrity of the story. (In an interview with Spignesi for *The Shape Under the Sheet,* Chris Chesley recalled an early promise of King, then fourteen years old: "You know what I'm gonna do the first time I hit it big, Chris? I'm gonna get myself a great big Cadillac." And, Chesley notes, King did.)

☐ **Dolores Claiborne** (scheduled for September 1992). This novel is to be the final offering of the four-book deal engineered by Arthur Greene. There has been no word as to its contents or length.

■ **The Doors** is, according to Michael Collings, an "unpublished, unfinished, unscheduled, and previously unknown novel." No more information is available.

☐ **The Eyes of the Dragon** (Philtrum Press, 1984). For those who think that King can write only horror, this book should come as a pleasant surprise. A writer is likely to turn up anything in his "toolbox," capable of constructing all kinds of stories.

King, who has heard enough comments from readers who think it's a child's tale because he wrote it for his daughter, points out that it's a story for *all* ages. The jacket copy confirms: "Stephen King has taken the classic fairy-tale form and transformed it into a masterpiece of fiction that will captivate readers of all ages."

L. Sprague de Camp—author of over a hundred books, including many works of fantasy—stated that it is neither a "child's fairytale" nor a "modern adult heroic fantasy." If anything, de Camp asserted, it can be "justly compared" to *The Lord of The Rings,* a work with which King is familiar, as **The Stand** and also **The Talisman** bring to mind Tolkien's trilogy. The comparison, to my mind, is apt.

The ending of **The Eyes of the Dragon** is wide open, leaving plenty of room for a sequel, though it's unlikely King will do so.

☐ **Firestarter** (Viking, 1980) is in a way a twist on **Carrie** and **The Shining**; in all three a child has an unwanted psychic ability. In **Firestarter** Charlene (Charlie) McGee has pyrokinesis.

☐ **Four Past Midnight** (Viking, 1990) comprises four novellas, all supernatural tales. (In comparison, the four novellas in **Different Seasons** were mainstream, though one story could be deemed marginally supernatural, "The Breathing Method.") In an introductory note and separate notes on each story, King tells the story behind each story.

In a videotaped interview produced by Equitable Group, King explained

that novellas are popular because "they have some of the stripped-down feel—
just the essentials." That, to me, also explains why King—a consummate short-
story writer but at times too self-indulgent as a novelist—shines as a writer of
novellas. As he said, it's like "taking off all the nonessentials and leaving this
bullet projectile."

On "The Langoliers," King said he wanted to explore the idea of "people
trapped on an airplane . . . I was able to make it work in a different way." Like
King's novella "The Mist" (people trapped in a Maine supermarket), "The
Langoliers" shares, as King pointed out, "an apocalyptic feel. . . ."

"Secret Window, Secret Garden," according to King, is an exploration of a
writer's nightmare. "I knew I had something because if there's anything that any
writer is deathly afraid of, it's writer's Kryptonite—plagiarism. . . . Of the
writer stories, it's easily the best from my viewpoint."

"The Library Policeman" had its genesis in a conversation with his son
Owen. The story *behind* the story provides a glimpse of the creative mind in the
process of building a story.

At a public lecture in Pasadena, California, King spoke extemporaneously
and spun out this tale of how his son Owen, who had his own library card,
wanted his father to check out the books with his card. When King asked why,
his son began: "I'm afraid . . ." and mumbled the rest of the sentence.

"I didn't get anything except the first two words, and immediately my
antenna comes right up and I want to know what this kid's afraid of . . . there
might be millions of dollars in this. Immediately, I become the concerned
parent," recalled King.

Owen said, "Well, I'm afraid of the library police." After some discussion
Owen told his father that his aunt, Stephanie Leonard, told him that he'd have
to return the library books on time, or the library police will come to the house
and get the books and *hurt* you.

King recalled, "It was like this total blast when things comes together and I
remembered the terror of the library when I was a kid. When I took the books
out, I always have to check the date. In those days, they just stamped the back of
the book: June 24. And that was the edge of the known universe. In theory, what
happened if you brought them back on June 25th instead? But you wonder to
yourself, 'What if I don't bring them back for a year?'

"And then I could remember as a kid the times when I couldn't find my
library books. I would just go totally skyhigh. . . . What do they *do* to children
who don't find their library books?

" 'But what if you don't have the books anymore?' And I started to turn this
thing over in my mind, started to wonder what a library policeman would look
like. I know what librarians look like—they look like regular people. Now think
about this: When you go out of this place [the Pasadena public library], you
look at all the unmarked doors and you go by doors [marked] 'AUTHORIZED

PERSONNEL ONLY.' Somewhere, behind one of those doors, there are two guys who are about seven feet tall, silver eyes, trench coats, and horrible, horrible weapons.

"So I started to write this story and I set it in Iowa, because Iowa seemed like Library Police country to me. I can't say why. . . .

"I think that what I'm trying to get at is the specific uses of the imagination. I started with a concept and started to build this thing up about what they would do to you. And the way I was able to work this story up was that I was able to take a guy who needed a couple of books quick, who hadn't been to the library in a long time, and went and got a couple of books from a very odd librarian who turns out to have been dead for thirty years. He uses the books to help him make a speech to the rotary club, and when he's done, he puts the books in a box in his kitchen, which happens to be a box that's full of old newspapers."

As King explained, the books were pulped and inevitably the library police come . . .

The last story in the book, "The Sun Dog," is a prelude piece for **Needful Things**.

Interestingly, the story may have been germinating for some time. On a horror panel with Ira Levin, Peter Straub, and George Romero on the "Dick Cavett Show," which aired on October 30 and 31, 1980, King talks about his fan mail, and one letter in particular:

> I can remember getting a letter from a fellow who wanted to come up. He said he had a magic Polaroid camera. And he could take my picture, and I would see all my ancestors standing behind me in a diminishing line. There'd be my father, my grandfather, [my great grandfather]—you know, on and on, presumably back to primordial depths, I don't know. I don't answer that sort of letter.

❑ **IT** (Viking, 1986), according to King's note at the end of the novel, was approximately four years in the writing—from germination to completion of the final draft. It's a long time to live with a novel, but King wanted to put everything in this novel about children and monsters, and did so. King said on the "Larry King Show":

> This novel percolated for about three years. The idea just sort of pogoed into my mind. I was walking over a wooden bridge; it was almost dark. I was wearing a pair of boots and I could hear my footsteps on the bridge. I flashed on the story "Billy Goat's Gruff" with the troll under the bridge ("Who's that trip-trapping over this bridge?"), and I thought, *Okay, that's what I want to write about.* So two or three years went by, and finally I sat down to write it. Four years later and 1,600 pages later, it was done.

An admittedly ambitious but fundamentally flawed novel—it's difficult for me to believe that the creature could have been initially bested by a handful of children, who years later, as adults, manage to kill it—the first half of the book, the story of the children, is much better than the second half, the story of the children as adults.

An exploration of myth, **IT** also explores one of King's fundamental beliefs. As King told an interviewer:

> Above all else, I'm interested in good and evil, whether or not there are
> powers of good and powers of evil that exist outside ourselves. I think that
> the concepts of good and evil are in the human heart, but because I was
> raised in a fairly strict religious home [Methodist], I tend to coalesce those
> concepts around God symbols and evil symbols, and I put them in my work.

In an earlier novel, **The Stand**, King also wrestled with those fundamental questions, and like **IT**, **The Stand** perforce required a large canvas.

☐ **The Long Walk** (Signet, 1979; see **The Bachman Books**) is one of King's few stories that could be termed science fiction; more precisely, this kind of story is "alternate history." In other words, it's the world as we know it, but it's dissimilar in critical ways, and usually set in the future.

Although King admits the novel is "full of windy psychological preachments . . . there's still a lot of story in those novels," he wrote in an introduction to **The Bachman Books**.

■ **Milkman** is an aborted novel. From the two segments published in **Skeleton Crew**, one can see the grittiness of blue-collar life in Maine (captured so well in **'Salem's Lot**) colored by a surreal, bizarre twist. This is one novel I wish King would write.

☐ **Misery** (Viking, 1987) is one of King's best novels. In this psychological suspense story Annie Wilkes emerges as one of the most horrific of all of King's characters, although she doesn't see herself as the death angel she is.

The inspiration for the novel came from the far-out fringe fans who write to him. In an interview with David Sherman for *Fangoria* magazine, King said that the fan mail from "[t]he lunatic fringe is less than one percent. It's a rare week when we find one. We just sort of all gather together and exclaim over it. Most of the letter writers look to be from people who are, I would say, just middle-to-upper-class people."

Misery also highlights King's relationship with his normal readers, which as he said in a recent interview with *Publishers Weekly* is one of duality:

> I feel a certain pressure about my writing, and I have an idea of who reads
> my books; I am concerned with my readership. But it's kind of a combination
> love letter/poison-pen relationship, a sweet-and-sour thing. . . . I feel I

ought to write something because people want to read something. But I think, "Don't give them what they want—give them what you want."

It's a frustration that stems from the pigeonholing of King as a horror writer, which, I think, has kept King from a larger audience. I've met a number of readers who simply condemn and dismiss King out of hand, prejudging the work by what's on the surface.

In *Grimoire* Clive Barker stressed that the horror label is too restrictive when describing King's work:

> Steve's contribution, I don't think, is as much to horror fiction as to what I would call *fantastique,* fantasy fiction, the fiction of the imagination. Clearly, there are massive overlaps in his fiction between science fiction and horror, between fantasy fiction and horror, and indeed mainstream fiction and horror. It almost becomes redundant to say, *What does Steve offer to the horror genre?* What we should be asking is, *What does he offer to writing, to the business of prose?*

❏ **My Pretty Pony** (Whitney Museum, 1989). In recent years a number of King's stories, including this one, have had as their topic what King called the "essential conundrum of time," as he wrote in an introduction to **Four Past Midnight**.

A gentle short story about a boy and his grandfather, *My Pretty Pony* will likely see inclusion in King's third short-fiction collection.

❏ **Needful Things** (Viking, October 1991) is King at his storytelling best; it was optioned for a feature-length film by Reiner's company, Castle Rock Entertainment. A fictional nod to King's own **'Salem's Lot** (in its evocation of the Maine milieu) and to Matheson's short story "The Distributor," **Needful Things** also recalls the Faust legend and Mark Twain's "The Mysterious Stranger."

King could mine Castle Rock for many more stories, but he's chosen not to. His imagination is such that, as Stevens reminds us in "The Breathing Method," there are *always* more tales.

King's ability to surprise his readership—to give them what he wants, as opposed to what they *think* they want—is King's most impressive aspect. As Douglas E. Winter said in *Grimoire*:

> I think Steve is trying to challenge his readers, perhaps not with every book, but with many of them. It's what I love most about him. Just when I think that I have a handle on his awesome capabilities and capacities, he surprises the hell out of me with his very next book. I am in genuine awe of his talent to do that. And I think that's something people are beginning to take for granted, which they shouldn't. Each time I see one of his new books, every second or third one, I'm just bowled over by the breadth of his talent.

❏ **Night Shift** (Doubleday, 1978) is one hell of a good collection. King's introduction on why he writes horror and why people read it is worth your reading—an appropriate prelude piece to **Danse Macabre**.

Even though there's no money for King in writing short stories—unless they grow into novels—he writes them because, as he wrote in **Skeleton Crew**, he has no choice: "All the same, you don't do it for money, or you're a monkey. . . . You do it because to not do it is suicide."

Clive Barker, whose short stories in *Books of Blood* drew King's high praise and endorsement, said, "I think the short fiction remains perhaps the most vital of his output, and I regret that there isn't more of it."

❏ **People, Places, and Things—Volume I** (Triad Publishing Company, 1963). It's common for young writers to self-publish, simply so they can see their work in print. For those in the fantasy circles, fanzines—fan magazines—are frequently early showcases. King wisely avoided involvement with organized fandom, unlike H. P. Lovecraft, who immersed himself in "fanac" (fan activity) to the detriment of his professional output.

Although King is understandably embarrassed by these teenage efforts, the important thing is that the stories in this early "book" clearly show promise. And at that age, that's the best any writer can hope for.

❏ **Pet Sematary** (Doubleday, 1983) is one of King's best novels precisely because King visualized his worst nightmare come true—the death of one of his children—and in writing this novel made it *every* parent's nightmare.

A writer seldom *chooses* a story; the story chooses *him,* especially in stories where art imitates life. With King, it seems, everything springs from fear. Said King:

> People say, "Well, you probably jumped on this bandwagon." The fact, is,
> I've been writing this stuff forever. There was just a time when it seemed as
> though there were no market for it. A lot of this rises out of a clear sense of
> terror. I'm afraid of almost everything in the world. . . . At the same time,
> I'm fascinated by what I'm terrified by.

❏ **The Plant** (Philtrum Press, 1982, 1983, 1985), as King said, is "an epistolary novel-in-progress." A marvelously inventive story centering around an unsuspecting book editor at a failing publishing company and the strange plant he gets in the mail, **The Plant** may not see completion, for, according to King, "I went to see *The Little Shop of Horrors* between the [writing of] the second and third installment, and realized that was what I was writing. So I decided to stop right away."

❏ **Rage** (Signet, 1977; see **The Bachman Books**). Appropriately the first Bachman book published—King's first attempt at a serious novel—**Rage** is a necessary prelude to **Carrie**. Like **The Long Walk**, **Rage** was "full of windy psychological preachments," according to King. However, he admits, "there's still a lot of story" in that novel.

While in grammar school King wrote a story that sounded very much like **Rage**. Years later the story took its final form.

❏ **Roadwork** (Signet, 1981; see **The Bachman Books**). In an introduction to **The Bachman Books**, King reveals that he wrote it between **'Salem's Lot** and **The Shining**, and as "an effort to write a 'straight' novel" because people had asked him when was he going to write something serious.

Instead of focusing on a supernatural or horror element, **Roadwork** taps into more commonplace fears—specifically, a fear of cancer.

❏ **The Running Man** (Signet, 1982; see **The Bachman Books**). Set in 2025, this work—one of King's few forays into science fiction—is one of King's favorite novels, according to Douglas Winter. King wrote that this novel "moves with the goofy speed of a silent movie," like a stripped-down car.

❏ **'Salem's Lot** (Doubleday, 1975; originally titled **Second Coming**, then **Jerusalem's Lot**) is one of the few novels to which King has, over the years, thought of writing a sequel. But recently, at a public speech in Pasadena, California, he was asked about the sequel and replied that too much time had elapsed; he didn't think he'd write it, though he did write a short story, "One for the Road," that picked up where **'Salem's Lot** left off.

In a 1982 issue of *Fangoria* magazine King told an interviewer what the sequel, if written, would address:

> When I wrote "One for the Road" I knew that things weren't over in Jerusa-lem's Lot, the same way that I know they aren't over now. I think about a sequel a lot. I even know who would be in it and how it would launch . . . it's Father Callahan. I know where he is. People ask me, "You see Father Calla-han [get on] that Greyhound bus; what happened to him?" Well, I know what happened to him. He went to New York City and from New York he drifted across the country and he landed in Detroit. He's in the inner city and he's running a soup kitchen for alcoholics, mostly black, and he's been attacked a couple of times and he's been in the hospital and people think he's crazy. He doesn't wear the turned-around collar anymore, but he's doing this anyway and he's trying to get right with God. So one day this guy comes in. He's dying and he says, "I have to talk to you, Father Callahan." And Callahan says, "I'm not a Father anymore and how did you know that?" Finally, the guy is actually dying and coughing up blood and the last thing he says as he grabs Callahan by the shirt and pulls him down into this mist of beer and whiskey and puke and everything else is, "It's not over in the Lot, yet." Then he drops dead. So that's when it starts and Callahan realizes that if he's going

to get right he has to go back and do it there; that he can't do it in Detroit saving bums. He's got to do it where he got wrong with God. I even know how the book ends, but I just don't know what the transmission of it all is. Something's got to run it and it can't be vampires. The vampires have got to figure in it, but that can't be the major thing. Someday it'll come to me and I'll write it.

❏ **The Shining** (Doubleday, 1977), one of King's best novels, impressed Peter Straub so much that, for *Horror: 100 Best Books,* he wrote: "The fact is that **The Shining** is a masterwork, a bold product of an original vision, a novel of astonishing passion, urgency, tenderness, understanding, and invention."

King's archetypal Bad Place—like Shirley Jackson's Hill House in *The Haunting of Hill House*—**The Shining** (book) is very different from **The Shining** (film). In an introduction to the restored edition of **The Stand**, King wrote that you couldn't read Ken Kesey's *One Flew Over the Cuckoo Nest* without seeing "Jack Nicholson's face on Randle Patrick McMurphy. That is not necessarily bad . . . but it *is* limiting." The same can be said for **The Shining** (movie), for you cannot see it without seeing Jack Nicholson's face on Jack Torrance.

Read the book, *then* see the movie.

❏ **Silver Bullet** (Signet, 1985; see **Cycle of the Werewolf**).

❏ **The Stand** (Doubleday, 1978). The original version of **The Stand** remains King's most popular—and in many ways, most enduring—novel. It showcases King's imagination, breadth, and inventiveness in a way that recalls *Lord of the Rings,* and thus makes you wish it was a never-ending story. The last of his early novels at Doubleday, it is a testament to King's success that Doubleday not only reissued the book in a restored edition, but did so in an attractive trade edition and sumptuous limited edition, for which it deserves credit.

❏ **Stephen King** (William Heinemann, 1978) is an omnibus edition that collects—depending on the edition you get—**The Shining**, **'Salem's Lot**, **Night Shift**, and **Carrie**, or collects just the novels.

■ **Sword in the Darkness** (also called **Babylon Here** to distract people from linking King to Bachman) exists only in manuscript form at the Special Collections at the University of Maine at Orono. In all likelihood it will never see publication. On the "Larry King Show" Stephen King talked about his "trunk" books: "I probably have four novels in the trunk that just happen to be dead-on-arrival. They're not good books. My definition of how you know when a book's a bad book is that even when you're drunk, you can't read it and say, 'This is a good book.' "

❏ **The Talisman** by Stephen King and Peter Straub (Viking and G. P. Putnam's Sons, 1984) remains King's only book-length collaboration.

In the wake of its success, Straub found himself inextricably linked to King, sometimes to his dismay. In the *Castle Rock* interview, he said, "I must confess that I have grown tired of being forced to talk about my friend Steve King on nearly every public occasion. I'm especially tired of those questioners who are in reality seeking juicy gossip about him, about us, or about our collaboration. There is no juicy gossip, and even if there was, I'd keep it to myself."

Donald M. Grant, Publisher, Inc., issued a beautiful two-volume, slip-cased, limited edition of **The Talisman**, with decorations by Thomas Canty and full-color illustrations by several prominent artists in the field, including Jeffrey Jones, Don Maitz, Rowena Morrell, Phil Hale, and Ned Dameron.

❑ **Thinner** (NAL, 1984) was originally a short story that grew—an inversion of the plot, in which the protagonist of the novel steadily lost weight. Unlike the other Bachman books, this one *read* like a Stephen King novel. Although its sales in hardback were impressive as a Bachman book, its sales after King's authorship became known showed the commercial value of the brand name.

❑ **The Tommyknockers** (Putnam, 1987) is, according to King, one of the few novels—like **The Eyes of the Dragon** and the **Dark Tower** books—that have not been optioned for the movies. Instead, it has been optioned by ABC-TV for a four-hour mini-series in Spring 1992.

■ **Under the Dome** (see **The Cannibals**).

■ **Weeds** was originally an aborted novel, though it saw publication as a short story in *Cavalier* and was adapted for the comic-book format of **Creepshow**. Approximately 20,000 words were written, but as King told interviewer Paul Gagne:

> I ran out of inspiration for the thing. . . . It took place during the Fourth of July, and there were fireworks in the sky throughout it all, which made it nice. Jordy [Verrill] originally had this neighbor who was a lot smarter and a better farmer than he was, and the weeds started to spread to his side. But once the weeds started to grow beyond that closed world and toward the town, I couldn't find any more to say. It seemed to me that that was all I really cared about, and I ran out of caring about it.

■ **Welcome to Clearwater** is an aborted novel that, according to Winter, was begun in 1976.

■ **Western** novel, untitled, aborted. In a 1989 public speech King said: "A few years ago, I did try very hard to write a western, because it's a form I like. I wrote about 160 pages and the only scene that really had any power was when this old guy got drunk outside this farmhouse and fell into the pigsty, and the pigs ate him. That one scene has some real drive and punch. This is what turned on my lights, for reasons I don't understand."

■ **You Know They've Got A Helluva Band**, a "short novel." In *Fangoria #105* (August 1991), Brad Ashton-Haiste recounts in "Bleedful Kings" the talk King gave at the Landmark Theatre in Syracuse, New York, on April 26, 1991. In the article, Ashton-Haiste wrote:

> Another project on the King writing front is the just-completed short novel
> **You Know They've Got A Helluva Band.** Set in Oregon, it concerns a
> group of people who "get lost on a back road, the back road goes from bad to
> worse, they end up in a little town called Rock 'n' Roll Heaven, Oregon, and
> everybody is there. The waitress at the restaurant is Janis Joplin; the town
> bad boy is Jim Morrison; Ronnie Van Zandt hangs out at the pool hall with
> Jim Croce. And the thing is, the group has to stay because the rockers need
> an audience."

Initially reported as a "short novel," this is in fact a long short story (approximately 18,000 words) which will be published in an anthology edited by Jeff Gelb, *Shock Rock: The New Sound of Horror,* a $4.99 mass market paperback original from Pocket Books to be published in January 1992.

Other Projects

❏ In the papers at the Special Collections at the library at the University of Maine at Orono, there are two unpublished essays that were intended for inclusion in a nonfiction collection, which was to bear a dedication to King's mother. It does not appear that its final contents had been determined, though at least two pieces were completed. One discussed Ray Kroc and McDonalds ("Your Kind of Place"). In the other King reflected on his childhood days in Stratford, Connecticut. There he and his brother once were taken by their mother to a shoestore where they saw a machine for X-raying feet. Naturally curious, they asked their mother what it was. "Culch" (pure junk), she responded. Later the boys returned to the store and Stephen put his foot in the machine and saw a ghostly green X-ray of his foot—his bones were wiggling. As King recalled, he didn't care for it at all. Later the machine was removed from the store because of its cancer-inducing characteristics.

In recent years King has discussed the possibility of putting together a third collection of short fiction. My best guess is that he will do so, since he has on hand sufficient material. I'll also hazard a guess that this book will appear as a trade hardback in 1992 (1993, at the latest).

In a recent interview with *W•B* King said that there were a number of novels he wanted to write:

1. His Viking editor, Chuck Verrill, suggested he write *Steel Machine,* an excerpt of which appears in **The Dark Half**. *Steel Machine,* credited to Richard Stark, would be published as a Richard Bachman novel. "And so I'm actually thinking about writing [it]," King said.

2. "There is a baseball book in me. I didn't mention it because that's the one that's closest to actually happening." (Recently, October 1990, at a press conference for *Stephen King's Graveyard Shift* in Bangor, King reiterated that he wanted to write a baseball novel.)

3. "I'd like to write a novel about an evangelist, not necessarily an Elmer Gantry novel, but I'd like to write about religion."

4. "I'd like to write a novel about Christ."

5. "I've got an interest in writing a novel about what happened at Jonestown."

2. Short Fiction

This checklist of short fiction lists published, uncollected (indicated by a black box, ■), and forthcoming stories. If collected, it gives the name of the book. If uncollected, it gives the publication name and year of publication.

Stories in *People, Places, and Things—Volume One* are juvenilia and, as such, will not likely be reprinted. For that reason I have not marked these stories with the black-box symbol.

"Apt Pupil" (in *Different Seasons*). Early in King's career the trappings of horror took traditional forms: ghosts, werewolves, and vampires. Later King explored the monsters that were within *us,* and in doing so found rich material indeed. One of his most horrific stories, this one is mainstream fiction and one of his best stories.

"The Ballad of the Flexible Bullet" (in *Skeleton Crew*).

"Battleground" (in *Night Shift*).

"Beachworld" (in *Skeleton Crew*).

"The Bear" (*F&SF,* December 1990; an excerpt from **The Dark Tower III: The Wastelands**).

■ **"Before the Play"** (*Whispers* 17/18, August 1982). A prelude piece, a stage setter for *The Shining,* this tells the history of the Overlook—its construction and its haunted past. Although it was to be reprinted in *The Shape Under the Sheet*, King pulled it at the last minute. Both "Before the Play" and an end piece "After the Play" were originally cut from the book at the behest of King's editor, who said that by doing so, the publisher could shave $1 off the retail price. Unfortunately, "After the Play," an unpublished piece, was later lost by King.

"Big Wheels: A Tale of the Laundry Game (Milkman #2)" (in *Skeleton Crew;* see **Milkman** in list of books).

"The Bird and the Album" (*A Fantasy Reader: The Seventh World Fantasy Convention Program Book*, edited by Jeff Frane and Jack Rems; 1981. An excerpt from *IT*).

■ **"The Blue Air Compressor"** (*Onan*, January 1971; heavily revised for its appearance in *Heavy Metal*, July 1981).

"The Body" (in *Different Seasons*). This is one of King's finest works, which to my mind would be strengthened if the two pieces of fiction within the work—stories within the main story—were deleted. Of King's work, this is his all-time favorite, as he said at the 1989 Pasadena lecture.

"The Boogeyman" (in *Night Shift*).

"The Breathing Method" (in *Different Seasons*).

"Cain Rose Up" (in *Skeleton Crew*).

■ **"The Cat from Hell"** (*Cavalier*, June 1977). This was inspired by a newspaper photograph that King received from *Cavalier's* Nye Willden. The original idea was for King to write the beginning, then have the readers write their endings for a *Cavalier* contest. King, however, could not resist completing the story, and Willden could not resist publishing it.

"Children of the Corn" (in *Night Shift*) is set in Nebraska, a place that, to King, is the perfect place for a horror story. In a videotaped interview from Equitable Group, King said that "I love it out there because reality's thinner; I don't know how to describe it any better than that." King explained that the eeriness evoked by Nebraska has much to do with its isolation and straight roads, with few towns, and radio stations dropping off the air. "And you say to yourself: *Anything* can happen out here. And I know where some of the byways are that I've gotten people to travel along with me. I like to take them out there and leave them out there."

"The Crate" (originally published in *Gallery*, July 1979; adapted as a comic-book story for *Creepshow*). The original inspiration came from a real-life incident at the University of Maine at Orono, where an old crate dating back to the previous century had been discovered in the basement of one of the buildings on campus. What, King thought, *could* have been in that crate?

■ **"Crouch End"** (anthologized in *New Tales of the Cthulhu Mythos*, edited by Ramsey Campbell; 1980). When King was in England visiting Peter

Straub, he got lost in the Crouch End section of London, where Straub lived. That was the original inspiration for this tale set against H. P. Lovecraft's Cthulhu Mythos.

"Cujo" (*Science Fiction Digest,* January–February 1982; see **Cujo** in list of books).

"The Cursed Expedition" (*People, Places, and Things—Volume One*).

"Dedication" (in a collection, *Night Visions 5,* edited by Douglas E. Winter; 1988).

"The Dimension Warp" (*People, Places, and Things—Volume One*).

"The Doctor's Case" (anthologized in *The New Adventures of Sherlock Holmes: Original Stories by Eminent Mystery Writers,* edited by Martin Greenberg and Carol-Lynn Rossel; 1987). A mystery fan, King wrote a "locked room" story for this collection.

"Dolan's Cadillac" (see **Dolan's Cadillac** in book listing). This is a tale of revenge recalling Poe's "The Cask of Amontillado."

"Do the Dead Sing?" (see "The Reach"). For this elegiac story, King received the World Fantasy Award in 1981. Inspired by a real-life Stella Flanders who refused to cross the body of water known as the Reach to the mainland from her home on Goat Island, this story evinces King's ability at once to evoke the texture of life in Maine and to dab it with a touch of the supernatural. It also addresses two of King's central concerns in his fiction: the enduring power of love (do you love?) and the inevitability of death.

"The End of the Whole Mess" (*Omni* magazine, October 1986).

"Father's Day" (in *Creepshow*).

"The Fifth Quarter" (under the pen name John Swithen, King's only other pen name ever used; *Cavalier,* April 1972).

"For the Birds" (*Bred Any Good Rooks Lately* "gathered" by James Charlton; Doubleday, 1986). The punchline of King's story was used for the title of this short, fun collection of puns using birds as its theme; presumably, the contributors simply winged it.

"The Glass Floor" (*Startling Mystery Stories,* fall 1967; reprinted with minor changes in *Weird Tales,* fall 1990, with an introductory essay by King on the history of the piece).

"Gramma" (in *Skeleton Crew*). In an interview in *The Shape Under the Sheet,* Chris Chesley tells Spignesi that as a child, King "saw and felt too much for his age," that King couldn't filter out the world around him. As a result, King transmuted his life experiences into fiction, as he did in this story, which is based on King's days in Durham when his mother took care of her parents. King, then eleven years old, saw his invalid and sick grandmother as a "horrifying presence," said Chesley. The result: a "hair-raising story," according to Chesley, which "raised the hackles on my neck, even though I knew from whence the story was derived."

"Graveyard Shift" (in *Night Shift*). During high school and in the summer, King worked at a textile mill, the inspiration for this story.

"Gray Matter" (in *Night Shift*).

"The Gunslinger" (*F&SF,* October 1978; see **The Dark Tower: The Gunslinger** in list of books).

"The Gunslinger and the Dark Man" (*F&SF,* November 1981; see **The Dark Tower: The Gunslinger**).

"Here There Be Tygers" (in *Skeleton Crew*).

"Heroes for Hope Starring the X-Men" (Marvel Comics Group, 1985; a benefit book for famine relief in Africa, King contributed three pages to the project).

■ **"Home Delivery"** (anthologized in *Book of the Dead,* published by Mark V. Ziesing, edited by John Skipp and Craig Spector; 1989). A short story for an anthology of zombie stories, this horrific tale satisfies the third level of gross-out that King aims for when he can't achieve terror or horror.

"Hotel at the End of the Road" (*People, Places, and Things—Volume One*).

"I Am the Doorway" (in *Night Shift*).

"I Know What You Need" (in *Night Shift*).

"I'm Falling" (*People, Places, and Things—Volume One*).

■ **"In A Half-World of Terror"** (see "I Was a Teenage Grave Robber").

■ **"It Grows on You"** (originally published in a college literary magazine, *Marshroots,* in 1975; reprinted in the Stephen King issue of *Whispers,* 17/18, August 1982).

"I've Got to Get Away" (*People, Places, and Things—Volume One*).

■ **"I Was a Teenage Grave Robber"** (originally published in a fanzine, *Comics Review,* in 1965; reprinted in 1966 in Marvin Wolfman's fanzine, *Stories of Suspense,* as "In a Half-World of Terror," the title King preferred). In an interview with Bhob Stewart in *Starship,* King commented on fanzines and fan activity in general: "One of the things I think has been good for me— really, really good—is that I stayed out, mostly by luck, of that circle of fanzines and fans that club together."

"The Jaunt" (in *Skeleton Crew*).

"Jerusalem's Lot" (in *Night Shift*). This epistolary story predates **'Salem's Lot** and is the only tale in **Night Shift** that, for obvious reasons, has not been optioned for the movies. Owing much to H. P. Lovecraft's "The Rats in the Walls" and Stoker's *Dracula,* it laid the groundwork for *'Salem's Lot.*

"The Langoliers" (in *Four Past Midnight*).

"The Last Rung on the Ladder" (in *Night Shift*). In his introduction to *Night Shift,* John D. MacDonald cited this story as "[o]ne of the most resonant and affecting stories in this book. . . . A gem. Nary a rustle nor breath of other worlds in it." MacDonald's contention—borne out by the range of work that followed this book—is that in focusing on what's most obvious about King's work, the monsters, we overlook the more important element: story. In short, we should judge King not by *what* he writes but by *how* he writes. That would probably suit King just fine, since his linkage with the field has had its detrimental effects: "The thing about this field—if you visualize American Literature as a town, then the horror writer's across the tracks on the poor side of town, and that's where the 'nice' people won't go," he told Charles L. Grant in an interview for *Twilight Zone*.

"The Lawnmower Man" (in *Night Shift*).

"The Ledge" (in *Night Shift*).

"The Library Policeman" (in *Four Past Midnight*).

"The Lonesome Death of Jordy Verrill" (in *Creepshow*).

"The Mangler" (in *Night Shift*).

"The Man Who Loved Flowers" (in *Night Shift*).

"The Man Who Would Not Shake Hands" (in *Night Shift*).

■ **"The Man with a Belly"** (*Cavalier*, December 1978).

"The Mist" (in *Skeleton Crew*).

"The Monkey" (in *Skeleton Crew*).

"The Monster in the Closet" (*Ladies' Home Journal*, October 1981; an excerpt from **Cujo**).

"Morning Deliveries (Milkman #1)" (in *Skeleton Crew*).

■ **"The Moving Finger"** (in *F&SF*, December 1990).

"Mrs. Todd's Shortcut" (in *Skeleton Crew*).

■ **"My Pretty Pony"** (see **My Pretty Pony** in the book listing).

"Never Look Behind You" (a collaboration with Christopher Chesley, in *People, Places, and Things—Volume One*).

■ **"The Night Flier"** (anthologized in *Prime Evil: New Stories by the Masters of Modern Horror*, edited by Douglas E. Winter; as a limited edition by Donald M. Grant, and as a trade hardback by NAL, both in 1988). This vampire story shows King's ability to pump new life into a traditional horror creature.

■ **"Night of the Tiger"** (*F&SF*, February 1978). Originally submitted to Robert Lowndes, the story was rejected on the grounds that he published mostly reprints in his magazines; besides, the story was too long. When King finally broke into print professionally, his first sale to Lowndes was for *Startling Mystery Stories*. An editorial comment prefacing the piece noted that this story had been formerly rejected because of length.

"Night Surf" (in *Night Shift*).

"Nona" (in *Skeleton Crew*).

"One for the Road" (in *Night Shift*).

"The Oracle and the Mountains" (*F&SF*, February 1981; see **The Dark Tower: The Gunslinger** in the list of books).

"The Other Side of the Fog" (*People, Places, and Things—Volume One*).

■ **"Popsy"** (anthologized in *Masques II: All-New Stories of Horror and the Super-natural,* edited by J. N. Williamson; Maclay & Associates, 1987).

"Quitters, Inc." (in *Night Shift*).

"The Raft" (rewritten for inclusion in *Skeleton Crew;* see King's explanation in the afterword to the collection).

"Rainy Season" (*Midnight Graffiti,* spring 1989).

"The Reach" (in *Skeleton Crew*).

"The Reaper's Image" (in *Skeleton Crew*).

"The Reploids" (collected in *Night Visions 5,* edited by Douglas E. Winter; Dark Harvest, 1988).

"The Return of Timmy Baterman" (*Satyricon II Program Book,* edited by Rusty Burke, for a 1983 convention; an excerpt from *Pet Sematary*).

"The Revelations of 'Becka Paulson' " (*Rolling Stone,* July 19–August 2, 1984, reprinted in Scream Press edition of *Skeleton Crew;* an excerpt from *The Tommyknockers*).

"The Revenge of Lard Ass Hogan" (originally published in *Maine Review* in 1975, it was revised for inclusion as a story-within-a-story by Gordon Lachance in "The Body" in *Different Seasons*).

"Rita Hayworth and Shawshank Redemption" (in *Skeleton Crew*).

"Secret Window, Secret Garden" (in *Four Past Midnight*).

"Skybar" (in *The Do-It-Yourself Bestseller—A Workbook,* edited by Tom Silberkliet and Jerry Biederman; Doubleday under its Dolphin imprint, 1982).

"Slade" (serialized in eight weekly installments in *Maine Campus,* June 11–August 6, 1970).

"The Slow Mutants" (*F&SF,* July 1981; see **The Dark Tower: The Gunslinger** in list of books).

"Sneakers" (collected in *Night Visions 5,* edited by Douglas E. Winter; Dark Harvest, 1988).

"Something to Tide You Over" (in *Creepshow*).

"Sometimes They Come Back" (in *Night Shift*).

"Squad D" (to be anthologized in the third volume of Harlan Ellison's *Dangerous Visions* trilogy, *The Last Dangerous Visions;* no publication date has been announced).

"The Star Invaders" (self-published by King; Triad Publishing Company, under its Gaslight Book imprint, 1964).

"The Stranger" (*People, Places, and Things—Volume One*).

"Strawberry Spring" (originally in *Ubris,* then rewritten for its appearance in *Night Shift*).

"Stud City" (originally published in *Greenspun Quarterly* in 1970, it was revised for its appearance as a story-within-a-story by Gordon Lachance in "The Body" in *Different Seasons*).

"Suffer the Little Children" (*Cavalier,* February 1972).

"**The Sun Dog**" (in *Four Past Midnight*).

"**Survivor Type**" (in *Skeleton Crew*).

"**They're Creeping Up on You**" (in *Creepshow*).

"**The Thing at the Bottom of the Well**" (*People, Places, and Things—Volume One*).

"**Trucks**" (in *Night Shift*).

"**Uncle Otto's Truck**" (in *Skeleton Crew*).

"**The Way Station**" (*F&SF*, April 1980; see **The Dark Tower: The Gunslinger** in list of books).

"**The Wedding Gig**" (in *Skeleton Crew*).

"**Weeds**" (in *Cavalier*, May 1976; adapted as "The Lonesome Death of Jordy Verrill" for *Creepshow*).

"**The Woman in the Room**" (in *Night Shift*). One of King's most memorable stories, this one hit close to home. King wrote in *The Complete Masters of Darkness* that the story served a cathartic purpose for him—the healing power of fiction, not for the reader but, this time, for the storyteller.

"**Word Processor of the Gods**" (in *Skeleton Crew*).

Notes

Because this book is a popular study, I have not numbered the notes in the main text. Instead, I have numbered the endnotes sequentially, referenced by chapter and page number.

In some cases I worked with photocopied material and was not able to extract full bibliographic information. I am hopeful future editions will reflect full citations.

Throughout these notes the following abbreviations are used:

BDN—Bangor Daily News
CR—Castle Rock: The Stephen King Newsletter
DEW—Douglas E. Winter
GB—the author
NAL—New American Library
SK—Stephen King

Preface

1. P. 7: "I think that maybe the one value literary critics have is that they can chart a career after it's gone past a certain point." SK, quoted in "Taking You Blindfolded to the Cliff Edge," *19* magazine (British), March 1980, p. 6.

2. P. 7: "master of pop dread," the "indisputable King of horror, a demon fabulist who raises gooseflesh for fun and profit. . . . [H]e seems to be the country's best-known writer." Stefan Kanfer, "King of Horror," *Time,* October 6, 1986, p. 74.

3. P. 8: "Bestsellasaurus Rex." SK, "The Politics of Limiteds—Part II," *CR,* July 1985, p. 1.

4. P. 8: "middle-aged white rapper." SK, quoted by John Healy, "The 'King of Horror' to Pack City Hall Tuesday Night," *Evening Express* (Portland, ME), March 1, 1990.

5. P. 8: a writer who doubts he'll ever "be taken seriously." SK, interview in *Bare Bones: Conversations on Terror with Stephen King,* ed. Chuck Miller and Tim Underwood (New York: McGraw–Hill Book Company, 1988), p. 210.

6. P. 8: a "marketable obsession." SK, Foreword, *Night Shift* (New York: NAL, Signet, February 1979), p. xiii.

7. P. 8: He is "America's Horror Writer Laureate," according to the president of the American Bookseller's Association. Joyce Meskis, quoted by Roger Cohen, "Hot Authors with a Common Goal: Promotion," *New York Times,* June 3, 1991.

8. P. 8: "America's literary boogeyman." SK, "Straight Up Midnight: An Introductory Note," *Four Past Midnight* (New York: Viking, 1990), p. xiii.

9. P. 8: "All I can say is that I feel a bit overexposed." SK, quoted by Kelli Pryor in

"1990 Entertainers: Stephen King, 6 [of 12, in descending order]," *Entertainment Weekly,* 1990 Year End Special, December 28, 1990, p. 30.

10. P. 9: "Nothing really changes." SK, quoted by Bill Goldstein, "King of Horror," *Publishers Weekly,* vol. 238, no. 4 (Spring 1991), p. 8.

11. P. 9: "the high priest of horror" with 140 million copies of his books in print worldwide. Profile on ABC–TV, "Prime Time Live: King Fear," Diane Sawyer, August 23, 1990.

12. P. 9: what King calls "The Question," a tipoff that the interview will be just another personality profile. SK, "On *The Shining* and Other Perpetrations," *Whispers,* vol. 5, no 1–2 (August 1982), p. 11.

13. P. 10: "a critical appreciation . . . an intermingling of biography, literary analysis, and unabashed enthusiasm. . . ." DEW, Foreword, *Stephen King: The Art of Darkness* (New York: NAL, 1984), p. xiii.

14. P. 10: "I feel a certain pressure about my writing, and I have an idea of who reads my books. . . ." SK, quoted by Goldstein, "King of Horror," p. 6.

Chapter 1: War Baby

1. P. 15: "We were fertile ground for the seeds of terror, we war babies; . . ." SK, *Stephen King's Danse Macabre* (New York: Everest House, 1981), p. 23.

2. P. 15: "After my father took off, my mother landed on her feet, scrambling." Ibid., p. 99.

3. P. 16: "I can remember one night coming in after she'd been to one of these little bookshops where you go and they had the recycled paperbacks. . . ." SK, extemporaneous speech, at "Sunday Book & Author Breakfast: Stephen King, Dr. Ferrol Sams, Gloria Steinem," ABA Annual Meeting, New York, June 2, 1991. Recorded by GB.

4. P. 16: That night he slept "in the doorway, where the real and rational light of the bathroom bulb could shine on my face." SK, *Danse Macabre* (New York: Berkley Books, 1982), p. 121.

5. P. 16: "This memory is interesting because it is *not* a memory of literature. . . ." SK, "Dr. Seuss & the Two Faces of Fantasy," address at Swanncon 5, published in *Fantasy Review,* June 1984, p. 10.

6. P. 17: "She had a thin book from the library—obviously a grown-up book." SK, at "Sunday Book & Author Breakfast."

7. P. 17: On his own, King read Dr. Seuss, whose "grim situation comedy" *The 500 Hats of Bartholomew Cubbins* made a powerful impact on him. . . . SK, "Dr. Seuss & the Two Faces of Fantasy," p. 12.

8. P. 17: the idea that "sudden weirdness can happen to the most ordinary people, and for no reason at all." Ibid.

9. P. 17: as Leonard Wolf wrote in *Horror,* "is a darling of horror film aficionados." Wolf, *Horror: A Connoisseur's Guide to Literature and Film* (New York: Facts on File, 1989), p. 49.

10. P. 17: "I still see things cinematically." SK, quoted by Mel Allen in untitled newspaper article, *Maine Sunday Telegram,* October 31, 1976, p. 3D.

11. P. 18: In one account, in a college newspaper column, he wrote that he was

"waiting in the barber shop to get a haircut when that happened." SK, "King's Garbage Truck," *Maine Campus,* May 7, 1970.

12. P. 18: "I want to tell you that the Russians have put a space satellite into orbit around the earth." SK, *Danse Macabre,* p. 21.

13. P. 18: "I am certainly not trying to tell you that the Russians traumatized me into an interest in horror fiction. . . ." SK, Ibid., p. 27.

14. P. 19: In the late fifties Durham was, as King's childhood friend Christopher Chesley recalled, "a working-class town. . . ." Chesley, interviewed by GB in Durham, Maine, October 22, 1990.

15. P. 19: "We didn't have desserts when I grew up." SK, quoted by Mel Allen in untitled article, *Maine Sunday Telegram.*

16. P. 20: David King remembered that his mother "was taking care of her parents with support from her sisters. . . ." David King, interviewed by Stephen J. Spignesi, "Growing Up with the Boogeyman," in *The Shape Under the Sheet: The Complete Stephen King Encyclopedia* by Stephen J. Spignesi (Ann Arbor, MI: Popular Culture, Ink., 1991), p. 36.

17. P. 20: "My mother . . . worked at the bakery from eleven to seven, making the goods." SK, quoted by Mel Allen, *Maine Sunday Telegram.*

18. P. 20: "He looked like a kid with those old-fashioned, black-rimmed glasses." Chesley, interviewed by GB.

19. P. 20: "Steve was a big, klutzy kid." Brian Hall quoted by Jeff Pert, "The local Haunts of Stephen King," *Times Record* (Brunswick, ME), October 29, 1990.

20. P. 20: "He looked like Vern [Tessio] in the film *Stand by Me.*" David King, interviewed by Spignesi, *The Shape Under the Sheet,* p. 36.

21. P. 20: "King, in effect, learned *how* to write from what he saw on the screen at the Ritz. . . ." Chesley, interviewed by GB.

22. P. 21: "This was *not* a takeoff on the story." Ibid.

23. P. 21: "It was all of twenty pages." Ibid.

24. P. 21: "I could write, and that was the way I defined myself, even as a kid." SK, quoted by Charles Platt, "Stephen King," *Dream Makers: Volume II,* interviews by Charles Platt (New York: Berkley Books, 1983), p. 278.

25. P. 21: "I grew up in a real rural environment, and I've been writing about it ever since." SK, interviewed on videotape, "Stephen King/Four Past Midnight/Stephen King Speaks/Dark Half" (New York: Equitable Production Group, 1990). Note: The tape was accompanied by a memo dated June 6, 1990 from Christine Caruso of Penguin USA to "All Sales Reps."

26. P. 21: It was "a cold day in 1959 or 1960, the attic over my aunt and uncle's garage was the place where that interior dowsing rod suddenly turned over. . . ." SK, *Danse Macabre,* p. 100.

27. P. 21: In what King termed the "family museum," the attic over the garage. . . . Ibid.

28. P. 22: "the only man on the sales force who regularly demonstrated vacuum cleaners to pretty young widows at two o'clock in the morning." SK, interviewed by Eric Norden, "The *Playboy* Interview: Stephen King," reprinted in *The Stephen King Companion* ed. GB (Kansas City and New York: Andrews and McMeel, 1989), p. 29.

29. P. 22: The son described his father as being of "average height, handsome in a 1940s sort of way. . . ." SK, *Danse Macabre,* p. 99.

30. P. 22: As his son later observed, "None of the stories sold and none survives." SK, interviewed by *Playboy*, reprinted in *The Stephen King Companion*, p. 29.

31. P. 22: Lovecraft "struck . . . with the most force. . . ." SK interview, "Stephen King on *Carrie, The Shining*, etc.," conducted by Peter S. Perakos, *Cinefantastique*, Vol 8:1, p. 12.

32. P. 22: "When Lovecraft wrote 'The Rats in the Walls' and 'Pickman's Model,' he wasn't simply kidding around. . . ." SK, *Danse Macabre*, p. 102.

33. Pp. 22–23: "What Steve learned from Lovecraft was the possibility of taking the New England atmosphere and using that as a springboard." Chesley, interviewed by GB.

34. P. 23: "As a kid growing up in rural Maine, my interest in horror and the fantastic wasn't looked upon with any approval whatsoever. . . ." SK, "The Importance of Being Forry [Forrest J. Ackerman]," *Mr. Monster's Movie Gold* by Forrest J. Ackerman (Norfolk, VA: Donning Company/Publishers), p. 9.

35. P. 23: "Everybody thought—considering how much he read and how much he wrote—that he spent way too much time in his room. . . ." Chesley, interviewed by GB.

36. P. 23: Ackerman, wrote King, "stood up for a generation of kids who understood that if it was junk, it was *magic* junk." SK, *Mr. Monster's Movie Gold*, p. 12.

37. P. 24: As Chesley wrote, "The country dirt roads, the stands of pine trees, the hayfields run to seed. . . ." Christopher Chesley, "The Real Stephen King," introduction of King at public lecture, Truth or Consequences, New Mexico, November 19, 1983.

38. P. 24: "When I went to Stephen King's house to write stories with him, there was the sense that these things weren't just stories. . . ." Chesley, interviewed by GB.

39. Pp. 24–25: "The reason I write this stuff is a sense of wonder. . . ." SK, extemporaneous speech, Truth or Consequences, New Mexico, November 19, 1983. Recorded by Ellanie Sampson.

40. P. 25: "Until I get a mimeograph machine things are going to be rather rushed." David King, quoted by Don Hansen, "3 Durham Lads Publishing Bright Hometown Newspaper," *Record* (Brunswick, ME), April 23, 1959.

41. Pp. 25–26: "Well, the fall T.V. season is in full swing. . . ." SK, "T.V. News," *Dave's Rag* (Pownal, ME), "Summer Special," 1959.

42. P. 26: David King offered "Pictures expertly taken of any subject. . . ." Ibid.

43. P. 26: "New book by STEVE KING!" Ibid.

44. P. 26: "WATCH FOR THE NEW KING STORY!!!!" *Dave's Rag*, quoted by Don Hansen, "3 Durham Lads," *Record*.

45. P. 26: "I started to submit stuff when I was about twelve, to magazines like *Fantastic* or *Fantasy and Science Fiction*." SK, quoted by Charles Platt, *Dream Makers: Volume II*, pp. 276–77.

46. P. 27: his brother was "constantly at the typewriter" . . . David King, interviewed by Spignesi, *The Shape Under the Sheet*, p. 35.

47. P. 27: "In an odd way, they were trophies." Chesley, interviewed by GB.

48. P. 27: "I think that writers are made, not born or created out of dreams or childhood trauma. . . ." SK, *Danse Macabre*, p. 92.

49. P. 27: "Stephen King is aware of what he needs to preserve himself—the time and space and distance that allow him to write." Chesley, interviewed by GB.

50. P. 27: Through King's imagination, Durham became a microcosm of the universe, where his "lens of imagination" focused on the people. . . . SK, "A Preface in Two Parts/ Part 2: To Be Read After Purchase," *The Stand* [II] (New York: Doubleday, 1990), p. xii.

51. P. 27: Behind the King home was a shed where Stephen and David King and their friends would meet to "play cards, read magazines, things like that." Chesley, interviewed by GB.

52. Pp. 27–28: Near the Chesley home is the Harmony Grove Cemetery where, as Chesley recalled, he and King "went . . . under the light of the late, sinking summer moon." . . . Chesley, "The Real Stephen King," introduction of King, public lecture, Truth or Consequences, New Mexico, November 19, 1983.

53. P. 28: "We got hold of a movie camera." Chesley, interviewed by GB.

54. P. 28: King wrote: "Outsiders think they are the same, these small towns—that they don't change." SK, "It Grows on You," *Whispers*, vol. 5, no. 1–2 (August 1982), p. 59.

55. Pp. 28–29: "I was twelve going on thirteen when I first saw a dead human being." SK, "The Body," *Different Seasons* (New York: Viking Press, 1982), p. 301.

56. P. 29: In an interview with Brian Hall . . . Jeff Pert wrote that "Durham couldn't afford a school bus for only a few kids. . . ." Jeff Pert, "The Local Haunts of Stephen King," *Times Record* (Brunswick, ME), October 29, 1990.

57. P. 29: Chris Chesley . . . "saw Steve periodically on the weekends. . . ." Chesley, interview with GB.

58. P. 29: Academically, he was an above-average student; though he remembered getting "C's and D's in chemistry and physics." . . . SK, quoted in *Bare Bones*, p. 57.

59. P. 30: John Gould, its editor, was the one "who taught me everything I know about writing in ten minutes." SK, "Everything You Need to Know About Writing Successfully—in Ten Minutes," *The Writer*, July 1986, p. 8.

60. P. 30: "I would observe what happened to people who were totally left out and picked on constantly." SK, quoted in *Pub* (English magazine), May 1980, p. 33.

61. P. 30: "Gotta Read" or "Wanna Read." SK, "What Stephen King Does for Love," *Seventeen*, April 1990, p. 241.

62. P. 30: . . . King particularly enjoyed Ed McBain (who taught King "some of the stylistic devices Steve uses—putting thoughts in italics, and snappy dialogue"). . . . Chesley, interview with GB.

63. P. 30: In another magazine, *Scholastic Scope*, King cited his "favorite books . . . when he was a student." Stephanie Leonard, Editor's Column, *CR*, June 1986, p. 8.

64. P. 31: "He always wrote intuitively." Chesley, interviewed by GB.

65. P. 31: "I had gotten into the habit of visiting Steve, who liked to make up scary stories." Chesley, "The Real Stephen King," introduction of King at public lecture, Truth or Consequences, New Mexico, November 19, 1983.

66. Pp. 31–32: "*People, Places, and Things* is an Extraordinary book." Christopher Chesley and Stephen King, Forward [Foreword], *People, Places, and Things—Volume I* (Durham, ME: Triad Publishing Company, 1963).

67. P. 32: "What I remember is a progression." Chesley, interviewed by GB.

68. P. 33: "Look to your skies . . . a warning will come from your skies . . . look to your skies. . . ." SK, quoting dialogue from *Earth vs. the Flying Saucers,* in *Danse Macabre*, p. 25.

69. P. 33: "In Part I, Jerry Hiken, one of the last defenders of the Earth, has been captured by the Star Invaders. . . ." Michael R. Collings, *The Shorter Works of Stephen King* by Collings and David Engebretson (Mercer Island, WA: Starmont House, 1985), p. 10.

70. P. 33: "I was never part of a fan network." SK, quoted by Charles Platt, *Dream Makers: Volume II*, p. 276.

71. Pp. 33–34: "An orphaned teenager accepts a job as a grave robber. . . ." Collings, *The Shorter Works of Stephen King*, p. 13.

72. P. 34: "A huge, white maggot twisted on the garage floor. . . ." SK, "I Was a Teenage Graverobber," reprinted as "In a Halfworld of Terror," in *Stories of Suspense*, a fanzine published by Marv Wolfman, p. 11.

73. P. 34: "Look to your skies. . . ." *Danse Macabre*, p. 25.

74. P. 35: "They don't call that stuff 'juvenilia' for nothing, friends 'n neighbors." SK, Foreword, *Stalking the Nightmare* by Harlan Ellison (Huntington Woods, MI: Phantasia Press, Book Club Edition, 1982), p. 5.

75. P. 35: ". . . there comes a day when you say to yourself, *Good God! If I was this bad, how did I ever get any better?*" Ibid.

76. P. 35: "My high school career was totally undistinguished." SK, quoted by Richard Rothenstein, "Interview with Stephen King," *Pub,* May 1980, p. 33.

77. P. 35: "I've always assumed that he didn't have a wonderful high school experience. . . ." Chesley, interviewed by GB.

78. P. 35: one of his childhood fears was of "not being able to interact, to get along and establish lines of communication." SK, interview, *Bare Bones,* p. 90.

79. P. 36: "He looked like the total all-American kid as he pedaled his twenty-six-inch Schwinn with the apehanger handlebars. . . ." SK, "Apt Pupil," *Different Seasons,* p. 105.

80. P. 36: King had originally applied to Drew University in New Jersey, but "his family finances were insufficient to enable him to attend. . . ." DEW, *Stephen King: The Art of Darkness,* p. 20.

Chapter 2: The College Years

1. P. 37: "There I was, all alone in Room 203 of Gannett Hall, clean-shaven, neatly dressed, and as green as apples in August." SK, "King's Garbage Truck," *Maine Campus* (Orono), July 25, 1969.

2. P. 37: "rather shy but brilliant," which is probably a fair assessment. David Bright, quoted by Sanford Phippen, "The Student King: The Master of Modern Horror at Maine," *Maine* (UMO alumni association magazine), Fall 1989, p. 23.

3. Pp. 37–38: Years later King, writing about his freshman year, recalled that although he'd "swagger around. . . ." SK, *Maine Campus,* July 25, 1969.

4. P. 38: . . . and then there was the nervousness when dating "your first Sophisticated College Girl." Ibid.

5. P. 38: he "shaved three times in twenty minutes, and that was just to call her up and ask her." Ibid.

6. P. 38: "And you never—I repeat, *never*—removed your beanie in public. . . ." Ibid.

7. P. 38: "Jim Bishop was the first person Steve King met on campus who was responsive to his work." Burton Hatlen, interviewed by GB in Bangor, Maine, October 27, 1990.

8. P. 38: "Jim Bishop . . . remembers, 'Steve's big physical presence'. . . ." Bishop, quoted by Phippen, "The Student King," *Maine,* p. 20.

9. P. 39: "I would encourage every American to walk as often as possible." John F. Kennedy quoted by SK as epigraph to *The Long Walk,* collected in *The Bachman Books: Four Early Novels by Stephen King* (New York: NAL Books, 1985), p. 137.

10. P. 39: "I brought it home and laid it on the dining room table." Hatlen, interviewed by GB.

11. P. 39: "Professor Hatlen said I should give this to you to read." SK, quoted by Carroll F. Terrell, *Stephen King: Man and Artist* (Orono, ME: Northern Lights Publishing Company, 1991), p. 44.

12. P. 39: "It was called *The Long Walk* and posed certain technical problems which would require more practice for him to solve." Ibid.

13. P. 39: "I am conscious now that I thought *The Long Walk* was a first novel." Ibid., p. 48.

14. P. 40: "I was too crushed to show that book to any publisher in New York." SK, "On Becoming a Brand Name," Foreword to *Fear Itself: The Horror Fiction of Stephen King,* ed. Tim Underwood and Chuck Miller (San Francisco and Novato, PA: Underwood–Miller, 1982), p. 16.

15. P. 40: "Stephen King has been sending us stories for some time. . . ." Editorial comment on SK's "The Glass Floor," *Startling Mystery Stories,* Fall 1967, p. 23.

16. P. 40: That first published story, according to King, was "the product of an unformed storyteller's mind," written so he could "*see better.*" SK, Introduction to "The Glass Floor" by SK, *Weird Tales,* vol. 52, no. 1 (Fall 1990), p. 36.

17. P. 40: "We read Steinbeck's *In Dubious Battle,* and I remember him being very struck with that." Hatlen, interviewed by GB.

18. P. 41: "The creative writing courses at the college level are very important, but I don't think they're necessary." SK, quoted by Phippen, "The Student King," *Maine,* p. 20.

19. P. 41: "University officials were at a loss to explain Whitman's actions." Article, "Sniper on Tower Terrorizes Campus, Slays 12," in *Chronicle of the 20th Century,* ed. Clifton Daniel (Mount Kisco, NY: Chronicle Publications, 1987), p. 952.

20. P. 41: "Maybe you get loaded on Thursday afternoon." SK, "King's Garbage Truck," *Maine Campus,* May 8, 1969.

21. P. 42: With that "false spring, a lying spring" comes "Springheel Jack." . . . SK, "Strawberry Spring," in *Night Shift* (New York: NAL, Signet, 1979), p. 177.

22. P. 42: "It was a very dynamic experience for a lot of people." Hatlen, interviewed by GB.

23. P. 42: King remembered having written "about forty to fifty poems." . . . SK, interviewed by Rodney Labbe, *Ubris II,* 1984, p. 46.

24. P. 42: "From that seminar . . . came a half dozen or so energetic and highly individual young poets. . . ." Jim Bishop, quoted by Phippen, "The Student King," *Maine,* p. 20.

25. P. 42: she saw an "enormous, shambling person in cut-off gum rubbers." Tabitha King, quoted by DEW, *Stephen King: The Art of Darkness,* p. 23.

26. P. 43: "Steve came into the campus office and said he wanted to write a column." David Bright, interviewed by GB in Bangor, Maine, October 25, 1990.

27. P. 43: "The guy is very prolific; he likes to write and is excellent at it." Ibid.

28. P. 43: According to another staffer, "King was always late." *Feast of Fear:*

Conversations with Stephen King "compiled by Don Herron" (San Rafael, CA and Novato, PA: Underwood–Miller, 1989), p. 2.

29. P. 44: as an undergraduate "King was so different from most students." Hatlen, interviewed by GB.

30. P. 44: "I remember a meeting in which the students and faculty got together to talk about the curriculum of the English department." Ibid.

31. P. 44: "highly imaginative, and he had a pretty good organization." Edward Holmes, interviewed by GB in Winterport, Maine, on October 24, 1990.

32. Pp. 44–45: "We wrote independently but then got together once a week and it was great fun, often hilarious." Diane McPherson, quoted by Phippen, "The Student King," *Maine,* p. 20.

33. P. 45: "After he'd finished about half of it, he asked me if it would be a good idea to send it to a publisher to get an advance." Terrell, *Stephen King: Man and Artist,* pp. 52–53.

34. P. 45: "a badly busted flush." SK, "On Becoming a Brand Name," *Fear Itself,* p. 17.

35. P. 45: "I can't even like it when I'm drunk." Ibid.

36. P. 45: He had, he began, "a few hard words to say about clothes, hair, and the general state of the young." SK, "King's Garbage Truck," *Maine Campus,* February 12, 1970.

37. Pp. 45–46: King then lashed out at "a few of the things I'm sick of." . . . Ibid.

38. P. 46: "Can you imagine a country supposedly based on freedom of expression telling people that they can't grow hair on their head or their face?" Ibid.

39. P. 46: "When I was in school, Vietnam was going up in flames. . . ." SK, interviewed by Rodney Labbe, "Stephen and Tabitha King," *Ubris II* (Orono, ME), vol. 1, no. 1, 1984.

40. P. 46: "At that time, college campuses were in revolt—utter revolt." Ibid.

41. P. 47: "They are unreal symbols of very real fears." (Bibliographic information not available.)

42. P. 47: . . . metamorphosed into what he self-termed "a scummy radical bastard." SK, "King's Garbage Truck," *Maine Campus,* April 16, 1970.

43. P. 47: "Declaration of Independence, the Constitution, and even the Articles of Confederation." Ibid.

44. P. 47: King took a ream of "bright green" paper. . . . SK, Afterword, *The Dark Tower: The Gunslinger* (West Kingston, RI: Donald M. Grant, Publisher, 2d ed., 1984), p. 220.

45. P. 47: Putting his ream to good use, King—"living in a scuzzy riverside cabin not far from the University. . . ." Ibid., p. 221.

46. P. 47: "The man in black fled across the desert and the gunslinger followed." Ibid., p. 222.

47. P. 48: "He was sitting by the stove. . . ." Chesley, interviewed by GB.

48. Pp. 48–49: "One morning, one sunshine morning, Kent State was a phrase. . . ." *Prism* (UMO yearbook), 1970.

49. P. 49: "in a few weeks . . . I can march along with the rest of the Class of '70 into the Outside World. . . ." SK, "King's Garbage Truck," *Maine Campus,* May 7, 1970.

50. P. 49: "A BLESSED (?) EVENT ANNOUNCED TO THE UNIVERSITY OF MAINE AT ORONO." Ibid., May 21, 1970.

51. Pp. 49–50: "This boy has shown evidences of some talent. . . ." Ibid.

52. P. 50: "Bachelor of Science degree in English. . . ." NAL press release on Stephen King.

Chapter 3: The Long Walk

1. P. 51: After graduation King moved into what he termed a "sleazy Orono, Maine, apartment." . . . SK, quoted by DEW, *The Art of Darkness*, p. 24.

2. P. 51: "It was almost dark when Slade rode into Dead Steer Springs." SK, "Slade," *Maine Campus,* June 11, 1970.

3. P. 52: "Almost all of the men's magazines are excellent markets for the beginning horror freelancer." SK, "The Horror Writer and the Ten Bears," Foreword to *Kingdom of Fear: The World of Stephen King,* ed. Tim Underwood and Chuck Miller (San Francisco and Columbia, PA: Underwood–Miller, 1986), p. 16.

4. P. 52: "They need lots of material, and most of them could care less if you're an unknown." Ibid.

5. P. 52: "If your story has sex interest and is still quality, I'd say send to *Adam* first." Ibid., p. 17.

6. P. 52: "Son, are those traffic cones yours?" SK, Notes, *Skeleton Crew* (New York: G.P. Putnam's Sons, 1985), p. 510.

7. Pp. 52–53: "I have a particular warmth for *Cavalier,* because they published my [own] first marketable horror stories." SK, *Kingdom of Fear,* pp. 16–17.

8. P. 53: "I wrote most of 'Graveyard Shift' in the office of the *Maine Campus.*" SK, at October 25, 1990, world premiere and press conference for *Stephen King's Graveyard Shift,* Hoyt Cinema, Bangor, Maine.

9. P. 53: "Oh, more! I think he ought to go around ripping the heads off rats and eating them!" Ibid.

10. P. 53: Though the premise is on the surface humorous, it was "the ultimate labor versus management story." Ibid.

11. P. 53: "The real impetus to write this particular story was the mill I worked in." Ibid.

12. P. 54: According to his friend, "some of them were as big as puppies." Ibid.

13. P. 54: It was this same friend who told King that for recreation, they'd "put the rats in the dye bins and see how fast they would run when they started to roll the drums." Ibid.

14. P. 54: . . . he "blocked out all the ads for glossy photos and films" of young women in highly suggestive poses. Ibid.

15. P. 54: "The only important thing I ever did in my life for a conscious reason was to ask Tabitha Spruce . . . if she would marry me." SK, "Why I Was Bachman," *The Bachman Books: Four Early Novels by Stephen King* (New York: NAL Books, 1985), p. v.

16. P. 54: "on Thursday nights in a hall that had a poster on the wall that said, 'Methodists say: No thank you.'" SK, extemporaneous speech at "Sunday Book & Author Breakfast: Stephen King, Dr. Ferrol Sams, Gloria Steinem," ABA Annual Meeting, New York, June 2, 1991. Recorded by GB.

17. Pp. 55–56: Thompson later wrote that *Getting It On* "was a masterful study in

character and suspense. . . ." Bill Thompson, "A Girl Named Carrie," Introduction to *Kingdom of Fear,* p. 31.

18. P. 56: "Doubleday declined, a painful blow for me. . . ." SK, "On Becoming a Brand Name," *Fear Itself,* p. 18.

19. P. 56: "There I was, unpublished, living in a trailer, with barely enough money to get by. . . ." SK, quoted in interview; no other information available.

20. P. 56: "King was a promising teacher." Robert W. Rowe, interviewed by GB, October 26, 1990, Hampden, Maine.

21. P. 56: "It was hard to catch him without a book under his arm; if he had the spare time, he'd be reading a book." Ibid.

22. P. 56: A former student . . . remembered King as "a good teacher who had seven classes a day and a study hall." Brenda Willey, interviewed by GB, October 1990, Bangor, Maine.

23. P. 57: *The Running Man* . . . "was written during a period of seventy-two hours." . . . SK, Introduction, *The Bachman Books,* p. ix.

24. P. 57: and for him it was "a fantastic, white-hot experience." SK, "On Becoming a Brand Name," *Fear Itself,* p. 19.

25. P. 57: "it still wasn't magic time." Thompson, *Kingdom of Fear,* p. 31.

26. P. 57: "Three weeks after submission, I received my material back in the SASE with a note which was both cordial and frosty." SK, "Memo from Stephen King," *Rotten Rejections,* ed. Andre Bernard (Wainscott, NY: Pushcart Press, 1990), p. 25.

27. P. 57: "I was very impressed, sensing that there was something very out of the ordinary about [King's] writing." Nye Willden, "An Editor's Reminiscence," in *The Stephen King Companion,* ed. GB (Kansas City and New York: Andrews and McMeel, 1989), p. 253.

28. P. 58: "He was having a difficult time financially." Ibid.

29. P. 58: "It was like the horror could be in the 7–11 down the block . . . just up the street something terrible could be going on." SK, interviewed on "Dick Cavett Show," October 31, 1980 ("Horror Panel—II").

30. P. 58: Overworked and stressful, King began "drinking too much." SK, "On *The Shining* and Other Perpetrations," *Whispers,* vol. 5, no. 1–2 (August 1982), p. 13.

31. P. 58: "I began to have long talks with myself at night about whether or not I was chasing a fool's dream." SK, "On Becoming a Brand Name," *Fear Itself,* p. 19.

32. P. 58: "Tabitha was home with the kids. . . ." Chesley, interviewed by GB.

33. P. 59: " . . . it had never crossed my mind to write a horror novel." SK, "On Becoming a Brand Name," *Fear Itself,* p. 20.

34. P. 59: "Steve trusts Tabitha's opinion. . . ." Chesley, interviewed by GB.

35. P. 59: "I persisted," King later wrote, "because I was dry and had no better ideas." SK, "On Becoming a Brand Name," *Fear Itself,* pp. 22–23.

36. P. 59: "My considered opinion," King concluded, " was that I had written the world's all-time loser." Ibid., p. 23.

Chapter 4: The Doubleday Days

1. P. 60: Finally . . . "it was magic time." Bill Thompson, "A Girl Named Carrie," Introduction to *Kingdom of Fear,* p. 31.

2. P. 60: "Thompson's ideas worked so well that it was almost dreamlike." SK, "On Becoming a Brand Name," *Fear Itself,* p. 24.

3. P. 60: "Basically, the editorial process means understanding what the author wants to do and helping him get there." Thompson, "A Girl Named Carrie," *Kingdom of Fear,* p. 32.

4. P. 60: Now it was up to Thompson to sell the book to "the profit-center types—sales, publicity, subsidiary rights." Ibid.

5. Pp. 60–61: King drank two gin-and-tonics on an empty stomach and, as he put it, was "almost immediately struck drunk. . . ." SK, "On Becoming a Brand Name," *Fear Itself,* p. 25.

6. P. 61: As Thompson recalled, "When the rights director's eyes lit up and, when the advertising manager called it a 'cooker,' I knew we were home free." Thompson, "A Girl Named Carrie," *Kingdom of Fear,* p. 32.

7. P. 62: " 'Carrie' Officially A Doubleday Book." Thompson to SK, March 1973, quoted by SK in *The Writer,* June 1975, p. 25.

8. P. 62: "After I hitchhiked home, I came down the little dirt road his house was on." Chesley, interviewed by GB.

9. P. 62: After the contract was signed and the advance money arrived, the Kings used some of it to buy "a new blue Pinto" and moved out of their trailer and into an apartment on Sanford Street in Bangor. Ibid.

10. P. 62: "To say that Tabby and I were flabbergasted by this news would be to understate the case. . . ." SK, "On Becoming a Brand Name," *Fear Itself,* p. 28.

11. P. 62: To mark the event, "I went out to buy something nice for Tabby." SK, in uncredited UPI story, "Hit Novelist Keeps His Perspective," *Hartford Courant* (Hartford, CT), October 16, 1979.

12. P. 63: "When *Carrie* was bought by Doubleday, my editor was Bill Thompson, and Doubleday. . . ." SK, speech at "Sunday Book & Author Breakfast: Stephen King, Dr. Ferrol Sams, Gloria Steinem," ABA Annual Meeting, New York, June 2, 1991. Recorded by GB.

13. P. 63: "Steve King can't quite make up his mind whether or not he should retire." David Bright, "Hampden Teacher Hits Jackpot with New Book," *BDN,* May 25, 1973.

14. Pp. 63–64: The "promising teacher," as Hampden Academy principal Rowe recalled, "worked next door. . . ." Robert W. Rowe, interviewed by GB.

15. P. 64: But King would never forget what lay behind him—the "shit work." . . . SK, quoted by NAL publicity flyer for paperback edition of *The Shining* in 1977.

16. P. 64: "It was a great feeling of liberation, because at last I was free to quit teaching. . . ." SK, interviewed by Eric Norden, "The *Playboy* Interview: Stephen King," in *The Stephen King Companion,* p. 27.

17. P. 64: "He wasn't *Stephen King* the famous writer then; . . ." Brenda Willey, interviewed by GB.

18. P. 64: "My own response was that reputation follows function as much as form does; . . ." SK, "On Becoming a Brand Name," *Fear Itself,* p. 31.

19. P. 65: "I think it was an effort to make some sense of my mother's painful death the year before. . . ." SK, "Why I Was Bachman," *The Bachman Books,* pp. ix–x.

20. Pp. 65–66: "Doubleday is pleased to present you with this special edition of

Carrie, by Stephen King." William G. Thompson, letter to booksellers from Doubleday, January 1974.

21. P. 66: "a terrifying treat for both horror and parapsychology fans." *School Library Journal*, February 1974, p. 584.

22. P. 66: " . . . [A] fine, eerie haunting tale. . . ." *Publishers Weekly*, February 25, 1974, p. 102.

23. P. 66: "This first novel is a contender for the bloodiest book of the year. . . ." *Library Journal*, April 15, 1974, p. 1150.

24. P. 66: Remarking that King discovered "not the American Dream but the American Nightmare," Hatlen wrote that King "knows the desolation of rural Maine. . . ." Burton Hatlen, "[*Maine*] *Campus* columnist publishes novel," *Alumnus*, spring 1974, p. 9.

25. P. 67: "Stephen King's story will stun your sensibilities. . . ." Back cover of first edition of *Carrie*.

26. P. 67: "It didn't get within hailing distance of anyone's bestseller list. . . ." SK, interview. (Bibliographic data not available).

27. P. 67: " '*Salem's Lot* had been read at NAL with a great deal of enthusiasm. . . ." SK, "On Becoming a Brand Name," *Fear Itself*, p. 33.

28. Pp. 67–68: "I had written *Carrie* and '*Salem's Lot* and they were both set in Maine, because that's where I'm from." SK, extemporaneous speech in Pasadena, CA, April 26, 1989; cassette recording transcribed by GB.

29. P. 68: Colorado, "a spooky state with mountains and high passes and the wild howling and the wolves." SK, quoted in "Taking You Blindfolded to the Cliff Edge," *19* magazine (British), March 1980, p. 6.

30. P. 68: As King recalled, "the story just wasn't marching." (No bibliographic data available.)

31. P. 68: "The idea came to me while I was in the shower, washing my hair." SK, "On *The Shining* and Other Perpetrations," *Whispers*, August 1982, p. 12.

32. P. 68: "I was wondering what would happen if you had a little boy who was sort of a psychic receptor, or maybe even a psychic amplifier." SK, speech, Pasadena, CA.

33. P. 69: "By then," King recalled, "whatever it is that makes you want to make things up . . . was turned on." Ibid.

34. P. 70: A luxury hotel "built against the roof the sky . . . looking out over the last rising jagged peaks of the Rockies." . . . SK, "Before the Play," *Whispers*, August 1982, p. 20.

35. P. 70: "Some of the most beautiful resort hotels in the world are located in Colorado, but the hotel in these pages is based on none of them." SK, disclaimer in front matter of *The Shining* (Garden City, NY: Doubleday & Company, 1977).

36. P. 70: "I seemed to be back in the trailer in Hermon, Maine. . . ." SK, "On Becoming a Brand Name," *Fear Itself*, p. 36.

37. P. 70: "I was able to invest a lot of my unhappy aggressive impulses in Jack Torrance, and it was safe." SK, speech, Pasadena, CA.

38. P. 70: For King, the novel explored a dark side of his psyche, "the idea that parents are not always good." Ibid.

39. P. 70: "This was a revelation to me in a way, because I grew up without a father." Ibid.

40. P. 70: King "spilled the plot of *The Shine* over roughly 2,000 beers in a pleasant

little hamburger place called Jaspers." SK, "On Becoming a Brand Name," *Fear Itself,* p. 36.

41. P. 71: Thompson "wasn't terribly enthusiastic" about *The Shine . . . .* Ibid.

42. P. 71: "First the telekinetic girl, then the vampires. . . ." SK, Afterword, *Different Seasons,* p. 521.

43. P. 71: King concluded that he "could be in worse company. . . ." Ibid.

44. P. 71: "It was going to be a *roman à clef* about the kidnapping of Patty Hearst. . . ." SK, *Danse Macabre,* p. 369.

45. P. 71: During those six weeks King was haunted by "a news story I had read about an accidental CBW . . . spill in Utah." Ibid., p. 370.

46. P. 72: The seemingly endless novel became, as King put it, "my own little Vietnam. . . ." Ibid., p. 371.

47. P. 72: "Its writing came during a troubled period for the world in general and America in particular; . . ." Ibid., p. 372.

48. P. 72: It's "rather puzzling cover." . . . SK, "On Becoming a Brand Name," *Fear Itself,* p. 32.

49. P. 73: . . . invariably resulting in "the sudden silence of country people on their guard." Profile of SK in *Maine* magazine. (Bibliographic information not available.)

50. P. 73: "I was moved by what he had to say about the town." SK, interviewed by Mel Allen, reprinted in *Bare Bones: Conversations on Terror with Stephen King,* ed. Tim Underwood and Chuck Miller (New York: Warner Books, 1989), p. 64.

51. P. 73: . . . it's easy to see how Thompson had "lost one entirely sunny summer weekend with Ben Mears, Susan Norton and company in the town of Jerusalem's Lot, Maine." SK, "On Becoming a Brand Name," *Fear Itself,* pp. 30–31.

52. P. 74: "While *Rosemary's Baby* and *The Exorcist* mined supernatural niches in the bestseller list. . . ." Al Sarrantonio on *'Salem's Lot* in *Horror: 100 Best Books,* ed. Stephen Jones and Kim Newman (New York: Carroll & Graf Publishers, 1988), p. 162.

53. P. 74: "When people talk about the genre, I guess they mention my name first, but without Richard Matheson, I wouldn't be around." SK, "From *Stephen King,*" in *Richard Matheson: Collected Stories* by Richard Matheson (Los Angeles: Dream/Press, "Special Advance Reading Copy/WFC Prevue Edition," 1989), p. 800.

54. P. 75: "One of the newest pressures is the demand from reporters, schools, clubs, service organizations and the like for interviews and appearances." Mel Allen, "Witches and Aspirin," *Writer's Digest,* June 1977, p. 27.

55. P. 75: " . . . [H]e's had his phone number changed. . . ." Lois Lowry, "King of the Occult," *Downeast* magazine, November 1977, p. 61.

56. P. 76: "And remember Stephen King's First Rule of Writers and Agent, learned from bitter personal experience. . . ." SK, "Everything You Need to Know About Writing Successfully—in Ten Minutes," *The Writer,* July 1986, p. 46.

57. P. 76: "I had heard of Steve, but frankly, when I went to the party I had only read one thing by Steve." Kirby McCauley, interviewed by Christopher Spruce, "SK Literary Agent Discusses Friend and Client," *CR,* May 1986, p. 1.

58. P. 76: "Of such inconsequential beginnings dynasties are begun." SK, *'Salem's Lot* (New York: Doubleday, 1975), p. 22.

59. P. 77: "I partly saw his success growing." McCauley, quoted by Spruce, "SK Literary Agent Discusses Friend and Client," *CR,* p. 7.

60. P. 77: "Naturally, I wanted Steve to consider having me represent him." Ibid., p. 1.

61. P. 77: . . . "the undisputed master of the modern horror story." Jacket copy of first edition of *The Shining,* 1977.

62. P. 77: "I won't mention any by name." SK, interview, *Bare Bones,* p. 190.

63. Pp. 77–78: "Bridgewater was such a lovely place to live, a quiet place where nothing ever happened. . . ." Sales literature from Pinnacle Books in *Paperback Talk* by Ray Walters (Chicago: Academy Chicago Publishers, 1985), pp. 70–71.

64. P. 78: "it was obviously a masterpiece, probably the best supernatural novel in a hundred years." Peter Straub, "Meeting Stevie," *Fear Itself,* p. 10.

65. P. 78: "In its uniting of an almost bruising literary power, a deep sensitivity to individual experience. . . ." Peter Straub, review of *The Shining* for *Horror: 100 Best Books,* p. 172.

66. P. 78: First, advance money: ". . . [A]fter he started raking in millions for Doubleday. . . ." Kim Foltz with Penelope Wang, "An Unstoppable Thriller King," *Newsweek,* June 10, 1985, p. 63.

67. Pp. 78–79: "The Doubleday policy on paperback money is a 50-50 split, a policy that is non-negotiable." SK, interview, *Fear Itself,* p. 26.

68. P. 79: According to King, that policy "finally led to our parting of the ways. . . ." Ibid.

69. P. 79: "A writer who is his own agent has a fool for a client." SK, quoted in "An Unstoppable Thriller King," *Newsweek,* p. 63.

70. P. 79: "It put me in a whole different league." McCauley, quoted by Spruce, "SK Literary Agent Discusses Friend and Client," *CR,* p. 7.

71. P. 79: That deal . . . marked "the widening trend of writers signing directly with paperback publishers." SK, quoted in "Stephen King Signs Contract with New American Library," *Publishers Weekly,* July 4, 1977, p. 50.

72. P. 79: ". . . the paperback industry is now the giant of the publishing world." SK, "On Becoming a Brand Name," *Fear Itself,* p. 40.

73. P. 79: "The Bachman novels were 'just plain books,' paperbacks to fill the drugstore and bus-stations of America." SK, "Why I Was Bachman," *The Bachman Books,* p. ix.

74. P. 80: "Even a lesson in Latin grammar would have been more involving than what goes on in the Maine classroom. . . ." *Publishers Weekly,* July 25, 1977, pp. 69–70.

75. P. 80: . . . King now elected to visit England so he could write a book "with an English setting. When the novel is finished . . . it will be set back in a fictitious place. . . ." *Fleet News* (English newspaper), October 7, 1977.

76. P. 80: "Wanted, a draughty Victorian house in the country with dark attic and creaking floorboards, preferably haunted." Ibid.

77. P. 80: Owen, seven months old, according to the *Fleet News,* was "already getting his teeth into dad's books—literally." Ibid.

78. Pp. 80–81: "With its history of eerie writers and its penchant for mystery, England should help Stephen King produce a novel even more bloodcurdling than his previous ones. . . ." Press release, NAL, Signet, December 1977.

79. P. 81: "This little kid was savaged by a Saint Bernard and killed." SK, interview, *Bare Bones,* p. 114.

80. P. 81: . . . he got his motorcycle out of the garage "and it wasn't running right." SK, speech, Pasadena, CA.

81. P. 82. "The books are visual. . . ." SK, interview, *Bare Bones,* p. 108.

82. Pp. 82–83: "When Ted Holmes was forced to retire in 1975 at age sixty-five, we had the question of what to do with a creative writing position." Burton Hatlen, interviewed by GB.

83. P. 83: "I'm looking forward to teaching on a college level because we can focus more on creativity than grammar." SK, quoted in "Novelist King Teaching Creative Writing," *News-Times* (Danbury, CT), September 11, 1978.

84. P. 83: "This is great." SK, quoted in "Novelist to Teach," *Portsmouth Herald,* September 11, 1978.

85. P. 83: . . . King "outdoes himself in this spine-chilling moral fantasy. . . ." *Publishers Weekly,* November 28, 1977, p. 46.

Chapter 5: America's Literary Boogeyman

1. P. 84: "Why don't you do a book about the entire horror phenomenon as you see it?" Bill Thompson, quoted by SK, Forenote, *Danse Macabre,* p. 9.

2. P. 84: . . . King felt that "writing a book on the subject would complete the circle." Ibid., p. 11.

3. P. 84: "Naomi was really upset," recalled King. SK, quoted by John Nash in "Orrington's *Real* 'Pet Sematary.' " *BDN,* September 13, 1988.

4. P. 84: "On one side of the road, I wondered what would happen if that cat could come back to life." Ibid.

5. Pp. 84–85: "Death is it." SK, speech, Truth or Consequences, New Mexico, November 19, 1983.

6. P. 85: "If you are going to use real people in a story, you ought to play fair," King explained. (Bibliographic information not available.)

7. P. 86: "We are having a film series for this course." SK, quoted in "Stephen King Taking You Blindfolded to the Cliff Edge," in *19* (British magazine), March 1980, p. 6.

8. P. 86: "With nonfiction, there's all that bothersome business of making sure your facts are straight, that the dates jibe. . . ." SK, *Danse Macabre,* p. 10.

9. P. 86: "I still think *The Long Walk* is a first-rate book." Hatlen, interviewed by GB.

10. P. 87: "Both *The Long Walk* and *Rage* are full of windy psychological preachments. . . ." SK, "Why I Was Bachman," *The Bachman Books,* p. x.

11. P. 87: "I got the idea doing one of these dull chores where your wife says to you, 'Will you go to the market?' and hands you a list." SK, speech, Truth or Consequences, New Mexico.

12. P. 87: According to McCauley, the story went from seventy manuscript pages to eighty-five, then to "over a hundred. . . ." Kirby McCauley, Introduction, *Dark Forces* (New York: Bantam Books, 1981), p. xiv.

13. P. 87: "You're supposed to visualize that entire story in a sort of grainy black-and-white." SK, interview, *Feast of Fear,* p. 85.

14. P. 88: "*The Shining* cost roughly $19 million to produce as a film; . . ." SK, "Special Make-Up Effects and the Writer," *DQ,* no. 52, p. 6.

15. P. 88: "I went with Steve to see *The Shining.* . . ." Chesley, interviewed by GB.

16. P. 88: . . . *The Shining* struck King . . . as "a beautiful film." SK, interview, *Bare Bones,* p. 143.

17. P. 88: "When you sell something to the movies . . . there are two ways to go about it. . . ." SK, speech, Pasadena, CA.

18. P. 89: "It all began with me walking home one day and thinking about my car which was falling apart." SK, Speech, Truth or Consequences, New Mexico.

19. Pp. 89–90: "If you've ever done the tour, at the end of that period it feels like you've been in a pillow fight. . . ." SK, speech at ABA's "Sunday Book & Author Breakfast."

20. P. 90: "I like the jacket pretty well." SK, interview, *Bare Bones,* p. 131.

21. Pp. 90–91: "I like books that are nicely made, and with the exception of *'Salem's Lot* and *Night Shift,* none of the Doubleday books were especially well made." SK, Ibid.

22. P. 91: "I was, after all, rubbing elbows with writers I had idolized as a kid. . . ." SK, Foreword, *Silver Bullet* by SK (New York: NAL, Signet, 1985), p. 8.

23. P. 91: King agreed to write the calendar copy, writing "the *only* something which fits so neatly into the format Zavisa was suggesting." Ibid., p. 9.

24. P. 92: "Every now and then," King wrote, "I would look guiltily at the thin sheaf of pages gathering dust beside the typewriter. . . ." Ibid., p. 10.

25. P. 92: *Cycle of the Werewolf,* as King wrote, was a "stillbirth." Ibid., p. 11.

26. P. 92: Paul Monash's script was accepted, "a 200- or 225-page script—a four-hour miniseries script," recalled Hooper. (Bibliographic data not available.)

27. P. 92: "Considering the medium," King said, "they did a real good job." SK, quoted by Chris Palmer, "Watching 'Salem's Lot,' " *BDN,* November 17, 1979.

28. P. 92, "For five years I've wanted to write a book set in a fictional Maine city," King said. (Bibliographic information not available.)

29. P. 92: "I had a very long book in mind. . . ." SK, "A Novelist's Perspective on Bangor," *Black Magic & Music* (Bangor, ME: Bangor Historical Society, 1983), p. 4.

30. P. 93: Characterized by King as a "hard-drinking, working man's town." . . . SK, interview, *Feast of Fear,* p. 219.

31. P. 93: "I think a place is yours when you know where the roads go." Ibid., 268.

32. P. 93: King donated "six boxloads of manuscript papers." . . . Wayne Reilley, "King Donated Manuscripts to UMO," *BDN,* July 23, 1980.

33. P. 93: Flower asked about *'Salem's Lot,* citing its importance to "future researchers of Maine literature." . . . Eric Flower to SK, March 23, 1976.

34. P. 93: . . . King replied that he didn't feel there was much "Maineness" in his work. SK to Flower, April 6, 1976.

35. P. 94: "The U.S. government, or agencies thereof, has indeed administered potentially dangerous drugs to unwitting subjects on more than one occasion." SK, Afterword, *Firestarter* by SK (New York: NAL, Signet, 1981), p. 402.

36. P. 94: The world, King concluded, "is still full of odd dark corners and unsettling nooks and crannies." Ibid., p. 403.

37. P. 94: "Guilt rushed over me anew." SK, Foreword, *Silver Bullet,* p. 10.

38. P. 94: "The vignette form was killing me." Ibid., p. 11.

39. P. 95: Zavisa, wrote King, responded "with such enthusiasm" that King "wondered if it wasn't what he had sort of wanted all along. . . ." Ibid., p. 12.

40. P. 95: "Stephen King's stunning success as a novelist just may be unrivalled in publishing history." Jacket copy for *Danse Macabre.*

41. P. 96: "Knowledgeable and engaging, King is a perfect tour guide." *Publishers Weekly,* February 27, 1981, p. 144.

42. P. 96: "Richard Rubinstein, the producer, was real interested in filming 'Something to Tide You Over' in Maine." SK, *Graveyard Shift* world premiere/press conference, Bangor, ME.

43. P. 97: . . . J. G. Ballard's *High-Rise* in which "the inhabitants of a massive multistory apartment block gradually revert to savagery. . . ." Brian Ash, ed., *The Visual Encyclopedia of Science Fiction* (New York: Harmony Books, 1977), p. 241.

44. P. 97: *Cannibals,* as King told Winter, is "all about these people who are trapped in an apartment building." SK, quoted by DEW, *The Art of Darkness,* p. 157.

45. P. 98, "With a master's sure feel for the power of the plausible to terrify as much or more than the uncanny. . . ." *Publishers Weekly,* February 27, 1981, p. 144.

46. P. 98: "Cancer is everywhere; . . ." SK, speech, Truth or Consequences, NM.

47. P. 99: . . . he wanted "some new bread pans. . . ." *BDN,* (late) December 1981.

48. P. 100: King published in May 1981 his fourth Richard Bachman novel, *The Running Man,* which he felt "may be the best of them because it's nothing but story. . . ." SK, "Why I Was Bachman," *The Bachman Books,* p. x.

49. P. 100: "Somewhat contrary to the recollection reflected in the 'Afterword' to *Different Seasons,* it now appears that the four novellas were written by King in the following sequence. . . ." DEW, *The Art of Darkness,* p. 207.

50. P. 100: " 'Novellas,' Alan says. He is being a good sport, but his voice says some of the joy may have just gone out of his day; . . ." SK, Afterword, *Different Seasons,* p. 526.

51. Pp. 100–101: "at the risk of being an iconoclast I will say that I do not give a diddly-whoop what Stephen King chooses as an area in which to write." John D. MacDonald, Introduction, *Night Shift,* p. ix.

52. P. 101: "I got a really strong reaction to the 'Apt Pupil' story. . . ." SK, interviewed by Platt, *Dream Makers: Volume II*, pp. 279–280.

53. P. 101: "I took your idea and I wrote a story about these kids who walk down a railroad track to find the body of a boy." SK, interview, *Bare Bones,* p. 17.

54. P. 101: But an idea is not a story, so, said King, "I took a lot of things I had felt when I was a kid and put them in [Gordon Lachance]." Ibid.

55. P. 101: "The kid I had been playing with had been run over by a freight train. . . ." SK, *Danse Macabre,* p. 90.

56. Pp. 101–02: "A friend of mine said to me and Steve, 'Do you want to see a dead body?' " Chesley, interviewed by GB.

57. P. 102: "It ought to have THIS IS A PRODUCT OF AN UNDERGRADUATE CREATIVE WRITING WORKSHOP. . . ." SK, "The Body," *Different Seasons,* p. 335.

58. P. 103: "IT IS THE TALE, NOT HE WHO TELLS IT." SK, "The Breathing Method," *Different Seasons,* p. 473.

59. P. 103: "Here, sir, there are *always* more tales," he tells an inquisitive club member. Ibid., p. 518.

60. P. 103: *Publishers Weekly* called the stories "some of his best work." . . . *Publishers Weekly,* June 18, 1982, p. 64.

61. P. 103: "The important thing to acknowledge in King's immense popularity, and in the Niagara of words he produces, is the simple fact that he can write." Thomas Gifford, "Stephen King's Quartet," *Washington Post Book World,* August 22, 1982, p. 2.

62. P. 103: "I don't remember a single correspondent . . . who scolded me for writing something that wasn't horror." SK, "Straight Up Midnight: An Introductory Note," *Four Past Midnight* by SK (New York: Viking, 1990), p. xiv.

63. Pp. 103–104: "Written over a period of twelve years, *The Dark Tower: The Gunslinger* is the first cycle of stories in a remarkable epic. . . ." Donald M. Grant, advertisement for *The Dark Tower: The Gunslinger,* in *Whispers,* (whole) no. 17–18, August 1982, p. 17.

64. P. 104: "I didn't think anybody would want to read it." SK, quoted by Janet C. Beaulieu, "Gunslinger Stalks Darkness in Human Spirit," *CR,* March 1989, p. 1.

65. P. 104: "To issue such a book, of course, is one of the few ways I have left of saying that I am not entirely for sale. . . ." SK, "The Politics of Limiteds—Part II," *CR,* July 1985, p. 5.

66. P. 104: "The book was published at twenty dollars, and I was a little bit horrified by what happened." SK, speech, Pasadena, CA.

67. Pp. 104–105: "I am certain there is not a single person reading this who needs an introduction to Stephen King." Stuart David Schiff, Editorial, *Whispers,* August 1982, p. 2.

68. P. 105: "I'm still a fan at heart. . . ." SK, interview, *Feast of Fear,* p. 264.

69. P. 105: "Stephen King spent a lot of time in his suite, because he was mobbed wherever he went." *Locus* magazine, January 1983, p. 12.

70. P. 105: "I love conventions, but may have to give them up if this continues." *Locus,* August 1983.

71. P. 105: The conventions, King explained, were "no longer any fun." *Locus,* January 1983, p. 12.

72. P. 105: "Do you know me?" SK, celebrity ad for American Express, produced by Ogilvy & Mather, aired on television.

73. P. 106: King replied, "God, no! I'll be far away!" SK, quoted. (Bibliographic information not available.)

74. P. 106: "My idea of a perfect horror film would be one where you'd have to have nurses and doctors on duty. . . ." SK, videotaped interview, Equitable Group (New York, 1989).

75. P. 106: "It is the first book-length study of King's fiction. . . ." DEW, Foreword, *Stephen King* (Mercer Island, WA: Starmont House, 1982).

76. Pp. 106–107: "It's sort of an epistolary novel-in-progress" SK, interview, "Larry King Show," April 10, 1986; audiotape recording by Lion Recording.

77. P. 107: King now was unquestionably, as he put it, "America's literary boogeyman." SK, "Straight Up Midnight: An Introductory Note," *Four Past Midnight,* p. xiii.

Chapter 6: Bestsellasaurus Rex

1. P. 108: "It was the perfect time and place. . . ." SK, "Why I Wrote *The Eyes of the Dragon,*" *CR,* February 1987, p. 4.

2. P. 108: . . . King's attempt to reach out to his daughter Naomi, who had "read little of my work, and quite simply put, I wanted to please her and reach her." Ibid.

3. P. 108: "Although I had written thirteen novels by the time my daughter had attained an equal number of years, she hadn't read any of them." SK, jacket copy, *The Eyes of the Dragon* by SK (New York: Viking, 1987).

4. P. 108: Three months later King published *Christine*. ". . . I *love* my haunted car. . . ." SK, Afterword, *Different Seasons,* p. 526.

5. P. 108: "I wanted not to be taking a lot of cash which I didn't need, and it ties up money other writers could get for advances." SK, quoted in "King New Book Advance—$1," *Locus,* January 1983, p. 5.

6. P. 109: A dark *American Graffiti, Christine* is, according to King, "a monster story." SK, interviewed by Marshall Blonsky, "Hooked on Horror," *Washington Post,* p. B5.

7. P. 109: . . . it "contains some of the best writing King has ever done. . . ." *Publishers Weekly,* February 25, 1983, p. 80.

8. P. 109: "This one just seemed very, very special to me." Richard Kobritz, quoted by R. H. Martin in "Richard Kobritz and Christine," *Fangoria,* no. 32, p. 16.

9. P. 110: "A number of publishing houses, such as McGraw–Hill and World Publishing, initiated a royalty payout plan for a few of their successful authors." *Writer's Home Companion* by James Charlton and Lisbeth Mark (New York: Penguin Books, 1987), pp. 32–33.

10. P. 110: "At 36, [King] is not only far from running out of steam but becoming a better novelist." Waka Tsunoda, "King's 'Sematary' Unforgettable," *Sunday Portsmouth Herald,* December 4, 1983.

11. P. 110: "King's newest novel is a wonderful family portrait. . . ." *Publishers Weekly,* September 23, 1983, pp. 61–62.

12. P. 111: "I wanted to do something about it, and Don [Grant] wanted to do something about it." SK, speech, Pasadena, CA.

13. P. 111: . . . "King himself has expressed discomfort with the high price tag." SK, interview, *Feast of Fear,* p. 58. In that interview King also said of the Land of Enchantment edition of *The Cycle of the Werewolf:* "I wish that it could have been either more or less, in terms of the book project, because it sorta got out of hand there. It seems thin to me, for the price" (p. 58).

14. P. 111: "I had not intended that it should be reprinted. . . ." SK, Foreword, *Silver Bullet* by SK, p. 12.

15. Pp. 111–12: "I started out as a writer and nothing more." SK, "On the Politics of Limiteds—Part II," *CR,* July 1985, p. 1.

16. P. 112: "We were living in a trailer on top of a bleak, snow-swept hillside in Hermon, Maine." SK, interviewed by *Playboy,* reprinted in *The Stephen King Companion,* p. 25.

17. P. 112: . . . furthermore, plans for the "King Museum, originally sited upon his old trailer pad, are terminated." Hermon town manager Ethan W. Aronoff, "Hermon Is Miffed at Stephen King," *BDN,* June 21, 1983.

18. P. 112: King, in a letter to his hometown newspaper, wrote that Hermon was never one of his "favorite places." SK, letter to editor, *BDN,* June 22, 1983.

19. Pp. 113–14: On SK's visit to Truth or Consequences, New Mexico, Ellanie Sampson, a librarian there, supplied all the information.

20. P. 114: "I didn't do it for the money. . . ." SK, "Entering the Rock Zone, Or, How I Happened to Marry a Rock Station from Outer Space," *CR,* October 1987, p. 5.

21. P. 114: "When I write, I just crank the music." SK, interviewed by Equitable Group.

22. Pp. 114–15: The winter is the "preferred time" for writing a novel. . . . Ibid.

23. P. 115: On January 14, 1984, Douglas Winter and King were "huddled before a woodstove fire. . . ." DEW, *The Art of Darkness* (New York: NAL, Signet, 1986), p. 194.

24. P. 115: "Richard Bachman is an incredibly talented writer. . . ." Letter to booksellers from NAL, distributed with advance reading copies of *Thinner* at the American Bookseller's Convention in 1984.

25. Pp. 115–16: In "Lists That Matter (Number 8)," King cited ten films that, if they weren't the worst movies of all time, were certainly "right up there." . . . SK, "Lists That Matter (Number 8)," *CR,* September 1985, p. 7.

26. P. 116: . . . Stephen King's incendiary remarks about the film—"the worst of the bunch." . . . SK, quoted by Gary Wood in "Firestarter," *Cinefantastique,* vol. 21, no. 4 (February 1991), p. 34.

27. P. 116: "When you make a film, you try your best." Ibid.

28. Pp. 116–17: "I see that Mark Lester has finally revealed my dark secret; . . ." SK, "King on *Firestarter*: Who's to Blame?" letter to *Cinefantastique,* p. 35.

29. P. 117: . . . as Tabitha King later wrote, explored "[t]he very connection that exists . . . between the writer and the reader. . . ." Tabitha King, "Co-miser-a-ting with Stephen King," *CR,* August 1987, p. 5.

30. P. 117: . . . which "inevitably draws those most in need of connection with anyone, anything. . . ." Ibid.

31. P. 117: "I love these people." SK, quoted by David Streitfeld, "Stephen King's No. 1 Fans," in *CR,* August 1987, p. 5.

32. P. 117: He owes his fans "[s]omething to read." Ibid.

33. P. 117: Even with all that, as Streitfeld wrote, "[King] doesn't worry about a deranged, passionate fan coming after him." Ibid.

34. P. 118: "In horror fiction, two heads are better than one. . . ." "Worst of Pages," *People,* December 24–31, 1984, p. 18.

35. P. 118: *Esquire,* styling King and Straub "Shockmeisters," attempted to put both authors in their place. . . . Barney Cohen, "The Shockmeisters," *Esquire,* November 1984, p. 231.

36. P. 118: "King, whose own style is American yahoo. . . ." Ibid.

37. P. 118: "infused with warmth, vivid characterization and dramatic intensity. . . ." *Publishers Weekly,* September 20, 1985, p. 107.

38. P. 118: A literary experiment, *The Talisman* was "a definite departure from [King's] previous ventures into the supernatural." . . . *Booklist,* January 15, 1985, p. 686.

39. P. 118: "As Casey Stengel used to say, you've got to put an asterisk by it." . . . SK, quoted by DEW, *The Art of Darkness,* p. 143.

40. P. 119: Mark Graham cited the NAL connection in "Fit for a King: This Thriller Raises an Authorship Question," *Rocky Mountain News Sunday Magazine/Books* (Denver), December 23, 1984.

41. P. 119: "You were starting to sound a little like a Stephen King novel for a while

there. . . ." Stephen King, writing as Richard Bachman, *Thinner* (New York: NAL Books, 1984), p. 111.

42. P. 119: . . . which he termed "a very humble storefront in a world dominated by a few great glassy shopping malls." SK, "The Ideal, Genuine Writer: A Forenote," *The Ideal, Genuine Man* by Don Robertson (Bangor, ME: Philtrum Press, 1987), p. ix.

43. Pp. 119–20: Opposed to what he termed "autographs masquerading as books. . . ." SK, "The Politics of Limiteds—Part II," *CR*, p. 2.

44. P. 120: "With good care," wrote Alpert, " *The Eyes of the Dragon* will stay in fine condition for centuries." Michael Alpert, "Designing *The Eyes of the Dragon*," *CR*, August 1985, p. 6.

45. P. 120: Limited editions, in King's mind, recalled the nineteeth century when "books were viewed as things of great value, and were jealously guarded." SK, "The Politics of Limiteds—Part II," *CR*, p. 5.

46. P. 120: "A real limited edition, far from being an expensive autograph stapled to a novel, is a treasure." Ibid.

47. P. 120: "Our goal is to keep you up-to-date on the work of this prolific writer." . . . Stephanie Leonard, *CR*, January 1985, p. 1.

48. P. 120: . . . would also "serve as a vehicle for communication between the fans." Stephanie Leonard, interviewed by Stephen J. Spignesi, "Living in Castle Rock: An Interview with Stephanie Leonard, the Founding Editor of *Castle Rock: The Stephen King Newsletter,*" in *The Shape Under the Sheet,* p. 97.

49. P. 121: In the second issue Leonard hinted that there would be "a secret revealed at long last. . . ." Stephanie Leonard, *CR*, February 1985, p. 8.

50. P. 121: . . . what King termed "cancer of the pseudonym." . . . SK, quoted by Stefan Kanfer, "King of Horror," *Time,* October 6, 1986, p. 78.

51. P. 121: "You know how when you're carrying home some groceries in the rain and the whole bag just kind of falls apart?" SK, quoted by Joan H. Smith, "Pseudonym Kept Five King Novels a Mystery," *BDN.* February 9, 1985.

52. P. 121: "That is so mean. Cruel, too." Jo Koskela, "No Fair, Stephen King," letter to editor, *BDN.* (Date not known; most likely February or March 1985.)

53. P. 122: King pointed out that they confused "enjoyment with ownership." SK, letter to editor, *BDN,* March 5, 1985.

54. P. 122: . . . which "might tell you something. . . ." SK, "Why I Was Bachman," *The Bachman Books,* p. ix.

55. P. 122: "I was pissed." SK, quoted by Loukis Louka, "The Dispatch Talks with: Writer Stephen King," *Maryland Coast Dispatch,* August 8, 1986.

56. P. 123: "As to whether or not he has any other pseudonyms, except for using the name John Swithen. . . ." Stephanie Leonard, *CR*, April 1985, p. 1.

57. P. 123: It would be, as NAL's Elaine Koster termed it, "a Stephen King firestorm." Koster, quoted in "An Unstoppable Thriller King," *Newsweek,* June 10, 1985, p. 62.

58. P. 123: "Some critics will want to dismiss it as a grandstand act. . . ." SK, quoted in "People: Stephen King's Torrent of Horror," *USA Today,* July 11, 1985.

59. P. 124: "a showcase for his enormous talent and range. . . ." *Library Journal,* May 1, 1985, p. 78.

60. P. 124: "hefty sampler from all stages of his career. . . ." *Publishers Weekly,* April 19, 1985, p. 72.

61. P. 125: "Seven books about Stephen King. . . ." Back-cover copy on Starmont's SK books.

62. P. 125: *Castle Rock* reported that he "hopes to direct this one." Stephanie Leonard, *CR,* March 1985, p. 1.

63. P. 126: "A lot of people have made movies out of my stories. . . ." SK, quoted by Jessie Horsting, *Stephen King at the Movies* (New York: Starlog Press [dist. by NAL], 1986), p. 70.

64. P. 126: "With King working as both screenwriter and director, *Overdrive* has become an intriguing project." Michael R. Collings, *The Films of Stephen King* (Mercer Island, WA: Starmont House, 1986), p. 159.

65. P. 127: "I got paid $70,000 to direct this thing, and as far as I'm concerned it was disaster pay." SK, quoted by Calvin Ahlgren, "King of Horror Finds Directing Unnerving," *San Francisco Chronicle,* July 22, 1986.

66. P. 127: "I didn't. I didn't care for it at all." Ibid.

67. P. 127: That summer North Carolina passed what King called an "anti-porn statute. . . ." SK, "Say 'No' to the Enforcers," *CR,* August 1986, p. 7.

68. P. 127: "In North Carolina, bare breasts and cocaine are both crimes." Ibid.

69. P. 127: . . . King concluded that "it's our responsibility. . . ." Ibid.

70. P. 128: . . . the public "favored restrictions on pornography." George A. Smith, "We Fought the Good Fight," *Christian Civic League Record,* p. 8.

71. P. 128: "The purpose of this bill is to make it a crime. . . ." Header from Legislative Document No. 2092, Bill 2, House of Representatives, February 28, 1986. (Much of the information I have on hand about the anticensorship movement in Maine was sent to me by Bill Maroldo, the director of public affairs at WCBB, channel 10, in Lewiston, Maine.)

72. P. 128: "Do It for the Children." Christopher Spruce, "Stephen King Helps Spearhead Censorship Referendum Defeat" in *The Stephen King Companion,* p. 142.

73. P. 128: "Don't Make Freedom a Dirty Word." *Christian Civic League Record.*

74. P. 129: . . . two ads "stressing the link between pornography and child sexual abuse." Ibid.

75. P. 129: "Hard-core and violent pornography debases and destroys lives, families and marriages." Jasper S. Wyman, "Another Viewpoint: Hard-core, Violent Pornography Debases and Destroys," *BDN,* February 28, 1986.

76. P. 129: "Want to hear something *really* scary?" *Locus* magazine. (No other bibliographic information available.)

77. P. 129: "I think the idea of making it a crime to sell obscene material is a bad one. . . ." SK, quoted by Christopher Spruce, "Stephen King Helps Spearhead Censorship Referendum Defeat," in *The Stephen King Companion,* p. 143.

78. P. 129: "There are a few holes in the idea of an obscenity law." Joseph King, "Another Viewpoint: An Obscenity Law Is Obscene," *BDN,* June 5, 1986.

79. P. 129: "If the censorship referendum passes, your freedom could go up in smoke." *Christian Civic League Record.*

80. P. 129: "I hate that ad." SK, quoted by Christopher Spruce, "Stephen King Helps Spearhead Censorship Referendum Defeat," in *The Stephen King Companion,* p. 142.

81. P. 130: "Stephen King, who has had his books banned from some school libraries. . . ." Ibid.

82. P. 130: "We fought the good fight." *Christian Civic League Record,* p. 19.

83. P. 130: As King wrote in an article . . . "Ratings can sell tickets or destroy movies." SK, "The Dreaded X," *Gauntlet* (Springfield, PA: Gauntlet, Inc., 1991), p. 70.

84. P. 130: "For the record, I don't think the picture is going to review badly." . . . SK, quoted in "Full Throttle with Stephen King," *New Times* (Phoenix, AZ), July 30–August 5, 1986.

85. P. 130: "As I left, I felt the urgent need of a hot bath. . . ." Robert H. Newall, "King's Film Lacks Taste," *BDN,* July 29, 1986.

86. Pp. 130–31: King "has taken a promising notion—our dependence on machines—and turned it into one long car-crunch movie, wheezing from setups to crackups." Jon Pareles, "Film: By Stephen King, 'Maximum Overdrive,'" *New York Times,* July 25, 1986.

87. P. 131: "Stephen King's latest movie . . . is a factory reject." Robert Garrett, "'Overdrive': Bodies by King," *Boston Globe,* July 26, 1986.

88. P. 131: "I don't have any plans to direct, but sooner or later I would like to do it again . . . in Maine." SK, press conference for *Stephen King's Graveyard Shift,* Bangor, ME.

89. P. 131: "Hollywood is always looking for some way to *market* films, more than they're looking for a good story." Rob Cohen, quoted by Gary Wood, "The Dark Half," *Cinefantastique,* p. 27.

90. P. 131: "A boy and his buddies set out on a hike to find a dead body." Television listing, *USA Today,* March 2, 1990.

91. P. 132: "When you read [King's] books, and because so many people have seen his films, people assume that Stephen King is just a schlocky kind of horror writer; . . ." Rob Reiner, interviewed by Gary Wood; transcription of unpublished 1989 interview provided by Wood.

92. P. 132: "Who could have predicted that a movie, let alone a good movie, could be made from a story about 12-year-olds hiking to find a dead body?" David Brooks, "What Is Death, What Is Goofy?" *Insight,* September 1, 1986.

93. P. 132: "Considering what a disaster Stephen King's *Maximum Overdrive* is, directed by the best-selling horror novelist himself. . . ." Richard Freeman, "Boys Will Be Boys in Refreshing 'Stand by Me,'" *Newark Star-Ledger,* August 8, 1986, p. 49.

94. P. 133: . . . *Time* considered him the "King of Horror." Stefan Kanfer, "King of Horror," *Time,* October 6, 1986.

95. P. 133: "The Master of Pop Dread." Ibid.

96. P. 133: "the apotheosis of my public life." . . . SK, speech at ABA's "Sunday Book & Author Breakfast."

97. P. 133: "I had dinner with Bruce Springsteen—the Boss himself—just before they all went on the 'Born in the USA' tour. . . ." Ibid.

98. P. 133: "I knew *IT* would be long since I was trying to focus and understand all the things I had written before." Book ad, *Book of the Month* (Book-of-the-Month-Club).

99. P. 134: [T]here was an age—it ended around 1950, I should judge—when the long novel was accepted on its own terms. . . ." SK, "Love Those Long Novels" (book review column), *Adelina,* November 1980, p. 12.

100. P. 134: "*IT* literally transcends itself, to stand as the most powerful novel King has written." Michael Collings, "IT: Stephen King's Comprehensive Masterpiece," *CR,* July 1986, p. 5.

101. P. 134: "Thank you for your kind letter and the accompanying essay." SK to Michael Collings, in "Stephen King's Comments on *IT*," *CR,* July 1986, p. 1.

102. P. 134: "The exciting and absorbing parts of *IT* are not the mechanical showdowns and shockeroos. . . ." David Gates, "The Creature That Refused to Die," *Newsweek,* September 1, 1986, p. 84.

103. P. 134: . . . King, "who is in many ways the Thomas Wolfe of our times. . . ." E. F. Bleiler, "Books," *Twilight Zone,* February 1987, p. 8.

104. Pp. 134–35: I am a writer who exists more on nerve-endings than the process of intellectual thought and logic." SK, untitled essay in *Nightmares in the Sky: Gargoyles and Grotesques,* with f-stop Fitzgerald (photographs) (New York: Viking Studio Books, 1988), p. 7.

105. P. 135: "Where did Stephen King, the most experienced crown prince of darkness, go wrong with *IT*?" Walter Wagner, "More Evil Than a 15-foot Spider," *New York Times Book Review,* August 24, 1986.

106. P. 135: "Get *IT.* Buy *IT.*" *Publishers Weekly,* June 27, 1986, p. 74.

107. P. 135: "I wait for each new King novel as an alcoholic waits for that next drink." Whoopi Goldberg, in *Reign of Fear: Fiction and Film of Stephen King,* ed. Don Herron (Los Angeles, and Columbia, PA: Underwood–Miller, 1988), p. 9.

108. P. 136: "I would do stuff and it would fall apart like wet tissue paper." SK, speech, Pasadena, CA.

109. P. 136: "All I know is, if I don't do it, I go crazy." Tabitha King, interviewed by Rodney Labbe, "Tabitha King: Resisting the Star-Maker Machinery." *CR,* December 1987–January 1988, p. 5.

110. P. 136: "It is—or if it succeeds—a tale. . . ." SK, "Why I Wrote *The Eyes of the Dragon,*" *CR,* February 1987, p. 4.

111. P. 137: "Why? Because Mr. King had written for a thirteen-year-old, and not for me." Margi Washburn (Tucson, AZ), letter to editor, " 'Eyes' Has It," *CR,* December 1987–January 1988.

112. P. 137: "It took me three days to finish this treasure. . . ." Ibid.

113. P. 137: . . . she had taken the manuscript "with a marked lack of enthusiasm. . . ." SK, jacket copy, *The Eyes of the Dragon.*

114. P. 137: . . . changed into "rapt interest as the story kidnapped her." Ibid.

115. P. 137: When she finished, she told him that "the only thing wrong with it was that she didn't want it to end." Ibid.

116. P. 137: "That, my friends, is a writer's favorite song, I think," concluded King. Ibid.

117. P. 137: "I have read several pained, angry, and offended letters from fans. . . ." Tabitha King, "Co-miser-a-ting with Stephen King," *CR,* August 1987, p. 1.

118. P. 137: "The public is frequently possessive and unforgiving, without seeming to understand that what they are attempting to exercise is a kind of emotional slavery." Tabitha King, interviewed by Labbe, "Resisting the Star-Maker Machinery," *CR,* p. 10.

119. P. 138: "I thought it would be about escape, pure and simple." SK, interview, Book-of-the-Month Club *News Magazine,* June 1987.

120. P. 138: "They wanted Misery, Misery, Misery." SK, *Misery* (New York: Viking, 1987), p. 25.

121. P. 138: "People really like what I do." . . . SK, speech, Pasadena, CA.

122. P. 138: "This is for Stephanie and Jim Leonard. . . ." Dedication, *Misery.*

123. P. 139: "King's new novel, about a writer held hostage by his self-proclaimed 'number-one fan,' is unadulteratedly terrifying." *Publishers Weekly.* May 1, 1987, p. 52.

124. P. 139: . . . "[Chapman] was living in Hawaii, and his constrained financial circumstances made it unlikely he had come to New York." David Streitfeld, "Stephen King's No. 1 Fans," *CR,* August 1987, p. 1.

125. P. 139: "At this point, nobody can make me change anything." SK, interviewed by Lynn Flewelling, "King Working on a Book He Believes Could Be His Best," *BDN,* September 11, 1990.

126. Pp. 139–40: . . . it was "not one of King's more original novels." . . . *Library Journal,* January 1988, p. 99.

127. Pp. 139–40: "we smugly tell ourselves that no one could be as stupid as the people in this book." *Booklist,* October 1, 1987, p. 170.

128. P. 140: "*The Tommyknockers* is consumed by the rambling prose of its author." *Publishers Weekly,* October 9, 1987, p. 79.

129. P. 140: King acknowledged that Grant had "taken a chance on these *novels,* one by one." Dedication, *The Dark Tower II: The Drawing of the Three.*

130. P. 140: "This work seems to be my own Tower, you know; these people haunt me, Roland most of all. . . ." SK, Afterword, *The Dark Tower: The Drawing of the Three* (West Kingston, R.I.: Donald M. Grant, Publisher, 1987), p. 400.

131. P. 141: "Publishing this book is no thank-you note, but a simple necessity." SK, "The Ideal, Genuine Writer: A Forenote," *The Ideal, Genuine Man* by Don Robertson (Bangor, ME: Philtrum Press, 1987), p. ix.

132. P. 141: Placing Robertson as the "latest . . . in a brawny bunch of American story-tellers who wrote naturalistic fiction." . . . Ibid., p. xx.

133. P. 141: "from Mark Twain to Stephen Crane to Frank Norris. . . ." Ibid.

134. P. 141: *The Ideal, Genuine Man* "is, quite simply, a great book by an ideal, genuine writer." Ibid.

135. P. 141: . . . the "American naturalists of a dark persuasion. . . ." SK, *Danse Macabre,* p. 306.

136. P. 141: . . . King admitted was "a critical and financial flop." SK, "A Postscript to 'Overdrive,' " *CR,* February 1987, p.1.

137. P. 142: "It was undoubtedly one of the worst movies I have ever seen. . . ." Lisa Dunn, letter to editor, "Lot-ta Yuck," *CR,* November 1987.

138. P. 142: "It's actually gotten some good reviews, but I think it's dreadful." SK, interviewed by Gary Wood, 1989 (unpublished).

139. P. 142: "Finally, I wrote a little story called 'Rainy Season' and all at once, everything opened up and flooded out." SK, speech, Pasadena, CA.

140. Pp. 142–43: NAL's Robert Diforio declared that King was "as mesmerizing in audio as he is in print." Robert Diforio quoted in "Stephen King Tapes Readings Coming from NAL," *Publishers Weekly,* February 19, 1988.

141. P. 143: "I thought that even though I don't have a professional voice, I know what the story means to me, which is a great deal." SK, quoted in "Stephen King Tapes Readings Coming from NAL," *Publishers Weekly,* February 19, 1988.

142. P. 143: "All the change means is that Z-62 will offer its programming commercial-free." SK, "Stephen King's WZON Rocks On," *Castle Rock,* October 1988, p. 3.

143. P. 143: "A recent article in *Fantasy Newsletter* mentioned a shake-up at the Kirby McCauley agency." Stephanie Leonard, editorial comments, *CR,* September 1988, p. 2.

144. P. 144: "This is simply wonderful to report." Robert Diforio, quoted by Spruce, "Happy New Year . . . ," *CR,* February 1989.

145. P. 144: "After that time off from writing . . . the ideas and creativity started up again. . . ." Ibid.

146. P. 144: "It is a strange thing." DEW, interviewed by Howard Wornom and GB, "An Interview with Douglas Winter," *Grimoire* (Williamsburg, VA: GB Publishing, 1990), p. 75.

147. P. 145: "I think that they responded the way that we hoped that they would, the way we dreamed they would. . . ." SK, press conference for *Stephen King's Graveyard Shift,* Bangor, ME.

148. P. 145: "Because *Pet Sematary* of all my novels was the one I thought would be the most difficult to film, I just simply made it an unbreakable part of the deal. . . ." Ibid.

149. P. 146: "If you're going to tell about Maine, why not come here?" Ibid.

150. P. 146: . . . the Kings made a "hefty donation." . . . Christopher Spruce, Editor's Column, *CR,* December 1989, p. 2.

151. P. 146: "As children, we need to have our dreams encouraged and nurtured." Ibid.

152. P. 147: "Steve's office, where he writes personal letters and answers mail. . . ." In a letter from David Lowell to GB, February 1991.

153. Pp. 147–48: . . . called "the new King thriller . . . so wondrously frightening that mesmerized readers won't be able to fault the master. . . ." *Publishers Weekly,* September 1, 1989, p. 76.

154. P. 148: "I'm not sure he has ever been entirely comfortable with the idea of a newsletter devoted to 'Stephen King.'" Christopher Spruce, "Say Goodnight, Lucy," *CR,* September–October 1989, p. 1.

155. P. 148: "It's been around for five full years. . . ." Ray Rexer, excerpt from "I Don't Care What People Say, Castle Rock Is Here to Stay," *CR,* December 1989, p. 1.

156. P. 148: "I'm forty-two now, and as I look back over the last four years of my life I can see all sorts of cloture." SK, "Two Past Midnight: A Note on 'Secret Window, Secret Garden,'" *Four Past Midnight,* p. 250.

157. P. 149: . . . "the oldest radio station in Bangor" became "the city's newest station. . . ." Dale McGarrigle, "WZON radio Goes from Rock 'n' Roll to Talk 'n' Sports," *BDN,* October 9, 1990.

158. P. 149: King wrote that "approximately four hundred pages of manuscript [100,000 words] were deleted from the final draft." SK, "A Preface in Two Parts:/Part 2: To Be Read After Purchase," *The Stand,* p. x.

159. P. 149: "The cuts were made at the behest of the accounting department." Ibid.

160. P. 149: "King's editor at that time, William G. Thompson, who is now with another publisher. . . ." *Science Fiction Chronicle,* March 1990, p. 4.

161. P. 149: ". . . [T]here was no damning of the old Doubleday, and there was no rancor." Edwin McDowell, "King's 'The Stand' To Be Reissued," *The New York Times,* February 4, 1990; reprinted in *Maine Sunday Telegram.*

162. P. 150: . . . not for himself but "to serve a body of readers who have asked to have it." SK, "A Preface in Two Parts," . . . *The Stand,* p. x.

163. P. 150: . . . "long tale of dark Christianity." . . . Ibid., p. xii.

164. P. 150: Although not his favorite novel, "it is . . . the one people who like my books seem to like the most." Ibid.

165. P. 150: . . . the new edition remained the "same excellent tale." . . . *Publishers Weekly,* March 16, 1990, p. 60.

166. P. 151: "Randall Flagg to me is everything that I know of in the last twenty years that's really bad. . . ." SK, interview, *Feast of Fear,* p. 29.

167. P. 151: "When this book is published, in 1990, I will have been sixteen years in the business of make-believe." SK, "Straight Up Midnight: An Introductory Note," *Four Past Midnight,* p. xiii.

168. P. 151: . . . King described, "tales of horror." Ibid., p. xv.

169. P. 151: . . . King wrote his "last story about writers and writing. . . ." SK, "Two Past Midnight: A Note on 'Secret Window, Secret Garden,' " *Four Past Midnight,* p. 250.

170. Pp. 151–52: "I'll never leave Maine behind, but Castle Rock became more and more real to me." SK, quoted by Bill Goldstein, "King of Horror," *Publishers Weekly,* p. 9.

171. P. 152: "More than just good yarns, these are can't-tear-your-eyes-away stories. . . ." Digby Diehl, "Books," *Playboy,* October 1990, p. 30.

172. P. 152: . . . acknowledged King as "above all a master storyteller. . . ." Michael A. Morrison, "Stephen King: Time Out of Joint," *Washington Post Book World,* August 26, 1990, p. 9.

173. Pp. 152–53: "*Graveyard Shift* was written by this 22-year-old kid who sold two pieces of fiction beforehand, both to specialty magazines." SK, press conference at Hoyt Cinema for *Stephen King's Graveyard Shift,* Bangor, ME.

174. P. 153: . . . passed "quickly into that great video graveyard in the suburbs." Richard Harrington, " 'Graveyard': Dead on Arrival," *Washington Post,* October 29, 1990, p. B8.

175. P. 153: "The acting and directing are substandard." Ibid.

176. P. 154: "The thing that drew me to the film was not that it was a suspense thriller genre." Rob Reiner, interviewed by Gary Wood, 1989.

177. P. 154: "It's an old, tired joke." Kathy Bates quoted by Glenn Lovel, " 'Psycho' Jokes Aside, Actress Kathy Bates Refuses to Be Typecast," *Daily Press* (Newport News, VA), December 8, 1990.

178. P. 154: "I've admired King's work over the years, but I'm not a horror devotee." Ibid.

179. P. 155: "Though *Pet Sematary* and *Graveyard Shift* have inspired countless moviegoer moratoriums on Stephen King adaptations. . . ." Mike Clark, "Reiner's 'Misery' Makes Scary Company," *USA Today,* November 30, 1990.

180. P. 155: "The film seems best when it centers on the children." Mal Vincent, "Childhood's Worst Fears Resurface When 'It' Returns to a Small Town,' " *Virginian-Pilot and Ledger-Star* (Norfolk, VA), November 1990, p. G3.

181. P. 156: "(King) feels embarrassed by these early columns and considers them juvenilia. . . ." Arthur B. Greene, quoted in "Novelist Opposes Republication of Student Columns," AP story, *BDN,* December 5, 1990.

182. P. 156: Its attorney said, "My general understanding is, if you write a column for a newspaper, it belongs to the newspaper." Ibid.

183. P. 156: "We just don't have the kind of funds to take on protracted litigation." Doug Vanderweide, quoted in "Campus Paper Drops Plans to Reprint Old King Columns," AP story, *BDN,* December 6, 1990.

184. P. 156: "For what is easy to see in King's writing is a growing awareness. . . ." Douglas Rooks, "Commentary: Stephen King's Coming of Age," *Morning Sentinel,* December 24, 1990.

185. Pp. 156–57: . . . had started out as "a young man who knew no one in the publishing world and who had no literary agent. . . ." SK, "On Becoming a Brand Name," *Fear Itself,* p. 15.

186. P. 157: "Stephen King is unique." Edward L. Ferman, "In This Issue," *The Magazine of Fantasy and Science Fiction* (Cornwall, CT: Mercury Press, 1990), p. 6.

187. P. 157: "The idea of doing a piece, an overview on why these films haven't worked, is really interesting to me." SK, quoted by Gary Wood, "Stephen King and Hollywood," *Cinefantastique,* p. 29.

188. P. 157: "Love them or loathe them, you couldn't have had the '80s without them. . . ." "Love Them or Loathe Them," *People Weekly,* Fall 1989, p. 45.

189. P. 157: "Nothing is as unstoppable as one of King's furies. . . ." Ibid.

190. P. 158: Sales of King books from *Publishers Weekly,* January 5, 1990, p. 24.

191. P. 158: " . . . the 1980s saw him become America's bestselling writer of fiction." Jacket copy, *Four Past Midnight.*

Chapter 7: The Wastelands—and Beyond

1. P. 159: "The publishers of the first two *Dark Tower* volumes and the collector's editions of *The Talisman* and *Christine.* . . ." Ad copy in *F&SF* (December 1990), Donald M. Grant, Publisher, Inc.

2. P. 159: "We have been inundated with calls and letters concerning the long-awaited third book in Stephen King's *Dark Tower* series." Brochure to in-house mailing list, Donald M. Grant, Publisher, Inc., March 1991.

3. P. 160: King said that the act of writing is analogous to looking through "an almost forgotten window. . . ." *SK,* "Two Past Midnight: A Note on 'Secret Window, Secret Garden,' " *Four Past Midnight,* p. 251.

4 P. 160: King continued, "But sometimes windows break." Ibid.

5. P. 160: "You stole my story and something's got to be done about it." SK, "Secret Window, Secret Garden," *Four Past Midnight,* p. 253.

6. P. 160: "A woman is suing author Stephen King. . . ." "Woman sues King," *Daily Press* (Newport News, VA), April 18, 1991.

7. Pp. 160–61: "Anne Hiltner is suing King in New Jersey courts. . . ." John Ripley, "King Target of Scare," *BDN,* April 1991.

8. P. 161: Keene "told police . . . he had planned to do something to gain publicity." Ibid.

9. P. 161: According to the *News,* "Marsha DeFilippo, who works in the office, said Keene wanted King to help him write a book." Renee Ordway, "Kings Plan to Increase Security After Weekend Break-In," *BDN,* April 23, 1991.

10. P. 161: "He had become enough of a concern that I told a couple of people who

work with me to call the police if he came back around." . . . SK, quoted by Ordway, *BDN,* April 23, 1991.

11. P. 161: . . . she "heard glass breaking in the kitchen." Ibid.

12. P. 161: She thought "it was the glass cupboard over the sink and . . . the cat had gotten up there." Tabitha King, quoted by Ordway, *BDN,* April 23, 1991.

13. P. 161: "I didn't have time to be scared. . . ." Ibid.

14. Pp. 161–62: The "hand-held detonator unit" Keene had was only some "cardboard and some electronic parts from a calculator." Ibid.

15. P. 162: "I wanted to get into that attic." Erik Keene, quoted by Ordway, "King Home Attic Was Focus of Keene Break-In," *BDN,* April 26, 1991.

16. P. 162: "I don't know what I would have done, but it's an amusing thing to contemplate, isn't it?" Ibid.

17. P. 162: Keene was "on parole from Dallas County in Texas for theft." Ibid.

18. P. 162: "the Texas man said he has been diagnosed as a schizophrenic. . . ." Ibid.

19. P. 162: "Keene said he wants to write a book with King." Ibid.

20. P. 162: . . . "he pleaded innocent to a burglary charge and innocent by reason of insanity to a terrorizing charge." Margaret Warner, "Man Accused in King Break-In Gets New Attorney Admonition," *BDN,* May 16, 1991.

21. P. 162: "Keene said he has many troubles." Ordway, "King Home Attic Was Focus of Keene Break-In," *BDN,* April 26, 1991.

22. P. 162: . . . that Keene termed "my little episode of terror. . . ." Ibid.

23. P. 162: "after all, we've lived here for 12 years and this is the first time somebody has tried to plant a bomb in the attic." SK, quoted by Ordway, "Kings Plan to Increase Security after Weekend Break-In," *BDN,* April 23, 1991.

24. P. 162: "Usually those people write, but they don't show up," King said. Ibid.

25. P. 162: . . . "security at their house . . . will be increased." Ibid.

26. P. 163: he was "a lightning rod" for his fans. "I had one drop by to visit my wife last week." "King Tells Eager Fans in Syracuse about 'Odd State' of Being Famous," AP story, in *BDN,* April 29, 1991.

27. P. 163: . . . King "said Castle Rock had become something of a safe haven for him. . . ." Ibid.

28. P. 163: "*Needful Things* is about buying and selling American." SK, press conference with Gloria Steinem, Javits Convention Center, New York, June 2, 1991. Audiotape recording transcribed by GB.

29. Pp. 163–64: "It's easy to dig yourself a rut and furnish it." Ibid.

30. P. 164: "Castle Rock, Maine, where Polly Chalmers runs You Sew 'n' Sew and Sheriff Alan Pangborn is in charge of keeping the peace." Copy for *Needful Things,* Viking's fall–winter catalogue (September–December 1991), p. 16.

31. P. 165: "Probably the worst of it is that the phone rings all the time. . . ." SK, interviewed by *W•B* (Waldenbooks consumer magazine), November–December 1989, p. 18.

32. P. 165: "What comes out of your fiction is what you live." SK, quoted by Dennis Etchison, Foreword, *Reign of Fear,* p. 2.

33. P. 166: " . . . New Criticism insisted on close reading of the text and awareness of verbal nuance. . . ." *The Oxford Companion to English Literature,* ed. by Margaret Drabble (Oxford and New York: Oxford University Press, 1985), p. 693.

34. P. 166: With the explosion in what *Newsweek* termed "the boom in trash biography." . . . Cover artwork by Risko, jacket for fictitious book titled "*Poison Pen: The Boom in Trash Biography,* Kitty [Kelley] vs. Nancy [Reagan]," *Newsweek,* April 22, 1991.

35. P. 166: "[Tolkien] finds the attentions of his enthusiastic following rather embarrassing and his notoriety a bit of a bore." J. R. R. Tolkien, quoted by Lin Carter, *Tolkien: A Look Behind "The Lord of the Rings,"* (New York: Ballantine Books, March 1969), p. 29.

36. P. 166: Justin Kaplan . . . maintains that "no biographer, even the best disposed and admiring, who has any gumption and integrity can be altogether a friend to the person he or she is writing about. . . ." Justin Kaplan, "Biographies Should Tell All," *Newsweek,* April 22, 1991, p. 58.

37. P. 166: "I think there is something salutary even in carnival excess. . . ." Ibid.

38. P. 167: "My thoughts are that the real Stephen King is much more interesting than the external myth that surrounds him now." Chesley, interviewed by Spignesi, *The Shape Under the Sheet,* pp. 49–50.

39. P. 167: King has a "sense of himself as being outside the mainstream. . . ." Ibid.

40. P. 167: "We do business with him like no one else." Jonathan Levin, quoted by Matt Roush, "Stephen King Scares Up a Summer Series," *USA Today,* May 7, 1991, p. 3D.

41. P. 168: "I'm not sure what you do about it." SK, press conference with Gloria Steinem, Javits Convention Center, New York, June 2, 1991. Audiotape recording transcribed by GB.

42. P. 168: "What do you read when you want to be frightened?" Reporter's question for SK, press conference, Javits Convention Center.

43. Pp. 168–69: "The answer is the answer that I gave." SK, press conference, Javits Convention Center.

44. P. 169: "*American Psycho* is a disturbing book." Ibid.

45. P. 170: "At the jamboree for Stephen King, held in a downtown club with tighter security than a presidential candidate gets. . . ." "Style" section, *Washington Post,* June 1991.

46. P. 170: "It was the first work of a man who in catering to a public's worst nightmares would become a publisher's dream." Joyce Meskis, introducing SK at "Sunday Book & Author Breakfast: Stephen King, Dr. Ferrol Sams, Gloria Steinem," ABA Annual Meeting, New York, June 2, 1991.

47. Pp. 170–71: "Writers, novelists in particular, are actually supposed to be secret agents." SK, speech at "Sunday Book & Author Breakfast."

48. P. 171: "You are the people who have allowed me to do for money what I would otherwise have done for free anyway." Ibid.

49. P. 171: " . . . the writer's job is to write. . . ." SK, "On Becoming a Brand Name," *Fear Itself,* pp. 41–42.

Chapter 8: Stephen King in the Heart of Darkness

1. P. 172: "The novelist is, after all, God's liar. . . ." SK, *Danse Macabre,* p. 369.
2. P. 172: "Thanks but no thanks to the five or six people who offered to let me

write their complete life stories. . . ." Amy Tan, "Angst & the Second Novel," *Publishers Weekly,* April 5, 1991, p. 6.

3. P. 173: "I get them from the lord Satan." SK, speech, Portland (ME) City Hall Auditorium, March 7, 1990.

4. P. 173: "I get mine from Utica [New York]." SK, interview. (No bibliographic information available.)

5. P. 173: "Twenty different sexual encounters may result in twenty different children. . . ." SK, "On *The Shining* and Other Perpetrations," *Whispers,* August 1982, p. 12.

6. P. 173: "A story or a novel is, after all, only a chain of coherent imaginative thoughts. . . ." Ibid., p. 11.

7. P. 173: "With 'The Langoliers,' that image was of a woman pressing her hand over a crack in the wall of a commercial jetliner." SK, "One Past Midnight: A Note on 'The Langoliers,' " *Four Past Midnight,* p. 4.

8. P. 173: "For a while I started to think, 'Suppose Bachman wasn't dead?' " SK, interviewed by *W•B,* November–December 1989, p. 18.

9. P. 174: "I took my daughter to see 'Les Miserables' in New York. . . ." Ibid.

10. P. 174: "Sick" or healthy, all creative activity—including writing—is the product of individual imagination. . . ." Robert Bloch, "Heritage of Horror," Introduction to *The Best of H. P. Lovecraft* (New York: Del Rey Books, 1982), p. 3.

11. P. 174: "By now, I really am sick of questions about word processors. . . ." Peter Straub, interview, "Straub Talks About *Talisman,* " *CR,* July 1985.

12. P. 175: "I like to write three drafts. . . ." SK, interviewed by Charles Platt, *Dream Makers: Volume II,* p. 282.

13. P. 175: "I think that if there was any change suggested to me that I didn't want, all I would need to say would be, 'No, I won't do that.' " Ibid.

14. P. 175: "It's a terrible position to be in." Ibid., p. 283.

15. P. 176: King wrote, "I agreed willingly enough. . . ." SK, "On *The Shining* and Other Perpetrations," *Whispers,* p. 15.

16. P. 176: "People think the muse is a literary character, some cute little pudgy devil. . . ." SK, quoted in "King of Horror," *Time,* reprinted in *The Shape Under the Sheet,* p. 19.

17. Pp. 176–77: "I gathered my research materials . . . and then I attacked the novel." SK, *Danse Macabre,* pp. 369–70.

18. P. 177: " . . . I'm never completely sure where I'm going. . . ." SK, Afterword, *The Dark Tower: The Gunslinger,* p. 223.

19. P. 177: Ralph Vincinanza's assessment of King's career from Bill Goldstein, "King of Horror," *Publishers Weekly,* vol. 238, no. 4 (Spring 1991), p. 9.

20. P. 178: " 'What's this story?' Vern asked uneasily." SK, "The Body," *Different Seasons,* p. 377.

21. P. 178: "All my life as a writer I have been committed to the idea that in fiction the story value holds dominance. . . ." SK, Foreword, *Night Shift,* p. xx.

22. P. 178: "I'm not afraid of spiraling down into a very unpleasant conclusion." SK. (Bibliographic data not available.)

23. P. 178: "We're afraid of the body under the sheet." SK, Foreword, *Night Shift,* p. xvi.

24. P. 179: "I think if I had been publishing twenty years ago, if I had started in the mid-sixties, I would have become a fairly popular writer." SK, interview, in *Feast of Fear,* p. 52.

25. P. 179: "To have a broad sales potential, a book must have scope." Dean R. Koontz, "Breaking Through," *Horror Writers of America Newsletter,* October 1988, pp. 8–9.

26. P. 179: "I have redefined the genre of horror-writing in this country." SK, quoted by Goldstein, "King of Horror," *Publishers Weekly,* p. 9.

27. P. 180: "One would have to . . . say that [King's] definition of horror is so broad and so populist. . . ." Clive Barker, interviewed by GB and Howard Wornom, "An Interview with Clive Barker," *Grimoire,* p. 20.

28. P. 180: "Most of all, I think that trapped inside King is one of the finest writers of our time." A. J. Budrys, "Stephen King," *F&SF,* p. 55.

29. P. 180: "he is the first writer, ever, to have truly baffled the critics." Ibid.

30. P. 180: "I didn't write them for money; . . ." SK, Foreword, *Night Shift,* p. xiii.

31. P. 181: "The fact is, almost all of the stuff I have written—and that includes a lot of the funny stuff—was written in a serious frame of mind." SK, "Four Past Midnight: A Note on 'The Sun Dog,' " *Four Past Midnight,* pp. 607–8.

32. P. 181: "King says he always wanted to 'build a bridge between wide popularity and a critical acceptance . . . .' " SK, quoted by Goldstein, "King of Horror," *Publishers Weekly,* p. 8.

33. P. 181: Out of King's "small amount of talent." . . . Ibid.

34. P. 181: . . . have issued the "great things." . . . Ibid.

35. P. 182: "All the same, you don't do it for money, or you're a monkey." SK, Introduction, *Skeleton Crew,* p. 15.

36. P. 182: "The only thing that matters is the story, not the person who writes it." SK, interviewed by *W•B,* November–December 1989, p. 7.

37. P. 182: "These days I sometimes look at this typewriter and wonder when it's going to run out of good words." SK, "The Body," *Different Seasons,* p. 377.

38. P. 182: "One thing hasn't changed during those years. . . ." SK, "Straight Up Midnight: An Introductory Note," *Four Past Midnight,* p. xiii.

39. P. 182: "The act of writing is beyond currency." Ibid., p. xv.

40. P. 182: "the mouth can speak, but there is no tale unless there is a sympathetic ear to listen." Ibid., p. xiv.

41. P. 182: . . . to experience what he termed the "restorative powers of fiction" and fiction's magical ability to take them away from the mundane world. SK, speech at "Sunday Book & Author Breakfast."

Selected Bibliography

The sheer volume of material by and about Stephen King has resulted in several major bibliographies, with more to come. A good place to start is *Stephen King: The Art of Darkness* by Douglas E. Winter, a Signet paperback, revised in 1986. For more information, consult *The Annotated Guide to Stephen King* by Michael R. Collings. It covers both the primary and the secondary works, and was published in 1986.

For Borgo Press, Collings has updated his Starmont edition. I have a manuscript copy of the book and commend this edition to your attention (see Appendix 1). *The Work of Stephen King: An Annotated Bibliography & Guide* promises to be the definitive reference work on King.

In the research for this book I was fortunate to have access to the holdings at the Special Collections at the Fogler Library at the University of Maine at Orono, to the collections of several King collectors, in addition to the files of Dr. Michael R. Collings. And as a result of my own research when working on *The Stephen King Companion,* I had collected several shelves of books and assorted publications by and about King. I also had several file drawers packed with hundreds of articles, reviews, profiles, and interviews that are crucial to background research.

Not least, I have viewed many of the movies on videocassette, listened to audiotape adaptations, monitored taped interviews and public speeches, and viewed several videotapes that are not generally available.

This selected bibliography, then, lists the books and other key resources most useful during the course of researching this book. (For additional information on quoted material, see Notes.)

If a book is *out of print,* I have indicated it with an abbreviation: OP. In cases where I feel clarification is necessary, I have done so following the entry itself.

For forthcoming titles, see the detailed information in Appendix 1.

No additional comments are made about the primary King books, since they have been discussed in both *The Stephen King Companion* and the text of this book.

Unless otherwise noted, the books below are first editions.

Bachman, Richard [Stephen King]. *Thinner.* New York: New American Library, NAL Books, 1984.

Barron, Neil, ed. *Horror Literature: A Reader's Guide.* Garland Reference Library of the Humanities (vol. 1220). New York and London: Garland Publishing, 1990. This comprehensive reference book is the place to begin for research in the field. It is exhaustively researched and covers horror literature from 1762 to the present, in four periods, with detailed research aids and useful author, title, and theme indices. This tome is indispensable for an overview of the field and its rich traditions.

Beahm, George, ed. *Grimoire.* Williamsburg, Virginia: GB Publishing, 1990. OP. A limited-edition trade paperback for those who bought the deluxe edition of *The Stephen King Companion* (250 copies in hardback), *Grimoire* had overflow material not available in any other edition: interviews with Clive Barker, Douglas E. Winter, and Kenny Linkous; an art portfolio by Linkous and by Timothy O' Shaughnessy, and miscellaneous material.

————, ed. *The Stephen King Companion.* Kansas City and New York: Andrews and McMeel, 1989. Principally a general introduction to King, reference guide, and buyer's guide to King material, as well as the companion book to this book.

Bernard, Andre, ed. *Rotten Rejections.* Wainscott, New York: Pushcart Press, 1990.

Bradbury, Ray. "Coda." *Fahrenheit 451.* New York: Ballantine Books, A Del Rey Book, 1988. This essay on censorship cuts to the heart of the controversy. Recommended reading for anyone with an interest in the subject, especially literary censorship.

————. *Zen in the Art of Writing.* Santa Barbara, California: Capra Press, Joshua Odell Editions, 1989. Valuable insights into the writing process by a writer who has influenced several generations of writers in the fantasy field.

Brown, Ray B., and Hoppenstand, Gary, eds. *The Gothic World of Stephen King: Landscape of Nightmares.* Bowling Green, Ohio: Bowling Green State University Popular Press, 1987. A scholarly collection of articles about King's work. Not for the casual reader.

Budrys, Algis. "Stephen King." *The Magazine of Fantasy & Science Fiction* 79 (1990):44–55. Budrys is a respected author and critic, well known in science-fiction and fantasy circles. The book reviewer for this magazine, Budrys wrote this thought-provoking essay examining King's stormy relationship with critics (a one-sided affair).

Charlton, James, and Mark, Lisbeth, eds. *The Writer's Home Companion.* New York: Penguin Books, 1987.

Collings, Michael R. *The Annotated Guide to Stephen King: A Primary and Secondary Bibliography of the Works of America's Premier Horror Writer.* Starmont Reference Guide No. 8. Mercer Island, Washington: Starmont House, 1986. (See *The Work of Stephen King,* below.)

————. *The Films of Stephen King.* Starmont Studies in Literary Criticism No. 12. Mercer Island, Washington: Starmont House, 1986. Although there are no photographs in this book, Collings provides a useful discussion comparing and contrasting each visual adaptation against the original text, shedding light on the critical success (or failure) of each work.

————. *The Many Facets of Stephen King.* Starmont Studies in Literary Criticism No. 11. Mercer Island, Washington: Starmont House, 1985. A thought-provoking thematic grouping and discussion of King's book-length fiction.

————. *Stephen King as Richard Bachman.* Starmont Series in Literary Criticism No. 10. Mercer Island, Washington: Starmont House, 1985. An exhaustive work with discussions of each book, in addition to discussions of events before and after the revelation of the Bachman pen name.

————. *The Stephen King Phenomenon.* Starmont Studies in Literary Criticism No. 14. Mercer Island, Washington: Starmont House, 1987. A useful examination of King as a phenomenon in his own right. Useful in understanding King in light of his popularity beyond the books themselves.

————. *The Work of Stephen King: An Annotated Bibliography & Guide.* Bibliographies of Modern Authors Series, edited by Boden Clarke. San Bernardino, California: Borgo Press, forthcoming. See my extended notes in Appendix 1.

Collings, Michael, and Engebretson, David. *The Shorter Works of Stephen King.* Starmont Series in Literary Criticism No. 9. Mercer Island, Washington: Starmont House, 1985. Though somewhat outdated, this book covers the short fiction, both collected (by book) and uncollected. Each story synopsis is scoped out by a discussion of the work itself.

Conner, Jeff. *Stephen King Goes to Hollywood.* "Produced" by Tim Underwood and Chuck Miller. New York: New American Library, A Plume Book, 1987. The most recent of the books on King's films, this book is an informal overview illustrated with many stills, with an emphasis on the art of the deal—the minutiae of putting a movie deal together, details which are not likely to be of great interest to the average King reader. In that regard, it offers new (although admittedly esoteric) information for the lay reader. However, the plot summaries and the general story-behind-the-story essentially duplicate what had been published in the Horsting book, *Stephen King at the Movies.*

de Camp, L. Sprague. *Lovecraft: A Biography.* London: New English Library, 1975.

de Camp, L. Sprague; de Camp, Catherine Crook; and Griffin, Jane Whittington. *Dark Valley Destiny: The Life of Robert E. Howard.* New York: Bluejay Books, 1983.

Engel, Joel. *Rod Serling: The Dreams and Nightmares of Life in the Twilight Zone.* Chicago: Contemporary Books, Inc., 1989.

Herron, Don, ed. *Feast of Fear: Conversations with Stephen King.* Edited by Underwood–Miller. San Rafael, California, and Lancaster, Pennsylvania:

Underwood–Miller, 1989. This limited edition of 600 copies ($75) collects forty-seven interviews conducted with King.

Over the years King has given countless interviews—so many that, as he has often said, he's "interviewed out."

Typically, the questions are asked by people who interview him as a celebrity, not as a writer. Thus, the queries are usually inane: "Where do you get your ideas?" is a favorite. (Depending on his mood, he's replied: "I get them from the lord Satan." "I get them at 239 Center Street in Bangor, just around the corner from the Frati Brothers Pawnshop." My favorite: "They come from any place and no place at all," which is the most accurate.)

The value of collections like this is that they compile several dozen interviews that, otherwise, are difficult to obtain—expensive and time-consuming. I, for one, am glad to see such collections; King, who unlike other authors has spoken frequently about his work and the creative process, is obviously the preferred source for such commentary.

The problem, though, with these collections is that unless King has reviewed the interview before publication, his unedited words can't be taken at face value as an accurate representation of what he *intended* to say. The better interviews are rigorously checked before publication, such as the *Playboy* interview. But others read as if they had not been edited, and in numerous cases I've found inaccuracies and misspellings that cloud, rather than illuminate, the discussion at hand.

The final problem with such collections, noted by several critics, is that without an index and without corrections to the text—many of the interviews, after all, were never meant for eventual compilation—they have little use beyond background reading. The lack of an index makes it difficult to find subjects by topic; and the uncorrected errors make the interview a minefield of potential problems if one relies on it as an informational source for research.

I hope future compilations—from Underwood–Miller or any other publisher—will address these basic concerns so that such books will *illuminate* and not *obscure* the discussions at hand.

————, ed. *Reign of Fear: Fiction and Film of Stephen King.* Los Angeles, and Columbia, Pennsylvania: Underwood–Miller, 1988. The third collection of essays from U–M, this is the least of the three. A mixed bag of articles, from the insightful (Burton Hatlen writing about two Bachman books) to the slight (Whoopi Goldberg's review of *IT*), to the annoying (editor Don Herron's "Summation," with his decidedly sarcastic writing tone guaranteed to alienate readers). Of the three collections of essays, this is the least valuable, because of its hit-and-miss selections.

Horsting, Jessie. *Stephen King at the Movies.* New York: Starlog Press (dist. by NAL), 1986. OP. The best (though now outdated) general introduction to

King's movies, with stills from the movies and an informal writing style that provides detailed information on the adaptations.

Jackson, Shirley. *The Lottery and Other Stories. The Haunting of Hill House. We Have Always Lived in the Castle.* Reprint (3 vols. in 1). Camp Hill, Pennsylvania: Book-of-the-Month-Club, Quality Paperback Book Club, 1991.

King, Stephen. *Carrie.* Garden City, New York: Doubleday & Company, 1974.

——. *Christine.* New York: Viking Press, 1983.

——. *Danse Macabre.* New York: Berkley Books, 1982. This is the preferred edition. King, who asked readers to send in corrections, got enough that he had to send a box of them to Dennis Etchison, who ensured the corrections were made for this edition.

——. *The Dark Half.* New York: Viking Penguin, 1989.

——. *The Dark Tower: The Gunslinger.* New York: New American Library, A Plume Book, 1988.

——. *The Dark Tower II: The Drawing of the Three.* New York: New American Library, A Plume Book, 1989.

——. *The Dead Zone.* New York: Viking Press, 1979.

——. *Different Seasons.* New York: Viking Press, 1982.

——. *The Eyes of the Dragon.* New York: Viking Penguin Inc., 1987. There are textual changes between this edition and the original Philtrum Press edition.

——. *Firestarter.* New York: New American Library, Signet, 1981.

——. *Firestarter.* New York: Viking Press, 1980.

——. Foreword to *Stalking the Nightmare,* by Harlan Ellison. Huntington Woods, Michigan: Phantasia Press, 1982.

——. *Four Past Midnight.* New York: Penguin Books USA, Viking, 1990.

——. "The Glass Floor: Introduction." *Weird Tales* 52 (1990):36–37. This marks the only reprinting of King's first published story, especially useful for the comments provided by King in his introductory remarks.

——. *IT.* New York: Viking Penguin, 1986.

——. *Misery.* New York: Viking Penguin, 1987.

——. *Needful Things.* New York: Viking, 1991. "Unrevised and Unpublished Proofs" state.

——. "On *The Shining* and Other Perpetrations." *Whispers* 5 (1982):11–16. OP. This essay made its only appearance here, a specialty magazine in the fantasy field. For anyone with an interest in *The Shining,* this is required reading.

——. *Pet Sematary.* New York: Doubleday & Company, 1983.

——. *'Salem's Lot.* New York: Doubleday & Company, 1975.

——. *The Shining.* New York: Doubleday & Company, 1977.

——. *Silver Bullet.* New York: New American Library, Signet, 1985. This is the reissue of *The Cycle of the Werewolf,* with additional material added: King's final screenplay, King's essay on the story behind the book and the movie, and an eight-page photo section of movie stills.

————. *Skeleton Crew.* New York: G. P. Putnam's Sons, 1985.

————. *The Stand.* New York: Doubleday & Company, 1978.

————. *The Stand: The Complete & Uncut Edition.* New York: Bantam Doubleday Dell Publishing Group, Doubleday, 1990. A restoration of the original, this also has a two-part introduction by King that sheds light on its history—a story in itself.

————. *Stephen King's Creepshow.* New York, and Scarborough, Ontario: New American Library, A Plume Book. 1982. A graphic novel (a book in cartoon format), this is an interesting addition to anyone's King collection. The artwork is by Berni Wrightson, who has worked with King on three other projects: *The Cycle of the Werewolf,* the revised edition of *The Stand,* and *Heroes for Hope.*

————. *Stephen King's Danse Macabre.* New York: Everest House Publishers, 1981. OP. This book is currently in print in a mass market paperback edition from Berkley, listed above. Required reading along with *Stephen King: The Art of Darkness.*

————. *The Tommyknockers.* New York: G. P. Putnam's Sons, 1987.

King, Stephen and Straub, Peter. *The Talisman.* New York: Viking Penguin, 1984.

————. *Twice the Power: Needful Things, Four Past Midnight.* Great Britain: Hodder & Stoughton, 1991. "An exclusive presentation proof" of the hardback edition of *Needful Things* (announced for October 4, 1991) and the paperback edition of *Four Past Midnight* (announced for October 4, 1991). From *Four Past Midnight,* one story is reprinted in this proof state: "Secret Window, Secret Garden."

Magistrale, Anthony. *The Moral Voyages of Stephen King.* Starmont Studies in Literary Criticism 25. Mercer Island, Washington: Starmont House, 1989.

Matheson, Richard. OP. *Richard Matheson: Collected Stories.* "Special Advance Reading Copy, WFC Prevue Edition." Los Angeles: Dream/Press, 1989. For anyone interested in King, Matheson is recommended reading, and this is a good place to start. From the publisher of the limited edition of *Skeleton Crew,* this collection has an introduction by Matheson, as well as several essays by notables in the field, including King. A trade edition may still be available from the publisher. (Publisher Jeff Conner issues the most imaginatively designed books in the field. You'll want to get his catalogue. Write to: Scream Press, PO Box 481146, Los Angeles, CA 90048.)

McCauley, Kirby, ed. *Dark Forces.* New York: Bantam Books, 1981. Contains the original appearance of "The Mist" by King.

Miller, Chuck, and Underwood, Tim, eds. *Bare Bones: Conversations on Terror with Stephen King.* New York: McGraw–Hill Book Company, 1988.

————, eds. *Bare Bones: Conversations on Terror with Stephen King.* New York: Warner Books, 1989. A collection of thirty interviews, the first of two compilations. See herein my general comments about *Feast of Fear* (Don Herron, ed.), which also apply here.

————, eds. OP. *Fear Itself: The Horror Fiction of Stephen King.* San Francisco, and Columbia, Pennyslvania: Underwood-Miller, 1982. The first of three essay collections, this is the best. It contains King's essay "On Becoming a Brand Name," which has not been reprinted elsewhere. Although King and Winter feel this is not a good book, I believe it offers important essays that make it worthwhile: by Burton Hatlen, Fritz Leiber, and Ben P. Indick—all of whom have contributed perceptive pieces available only in this collection. A mass-market paperback edition is in print from Signet.

————. eds. *Kingdom of Fear: The World of Stephen King.* San Francisco, and Columbia, Pennsylvania: Underwood–Miller, 1986. The second collection of essays, available in trade paperback from NAL. The book's few slight essays do not greatly detract from its many fascinating ones.

Platt, Charles. *Dream Makers: Volume II.* New York: Berkley Publishing Corporation, A Berkley Book, 1983.

Pollock, Dale. *Skywalking: The Life and Films of George Lucas.* New York: Ballantine Books, 1984. For anyone interested in a behind-the-scenes look at the movie industry, this book on filmmaker George Lucas is fascinating reading.

Reino, Joseph. *Stephen King: The First Decade, Carrie to Pet Sematary.* Twayne's United States Author Series, edited by Warren French. Boston: G.K. Hall & Co., Twayne Publishers, 1988.

Robertson, Don. *The Ideal, Genuine Man.* Bangor, Maine: Philtrum Press, 1987. One of King's favorite Robertson books, with an illuminating introduction (which King terms a "forenote") by King on Robertson. Read this and see where part of King's literary style developed.

Schweitzer, Darrell, ed. *Discovering Stephen King.* Starmont Studies in Literary Criticism No. 8. Mercer Island, Washington: Starmont House, 1985.

Skipp, John, and Spector, Craig, eds. *Book of the Dead.* Willimantic, Connecticut: Mark V. Ziesing, 1989.

Spignesi, Stephen J. *The Shape Under the Sheet: The Complete Stephen King Encyclopedia.* Trade hardback. Ann Arbor, Michigan: Popular Culture, Ink., 1991. Two books in one, this is a concordance to the fiction and a companion book, most useful for library collections and King readers with more than a casual interest. (See my comments in Appendix 1.)

————. *The Stephen King Quiz Book.* New York: Penguin Books USA, Signet, 1990.

Sullivan, Jack. *The Penguin Encyclopedia of Horror and the Supernatural.* New York: Viking Penguin, Inc., 1986. An excellent, photo-illustrated encyclopedia of the field: 600 entries and 50 essays, alphabetically arranged, covering a cross-section of the field and its practitioners—writers, artists, and movie material.

Terrell, Carroll F. *Stephen King: Man and Artist*. Orono, Maine: Northern Lights, 1991. A noted Pound and Eliot scholar, Professor Terrell had King as a college student. An important associational title as well as a study of King as a classical writer, this is principally for scholars.

Touponce, William F. *Ray Bradbury*. Starmont Reader's Guide 31, Roger C. Schlobin, ed. Mercer Island, Washington: Starmont House, 1989.

Wiater, Stanley. *Dark Dreamers: Conversations with the Masters of Horror*. New York: Avon Books, 1990. A journalist by trade, Wiater is an informed interviewer whose knowledge of the genre makes this book the interview collection of choice, along with Winter's *Faces of Fear*.

Winter, Douglas E. OP. *Faces of Fear*. New York: Berkley, 1985. Seventeen interviews of the most prominent practitioners in the genre. Winter knows the field, which makes his interviews so useful. (You've got to know the right questions to ask—and Winter does.)

————. OP. *Shadowings: The Reader's Guide to Horror Fiction: 1981–1982*. Starmont Studies in Literary Criticism I. Mercer Island, Washington: Starmont House, 1983.

————. *Stephen King*. OP. Starmont Reader's Guide 16, edited by Roger C. Schlobin. Mercer Island, Washington: Starmont House, 1982. The original guide, revised for the NAL editions.

————. *Stephen King: The Art of Darkness*. New York: NAL Books, 1984. OP. The single best book on King to date, Winter enjoyed the cooperation of King, who contributed interviews and provided otherwise unobtainable information on his life and work. An invaluable resource and highly recommended.

————. *Stephen King: The Art of Darkness*. 2d ed., rev. New York, and Scarborough, Ontario: New American Library, Signet, 1986. Revised and updated, with a new section on the Bachman books. This is the preferred edition of the first, best, and most authoritative book on King to date.

Wolf, Leonard. *Horror: A Connoisseur's Guide to Literature and Film*. New York and Oxford: Facts on File, 1989. Occasionally useful, but sketchy compared to the *Penguin Encyclopedia*.

Wood, Gary L. "Stephen King Phone Interview." Transcription of telephone interview, June 12, 1989, recorded in Virginia Beach, Virginia. The first of two interviews conducted by Wood, much of this information did not appear in print in the *Cinefantastique* issue on King, to which Wood contributed six pieces.

————. "Stephen King Phone Interview II." Transcription of telephone interview, July 26, 1990, recorded in Virginia Beach, Virginia.

Acknowledgments

Stephen King did not approve or authorize this book. In fact, his preference was that it not be written, which meant that there was no access to him, his immediate family, his professional associates (his office staff or agent), or his publishers. Relying, then, on my own readings, interviews with friends, and secondary sources, I was obviously not able to confirm information in this book directly with the source. Consequently, any errors herein are mine, and mine alone.

I am especially grateful to all of those who, in many ways, supported me on this project:

For research assistance and material: John Baker (*Publishers Weekly*); the Bangor Public Library; the Williamsburg Public Library, especially the reference librarians; Kimberly Barnett Flannery (editor of *TV-Plus* from Waterville, Maine); Melvin Johnson and Muriel Sanford (in Special Collections at the Fogler Library at the University of Maine at Orono); Ben Morgan Jones; Barry R. Levin (Barry R. Levin Science Fiction & Fantasy Literature); David Lowell; Bill Maroldo (public affairs producer of WCCB 10, Lewiston, Maine); Ellanie Sampson (architect of King's visit to her library, Truth or Consequences, New Mexico); Sandy Shriver and Chris Church (*Portland Press Herald,* Portland, Maine); and especially Charles Campo (librarian at the *Bangor Daily News,* Bangor, Maine) for the photographs and copies of news stories on King.

For interviews: John Esposito, screenwriter of *Stephen King's Graveyard Shift;* Lea Girardin from the Maine Film Commission; Burton Hatlen and Edward Holmes (retired) from the English department of the University of Maine at Orono; Rick Hautala, a Maine writer; and Christopher Spruce, former *Castle Rock* publisher and general manager of WZON.

For support, information, and much needed advice: Colleen Doran, artist; Stephen J. Spignesi, author of *The Shape Under the Sheet;* Douglas E. Winter; Gary Wood, *Cinefantastique* contributor; and Howard "Rusty" Wornom.

I am especially grateful to those who took time to contribute creatively to this project, who assisted behind the scenes in more ways than I can acknowledge in print: Christopher Chesley, Michael Collings, Kenny Ray Linkous, and Carroll Terrell.

I owe a special debt, once again, to Andrews and McMeel: to John McMeel and Kathy Andrews; to Thomas Thornton; to Patty Donnelly, Kathy Holder, Patty Rice, and Dorothy O'Brien. Thanks, too, are due to Jean Lowe and Lisa Shadid; they shepherded this book through production. These are the finest people in publishing I've met, and I'm proud of my association with them.

I owe very special thanks to my book editor at Andrews and McMeel, Donna Martin, for whom words fail me. As an editor, she has what Chuck Yeager calls the Right Stuff in spades, and what Kathy Holder calls the Write Stuff. This book is as much hers as mine. (Anytime you need a cab, Donna, I'll be glad to flag one down for you.)

And to Mary, my wife and best friend, I owe simply everything for always standing by me.

Index

About the Contributors

Michael R. Collings is a professor of English, now beginning his twelfth year at Pepperdine University in Malibu, California. In addition to working with the Composition Program, Professor Collings teaches courses in Milton and the Renaissance; Myth, Fantasy, and Science Fiction; and Creative Writing. He is director of the Seaver College Creative Writing Program.

Professor Collings has published over sixty articles, over one hundred fifty reviews, nearly three hundred poems, and a number of scholarly or creative monographs, including *In the Image of God: Theme, Characterization, and Landscape in the Fiction of Orson Scott Card* (1990), *Brian W. Aldiss* (1986), *Reflections on the Fantastic* (an edited anthology, 1986), and *Piers Anthony* (1983).

More central to this occasion, however, he has also published a number of articles, poems, and books examining horror literature in general and Stephen King in particular. His books on King include *Stephen King as Richard Bachman, The Many Facets of Stephen King, The Shorter Works of Stephen King* (with a student, David A. Engebretson), *The Annotated Guide to Stephen King, The Films of Stephen King,* and *The Stephen King Phenomenon,* all published through Starmont House, 1985–1987. *The Annotated Guide* has been updated and revised for future publication as *The Work of Stephen King* (Borgo Press). Professor Collings contributed a number of articles to *Castle Rock,* and has reviewed King's novels, stories, and films for *Fantasy Newsletter, Science Fiction and Fantasy Book Review Annual, Mystery Scene,* and others.

Professor Collings has also published three volumes of poetry—*A Season of Calm Weather* (1974), *Naked to the Sun: Dark Visions of Apocalypse* (1985), and *Dark Transformations: Deadly Visions of Change* (1990)—as well as a number of chapbooks.

Dr. Collings, his wife Judi, and their four children live in Thousand Oaks, California.

Christopher Chesley grew up in Durham, Maine, where he and Stephen King sometimes wrote stories, read books, and went to the movies together. Chesley got his undergraduate degree from the University of Maine. In his last year there, he was honored to be the recipient of the Virtue Award. He has been a substitute teacher in Last Chance, Colorado; and in Truth or Consequences, New Mexico, he was employed as an instructor with the Sierra Writers Association. Recently, he was favored by Stephen Spignesi with the opportunity to be a contributor to Spignesi's *The Shape Under the Sheet,* an encyclopedic work on Stephen King. Chesley maintains an interest in writing, and is working on several projects.

George Beahm's first book, *The Vaughn Bode Index*, was written when he was in high school and published the summer after college graduation. This was followed by *Kirk's Works*, the first of two art indexes on contemporary fantasy artists, published by Heresy Press. As a self-publisher, Beahm published three books of general interest. As the principal in GB Publishing, he published two nonfiction titles by local authors of regional interest, distributed principally in eastern Virginia. Formerly a marketing director for a book publishing company, a freelance book marketing consultant, and the U.S. distributor for an English book publishing company, Beahm is currently a full-time, freelance writer whose most recent book is *The Stephen King Companion*, published by Andrews and McMeel. His forthcoming book, a general-interest book on censorship, will be compiled in the companion book format, for Andrews and McMeel. He and his wife Mary, a high school English teacher, currently live in Williamsburg, Virginia.

Kenny Ray Linkous is a self-taught artist from a coal-mining town—Tams, West Virginia. His first professional assignment was illustrating the Philtrum Press edition of *The Eyes of the Dragon* by Stephen King. Linkous has subsequently rendered artwork for numerous projects, including *The Shape Under the Sheet* for Popular Culture, Ink., *Stephen King: Man and Artist* for Northern Lights, *Grimoire 1 and 2* and *The Stephen King Companion* for GB Publishing, and *Gauntlet* magazine. He is single and currently lives in Portland, Maine.

Carroll F. Terrell received his B.A. degree from Bowdoin (1940), his M.A. from the University of Maine (1950), and his Ph.D. at New York University (1956). The founder of the National Poetry Foundation, he is also the founder and editor of *Paideuna: A Journal Devoted to Ezra Pound Scholarship* and *Sagetrieb*, a journal devoted to poets in the Pound–W.C. Williams tradition, as well as editor the Man/Woman and Poet series. He has authored several books, including two volumes of *A Companion to the Cantos of Ezra Pound* (vol. 1 in 1981, vol. 2 in 1985); *Ideas in Reactions* (1991), a handbook to introduce students to the great poets and writers of the twentieth century; and *Stephen King: Man and Artist* (1991). He has also authored several volumes of poetry, including *On That Day, Smoke and Fire, Rod and Lightning,* and *Dark and Light*. He is currently the founder and director of Northern Lights, a nonprofit corporation devoted to publishing the work of promising young writers. He is currently working on *Dr. Seuss and the Two Faces of Fantasy*.

Q: **How would you like to be remembered?**
Stephen King: **As a good storyteller.**

—interview with *Cosmopolitan* magazine, 1985